The Machinery of Criminal Justice

The Machinery of
Criminal Justice

Stephanos Bibas

OXFORD
UNIVERSITY PRESS

OXFORD
UNIVERSITY PRESS

Oxford University Press, Inc., publishes works that further Oxford University's objective of excellence in research, scholarship, and education.

Oxford   New York
Auckland   Cape Town   Dar es Salaam   Hong Kong   Karachi   Kuala Lumpur   Madrid
Melbourne   Mexico City   Nairobi   New Delhi   Shanghai   Taipei   Toronto

With offices in
Argentina   Austria   Brazil   Chile   Czech Republic   France   Greece   Guatemala   Hungary
Italy   Japan   Poland   Portugal   Singapore   South Korea   Switzerland   Thailand
Turkey   Ukraine   Vietnam

Published by Oxford University Press, Inc.
198 Madison Avenue, New York, New York 10016

Oxford is a registered trademark of Oxford University Press
Oxford University Press is a registered trademark of Oxford University Press, Inc.

Library of Congress Cataloging-in-Publication Data
Bibas, Stephanos.
The machinery of criminal justice / Stephanos Bibas.
   p. cm.
Includes bibliographical references and index.
ISBN 978-0-19-537468-1 (hardback : alk. paper)
1. Criminal justice, Administration of—United States. I. Title.
KF9223.B53 2012
345.73'05—dc23   2011042174

Note to Readers
This publication is designed to provide accurate and authoritative information in regard to the subject matter covered. It is based upon sources believed to be accurate and reliable and is intended to be current as of the time it was written. It is sold with the understanding that the publisher is not engaged in rendering legal, accounting, or other professional services. If legal advice or other expert assistance is required, the services of a competent professional person should be sought. Also, to confirm that the information has not been affected or changed by recent developments, traditional legal research techniques should be used, including checking primary sources where appropriate.

(Based on the Declaration of Principles jointly adopted by a Committee of the American Bar Association and a Committee of Publishers and Associations.)

You may order this or any other Oxford University Press publication by
visiting the Oxford University Press website at www.oup.com

CONTENTS

AUTHOR BIOGRAPHY

Stephanos Bibas is a professor of law and criminology at the University of Pennsylvania and director of its Supreme Court Clinic. A graduate of Columbia, Oxford, and Yale, he clerked for Judge Patrick Higginbotham on the U.S. Court of Appeals for the Fifth Circuit and for Justice Anthony Kennedy on the Supreme Court of the United States. As a federal prosecutor in New York City, he successfully investigated, prosecuted, and convicted the world's leading expert in Tiffany stained glass for hiring a grave robber to loot priceless Tiffany windows from mausolea. He teaches and writes about criminal procedure, especially plea bargaining and sentencing, and litigates a wide range of cases before the Supreme Court. He lives in Philadelphia with his wife and three children.

ACKNOWLEDGMENTS

This book, drawing together and building on much of my previous writing, has been a decade in the making. My mentors in law school, especially Akhil Amar and John Langbein, first interested me in the subject with their starkly differing assessments of what modern American criminal justice is missing: Amar stresses the decline of popular involvement, while Langbein emphasizes how plea bargaining lets criminal justice professionals circumvent public trials for possibly self-interested reasons. Judge Patrick Higginbotham and Justice Anthony Kennedy, for whom I clerked, both taught me to appreciate the value of jury trials. And my countless supervisors and colleagues at the U.S. Attorney's Office, especially Vernon Broderick, Andy Dember, Cheryl Krause, Peter Neiman, and Rich Sullivan, taught me the ropes of jury trials and plea bargaining, opening my eyes to how far the reality had diverged from the historical ideal.

As an academic, I was the beneficiary of generous mentoring especially by Al Alschuler, George Fisher, and the late Dave Baldus and Bill Stuntz, each of whom taught me both by commentary and by example. Countless colleagues discussed, read, and commented on drafts of the book and its predecessor articles, including David Abrams, Matt Adler, Anita Allen, Al Alschuler, Laura Appleman, Regina Austin, the late Dave Baldus, Rachel Barkow, Amy Barrett, Chris Beauchamp, John Beckerman, A. J. Bellia, Doug Beloof, Doug Berman, Anita Bernstein, Randy Bezanson, Peter Blank, Josh Bowers, Don Braman, Curtis Bridgeman, Peg Brinig, Darryl Brown, Steve Burbank, Bill Burke-White, Emily Buss, Paul Butler, Paul Cassell, Gabriel Jack Chin, Jonathan Cohen, Tino Cuellar, Angela Davis, Antony Duff, Jeff Dunoff, Margareth Etienne, Jeff Fagan, Mary Fan, Nita Farahany, Kim Ferzan, Claire Finkelstein, George Fisher, Mike Fitts, George Fletcher, Dave Franklin, Carolyn Frantz, Doug Frenkel, Amanda Frost, Nicole Garnett, Rick Garnett, Brandon Garrett, Steve Garvey, Jill Gaulding, Adam Gershowitz, Gary Goodpaster, Craig Green, Lewis Grossman, Bernard Harcourt, Jill Hasday, Andy Hessick, Carissa Hessick, Adam Hirsch, David Hoffman, Herb Hovenkamp, Kyron Huigens,

Mark Janis, Dan Kahan, Leo Katz, Nancy King, Russell Korobkin, Seth Kreimer, Ken Kress, Anne Kringel, Herb Kritzer, John Langbein, Sophia Lee, Renée Lettow Lerner, Howard Lesnick, Doug Lichtman, Matt Lister, Erik Luna, Dan Markel, Terry Maroney, Toni Massaro, Serena Mayeri, Tracey Meares, Rob Mikos, Marc Miller, Jon Molot, Stephen Morse, Jeffrie Murphy, Bill Nelson, Nate Persily, Anne Joseph O'Connell, Sarah Paoletti, Gideon Parchomovsky, Todd Pettys, Eric Posner, Margaret Raymond, Kevin Reitz, Jenny Roberts, Paul Robinson, Ed Rock, Irene Merker Rosenberg, Jacqui Ross, Richard Ross, Dave Rudovsky, Ed Rubin, Ted Ruger, Hillary Sale, Barry Schwartz, Cathy Sharkey, David Skeel, Chris Slobogin, Bruce Smith, Carol Steiker, Kate Stith, Geof Stone, Lior Strahilevitz, Heather Strang, David Strauss, Cathie Struve, the late Bill Stuntz, Rick Swedloff, Sandy Guerra Thompson, Lea Vandervelde, Mike Wachter, Kevin Washburn, Amy Wax, Bob Weisberg, Peter Westen, Jerry Wetlaufer, David Wexler, Tess Wilkinson-Ryan, Norman Williams, the late Bruce Winick, Ron Wright, and Tung Yin.

This book has developed in fits and starts. About half of it has been substantially reworked from portions of several predecessor articles, including *Transparency and Participation in Criminal Procedure*, 81 *New York University Law Review* 911 (2006) (the genesis of most of chapter II plus some of the solutions in chapter VI); *Plea Bargaining Outside the Shadow of Trial*, 117 *Harvard Law Review* 2463 (2004) (the source of the last part of chapter II); *Harmonizing Substantive-Criminal-Law Values and Criminal Procedure: The Case of* Alford *and Nolo Contendere Pleas*, 88 *Cornell Law Review* 1361 (2003) (the source of the first part of chapter III); and *Forgiveness in Criminal Procedure*, 4 *Ohio State Journal of Criminal Law* 329 (2007) (which I wove into chapters III and IV). The second half of chapter III plus a bit of chapter IV of this work is derived from an essay previously published in *The Yale Law Journal. See* Stephanos Bibas & Richard A. Bierschbach, *Integrating Remorse and Apology into Criminal Procedure*, 114 *Yale Law Journal* 85 (2004).

A very special thanks goes to Rick Bierschbach, my sometime coauthor and dear friend, with whom I spent many hours batting around these ideas and who has read multiple drafts of much of this book. The second half of chapter III is the fruit of our profitable collaboration, and I am only saddened that he could not coauthor this book with me.

I could not have written this book without the terrific research assistance of Micole Allekotte, Jeffrey Andersen, Elizabeth Augustine, Joseph Baranello, Bryan Bennett, James Borod, Jacob Boyars, Jessica Chiarello, Pietro Deserio, Jordan Esbrook, Jonathan Fisch, Trevor Foster, Kate Gregory, John Harbin, Keith Kasten, Indira Khan, Agatha Koprowski,

Christopher Lee, Svetlana Mirkis, Ted Moore, Nick Moses, Brian Powers, Joline Price, Kerstin Rademacher, Brian Raimondo, Jenn Sasso, Kristen Scoville, Katrina Smith, Jessica Urban, and Yiyang Wu. Many librarians, especially Ed Greenlee, Ben Meltzer, Ellen Qualey, and Merle Slyhoff, have offered fantastic research help as well.

I fear that my feeble memory and shoddy recordkeeping has led me to slight many of the friends and colleagues who contributed to this work, and I apologize for my forgetfulness.

I am blessed to be where I am because of the enduring love and support of my parents Haritos and Cleo Bibas and my brothers Greg and Andrew. My two little sons provided many hours of glee and welcome distraction from the grind of writing, and the impending arrival of my baby daughter was a useful impetus to complete the manuscript on time. But most of all, I thank my wife and better half Juliana, a loving mate and friend who persistently supported me while prodding me to slog ahead. To her I dedicate this book.

INTRODUCTION

THE DIVERGENCE OF THEORY, REALITY, AND MORALITY

In popular imagination, criminal justice is a morality play, a form of educational social theater. As Thurman Arnold put it, "Trials are like the miracle or morality plays of ancient times. They dramatically present the conflicting moral values of a community in a way that could not be done by logical formalization." When values conflict, trials help to air and reconcile them; even when the values are settled, as they often are, trials teach and reinforce them. "In its very detail and drama . . . the trial becomes a morality play which impresses upon the public that the law is being enforced and that justice is being fairly administered." Crime thrillers, movies, and television portray courtroom dramas culminating in jury trials. In some, falsely accused defendants speak their piece and clear their names publicly. In others, victims have their days in court, literally see justice done, and sometimes even receive apologies from those who have wronged them. The jury serves as the chorus of a Greek tragedy, "the conscience of the community."[1] It applies the community's moral code, pronounces judgment, and brands or exonerates the defendant. Jury trials sort out who did what, what retribution (payback) wrongdoers deserve, and how to denounce crimes and vindicate victims. Ordinary citizens are key players, as victims and defendants have their say and jurors and the public sit in individualized judgment. They suffer, they make amends, and sometimes they even apologize or heal. Viewers evaluate who was right and wrong, empathize with the protagonists, and await catharsis and resolution by the end of the show.

Law students think they know better. The vision of criminal justice taught in most law schools emphasizes adversarial combat between prosecutors and defense lawyers at trial. On this account, lawyers duke it out over the facts and the law, and their combat separates the innocent from the guilty. Prosecutors seek to maximize convictions and punishment, to deter (scare off) and incapacitate (lock up) as many wrongdoers as possible.

Defense lawyers seek the opposite, to get their clients acquitted or at least the lowest possible sentence. They insist on procedural fairness and rights, questioning whether there is proof beyond a reasonable doubt. Victims are largely absent from this picture, defendants are pushed to invoke their rights to remain silent, and jurors meekly follow judges' technical instructions. Instead, lawyers run the show.

Newly minted lawyers soon find that the reality in the criminal justice trenches differs from both of these pictures. Unlike the popular imagination, the real world does not have much use for laymen. Victims rarely get to say much in court, certainly not at crucial proceedings such as bail, charging, and plea bargaining. Defendants stay silent, letting their lawyers do the talking for them. Discussions of right and wrong, of pain and blame, are almost absent. There is rarely a morality play. Punishment is largely hidden in far-away prisons, out of sight and out of mind.

Nor do new lawyers find much glamorous trial-lawyer combat in the real world. Indeed, plea bargaining is the name of the game. Many criminal lawyers assume that nearly everyone in the system is guilty and so negotiate settlements instead of fighting it out. Cookie-cutter plea bargains struck in conference calls or hallway conversations resolve most cases, so jurors and the public see few of them. These mass-produced bargains short-circuit elaborate constitutional procedures such as discovery, cross-examination, and jury instructions and deliberation. Lawyers trade defendants' constitutional rights, such as *Miranda* warnings and search-warrant requirements, as plea-bargaining chips for lower sentences. Some relevant factors, such as the badness of the crime and the defendant and the strength of the evidence, do influence plea bargains. But so do irrelevant factors such as the prosecutor's and defense lawyer's salaries and caseloads and the defendant's ability to afford bail. In other words, lawyers seldom seem to vindicate the innocent, vindicate the Constitution, weigh wrongdoers' just deserts, reform defendants, or heal victims. About all they do is move the plea-bargaining machinery as quickly and cheaply as possible, which maximizes the number of people the system can deter and incapacitate. The machinery of criminal justice, and its need for speed, has taken on a life of its own far removed from what many people expect or want. Efficiency has all but killed the morality play the public craves.

How did this happen in a democracy? After all, most criminal cases are titled something like *People of the State of X vs. John Q. Defendant*. Prosecutors still prosecute cases in the name of The People, and the public is passionately interested in them. How, then, did the criminal justice system become so far removed from The People, who are nominally in charge? How did it become so amoral, hidden, and insulated? And is there anything we can or should do about it?

To some extent, this distance between voters' interests and public officials' actions pervades representative government. Insiders' control of government is a chronic source of friction in a democracy, but the problem is most acute in criminal justice. In other areas of government, rational apathy and faith in expertise leads voters to defer to experts about, say, regulating fungicides or pension plans.[2] (No one would bother to watch reality television about tax auditors or dramas about public housing.) In contrast, many ordinary citizens do not defer to criminal justice experts but show passionate interest in how insiders handle criminal cases. Indeed, public outrage flares when politicians or the media sporadically bring perceived injustices to light.

In addition, the Sixth Amendment to the Constitution guarantees local, public jury trials. In other words, the public has a constitutional right to know about and take part in criminal trials, though in practice plea bargaining subverts those rights. The stakes are high as well: defendants' lives, liberties, and reputations compete with victims' rights, the public's security, and the law's expressive and moral messages. Also, crime victims, bystanders, and ordinary citizens have few procedural and no substantive legal rights in criminal justice. Judges, police, and prosecutors are not constrained by identifiable clients in the ways that, for example, teachers and welfare case workers are.[3] Thus, both the need for and the limits on democratic participation are particularly acute in the criminal arena.

Many scholars have written histories of plea bargaining, but that is not my precise focus here. As chapters II and III discuss, plea bargaining is part of a larger series of trends that have professionalized and mechanized the criminal justice system so much that it is out of touch with ordinary people's expectations and desires. Various explanations for these trends are partly true but incomplete. For example, some blame the Warren Court's creation and expansion of defendants' constitutional rights.[4] These rights ranged from *Miranda* warnings, to exclusion of evidence seized without search warrants, to habeas corpus petitions challenging final criminal convictions. These technicalities are often far removed from guilt, so factual guilt and innocence matter somewhat less to cases' outcomes. And these new rights gave prosecutors additional incentives to plea bargain, in exchange for defendants' surrendering of their rights. The plea-bargaining machinery, however, long predates the 1950s, and prosecutors were the ones who created it. These new defense rights created new bargaining chips and fueled prosecutors' incentives to bargain; these rights may have accelerated the machinery but did not start it.

Others lay the blame at the feet of rising crime and increased caseloads.[5] There is truth to this explanation as well. As courts became busier, they struggled to find faster ways to dispose of their business. Plea bargaining circumvented increasingly formal trials, allowing courts to move more criminal and civil cases. This partial explanation, however, leaves lawyers out of the picture. If victims and defendants were still handling their own cases amidst today's caseloads, they would not plea bargain in the same way that prosecutors and defense counsel do. Lawyers' outlooks, interests, and lack of accountability to laymen are integral to the mechanical mentality. Rising caseloads do not capture these factors.

Today, many people reflexively view this history as progress, as criminal justice moved from the bloody dark ages of our past to the more rational, enlightened present. The increases in lawyers, procedures, and plea bargaining have indisputably brought some benefits: they have increased some safeguards and accommodated staggering caseloads. Without denying these benefits, I want to critique these transformations and expose their overlooked costs. When one takes a few steps back to reflect on these developments, they appear far more troubling and costly. We cannot simply wax nostalgic for a bygone era, as the plea-bargaining machinery is not about to disappear, but we must see the past and present landscape clearly. Criminal justice used to be individualized, moral, transparent, and participatory but has become impersonal, amoral, hidden, and insulated from the people. It has thus lost some of its popular democratic legitimacy and support. Appreciating what we have lost can inspire reforms to revive these classic values in the modern justice system. Defendants, victims, and communities can play larger roles through grand juries, consultation with prosecutors, rights to be heard in court, restorative justice conferences, and requiring defendants to work to support their families and victims.

The ideal of the individualized morality play and personal confrontation lives on in our culture, waiting to be revived in practice. That does not mean we should or even can abolish plea bargaining and lawyers' leading role in criminal justice; they bring some benefits and are here to stay. But it does mean that we can attack the machinery's excesses. That means giving outsiders more information, more voice, and more influence, reintroducing key aspects of the redemptive morality play. Instead of remaining outsiders, victims, defendants, and ordinary citizens should actively participate as stakeholders alongside insiders.

OVERVIEW OF THE BOOK

Chapter I of this book retells the history of the criminal justice machine. Colonial Americans saw criminal justice as a morality play. Victims initiated and often prosecuted their own cases *pro se* (without lawyers), and defendants often defended themselves *pro se*. Laymen from the neighborhood sat in judgment as jurors, and even many judges lacked legal training. Trials were very quick, common-sense moral arguments, as victims told their stories and defendants responded without legalese. Communities were small, so gossip flew quickly, informing neighbors of what was going on. Even punishment was a public affair, with gallows and stocks in the town square. True, punishments could be brutal, procedural safeguards were absent, and race, sex, and class biases all clouded the picture. Nonetheless, the colonists had one important asset that we have lost: members of the local community actively participated and literally saw justice done.

Various forces changed this picture. Lawyers' dominance rose hand in hand with caseloads. Judges developed technical rules of evidence, boilerplate jury instructions, and procedure in tandem with the lawyers who were equipped to handle them. Lawyers are agents who are supposed to serve their principals: prosecutors are supposed to represent the public's and victims' interests in justice, while defense lawyers are supposed to represent defendants' interests. But lawyers had and still have strong self-interests in disposing of cases to lighten their own workloads and to avoid risky trials, and they tend to focus on quantifiable benefits.[6]

The rise of lawyers not only excluded victims, silenced defendants, and bypassed jurors through plea bargaining; it also hid criminal justice outside open court, just as prisons hid punishment behind high walls. Thus the system became not only less participatory, but also less transparent. Professionals greased the plea-bargaining machinery, speeding it up by bypassing laymen. In the process, the lawyers promoted case-processing efficiency and let the morality-play aspect wither. Laymen who encounter criminal justice for the first time see a yawning gulf between their popular expectation of justice and the lawyerized reality of amoral, cookie-cutter plea bargaining.

The point here is not to romanticize the past, to suggest that it binds us, or to advocate bringing back whipping or lynch mobs. But it helps to know where we have come from, if only to understand why we have expectations that our justice system does not satisfy. This historical account also illumines some of the forces that continue to shape our system to this day, so that we can critique it and consider possible reforms.

Some readers may wish to skip the historical overview and begin directly with the problems as they stand today, in chapter II. That chapter addresses the gulf between criminal justice insiders and outsiders. The insiders are the judges, prosecutors, defense counsel, police, and probation and parole officers who dominate criminal justice day to day. They are knowledgeable, powerful repeat players with distinctive senses of justice. They value disposing of cases efficiently over the means used to reach that result. The insiders can predict what that result will be, so they can strike bargains that reflect those expectations and save everyone time and money. Speedy bargains make all the insiders happy: prosecutors, defense lawyers, and judges all lighten their own workloads and move on to the next case. Insiders, then, see little reason to go through the motions of courtroom ritual just to reach predictable convictions and sentences. Nor do they see much need to include outsiders; as they see it, they themselves are professionals who know best how to run criminal justice to serve outsiders' interests.

Outsiders, in contrast, are laymen, not lawyers: victims, members of the public, and even to an extent defendants. To them, criminal justice seems opaque, technical, and amoral. Most of what they know is from sensational news anecdotes and glamorous crime dramas, which are far removed from the humdrum plea bargaining of open-and-shut smaller cases. They have few ways to participate in criminal cases. Finally, outsiders lack insiders' self-interests in clearing their dockets, and they do not grow jaded or mellow. Their dominant concern is to do justice.

To outsiders, doing justice does not mean inflicting the greatest punishment on the greatest possible number of defendants. While the public is often misinformed about average sentences, when properly informed it often finds actual sentences sufficient or even excessive. One cannot assume that current laws are harsh because that is what the public really wants; these laws often result from a warped, dysfunctional political process. Distortions arise in part because frustrated outsiders vent their dissatisfaction in the abstract by clamoring for more toughness in wholesale-level reforms. When they are given concrete cases, however, average citizens favor sentences as low as or even markedly lower than those required by a variety of criminal laws. A number of empirical studies by Julian Roberts, Paul Robinson, and others, discussed in chapter II.A.2, confirm this striking finding. At the individual, retail level, outsiders' judgments are far more nuanced and less harsh overall. Unfortunately, now that outsiders rarely serve on juries but instead influence legislation and referenda, the abstract, wholesale perspective has largely supplanted the contextualized, retail one. In addition to substantively just convictions and sentences, outsiders also want to see defendants held publicly accountable through fair, participatory procedures.

These differences in information, participation, and values create an enduring tension between self-interested insiders and excluded outsiders. The result is a game of tug-of-war. Insiders manipulate substantive rules and low-visibility procedures to dispose of cases as they like. Outsiders try to constrain insiders by changing substantive policy, say by creating new crimes and sentences. Insiders then subvert these constraints procedurally, and so on. Because insiders are better informed and continually involved, outsiders find it hard to win enduring victories but are periodically provoked to rise up in outrage.

This tug-of-war hurts criminal justice in many ways. It provokes voters to enact simplistic, crude laws. It makes it hard for outsiders to monitor insiders' performance. Insiders are thus too free to follow their own desires instead of victims' and the public's interests, which subverts democracy. The problem is particularly acute for insiders who are insulated from the decisions they make: a federal prosecutor or judge who commutes from the suburbs does not live with or hear from urban victims or defendants' families. The gulf between insiders and outsiders can cloud criminal law's efficacy, making the law too unclear to deter and condemn crimes effectively. It hinders criminal justice's ability to vindicate, heal, and provide catharsis to victims and the public. And it can sap public faith and trust in the law, making citizens less willing to follow the law.

There are also significant gaps between defense lawyers and their clients. Insider defense lawyers have strong interests in getting along with prosecutors and judges and disposing of their huge caseloads, particularly because most are overworked and underfunded. Defendants are overoptimistic, in denial, and prone to take risks. Huge differences in education, language, class, race, and sex impede communication. Defendants distrust their appointed lawyers because they are not paying for them. Defense lawyers do all the talking, effectively silencing and disempowering their clients. Lawyers see it as their job to minimize punishment and dispose of cases, but in doing so they can overlook clients' needs to express themselves, apologize, and heal. No political tug-of-war erupts, as defendants have little political or economic power, but these huge differences impair representation, oversight, and trust.

Chapter III focuses on one of the most serious failings of mechanical criminal justice: its failure to vindicate and heal. The professionals who run the machinery see their job as dispensing impersonal punishment, not sending moral messages or healing wounded relationships. The swiftness of the plea-bargaining machinery disposes of large caseloads quickly and cheaply, but at the expense of many other criminal justice values. Plea bargains and sentences reflect the individual defendant's badness, as well as the lawyers' interests, abilities, and workloads. At best, the question is how much retribution, deterrence, and incapacitation this defendant needs. While these factors are relevant, they are static, overlooking the dynamic potential of criminal justice to transform those who take part. Criminal justice could not only reduce future crimes, but also restore the relationships ruptured by crime. Currently, however, it largely ignores these goals.

In particular, criminal procedure enables defendants to remain in denial and does almost nothing to cultivate their expressions of remorse and apologies and victims' forgiveness. A criminal defendant who is in denial about his guilt may still be able to plead guilty and receive a guilty-plea discount; at most he need admit guilt only grudgingly. These equivocal guilty pleas deprive defendants, their families, victims, and the public of clear resolutions. They leave defendants in denial and more likely to repeat their crimes, and deprive victims of vindication. In contrast, jury trials and unequivocal guilty pleas vindicate victims, denounce crimes, and teach lessons. Defendants who remain in denial need jury trials to condemn or exonerate them, driving home clear messages to defendants, victims, and the public.

Criminal procedure has the same blind spot for expressions of remorse and apology. Crime is about more than just individual wrongdoing; it harms social relationships. Criminal procedure uses remorse and apology merely as poor gauges of how much retribution, deterrence, and incapacitation individual defendants need. But these tools have great power to heal wounded relationships, vindicate victims, and educate and reintegrate wrongdoers into the community.

Likewise, forgiveness used to play a much larger role in criminal procedure. But today, the state and its professionals dominate criminal procedure and largely exclude outsiders. They leave little room for outsiders such as victims and defendants to tell their stories, grieve, apologize, and forgive.

Part of the problem is that insiders' individual-badness model sees defendants as separate from the web of relationships and communities they have wounded. Another problem is that criminal procedure ignores many of the substantive justifications for punishment, such as educating defendants and the public and vindicating victims. In law school, we teach criminal law and criminal procedure as completely separate fields, but of course procedure exists to serve and implement substance. Criminal procedure needs to take more seriously the many values underlying the substantive criminal law, which it is supposed to serve. Right now, it does little more than minimize cost and maximize speed, incapacitation, and perhaps deterrence. Those aims are indeed substantively valuable, but procedure overlooks many other substantive values.

Chapter IV considers correcting these defects by adding new and different lay voices to criminal justice. The state's monopoly on criminal justice blinds it to the valuable human interests and needs that outsiders have. Crimes harm not just an impersonal state, but real people—people who deserve more consideration and power in criminal procedure. Mediation and other face-to-face interactions between victims and wrongdoers offer this hope. The state deserves a role and is useful in tempering vengeance and ensuring equality. But state control should not squeeze out the human needs and voices of real victims, defendants, and the public. Each ought to be able to have a say. That does not mean giving victims vetoes; neutral judges and juries must retain the final say. Victims and members of the public could check prosecutors at least by expressing their views. Empowering victims need not license vengeance. Victims care much less about controlling outcomes than about being heard and having a role in fair processes.

My suggestions for an individualized, participatory criminal justice system bear some resemblance to three recent criminal justice movements: victims' rights, restorative justice, and therapeutic jurisprudence. Each of these movements has valuable insights but offers only a part of the morality play for which the public thirsts. First, the victims' rights movement restores a crucial focus on the needs of victims, who often get lost in lawyer-dominated criminal procedure brought in the name of the state. Some victim advocates rightly emphasize the need to treat victims respectfully and hear their voices. But much of what passes for victims' rights rhetoric is unbalanced and vengeful, a cloak for law-and-order toughness. It often suggests that the only way to make victims happier is to punish defendants more, even though victims often care more about respectful treatment and apologies. Second, restorative justice emphasizes mediation to let victims, defendants, and their families confront and talk with one another. The idea of transcending a one-dimensional, zero-sum struggle between prosecutor and defense counsel is attractive, and participants seem to come away more satisfied. The difficulty is that most restorative justice enthusiasts, such as John Braithwaite, leave too little role for the state, blame, or punishment. Finally, the therapeutic jurisprudence movement rightly focuses on how the legal system's procedures can serve as (or obstruct) emotional and psychological therapy for wrongdoers, victims, and others. On the other hand, the rhetoric of therapy and psychology has a clinical ring, eschewing blame in favor of treatment. Here, as with restorative justice, the reluctance to blame and speak moral language leaves therapeutic jurisprudence incomplete.

All this moralistic talk may leave many readers uneasy. Our pluralistic society comprises a wide range of religious and moral beliefs, so we are uncomfortable engaging in morality-speak. It seems safer instead to rely on neutral criteria such as speed, cost, and numbers of cases processed. Lawyers can then run the system to maximize efficiency, obscuring the thorny moral judgments that are better suited to juries.

Chapter V addresses criminal procedure's embrace of efficiency as the antidote to moralizing. Criminal procedure tries to maximize efficiency, but lawyers rarely consider what it is supposed to be doing so efficiently. Criminal justice, more than almost any other area of law, is morally freighted in the popular imagination, and its moral significance is linked closely to its legitimacy. While controlling crime is one important concern of both insiders and outsiders, outsiders also want much more. They expect the criminal law to vindicate the innocent defendant or the wronged victim and denounce the guilty.

Why, then, is legal discourse about criminal procedure so divorced from popular moral discourse about the same subject? Some of the blame rests upon the artificial academic separation of criminal procedure from substantive criminal law. Some rests upon insiders' bureaucratic outlook and emphasis on quantity, speed, and cost. More of the blame, though, stems from intellectuals' fear that moral judgments are at best contentious, at worst arbitrary and intolerant. In contrast, the scientific language of efficiency and deterrence appears objective and indisputable. Academics and lawyers also fear that popular moralizing will be harsh and merciless; some prefer to trust their own sense of mercy and kindness.

Notwithstanding academic skepticism, however, Americans share a healthy enough moral consensus on the basic issues of criminal justice to support robust moral appeals and discourse, as chapter V.B shows. First, empirical research by Paul Robinson and others shows that laymen's judgments about crime emphasize retribution and show remarkable consensus in ascribing and ranking blame. The moral consensus about when and how much to blame is strongest for crimes against persons and property, but there is also substantial agreement even about so-called victimless and morals offenses. Second, when discussing hot-button topics such as the death penalty, laymen think it more polite to invoke neutral deterrence-speak than contentious moral language. What really drives their views, however, are expressive moral judgments about crime. Third, laymen bring these moral expectations to criminal procedure. They care not only whether legal procedures reach the right outcomes, but also whether they are fair and legitimate and whether they give laymen enough voice and control. They expect to have their say and their day in court, to be able to blame, grieve, and perhaps apologize and forgive. The machinery ignores these expectations. Fourth, laymen are not nearly as harsh as lawyers assume. Popular moral discourse accommodates both justice and mercy, punishment and forgiveness.

Taking these considerations more seriously, and bringing them out into the open, should enhance citizens' perceptions of the justice system's legitimacy without leading to excessive conflict over values. Fear of conflict over values should not lead us to squelch moral discourse, driving it underground into coded references and vigilantism. On the contrary, healthy moral discourse can strengthen, refine, and reinforce the community's moral code and expectations. Taking these ideas seriously, however, would require substantial reforms to the machinery of criminal justice.

Readers who are already convinced that the system is broken and out of touch may wish to skip ahead to the final chapter, which discusses how to solve these problems. Chapter VI begins to consider how one could return power to laymen within a lawyer-driven system. We cannot dynamite the entire machine and go back to lay-run criminal justice. The American criminal justice system could not handle its staggering caseloads that way, and the cost of sacrificing all procedural rights and expertise would be intolerable. But it is worth thinking seriously about how laymen could play more substantial and active roles in criminal justice.

First of all, punishment could be more visible, more focused on making amends, and better at reintegrating convicts after they have paid their debts to society. All able bodied inmates should have to work to repay victims, the state, and their own families. Work, perhaps even in the military or a civilian corps, would be prosocial, offsetting wrongdoers' antisocial crimes and teaching good habits. Likewise, mandatory educational and vocational training and drug treatment would teach valuable skills and help them to reintegrate as law-abiding citizens after release. Relaxing the collateral consequences of convictions would likewise promote inmates' reentry into society.

Alas, the macro-level reforms just suggested would collide head on with institutional barriers. Military leaders would resist admitting large numbers of poorly skilled convicts with disciplinary problems, and unions and businesses would oppose having to compete against prison labor. In the face of these entrenched barriers, the prospects for a national top-down fix are dim. Moreover, the problem is too diverse for a single national fix. No one statute or Supreme Court decision, or even a sequential reform program, will fix our broken system from above. Rather, we need bottom-up populism to pursue a multi-faceted approach. Reform is more likely to happen at the mid-level of counties, cities, and neighborhoods, and the micro-level of individual criminal cases. A variety of outsider pressures, organized and amplified through social-networking technology, can marshal outsiders' voices and their desire to participate at the retail level.

In criminal proceedings, defendants could be offered greater speaking roles, instead of having their defense counsel say everything while they remain mute. The system might encourage them to speak more, particularly after they plead guilty, when they need not worry about self-incrimination. Plea colloquies, sentencing hearings, and victim-offender mediation conferences before or after sentencing could offer defendants more opportunities to listen and speak. They could make public apologies and could pay back their families and victims through mandatory work. Having been held publicly accountable and paid their debts, defendants would be ready to be reintegrated rather than permanently shunned.

Victims too could play larger roles. From investigation onwards, police and prosecutors could use automated computer systems to notify victims of arrests, bail status and hearings, charges, plea discussions and bargains, and sentencings. Victims could have rights to consult with prosecutors throughout investigations and prosecutions. They could also have the option of greater speaking roles at these court hearings and in face-to-face conferences with defendants. Restorative procedures are possible, though imperfect, ways to give victims and defendants greater voices.

Even members of the public could receive better information and broader rights to consult with prosecutors and police, both in individual cases and through community-policing and -prosecution forums. And new restorative sentencing juries could blend restoration, retribution, and expressive condemnation. Victims and defendants would speak, prosecutors would justify their plea bargains, and juries would ultimately decide what sentences and discounts were deserved. That would radically change current law. Prosecutors could no longer bargain over the crime charged or over the facts. A plea bargain could recommend a lower sentence, but first a prosecutor would have to persuade a community jury that the punishment fit the crime. Thus, plea bargains would no longer be raw exercises of prosecutorial power, but persuasive public justifications ratified by juries.

Empowering victims could shift enforcement priorities toward violent and property crimes and away from so-called victimless crimes, except when particular indirect victims are aggrieved and complain. For example, drug enforcement might focus more on neighborhoods where gunfire, disorder, and other spillover effects harm the community. Police and prosecutors should not be completely beholden to victims, especially when they ask for disproportionate harshness or leniency. One does not want to give domestic abusers the power to get charges dropped by intimidating their victims into submission. But law-enforcement officials should heed and give more weight to victims' concerns.

These solutions, of course, carry costs. Including more parties will slow down proceedings, cost more, and reduce the volume of criminal cases that the system can process. In other words, reforms may reduce the aggregate amount of retribution, deterrence, and incapacitation that the system can mete out. But sometimes it is worth sacrificing quantity for quality. Some defendants or victims might receive better treatment than others, particularly those who are white, female, articulate, well-educated, and well-off. Greater personalization risks reducing formal equality and neutrality, which raises fears of bias. Many defendants will seek to game the system, feigning remorse and apology to win sentencing discounts. Yet many of these problems already exist in the status quo, and bringing them out into the open is likely to alleviate them. And one can at least hope that these short-term costs would be justified by the long-term benefits of restoring communities and ultimately bringing down crime.

THEMES OF THE BOOK

The overview exposes deep fault lines within criminal justice. Several themes recur in the account above. One pervasive theme is the divide between lawyers and laymen. Because lawyers tend to write the accounts of the legal system, they sometimes overlook this gulf, or else attribute it to the ignorance of non-lawyers. They trust themselves as the guardians of the rule of law and suspect public input as antithetical to law, equality, and reasoned moral judgment. From their internal point of view, which emphasizes quantity and results, they see themselves as doing as much justice as the system can handle.

But the insider-outsider gulf is too deep and too serious to dismiss so quickly. Insiders take for granted their own knowledge and power, forgetting that their dominance of the system is a relatively recent development. Thus, proposals for public disclosure seem to intrude upon sacred prosecutorial secrecy. Victims' rights seem like newfangled threats to lawyers' turf, instead of a re-empowerment to serve deeply felt needs once again. Likewise, insiders can overlook their self-interests. They are agents of principals, namely their clients or constituents. Yet insiders may not feel much pressure to conform to outsiders' expressed desires or interests because outsiders have so little power. There is no effective feedback loop nor check on agents' behavior. And because they are insulated from outsiders, insiders may not appreciate that their utilitarian emphasis on efficiency conflicts with outsiders' expressive, moralistic interests. Or insiders may dismiss outsiders' moralism as benighted and crude, instead of grappling seriously with outsiders' interests in quality and not just quantity. Outsiders are not irrational in seeking procedural justice in addition to substantive outcomes. They care about increasing the number of defendants punished, but they also care about the message expressed by the process. Nor are they wrong to think that their input can enrich dry legal processes. They understandably want to *see* justice done and take part in it, rather than taking insiders' word for it. The ailment of criminal justice is not excessive populism per se, as many scholars argue,[7] but insiders' excessive agency costs and outsiders' lack of healthy outlets, especially in individual cases.

As a matter of political theory, insiders ought to heed and hear the outsiders for whom they supposedly work. Insiders must not simply foist on the public their sense of efficiency, or crime control, or justice. In a democracy, outsiders' sense of justice must be central to both the substance and the process of criminal justice. For substantive criminal law, that means respecting what Paul Robinson calls empirical desert, the liability and punishment intuitions that most community members share upon reflection. The analogue in criminal procedure is procedural justice, the public's sense that procedures must treat people fairly and with respect and should give them a voice. Tom Tyler and other scholars explore what the public expects procedural justice to look like.[8] As chapter II explains, the reality has drifted far from the public's sense of procedural and substantive justice. It needs to be brought back into line. Thus, this book's normative argument is primarily populist and democratic. It advocates criminal procedures that reflect the enduring moral intuitions of the electorate, rather than some abstract philosophical theory. The pendulum should swing away from the rationalism, centralization, and statism that have come to dominate criminal justice since Cesare Beccaria wrote more than two centuries ago. Criminal justice insiders are fundamentally Weberian bureaucrats, but my emphasis is Tocquevillean.

A second theme of the book is the divorce between the values of criminal procedure and the values of substantive criminal law. Procedure is supposed to serve substance. But instead of weighing many substantive justifications for punishment, procedure emphasizes largely procedural values. For nearly half a century, criminal procedure scholars have debated within the famous dichotomy of procedural models sketched out by Herbert Packer. In Packer's scheme, the (softer) Due Process Model stresses fairness, rights, defendant autonomy, and accuracy in freeing the innocent. The (law-and-order) Crime Control Model emphasizes accuracy in convicting the guilty, speed, cost, finality, and efficiency.[9] Both ends of Packer's spectrum slight the substantive reasons why we punish and the roles victims and communities should play in criminal justice.

I do not want to overstate my case. Speeding up the machinery will maximize total years of imprisonment, thus promoting crime control through incapacitation and deterrence. And accuracy, emphasized by the Due Process Model, is essential to deter, incapacitate, and inflict retribution on the right people. Nevertheless, these substantive values are hardly overt, and other important substantive values drop out entirely. In practice, efficiency serves only the handful of values that are easy to quantify, like incapacitation. Missing is much discussion of retribution, vindicating victims, educating the public, or reconciling and healing defendants, victims, and communities. In other words, criminal procedure is largely divorced from the sibling it is supposed to serve, namely substantive criminal law. Our procedures maximize the quantity of output and slight the quality of the process and its softer goals.

Moreover, as Packer acknowledges, both models assume that the adversary clash of lawyers is central. Both thus implicitly buy into the insider world-view. Both also seem to treat criminal justice as a tug-of-war, a zero-sum contest between conservatives and liberals, prosecutors and defense counsel. Of course there is a zero-sum aspect: victims want some punishment, and defendants would prefer not to suffer it. But, I hope to show, there are changes that could make both sides better off, as victims, defendants, and communities often need to heal together. Sometimes this aspiration will prove too idealistic, but in other situations it can work.

This healing aspiration relates to a third theme of the book: a move from the individual-badness model to a more relational approach to crime. In gauging punishment, recent criminal procedure focuses on the individual defendant's badness: how much deterrence and incapacitation does he need? It draws a mechanistic picture of deterrence as pain and incapacitation as physical constraint. This approach is not so much wrong as incomplete. It ignores the other substantive-criminal-law values discussed above. Deterrence is not simply about pain and threat, but about reinforcing social norms and communicating public messages that discourage crime in other ways.

Equally, the individual-badness focus ignores the relational aspect of crime. Crime is not simply a discrete violation, a physical or monetary injury. It wounds relationships. Very often, wrongdoers, victims, and neighbors know one another, and crime estranges and embitters them. Even stranger-on-stranger and some victimless crimes tear the social fabric, sowing fear and distrust in neighborhoods and communities. In many situations, criminal justice has the potential to heal these wounded relationships, at least if the parties are willing to talk. Sometimes wrongdoers will admit guilt, accept blame, profess remorse, apologize, and make amends. Sometimes victims are willing or eager to tell their stories, vent, listen, accept apologies, and forgive, particularly if they see justice done. In other cases, all we can do is deter and incapacitate wrongdoers and inflict punishment. But in the right cases, criminal procedure can do more, helping to vindicate and heal the parties and their wounded relationships.

* * * * *

A note on terminology: Because public opinion and popular morality are central to my argument, I have tried to make the book accessible to non-lawyers and non-academics, writing as simply and clearly as possible. For instance, I explain concepts, terms, and ideas that will already be familiar to criminal procedure scholars, legal historians, and other lawyers and academics. I have consolidated my references down to one endnote per paragraph and minimized internal cross-references in order to limit distractions for the ordinary reader. I have also striven to use popular terminology where it is equally precise. For example, most criminal justice scholars habitually refer to offenders, perhaps because that word has a clinical, amoral ring. But a key part of my argument is that insiders' reluctance to speak the language of moral blame has distanced criminal justice from the lifeblood of popular moral judgment. I sometimes use the term offender to track the language of one of my sources, or in terms of art such as sex offender, repeat offender, first offender, and victim-offender mediation. Occasionally I use the term criminal, defendant, or inmate, where I want to stress the link to a crime or to one's status in a criminal case or prison. But for the most part I deliberately use the term wrongdoer, because it highlights the moral and legal wrong that the criminal justice system must try to heal. Academics' flight from the stigma attached to that term, I argue in this book, has backfired, breeding public dissatisfaction. The solution is to bring moral judgment out into the open instead of trying to squelch it.

CHAPTER I

c√ა

The Long Drift from Morality
Play to Machine

The popular ideal of criminal justice as a morality play, an educational
social drama unfolding before a jury of one's peers, harkens back to
colonial America. Deeply embedded in Americans' collective memory, it
profoundly shaped our Constitution and Bill of Rights. Yet, though we still
embrace those legal monuments, the tectonic plates have shifted beneath
our feet. The entire process has morphed from a public morality play into
a speedy plea-bargaining machine, hidden and insulated from the public.

Three major structural changes define this shift. First, while laymen
used to investigate and control prosecution of crime, the professional
criminal-justice bureaucracy has squeezed laymen out. Second, speedy,
hidden plea bargaining has supplanted public trials and juries' common
sense and moral judgment. Third, hidden imprisonment has displaced
public punishment, keeping the public from seeing justice done. Legal
historians are familiar with these changes and would find this stylized
portrait simplistic, as it glosses over subtleties and regional variations.
But most non-historians fail to appreciate how these structural changes
have warped today's justice system and caused it to diverge from our
collective historical memory.

Like continental drift, legal drift happens over centuries and millen-
nia, often without a single cataclysm or public recognition of the shift.
That is what has happened here. Our story begins in the seventeenth and
eighteenth centuries, before the American Revolution. Of course America
had inhabitants, settlers, and criminal justice long before the English
arrived at Jamestown and Plymouth Rock. The many American Indian
tribes had legal systems, as did the early Spanish and French settlers and

1

even the Vikings who may have preceded them. Dutch settlers arrived soon afterwards. But their laws left little mark on ours. Our criminal justice system originated with the English settlers who populated the thirteen original colonies, bringing English common law with them.[1] While the colonies' laws and customs varied significantly,[2] they also shared much heritage and perspective. To those English colonies we now turn.

A. CRIMINAL JUSTICE IN THE EARLY AMERICAN COLONIES

1. Small-Town Morality

Communities in the early American colonies were close-knit. Everyone knew everyone else. Villages were small, so word-of-mouth spread quickly. They were also fairly homogeneous. For the most part, people knew and agreed on what acts were right and wrong, which ones were permitted and forbidden. Consensus was especially strong in colonies like Massachusetts, which the Pilgrims and Puritans had founded for religious reasons—to establish a godly society. But even communities in non-religious colonies shared similar backgrounds and moral understandings.[3]

For the most part, law was not some newfangled imposition by distant bureaucrats. It reflected the communal moral consensus, the common-law sense of what had always been God's law and man's. Most crimes were not recent creations of the legislature, but the basic *mala in se*, the acts that everyone knew were wrong and forbidden. Of course these included violent crimes (murder, rape, robbery, and assault) and property crimes (burglary, arson, and theft). But especially in the Puritan colonies, crimes also included morals offenses (adultery, fornication, and drunkenness) and religious offenses (blasphemy, heresy, witchcraft, and dishonoring the Sabbath).[4] The community's moral consensus exerted social pressure to obey the law and to punish lawbreakers. Local judges and juries applied their local sense of right and wrong to the particular cases before them.

The downside of this moralistic approach to crime was its intrusiveness. The many seemingly victimless offenses, to our minds, violate one's liberty of conscience. We look back at Nathaniel Hawthorne's *The Scarlet Letter*, for example, and bristle at the self-righteous condemnation of Hester Prynne's adultery.[5]

But there was also an upside to the moralistic approach. The colonists recognized that everyone was weak, so anyone of any social class could succumb to temptation and crime. An erring criminal was a sinner just like everyone else. If he stumbled, gallows sermons would stress that those in the audience had likewise sinned and needed to repent. Most wrongdoers, then, were viewed as brothers whom fellow citizens should help up again after their falls. The job of the criminal justice system was to reclaim the errant sheep and reintegrate them into the flock. Society should hate the crime but love and redeem the criminal. Only the worst, most incorrigible wrongdoers were viewed as irredeemable threats who had to be killed or banished.[6]

2. Lay Justice

Colonial justice was the business of laymen. First, there were no organized police forces. In most colonies, each county had a sheriff or marshal to enforce the law, select juries, and oversee jails. But that was about the extent of law-enforcement professionalism. Ordinary white men took turns serving as night watchmen and making arrests as constables. If the sheriff needed help, a magistrate could call upon the posse comitatus, a group of men often indistinguishable from a mob. Likewise, if a victim or watchman let out a hue and cry, nearby citizens were supposed to rise up to help him catch a felon.[7] This was lay, amateur policing, far from the professional police forces that would begin in the nineteenth century.

Second, there were not many lawyers. At least at first, there simply were few lawyers in the colonies overall. A few men had some legal training from their days in England. There were, however, no formal law schools, certainly nothing like structured modern legal training. The few indigenous lawyers had learned simply by reading law books and apprenticing in a lawyer's office. Virginia, for example, repeatedly reversed efforts to license attorneys until 1732.[8]

Thus, many judges were not lawyers, but laymen representing the community's sense of justice and order. Many did not even have much experience with the justice system. Procedures, despite some technicalities, left magistrates or justices of the peace with broad discretion. Court proceedings were intelligible yet remained dramatic rituals, with imposing architecture, invocations, pomp, and distinctive judicial dress.[9]

Even if some judges were lawyers, at first the litigators were not. In England, victims prosecuted their own crimes *pro se*, without lawyers and at their own expense. They had the right to hire lawyers, but almost never did. Nominally a case was styled R. (*Rex*, Latin for *The King*) v. *David Defendant*, but the victim was in charge (except in homicide cases). The American colonies followed this practice for some time. We know surprisingly little about when and why our modern system of public prosecution eventually displaced victims, but it did not come to dominate criminal justice for quite some time. Even though, by the time of American Revolution, some colonies had officials who prosecuted some crimes, many prosecutions remained private well into the nineteenth century. Moreover, public prosecutors were local, often part-time officials who sometimes prosecuted on behalf of victims but also carried other work on the side. There were not yet public police forces; intricate, lawyer-dominated criminal trials; or state monopolies on investigating and prosecuting charges. Not until the nineteenth century did a publicly funded criminal-justice bureaucracy arise to pursue a crime-control agenda systematically. Often public prosecutors were appointed, not elected, and they had no systematic control of court calendars and dockets. Private citizens, not police or prosecutors, had to initiate proceedings by bringing complaints. Sometimes prosecutors could not proceed if a victim refused to cooperate, or they dropped charges at a victim's request. Until the mid-nineteenth century, New York prosecutors searched for evidence, drafted legal documents, and empanelled juries upon victims' paying them set fees.[10] Even after public prosecutors entered the picture, then, victims remained in charge for some time.

On the defense side, many defendants had to defend themselves without lawyers. Until the mid-twentieth century, the Sixth Amendment was understood to guarantee defendants the right to hire lawyers at their own expense. Many colonial defendants could not afford defense lawyers and had to represent themselves. In Maryland, for example, until the early nineteenth century not many defendants retained attorneys. Not until the mid-nineteenth century did half of London defendants have counsel; the numbers and timing in Massachusetts may have been comparable.[11] Though defense lawyers sometimes appeared, and some courts even appointed them, there was nothing like a public defender system to handle large blocks of cases. Thus, there were no systematic repeat players with incentives to plea bargain away their dockets.

Trials were exceedingly fast. Eighteenth-century English courts heard between twelve and twenty trials per day, each lasting about half an hour. Jury deliberation took only a few minutes; often jurors would not even retire from the courtroom, but huddle together and reach agreement. Trials in the colonies appear to have been almost as swift.[12]

These swift, informal trials were hardly today's stiff courtroom rituals, but rather arguments about who was right and who was wrong. They could be hectic and somewhat chaotic. Victims and any supporting witnesses testified under oath, very simply, about what the accused had done. The accused replied without being sworn in, responding to the

various accusations. Often the accused would deny the crime, but sometimes he would admit guilt and plead for mercy, as trials were merged with
sentencing considerations. In theory, crimes carried fixed punishments.
In practice, juries could mitigate sentences by convicting of lesser offenses,
such as petty rather than grand larceny. Particularly because many if not
most defendants had been caught red-handed or otherwise had no defense,
the main point of many trials was to weigh leniency.[13] In other words,
central to most trials was the issue of what punishment the accused
deserved.

Trials were thus morality plays. If the accused denied the crime, the
jury would determine who was lying and who was telling the truth. The
jury would also determine how bad the crime was, how bad or sympathetic
the criminal was, and what punishment seemed fitting. Ideally, the party
in the wrong (whether the criminal or false accuser) would confess and
repent, as in a courtroom drama. Confessing showed that the wrongdoer
had learned a lesson and paved the way to forgiving and reintegrating him
into society.[14]

Judges did not box juries in with technical legal instructions. Especially
before the eighteenth century, instructions were little more than remind-
ers of the statements they had heard from accusers and accused. Judges
freely commented on the testimony, strongly hinting at their views. They
questioned and cross-examined witnesses, helping witnesses to tell their
stories. They also limited abusive questioning and pointed out weaknesses
in each side's case. They frequently suggested that juries convict of lesser,
noncapital offenses. And they discouraged guilty pleas, so that defendants
could tell their stories and possibly show that they deserved mercy.[15]
(Defendants did plead guilty to many low-level victimless crimes punish-
able by fines, but not typically to higher-level offenses carrying more
serious punishments.) In other words, even judges' involvement focused
on the central, common-sense issues of who did what and what punishment defendants deserved. Trials were community searches for factual
and moral truth.

Though judges were active participants and expressed their opinions,
juries were also remarkably powerful and active. Far from sitting silently,
jurors occasionally interjected comments and questions, sometimes
through judges but also directly to witnesses mid-testimony. Judges sometimes gave conflicting instructions on the law, rudimentary guidance, or
no instructions at all. Even when judges instructed juries specifically and
unequivocally, litigants could argue their own views of the law to juries.
Juries had the power to interpret the law themselves, and judges could not
punish juries or set aside the verdicts of juries that disregarded their

instructions. In other words, juries were political institutions that judged factual and legal guilt as well as moral blame.[16]

Jury trials were transparent and easy to understand. There were few legal rules and little legalese to cloud the central issues of factual guilt and moral desert. Thus, the victim, defendant, and jury could easily understand what was going on. Likewise, the public could see the wheels of justice turning. Trials were very brief and courts were in session only sporadically. They were open to the public and held locally, so spectators could watch everything. They were public spectacles, crowded with spectators who had come into town to watch and gossip; criminal cases were the soap operas of their day. Neighbors' gossip quickly spread courtroom news throughout the small towns and villages where most Americans lived. Trials educated citizens about crime and the law and "satisf[ied] the public that truth had prevailed at trial," increasing public confidence in the justice system.[17]

Trials were not only transparent, but also participatory. Victims and defendants ran the system; they literally had their day in court. They not only saw justice done, but did it themselves. The public participated too. Bystanders at trial who happened to have relevant information could bring it forward, painting a more complete picture and checking witness perjury. And the (white male) public participated actively as jurors. As I have already mentioned, jurors interjected comments and questions and controlled convictions and sentences. By doing so, they shaped the law, monitored government officials, and prevented judicial favoritism and corruption.[18] Trials, in short, empowered the people.

3. Room for Mercy

When we look back at colonial-era punishments, we think of them as promiscuously bloody, far too quick to execute. But while there were many more capital crimes than today, colonial American criminal codes were much less bloody than England's. By the late eighteenth century, English law punished nearly two hundred offenses with the death penalty, becoming Europe's harshest penal code. Especially at first, the northern colonies in America did not authorize the death penalty for property crimes or did so only for recidivists (repeat offenders). For a time, some did not even authorize death for rape and manslaughter.[19]

The great blot upon this lenient picture is slavery. Southern colonies grew increasingly bloody towards slaves in an effort to control them. Slaves faced execution for trying to murder, rape, maim, or even bruise a white person, for burning or destroying goods, or for enticing other slaves to run away. Some Southern colonies also deprived slaves of jury trials, using justices of the peace to speed up executions. Perhaps as a result, North Carolina executed at least a hundred slaves between 1748 and 1772, far more than the number of whites it executed during its entire colonial history. Virginia executed 555 slaves between 1706 and 1784. Northern justice was sometimes racially tinged too. Reacting to a planned slave uprising, New York hanged or burned thirty-one slaves and four whites.[20]

But with the important exception of slave justice, the colonies were even more lenient in practice than in theory. Many colonies authorized execution for morals or consensual crimes, but executed almost no one for adultery, blasphemy, sodomy, or bestiality. Hanging for burglary, robbery, or theft was extremely rare. Before the Revolution, Pennsylvania convicted fewer than two people per year of capital offenses and executed only about one a year.[21]

Though crimes carried fixed penalties, colonial justice was more lenient in practice because criminal procedure left plenty of room for mercy. One avenue for mercy was the practice Blackstone famously termed "pious perjury." As previously noted, juries frequently convicted sympathetic defendants of lesser, noncapital offenses, often at the prompting of judges. In England, menacing property crimes, especially burglary by criminal gangs and highway robbery, almost never received mercy. More minor crimes, such as pickpocketing, almost always did. For the many crimes between these poles, juries calibrated their verdicts to the seriousness of the crime and the behavior and desert of the criminal. For example, shoplifters, as well as thieves who stole from houses, shops, and warehouses, frequently received lesser, noncapital convictions. "Pious perjury" was an imperfect and crude process, however, because juries could not always massage the facts into a lesser, noncapital charge. Because English law had no obvious noncapital substitute for sheep-stealing, for example, juries frequently acquitted sheep-stealers entirely.[22]

Another merciful holdover from English law was the legal fiction known as benefit of clergy. Originally, clergy and monks were exempt from execution by secular authorities because only the church could punish them. Because in the Middle Ages only clergy could read, the test for benefit of clergy was whether one could read a passage from the Bible. Over time, the passage was standardized as the first lines of Psalm 51: "Have mercy upon me, O God, according to thy loving-kindness: according unto the multitude of thy tender mercies blot out my transgressions." A first offender could memorize this passage, recite it, and save his life. (Over time,

legislatures abolished benefit of clergy for some of the most violent and
serious crimes.) Instead of being hanged, he would be branded on the
thumb with a letter indicating his crime. The brand marked him as a felon,
shamed him, and prevented him from claiming benefit of clergy a second
time. By the seventeenth century, though women could not be priests,
they could claim benefit of clergy. Even the Puritan colonies, which
abhorred the ritual form of benefit of clergy, limited capital punishment
for many offenses to repeat offenders. The commitment to mercy was so
pervasive that even slaves benefitted. Virginia let slaves claim benefit of
clergy and avoid the hangman's noose, softening some of the rigors of the
racist penal code.[23]

Judges exercised discretion in administering benefit of clergy. They
could strictly enforce literacy requirements for unsympathetic defendants. Conversely, judges could interpret literacy loosely and even overlook a prior conviction for sympathetic defendants charged with minor
crimes. Likewise, juries took convicts' branded thumbs into account in
their own discretionary judgments. They considered the prior record
relevant in deciding whether to convict of the latest offense.[24] No rules of
character evidence precluded common-sense inferences about whether
a thief was likely to steal again or deserved mercy if he had.

Finally, executive clemency frequently softened sentences. Juries that
convicted defendants of capital crimes would sometimes add recommendations of leniency. Most commonly the recommendation would come
from the judge, the official most knowledgeable about the case. Sometimes
judges harbored residual doubts about factual guilt or legal errors and
used pardons as appeals, to correct errors. The seriousness of the crime
was another factor. Nonviolent property crimes were far more likely to
draw pardons than violent ones such as robbery or burglary. Wrongdoers
who had been violent, made threats, or pointed weapons were much less
likely to receive pardons. Judges were especially likely to recommend
mercy for crimes for which juries could not return lesser verdicts, such as
sheep- and horse-stealing. Youths and neophytes were much more likely
to receive pardons, on the assumption that they had fallen under bad
influences and were not yet incorrigible. Women were not only much more
likely to be acquitted or receive lesser verdicts, but also much more likely
to receive pardons, as they were seen as less threatening. Wrongdoers who
turned in their accomplices could also earn pardons as rewards.[25]

One of the most important grounds for pardon was the convict's character. Character witnesses routinely testified about the defendant's
upbringing, employment, family support, sobriety, honesty, and trustwor-
thiness. (The victim's character was likewise relevant to how much weight

his testimony merited.) The reports of gentlemen and clergy of the area carried weight, which could introduce class and local bias. But most pardons occurred without intervention by anyone but a judge; thus, plenty of poor and powerless people received mercy.[26] While today we exclude much of this evidence as suspect, it did cast light on the wrongdoer's broader blameworthiness, dangerousness, and prospects for reform. The emphasis was not on formal, even blind equality before the law, but on fully textured evaluation of everything known about this particular person.

Perhaps the most interesting factor in clemency decisions was the role of remorse. Then, as now, one of the most powerful grounds for mercy was a convict's apparent remorse and change of heart. Thus, the colonists left plenty of time between sentence and execution for repentance. They even granted postponements so condemned men could prepare to meet their Maker and perhaps earn reprieves. Convicts often feigned repentance to put off death and possibly avoid the gallows entirely. For example, one condemned man's "present Pretensions and Desire of their Prayers, were with a View rather of being sav'd in this World than in the next." But then as now, officials saw through much of this fakery.[27]

4. Reintegrative Punishment

In the colonies, punishment was public, shameful, and even painful, but it was most often temporary. The point was to make the wrongdoer remorseful and get him to make amends, so the victim and community would forgive him and welcome him back into the community. Punishment let wrongdoers pay their material and moral debts to victims and society, wipe their slates clean, and return to the community as equals. It did not create a durable underclass of ex-cons, as our prisons do today.

Today, imprisonment has a near-monopoly on punishment. But in the colonies, imprisonment was not a common sanction. The dominant punishments were fines, corporal punishments, and shaming punishments. Fines were probably the most common punishment. Bonds and recognizances required wrongdoers or their sureties to post money, which they would forfeit if they misbehaved in the next year. Courts would also warn wrongdoers or require them to make restitution to victims. Another prevalent punishment was sitting bent over in the stocks or standing in the pillory. These devices locked the wrongdoer's feet, hands, or head in place. Whipping was also widespread, as was wearing a letter advertising one's crime. Mock execution was commonplace as well; many wrongdoers had to stand on scaffolds with nooses around their necks for a time.

Other punishments included standing in public wearing a gag, or being dunked in water on a ducking-stool. More severe punishments included branding, nailing and cutting off ears, and banishment. The main targets of these rare, severe, even brutal sanctions were wrongdoers who were repeat offenders or permanently dangerous.[28]

Many of these punishments were downright painful. Wrongdoers in stocks or pillories had to stand or sit for hours in uncomfortable positions, exposed to the elements and perhaps pelted with rotten tomatoes. But only branding and mutilation were permanently disfiguring; for most, the physical pain was transitory. What burned more was the humiliation of public shaming. In smaller, tightly knit communities with strong religious consciences, shame and guilt were tremendously powerful forces. As Hawthorne described the humiliation of wearing a scarlet letter: "The unhappy culprit sustained herself as best a woman might, under the heavy weight of a thousand unrelenting eyes, all fastened upon her, and concentred at her bosom. It was almost intolerable to be borne."[29]

Punishments were extremely visible. Until the nineteenth century they took place outdoors, typically in or near the town square. Often there was a procession to the scaffold. Though in England hangings degenerated into ghoulish merriment, in America they "were not macabre spectacles staged for a bloodthirsty crowd." Especially in the eighteenth century, they were well-behaved, orderly, somber, and dramatic rituals. The point of the death penalty was to be a visible and solemn spectacle, as those around watched the procession from jail to scaffold. As one condemned man supposedly versified:

> Ah! what a Spectacle I soon shall be,
>   A Corps suspended from yon shameful Tree.[30]

The same was true of noncapital punishments. Stocks, pillories, and shaming punishments were in full view of the community, often on a scaffold. Whipping too was visible; a Maryland court in 1664 specified that a woman be whipped "at the whipping Post in the Publicke View of the People."[31]

These punishment rituals educated viewers about the horrors of crime, drunkenness, and debauchery and reinforced communal moral teachings. Not only did people from miles around come to see hangings, but they also sent their children to watch. They came to gawk out of curiosity, but also to sympathize and learn. Ministers came to preach about the temptations and sins that lurked in each of our breasts and the dangers of giving in to those temptations. Their message was that anyone who kept giving in to small sins could fall prey to larger ones. The point was not to ostracize and demonize wrongdoers, but to recognize one's own sins too. Everyone needed to repent of his own sins and seek forgiveness. Condemned criminals were expected to play the same tune. They would recite the misdeeds that led them down the wrong path and warn spectators against doing the same.[32]

Those who attended were witnesses to the final act of the morality play, literally seeing justice done. But they were also participants in doing justice. By attending, they manifested "their disapproval of crime and the criminal." As Emile Durkheim put it, punishment day was a ritual that reinforced social solidarity by denouncing the transgression and vindicating the victim.[33] Just as ordinary citizens participated as spectators and jurors at trial, so too did they participate as spectators in punishment.

This morality play had a negative side, denouncing the crime. But it also had a positive side, offering forgiveness and redemption to the criminal. Most crime resulted from weakness of will and character, as some fell prey to temptations that assail each of us. The point was to teach a swift, memorable lesson and lead errant brethren to submit, repent, and make amends. The Puritans in particular tried exceedingly hard to get convicts to confess and repent, so they could cleanse their consciences. Once wrongdoers did so, the morality play could conclude with forgiving and welcoming them back into the fold. Community members had seen wrongdoers pay their debts to society. Having seen justice done, they were more ready to forgive.[34]

Colonial convicts paid their debts to society and victims not only symbolically, but also concretely. Restitution awards, fines, and extra damages were common, but there were also other ways to make amends. One hog thief was sentenced to acknowledge his crime publicly and then repair the county bridge. When on occasion wrongdoers were confined, they were not imprisoned and condemned to idleness, but placed in workhouses and made to labor. The theme linking these sanctions, Donald Braman notes, was that wrongdoers were held publicly accountable. They had not only to admit their guilt and apologize, but to work and make amends to their victims and fellow citizens. The antidote for antisocial behavior was enforced prosocial behavior.[35]

The system was paternal; the state was a stern but loving father, not a brutal Hobbesian dictator. Though the word paternalism sounds pejorative today, the paternal model had a bright side, namely love. Earthly fathers, like God the Father, stand ready to embrace prodigal sons who repent, reintegrating them into the community. Of course, the small minority of convicts who were branded or had to wear scarlet letters remained marked out, set apart as they are today. On the whole, though, society was far more ready to forgive and forget than it is today.[36]

Empirical evidence about colonial wrongdoers' reintegration comes from Middlesex County, Massachusetts. At least 67 criminal convicts who lived in Middlesex County between 1650 and 1686 were reintegrated into society in documented ways. Convicts routinely went on to hold town offices as selectmen, constables, surveyors, assessors, clerks, tythingmen, commissioners, and justices of the peace. Others served as militia officers, church elders, and even a foster parent. Though women could not hold public office, nine of ten convicted women went on to marry, suggesting that they were able to live down their shame and move on.[37]

The Quaker colonies of the Delaware Valley, today Pennsylvania and western New Jersey, were likewise eager to readmit convicts to social prominence. One historian studied more than a thousand criminal charges in these colonies between 1680 and 1710. Surprisingly, recidivists were slightly wealthier, more likely to own land, about as likely to be Quaker leaders, and much more likely to hold public offices than the general population.[38] In sum, by suffering their punishments, wrongdoers paid their debts to society and victims. After that, colonists stood ready to welcome them back as members of society in good standing. Their past convictions did not bar them from regaining society's good graces and high standing.

Forgiving wrongdoers was particularly important because, then as now, most crimes involved family members, friends, and neighbors. Most people had to go back to living among those whom they had wronged. Besides, a small society could hardly afford to kill, imprison, or exile more than a tiny fraction of its members. Everyone was valuable, too valuable to execute or lock away for years at great expense. Most wrongdoers returned from punishment to society, and remorse, apology, and forgiveness paved the way for their reentry.

Even capital punishment was designed to induce remorse and forgiveness. That explains why condemned criminals were given so long to see the error of their ways and repent. Remorse did not always induce earthly pardons, but it at least invited God's forgiveness and man's. When condemned convicts genuinely repented, the colonists rejoiced, forgiving them even as they hanged them. To some it seems hypocritical to forgive and yet execute. But the colonists saw no inconsistency between inflicting deserved punishment and sympathizing and releasing their resentment.

Forgiveness is about releasing resentment, not necessarily remitting earned punishment. Remorse and apology healed the rift torn by crime, symbolically reintegrating wrongdoers into the community. It was the final act of a cathartic morality play.[39]

* * * * *

There is much in our history to deplore. Race, sex,[40] class, and wealth biases infected colonial justice much more than they do today. Criminal law was far more invasive than it is today, encompassing many more morals and religious crimes. Colonial punishments could be brutal, too many crimes were capital, and there were few procedural safeguards to ensure accuracy. Laymen could be incompetent and inconsistent, and lack of eloquence could hurt *pro se* litigants. The colonists did not consciously choose their system, but, lacking lawyers and law books, were forced to make do with amateur morality plays. History is not hagiography. But it does correct the common assumption that everything old is backward, everything modern is better, and every change is progress. The colonials were not perfect, but neither were they simply benighted. Our popular image of the jury trial as a visible, participatory morality play has deep roots in our history. And our history confirms that this vision was not only possible but actually worked, albeit imperfectly.

B. CRIMINAL JUSTICE SINCE THE AMERICAN REVOLUTION

1. The Changing Aims of Criminal Justice

At first, the American Revolution carried forward the colonial spirit of populist, participatory justice. In the Declaration of Independence, the colonists specifically complained that King George III had deprived them of jury trials and manipulated their judges. The Constitution and Bill of Rights carried this vision forward. Article III specifically guaranteed criminal jury trials. Even that guarantee was not specific enough for the colonists, so the Sixth Amendment specified that criminal jury trials be speedy, public, impartial, and local. The Bill of Rights also contained seeds that would later sprout into the lawyerized model. These included the Fifth Amendment's privilege against self-incrimination and the Sixth Amendment's right to hire defense counsel.[41]

Before the Revolution, criminal law had been in large part about maintaining social and ethical cohesion. A central concern of the founders was checking the authority of arbitrary royal officials to punish without the assent of the community. The crown had used its powers to punish political opponents for spreading seditious libel and other political crimes. But between the founding and the nineteenth century, the target shifted from abuse of power to controlling ordinary street crime, and an increasingly professional administrative system displaced laymen.

Demography could explain some of this change. Some of the colonies, especially in New England, had begun as small, tight-knit, religiously and ethnically homogeneous groups fused together by religious fervor and mission. Over time they grew in population and area, waned in fervor, and eventually included different religions, ethnicities, and races. Weaker social cohesion and pluralism diluted whatever consensus had existed about enforcing morals, communal shame, and the identification of victims and wrongdoers as brothers.[42] But there were broader ideological forces at work as well.

These changes were in keeping with the nineteenth century's rationalism and scientism, which grew out of the eighteenth-century Enlightenment. The religious picture of wrongdoers as sinners like us, prey to ordinary temptation yet capable of redemption, waned. Instead, reformers saw wrongdoers as at best rationally selfish. Utilitarians such as Jeremy Bentham saw criminal law as a mechanism to inflict enough pain to outweigh the pleasure of crime and so deter rational wrongdoers. He of course dreamed up the Panopticon, the always-watched prison that epitomized social control. Enlightenment reformers such as Cesare Beccaria agreed that the goal was to deter crime rather than to exact deserved retribution; rational philosophy was to replace religious ignorance. Thus, Beccaria favored milder but certain punishments, without clemency or pardon.[43] The rule of law required equal application of consistent and codified rules, not ad hoc discretion and mercy.

Later nineteenth-century scientists had a more pessimistic but equally rationalist approach. They viewed crime as a genetic pathology, an incurable threat by beastly predators: Crime was not yielding to a human weakness with which we all could empathize; it manifested a dangerous deformity of body and brain. Wrongdoers were not fellow children of God, made in His image and likeness and capable of redemption, but ravenous beasts to be caged. Most famously, Cesare Lombroso promoted phrenology, which forecast crime based on physiognomy. He saw low foreheads and other Neanderthal characteristics as markers of criminality. On this view, wrongdoers were degenerates, throwbacks to primitive, less-evolved humans. Because most lacked free will, moral sense, and remorse, he thought, they could not repent or be reformed. Punishment was simply a way to deter and incapacitate these mutants, not to give just deserts, educate, empathize, or heal. He saw mercy as counterproductive, as it undercut equality and deterrence and bred crime.[44]

The criminal law, then, reflected America's shift from a republic of virtue to a stable social contract governed by rules, reason, and self-interest. As William Nelson adroitly summed up the legal changes in Massachusetts: "[b]y the turn of the century [1800], in short, the criminal was no longer envisioned as a sinner against God but rather as one who preyed on the property of his fellow citizens." Though the state continued to prosecute crime to preserve social stability, it forgot about criminal law's role in protecting communal ethical values and social cohesion.[45] Deterrence and incapacitation were the key guarantors of low crime rates and thus a secure market economy. Retribution and other more moral values did not fit well with this mechanistic conception of criminal law.

In the twentieth century, rehabilitation- and then retribution-speak resurged in popular and academic discussion. But these theories did not reverse the fundamental shape of criminal justice in practice. In the professionalized world of lawyers, criminal justice remained fundamentally a mechanism of social control through prison. As discussed below, once it began its inexorable advance, the plea-bargaining machine never again retreated to make room for the morality play.

2. Professionalization

If criminal justice was to be a predictable and reliable deterrent, it needed more than ragtag volunteers and conscripts to run it. This need gradually displaced laymen's roles as empowered participants. First, America needed professional law enforcers. Amateur constables and watchmen, drawn temporarily from the white male citizenry, were not enough. They lacked training, and some did not want to take part. Also, amateurs were no match for dangerous criminals, who often assaulted them or resisted arrest.[46]

Thus, America soon copied London's 1829 creation of a permanent, professional police force. After racial, ethnic, and anti-Catholic riots, a series of American cities established police forces in the mid-nineteenth century. Police adopted badges, uniforms, and rule books. America's police, however, were less professional. There were neither prerequisites nor training for the job. New York's police were much less disciplined than London's bobbies. Cops were locals who depended upon politicians for jobs and promotion and in turn helped their sponsoring politicians to get reelected. Political patronage bred corruption. Nevertheless, these forces were much more predictable and reliable than the amateur watches they superseded. In the past, prosecution had depended on complaints of victims and, secondarily, of neighbors. Now, however, police would instigate prosecution of those who disrupted public order, ranging from public intoxication to prostitution to gambling.[47] The move away from victim control thus shifted the emphasis of enforcement from vindicating aggrieved victims toward maintaining public order.

Reacting against police corruption and patronage, progressive reformers further insulated police from the communities they served. Beginning in the late nineteenth century, police work became more professional and specialized. Hiring standards, civil-service exams, and education requirements limited raw patronage hiring. By the twentieth century, police went from walking beats to driving patrol cars. They went from looking for problems to responding to radio-dispatch calls. These changes centralized control and monitoring, but in doing so distanced police from the people in their locale.[48]

Another change was that lawyers increasingly took control of initiating and prosecuting criminal cases. Though the colonies had few lawyers at first, during and after the Revolution the number of lawyers and law books multiplied. In the nineteenth century, public prosecution spread and displaced private prosecution. The increasing raft of victimless public-order crimes, such as liquor-law violations, required professionals because no victim had a personal stake. As with police forces, the growth of professional prosecutors gradually shifted emphasis towards these crimes and away from crimes with victims.[49]

Likewise, criminal defendants increasingly retained representatives to speak for them. Those who could afford it exercised their constitutional right to hire defense counsel. Thus, by the early to mid-nineteenth century, perhaps half of criminal defendants had lawyers. By the late nineteenth century, many states even began to appoint lawyers free of charge for those who could not afford to pay. In the early twentieth century, states began to form public defenders' offices to appoint free counsel. Interestingly, supporters touted these offices as cheaper, more pliable alternatives to confrontational shysters. One prominent defense lawyer even saw public defenders joining hands with prosecutors to ensure "that no innocent man may suffer or a guilty man escape"! In other words, their job was to grease the professional machinery and encourage guilty pleas rather than fight adversarial battles. Today, courts read the Sixth Amendment to guarantee free lawyers for all poor defendants who are charged with felonies or face actual imprisonment.[50]

Once prosecutors and defense lawyers had thoroughly displaced *pro se* victims and defendants, trials themselves changed. Prosecutors, not victims, made decisions about whether to initiate a complaint, how to investigate and charge, which witnesses to call, and which penalty to seek. Prosecutors, not victims, did the talking, relegating victims to being just one piece of the prosecutor's jigsaw puzzle. Once victims were mere witnesses, they would eventually be excluded from most of the trials for fear that hearing others' testimony could corrupt their stories.[51]

Likewise, defense lawyers did the talking. They made opening and closing statements, cross-examined adverse witnesses, and suggested reasonable doubts, explanations, and alibis. They also often advised their clients to stand mute, or else scripted what they would say. If defendants had criminal records, testifying would open them to impeachment and cross-examination about their prior convictions. Particularly for recidivists, the safest course was often to say nothing and let the defense lawyer poke holes in the prosecutor's case.[52]

Stories, therefore, came more from lawyers' mouths and less from laymen's. Even witness testimony was shaped more and more by lawyers. Witnesses did not simply tell open-ended stories, but responded to the prompting of lawyers' detailed questions. Lawyers investigated and built cases, marshalling and perhaps constructing or at least construing the facts. Lawyers began to prepare witnesses, interviewing them ahead of trial, questioning them, and subtly massaging or slanting their stories. Unscrupulous ones could even distort them or suborn perjury.[53]

The rules of evidence and procedure multiplied once expert lawyers dominated the system. Coming from larger cities and areas, jurors were less likely to know personally the victim's and defendant's characters and actions. Lawyers spent time selecting jurors and questioning them on voir dire, weeding out those with personal knowledge. Jurors thus became entirely dependent on the evidence that judges chose to admit. Judges, distrusting juries' common sense, increased their control by excluding evidence from their hearing. Rules of hearsay, character evidence, relevance, prejudice, privilege, and (later) exclusionary rules took issues away from juries. Some of these rules may have increased accuracy, but others distracted attention from the central question of guilt. These rules brought with them pretrial motions, objections, and sidebar conferences, lengthening trials and hiding evidence from juries and the public. Trials grew longer, from minutes to hours or days.[54] Moreover, these rules distracted from the central questions of guilt and blame.

Jury instructions also took shape and grew stiff. In the seventeenth and eighteenth centuries, judges offered their own views and comments on the evidence, but left jurors with only rudimentary legal instructions. Jurors applied their own common-sense understanding of the law in light of what seemed right. By the early nineteenth century, judges increasingly had legal training. They gave colorful, colloquial, concrete instructions, showing how juries might apply the law to the particular facts. But as appeals developed, appellate courts approved certain instructions and reversed others. Trial judges moved from talking about the specifics of the present case to reciting boilerplate copied from previous cases. Boilerplate protected against appellate reversal, but it also turned instructions into abstract legalese detached from the case at hand. And it hemmed in juries, eventually denying them the right to interpret the law themselves.[55] This series of changes lengthened and complicated trials and made jury service less empowering, which may have made jurors more reluctant to serve.

3. The Birth of Plea Bargaining

Public prosecutors were at first appointed, but by the Civil War, there was a strong trend toward electing them directly and locally. They were not necessarily full-time professionals. Most were part-time officials, hurrying to get back to their more lucrative private practices on the side. They received low salaries or fixed fees per case or conviction. Thus, they sought to dispose of their criminal cases quickly so they could earn additional money from their private clients.[56] And, of course, they lacked victims' personal stake in seeing justice done in court.

Prosecutors had far more work than they could handle. They had little or no support staff. Improved policing and enforcement of liquor laws may have meant more arrests and prosecutions. Carrying many hundreds of cases at a time, some prosecutors earned less than a dollar per case, even though some had to travel around judicial circuits. Legislatures balked at funding them adequately. And, as defendants hired lawyers, they filed more appeals. Some prosecutors also complained about their working conditions and paltry pay.[57]

Victims lacked the power to drop or compromise criminal charges and could be punished if they tried to do so out of court. Unlike victims, public prosecutors inherited the Attorney General's power to drop or dismiss charges. Prosecutors soon realized that they could promise defendants lower sentences by dismissing charges that carried fixed penalties. By dropping liquor-law charges, or downgrading murder to manslaughter, prosecutors could guarantee defendants lower sentences in exchange for their guilty pleas. This tactic—charge bargaining—is still prevalent today. By trading off longer sentences, prosecutors could lighten their workloads and ensure speedy convictions. Part-time prosecutors could thus earn more money from their private clients, and those paid by the case or conviction could also earn more public fees.[58]

Nineteenth-century crimes, however, often carried variable fines or prison sentences. Charge-bargaining these crimes did defendants little good, as judges retained broad discretion to sentence them. Prosecutors needed the power to bargain over sentences but could not promise what sentence a judge could give. For some more minor cases, prosecutors created a primitive form of probation. They could suspend prosecution or dismiss cases entirely.[59] More serious cases required judges to cooperate before prosecutors could promise sentences.

Though judges initially resisted prosecutorial bargains, they too became busy enough to acquiesce. The Industrial Revolution brought an explosion of tort suits to judges' courtrooms, including personal injuries from railroads, streetcars, mills, and factories. Often, the same judges carried both civil and criminal dockets. These new tort suits were fact- and time-intensive, so judges had little power to dispose of them by summary judgment. They could not bargain over outcomes, as juries set damages and each side wanted to maximize its wealth. The rising caseloads increased judges' incentives to dispose of what they could, namely criminal cases. So sometimes judges simply awarded lower sentences to those who pleaded guilty. Occasionally they made explicit promises or threats, bargaining directly with defendants. But more often, judges simply accepted the parties' sentencing recommendations. Defendants soon learned that most judges could be counted on to rubber-stamp these deals. Sometimes, defendants could withdraw their pleas if judges did not accept the recommended sentences, which gave them additional assurance.[60]

As defendants gained lawyers over the course of the nineteenth century, a stable criminal bar emerged. Prosecutors and defense counsel who dealt with one another regularly were repeat players. Both sides lacked personal stakes in the outcomes and had financial incentives to dispose of cases and get back to other business. The more cases they handled, the more money they made. Criminal lawyers got to know and trust one another. They soon learned the going rates or typical prices for standard crimes: a murder would go down to manslaughter, say, or a first-time burglar would get one year's imprisonment. Over time, a predictable market developed, which made the benefits of pleading guilty clearer and so encouraged more pleas. And defense lawyers worked with and on their clients, to sell them on the advantages of plea bargains.[61]

Thus, by the end of the nineteenth century, plea bargaining dominated American criminal justice. Just after the turn of the century, more than half of adjudicated defendants in Alameda County, California pleaded guilty. The fraction in New York City and New York State was four-fifths. In Middlesex County, Massachusetts, it was seven-eighths. The rates have only risen since then. Today, about nineteen out of twenty adjudicated defendants in America plead guilty.[62] Trials became the exception and plea bargains the rule.

4. The Hiding of Punishment Behind Prison Walls

The other big revolution in criminal justice after the Revolution was in punishment. In the colonies, prison was rare as a punishment for convicted criminals. The purpose of jail was to hold debtors and accused defendants pending trial or execution.[63] Capital punishment was common and public, as were corporal and shaming punishments.

An ideological change led to the great prison experiment. Reformers no longer saw the roots of crime in weakness of free will or in the devil's temptations. Rather, they blamed wrongdoers' families, associates, and vice-filled cities for dragging wrongdoers down into crime. The solution seemed to be to remove wrongdoers from their criminogenic environments and to instill new, law-abiding habits and discipline.[64]

For a few decades after the Revolution, reformers tried using imprisonment as a modified corporal and shaming punishment. Pennsylvania's 1776 state constitution, in making punishments less bloody, insisted on hard labor in public, on streets and roads, to humiliate prisoners. That scheme backfired, leading convicts and citizens to clash. Several states guaranteed the public access to prisons, so citizens could watch prisoners work.[65]

But a newer vision soon took hold, a radical break from the corporal and shaming past. Pennsylvania most eagerly embraced the penitentiary, literally a place for penitence and reform. In 1790 the Walnut Street Jail opened in Philadelphia, which classified, isolated, and disciplined prisoners but did not make them work. In 1829 the Eastern State Penitentiary (also called Cherry Hill) opened as a place for hard labor in solitude. Each prisoner remained in solitary confinement, separate from one another and in complete silence. The experiment was inspired by Enlightenment and Quaker faith in human nature. If each man was kept in silence, with only a Bible as his companion, his inner light or reason would supposedly convict his conscience and lead him to repent and reform.[66]

New York's Auburn prison was less austere, as inmates worked together in silence each day but slept alone at night. Both systems, however, involved at least some isolation, as well as almost military structure and discipline. Both had as their central aims to reform wrongdoers through structure, and in some cases work.[67]

These reformers were far too optimistic about human nature. Penitentiaries did not breed penitence. Where inmates were kept completely alone without work, they went insane or attempted suicide. Even prisoners who kept their wits were not reformed, committing more crime soon after release. True solitary confinement also proved too difficult and costly to maintain. As crime rose, Pennsylvania added cells to its prisons and housed multiple inmates per cell, destroying isolation. Once prisoners talked and bunked together, prison became a school for crime, providing criminal networks and contacts. Prison did keep inmates from victimizing those outside, but that was its main function, not reform.[68]

By the mid-nineteenth century, these experiments had abandoned their dreams of reforming inmates' souls through solitude and hard labor. The aim of spiritual and religious reform of souls gave way to a medicalized, rationalized, scientific goal of rehabilitating prisoners' habits. Morality was to rest on rational, scientific, utilitarian goals of concrete improvement. Professionalization and specialization swept prison administration just as it did the bench and bar, creating the social science of criminology. Prison reformers rejected retribution in favor of a medical model of crime. Warden Zebulon Brockway differentiated wrongdoers as "diseased, defective, and dependent" and sought to treat the "common scum" before the more "desperate characters" contaminated them. Crime was a moral or even physical disease, not weakness of will. Though Brockway was more optimistic than Lombroso, they shared the same pseudo-Darwinian differentiation of humans. Wrongdoers were aliens, deviants who risked contaminating society. When this medical model of rehabilitation failed,[69] the only alternative seemed to be to lock these aliens away in semi-permanent exile.

By the time prison had proved a failure at reforming wrongdoers, corporal and shaming punishments were all but gone. The public had grown unused to seeing corporal punishment, so whippings and the like came to seem barbarous, humiliating, and degrading. They smacked of punishing slaves, schoolboys, sons, and sailors, not free men. Beginning before the Civil War, Northern states in particular curtailed or abolished corporal punishments. They also stopped using shaming punishments, which worked less well in anonymous, transient cities and could backfire by hardening bad characters. Instead, they relied almost exclusively on modern, impersonal prisons. Though prison had failed, few people could stomach going back to bloodier punishments, and there was no obvious alternative. Thus, prison has remained our default punishment for two centuries. Inertia triumphed. But as Charles Dickens argued, prison's slow, concealed punishment of the mind in many ways inflicted graver wounds than corporal punishments had. It tore men from their families, friends, and livelihoods and "buried [them] alive . . . in horrible despair" and ennui.[70] Prison bred everything from abusive guards to gang violence to rape, but these brutalities were out of sight and mind. Punishment had changed from a transparent, public, communal exercise to the hidden domain of prison guards and parole boards. Rather than reintegrating convicts, it exiled them from society for years, making it hard for them to resume law-abiding lives when they returned.

One of the biggest barriers to reentry was that prisons bred idleness, not job skills and responsibilities. Though at first work had been central to prison administrators' ambitions to reform inmates, prison labor dwindled between 1870 and 1940. Though some humanitarian reformers criticized abusive treatment of prison laborers, the fatal blow was not humanitarian but economic. Opposition by labor unions and small businesses progressively constricted the amount that inmates could work. By 1940, Congress had outlawed the interstate transportation or sale of prison-made goods, choking the market for prison labor. Today, prisoners can work for private firms only at prevailing local wage rates. That requirement, on top of the added security costs in prison, makes prison labor uneconomical for private firms. Prisoners can instead produce goods for state governments' internal use, but that internal market is too small to keep most prisoners busy. As a result, only about one out of nine state prisoners, and one out of six federal prisoners, work in an industry or farm.[71] Thus many prisoners waste their days in mind-numbing idleness, watching television or killing time.

After replacing corporal punishment, imprisonment displaced capital punishment. Over the last two centuries, executions became much less frequent and reserved for the most serious crimes. For our purposes, what matters more than the death penalty's frequency is its privacy. Prison had already taken most punishment out of the public view, so people more rarely saw pain inflicted and became more delicate. Society grew disgusted by the spectacle of public executions. Some people thought they made spectators violent. Others thought they made viewers too sympathetic to the condemned. Elites looked down on spectators not as citizen-participants but as debauched mobs. They were disgusted in particular that women shed their delicacy to partake in such vulgar spectacles. These critics "were less concerned with the fate of the condemned prisoners than with the delicacy of their own feelings." (They were happy to overlook the brutality of prison life because it was hidden away.)[72]

Thus, in the mid-nineteenth century, the Northern states that retained capital punishment moved it from town squares to prison yards. Southern states later followed suit; the last public execution was in 1936. Smaller, more elite, more male crowds still managed to watch executions within prison yards. Spectators continued to come from miles around, to stand outside the walls or climb nearby trees and roofs to get a glimpse. And the press took the place of the public, as newspapers reported on and sensationalized the crime and execution. Once indoor electrocutions, gas chambers, and lethal injections replaced outdoor hangings in the twentieth century, only a handful of people could watch at all. These indoor executions could not be seen by the kinds of people who were supposed to be deterred by its example. And they required trained experts to run them at centralized locations, not the community collectively punishing crime in the locale where it occurred. As Stuart Banner puts it, "[i]t was the state, not the people, that was doing the killing."[73]

Those defendants who were not sent to prison were placed on probation. They returned to the streets within days or weeks and had only to check in with probation officers occasionally. This invisible punishment, without so much as a public condemnation or apology, may have appeared to be no punishment at all.

Whether because punishment had retreated from view or because formal law seemed too weak, some laymen took matters into their own hands. In the late nineteenth century on the western frontier, packs of vigilantes filled the vacuum left by absent or weak authorities. After the Civil War, racist lynch mobs inflicted their own summary punishment on accused blacks, especially in the South. Some sheriffs acquiesced or encouraged this violence; others were powerless to control these mobs.[74] These summary executions were the darkest outlet of the urge for swift, visible punishment.

5. The Decline of Mercy

Colonial justice embraced mercy as unfettered sovereign grace and individualized moral assessment. But to Enlightenment minds and scientists, mercy was arbitrary. Rational criminal justice, they thought, demanded equal, predictable deterrence, and mercy undercut deterrence. As a leading member of the American Philosophical Society wrote in the 1820s: "[T]he continual and monstrous abuse by Governors, of this great privilege [clemency], is a very powerful cause of the increase of crimes. . . . Governors have much to answer for, who thus defeat the laws, and offer a premium for vice."[75]

Sustained criticism of executive clemency gradually restricted its use. Between 1790 and 1837, Pennsylvania governors granted clemency well over a hundred times per year. Between 1839 and 1861 they averaged about twenty-six per year.[76]

Reacting to these criticisms, states gradually regulated the pardon power by constitution, statute, and regulation. Hearings became more formal (though not as formal as trials). Sometimes they were closed to the press and public. Often they were *ex parte*, meaning that only defendants and their lawyers were present. As Rachel Barkow has argued, the clemency power, like jury nullification, came to seem lawless and unpredictable. The administrative ideal of equality across cases seemed to conflict with individualized justice and with compassionate mercy. Thus, both executive clemency and jury nullification dwindled.[77]

In more recent years, pardons and commutations have plummeted still further. No governor wants to be remembered for releasing a rapist who went out to rape again. Our society is unwilling not only to reduce sentences, but also to reintegrate and restore ex-cons' rights after they are released from prison. Federal pardons, which usually restore civil rights after sentences are completed, dropped from a few hundred per year in the 1970s to a few dozen by the 1990s. Federal commutations, which reduce sentences, dropped from dozens per year in the 1960s to single digits in the 1990s, even as drug sentences skyrocketed. In twelve of the last twenty years, not a single person received a federal commutation; in six of them, there were no pardons either. Presidential clemency is criticized as a perk for the rich and powerful, ranging from vice-presidential aide I. Lewis Libby to fugitive commodities trader Marc Rich. Governors occasionally grant clemency, particularly if they are lame ducks about to leave office. But gubernatorial clemency has declined, too. Some governors finish their terms without granting any clemency. Around World War I, California governors and their pardon board granted a few dozen pardons and about as many commutations per year. But beginning in the 1990s, California pardons dropped from dozens to one or two per year; Governor Gray Davis did not pardon a single person in four years. These declines are quite typical. Across the country, pardons and commutations have steadily declined in recent decades.[78]

Another avenue for mercy was parole. The great penitentiary experiment sought to reform prisoners by incarcerating them for as long as necessary until they saw the error of their ways. Reformation required flexibility, so that prison officials could gauge each prisoner's reform and repentance. Thus, reformers called for indeterminate sentences, giving officials broad flexibility on when to parole prisoners. Judges imposed minimum and maximum sentences at the front end, leaving parole boards at the back end to set actual release dates.

Indeterminacy, however, took power from judges. It undercut parties' ability to forecast sentences in plea bargaining and risked inequality and arbitrariness. Thus, statutes and parole authorities began to standardize release dates. Good-time credits became a standard fraction of each sentence. Some statutes automatically entitled prisoners to release at the end of their minimum terms unless they had misbehaved in prison. Others established a presumption in favor of release at that time. Still others, such as in New York and New Jersey, granted parole "largely automatic[ally]" after the minimum term, "quite contrary to the theory of the indeterminate sentence." George Fisher argues persuasively that these limits on indeterminacy were tied to plea bargaining's rise and its need for predictability.[79] Parole and good-time credits thus became guaranteed rewards for pleading and not misbehaving, rather than avenues for mercy.

In more recent years, restrictions on parole have further constricted mercy. In the 1980s and 1990s, the truth-in-sentencing movement swept the country, eliminating or greatly limiting parole. The federal Sentencing Reform Act abolished parole and limited sentence reductions to an automatic 15% for good behavior. More than a dozen states likewise abolished discretionary parole, more than twenty others restricted it, and others became far stingier about granting it.[80] These truth-in-sentencing laws did make sentencing more transparent and accountable, but they also constrained mercy.

Another limit on mercy was the trend from indeterminate sentences to structured sentencing guidelines. Reformers, led by Judge Marvin Frankel, decried the dangers of arbitrariness, bias, and disparity in sentencing judges' unfettered discretion. Thus, the federal and more than a third of state sentencing systems enacted guidelines to cabin harshness and mercy. The main discount available under the federal guidelines is a 25% to 35% reduction for acceptance of responsibility. That discount in practice has little to do with remorse or repentance and everything to do with whether a defendant pleads guilty. The federal and most state systems also passed mandatory minimum sentences, tying judges' hands almost entirely. One refrain of reformers was that unelected judges should leave sentencing policy to politically accountable legislatures, as well as expert sentencing commissions. That complaint is valid in large part because nineteenth-century prison sentencing empowered judges, not jurors drawn from the community.[81]

Back in the colonial era, penalties were fixed and so nominally even less flexible than they are today. In practice, however, the rule-bound system was far more flexible than it seemed. Jurors frequently acquitted or convicted defendants of lesser offenses, and judges procured clemency for sympathetic defendants. Jurors knew the sentencing consequences of their decisions; indeed, judges advised them to take sentences into account in deciding whether to convict and for which crimes. Today, however, jurors usually do not know the penalties, and judges instruct them to disregard sentencing in reaching their verdicts. Jurors cannot serve as the conscience of the community when they do not know what punishments they are authorizing. The only partial exception is in capital sentencing, where jurors must at least find the defendant eligible for death.[82]

The one substantial source of leniency left is prosecutorial discretion. Prosecutors can decline to charge, drop charges, sign cooperation agreements, and recommend mercy in various other ways. Particularly sympathetic defendants may receive mercy as a result. More often, however, prosecutors use these tools as plea-bargaining chips, rewarding guilty pleas and punishing protracted litigation irrespective of the usual grounds for mercy. This discretion hardly conforms to the colonial model of transparent, accountable, individual moral evaluation. Unlike executives and juries, prosecutors retain discretion in part because their decisions are hidden from criticism and in part because they are supposedly making expert decisions about ranking priorities.[83] Far from serving substantive justice and mercy, the discretion that remains in the system drives the plea-bargaining machinery.

* * * * *

The rise of counsel, plea bargaining, and hidden punishment greatly diminished laymen's role in criminal justice. Victims no longer got to testify at trial—the one role left to them after prosecutors displaced them—nor did they have any say in plea bargaining. Defendants said nothing apart from giving scripted responses to plea colloquies and reading prepared statements. Even these responses and statements were usually coached by their lawyers ahead of time. Neither victims nor the public got to see cases unfold, as most plea bargaining takes place in private conversations, hidden from open court.

Nor did victims any longer watch punishment, which retreated behind prison walls. Rather than engaging in a cathartic morality play with convicts, we have in essence given up on them and locked them out of sight for years. We hold out little hope that prisoners can endure their shame, pay their debts to society and victims, and earn reintegration. Even if we eventually release them, a web of laws further ostracize ex-cons and hinder reentry. Prison has become banishment, and society remains indifferent or loath to forgive.

In short, criminal justice moved from a common-sense, public moral judgment to a technical, hidden, opaque process. It was no longer about communal expressions of justice and deserved punishment, but about speedy professional triage of threats.

CHAPTER II

⌀

Opaque, Unresponsive Criminal Justice

The professionalization of the last two centuries has created a gulf between criminal justice insiders and outsiders. The insiders are the lawyers and other professionals who run the machinery of criminal justice; the outsiders are the stakeholders in the system, namely victims, defendants, and the general public. The insiders supposedly represent the outsiders' interests and wishes, but there is often a gap between serving those interests and values versus serving their own. Economists call the result of this gap "agency costs," as insiders are imperfect agents of outsiders. Many scholars explore how agency costs skew the corporate world, requiring elaborate corporate governance mechanisms to counteract them. Public choice literature has applied the same lens to understanding legislatures and administrative agencies. But agency-cost understandings of criminal justice are surprisingly thin.

This chapter describes the tussle for control of today's hidden, lawyer-run, plea-bargaining machinery. That system looks quite different from the lay-run, public morality play that preceded it. I begin by defining rough categories of criminal justice insiders and outsiders. I explore the factors that divide the principals from their supposed agents, in particular prosecutors and how imperfectly they serve the public and victims. I then trace the game of tug-of-war that results: insiders manipulate criminal laws, outsiders episodically restrict them, insiders subvert these strictures, outsiders retaliate with new mandates, and so on. This downward spiral proves to be costly, as it clouds the law's effectiveness and legitimacy and hinders democratic monitoring of government. I end with a different set of agency problems, namely the ones that strain defendants' relations with their defense counsel. Defendants often mistrust appointed counsel, find it hard to talk and work with them, and see and comprehend little of what they do. These chronic agency problems hinder understanding, communication, and control. Nominally the people and the defendants are in charge, but in reality the lawyers run the show. The individual pieces of this game are familiar to many lawyers. Rarely, however, do lawyers step back and look at the broader picture of how the lawyer-run system diverges from lay preferences and how that gap warps criminal justice policy.

Five themes pervade this chapter. First is collaboration: Far from opposing each other as zealous adversaries, prosecutors and defense counsel work together to find their preferred solution. They are repeat players who establish going rates and habits of disposition. Neither the adversarial collision of truth and error nor the public spotlight checks lawyers' performance any longer: There is no neutral jury, and judges rubber-stamp bargains. In a sense, the real competitive game is between insiders and outsiders. Second is quantification: Every law or fact becomes quantified or commodified as a bargaining chip. In a collusive system, there is no ringing vindication of truth, but simply an adjustment of price. Rights are not about truth or fairness, but simply tilting the bargaining table. Third is hiddenness: This whole game is hidden from public view, frustrating outsiders' understanding and further undercutting any lessons the system might teach. Fourth is insulation: This hidden system is also insulated from outsiders' control. The public and victims have little say, and even defendants normally follow their lawyers' scripts rather than the other way around. Fifth is amorality: The insider-run system winds up being value-free. Rather than serving moral ends and valuing truths, it simply maximizes the number of cases processed. In its pursuit of quantity, it breezes by moral and healing qualities that outsiders expect and prize. Insiders play the system not as a morality play, but as a game.

To understand these themes, however, we must begin by describing the camps of insiders and outsiders. Only after exploring that background can we appreciate how and why the two camps erupt into conflict.

A. THE PLAYERS

1. Dominant Insiders, Savvy and Self-Interested

The professionalization described in the previous chapter created a clique of lawyers and other professionals who supplanted laymen in criminal justice. By the nineteenth century, public prosecutors had taken control of criminal cases away from victims. Defense lawyers had taken over for those defendants who could afford them. With the growth in numbers of public defenders and other appointed counsel in the twentieth century, they stood in for poor defendants as well. By then, judges came exclusively from the ranks of lawyers and shared their views. Trained police replaced amateur posses and night watchmen. Professional probation and parole officers, prison guards, and executioners flourished.

These trends created the modern gulf between insiders and outsiders in criminal justice. Insiders, especially lawyers, know and understand the complex legal rules that govern the system and the typical kinds of crimes, defendants, and punishments.[1] They see the investigative processes, witness interviews, police files, and backroom negotiations that result in plea bargains. In short, they are knowledgeable. Of course, their knowledge is not perfect, as hardly anyone has a comprehensive view of the system. But these insiders understand and control at least their own fiefdoms.

These insiders are no longer traditional adversaries, checking and keeping one another honest. On the contrary, their stance is collaborative. The insiders are courthouse regulars, repeat players who have strong incentives to get along. They form working groups, accommodating one another and bargaining away rights. Rather than unequivocally vindicating one side or the other, they split their differences and reach muddy compromises. The adversary system presupposes that a neutral decision-maker will keep each side on its toes. Now that jury trials are rare and judges automatically approve bargains, there are few adversarial checks.[2]

Nor do clients effectively check insiders. Nominally, insiders are agents of their principals. In practice, as the next part discusses, the public and victims have little role in criminal prosecution and so cannot constrain prosecutors. Prosecutors draw their fixed salaries regardless of how satisfied victims and the public are. Moreover, because plea bargaining is more hidden than trials, outsiders find it harder to monitor prosecutors' performance. Pleas result from back-room discussions, the terms of particular bargains often remain hidden, and prosecutors neither follow clear rules nor offer clear explanations for offering particular deals or not. Defendants have more say, as they decide whether to plead or go to trial. But of necessity they lean heavily on their lawyers' recommendations, and their lawyers do all the talking. As I discuss toward the end of this chapter, defendants lack good information and benchmarks for performance, so they largely acquiesce in their lawyers' advice. Moreover, most defense lawyers are appointed and not paid by their clients, removing another check on their performance.[3] Thus, insiders are largely insulated from oversight and supervision by their principals.

Insiders thus exercise a wide range of powers free of effective oversight. Police decide whom, where, and what to investigate; whether and whom to arrest or issue citations; and whether and which charges to file. Sometimes they even decide whether to refer a case to federal or state prosecutors. Prosecutors decide whether to accept charges and whether to downgrade them to misdemeanors or defer or dismiss them. They also decide whether to divert filed cases for drug treatment. They can agree to bail, strike cooperation agreements or plea bargains, and recommend lenient sentences. In a world of scarce resources, police and prosecutors exercise great power in deciding where and how hard to push. The same is true of defense counsel. Juggling dozens or hundreds of cases, they decide where to pick battles, how confrontational to be, and how hard to sell clients on deals.

Because insiders spend most of their time working in criminal justice, they have distinctive perspectives on how to run the criminal justice system. They have personal intuitions about just outcomes, which at first may coincide with the public's intuitions. Their assessment of just punishment tends to diverge from the public's over time, however, as they become jaded or mellower. After one has seen many armed robbery cases, for example, unarmed burglaries and thefts pale in comparison. Others may drift in the other direction, losing a sense of perspective and growing to accept harsh drug sentences as the norm. While prosecutors or parole officers may come to share a common insider sense of the relevant factors and going rates, this shared sense is unpublished, unwritten, and often unarticulated. Insiders also become jaded in another way, presuming guilt and being less willing than juries to credit defendants' defenses and excuses. While new insiders start out suspicious of plea bargaining, they grow used to the system and eventually find it difficult or impossible to imagine it any other way. In addition, insiders see defendants individually and up close, which may lead them to consider aggravating and mitigating factors that the public and victims never learn about or consider. Insiders may even become cynical enough to drop pretensions of doing justice, a concession to reality that outsiders would find startling.[4]

Insiders also have practical concerns about huge dockets and self-interests in disposing of cases. Plea bargains guarantee certainty of conviction and punishment. In exchange for certainty, risk-averse prosecutors sacrifice severity to avoid possible acquittals that could embarrass them and hurt their career prospects. In addition, most lawyers have little or no financial incentive to invest extra work in pending cases instead of disposing of them quickly. The press of large caseloads and limited funding and support staff also pushes many lawyers and judges to settle quickly, before investing much work. The sooner each pending case goes away, the earlier the lawyer or judge can go home to dine with friends and family. Swift dispositions mean not only more leisure time, but also better caseload and conviction statistics, the measures by which judges and prosecutors assess their performance.[5] Thus, insiders use their knowledge and power to speed the plea-bargaining machinery, maximizing pleas and minimizing time and cost.

I am not suggesting that insiders are consciously selfish. Though self-interest influences them at least at the margins, many insiders enter criminal justice out of public-spirited idealism. But even their idealistic understanding of how to serve the public interest differs systematically from outsiders' sense of the public interest. The jading and mellowing discussed above cause insiders to view the public interest differently from the way outsiders view it.

Another factor reinforces insiders' focus on case-processing statistics: legal training. Many law schools train future judges and prosecutors to use cost-benefit, net-present-value analysis when assessing outcomes.[6] Insiders, facing pressures to be efficient, may think that low-visibility procedures do not matter so long as ultimate convictions and sentences seem substantively acceptable to them. Most readers of this book, trained as lawyers, probably lean toward evaluating bottom-line outcomes the same way.

Lawyers' senses of justice also tend to emphasize neutral criteria such as equality, the need to treat like cases alike. Taken to its logical extreme, this approach to justice exalts equal, predictable rules at the expense of discretion and mercy. Mercy and compassion, Dan Markel argues, fail to give wrongdoers what they deserve and conflict with equality under the rule of law.[7] In many lawyers' minds, fears of arbitrariness and discrimination dominate evaluations of justice.

Of course, labeling all these groups as insider lawyers is too tidy; real life is messier. Some insiders, such as police and probation officers, are not lawyers, while some outsider victims may happen to be tax lawyers. Some lawyers who practice regularly in the same criminal court are quintessential insiders. In contrast, an immigration lawyer who handles the occasional criminal case may be much less familiar with and jaded by routines. Sometimes these variations matter, but usually it is simpler and clearer to lump insiders together. On average, insiders are knowledgeable, informed, powerful, legally trained, trusted repeat players. They share self-interests in disposing of cases quickly, care most about the bottom line, and lack the same personal stakes as the outsiders whom they supposedly represent.

Not every governmental actor or repeat player fits neatly on the insider half of my dichotomy. In particular, as I will explain, legislatures and the media straddle the fence. They are entrepreneurial and opportunistic, simultaneously working with insiders and demagoguing against them when doing so can win voters and viewers.

2. Excluded Outsiders, Yearning for Justice

Criminal justice outsiders see the system quite differently. To be sure, outsiders vary even more than insiders do. Each group varies in its interests, knowledge, concerns, and relative power. Victims of violent crimes may be more emotionally hurt and possibly vengeful than victims of property crimes. Victims who are relatives or neighbors of their defendants may care more about confronting and reconciling with them. Recidivist defendants may be more knowledgeable and jaded, while first offenders are more classic outsiders. Locals affected by particular crimes have interests, knowledge, and powers that may approach those of victims; indeed, they are indirect victims. Residents of high-crime neighborhoods have some personal concerns and knowledge, but may be politically powerless and poor. Finally, the rest of the general public likely has the least direct interest and concern and only general forms of power, such as the ballot box. Voters do, however, express outrage and concerns about crime to their elected representatives and candidates. Some of these groups, such as residents of high-crime neighborhoods, are more knowledgeable and personally concerned (though perhaps less powerful) than the general public. Thus, some groups are classic outsiders while others straddle the insider/outsider fence. Despite their differences, the various groups of outsiders share important interests and exercise power collectively, for example through elections. Thus, often I will refer to outsiders collectively, though sometimes I will separate out victims from the public. These subcategories of outsiders likely differ from one another in ways that I cannot always explore. Rather than lumping them with outsiders generally, I will discuss defendants and their families separately in the last part of this chapter. Until then, I will focus on police and prosecutor insiders versus victims and voter outsiders.

Much of the criminal justice system is hidden from outsiders' view. Police do not announce which motorists they will stop and what crimes and neighborhoods they will target. Prosecutors rarely explain publicly why they have declined prosecution, pursued felony charges, or bargained away imprisonment. Discovery occurs between the prosecutor and defense lawyer and is not made public. Strict secrecy requirements cloak grand jury proceedings. Plea bargaining usually happens in conference rooms, courtroom hallways, or on private telephone calls rather than in open court.[8] Important conferences take place at sidebar or in judges' chambers. Public jury trials are the exception, not the rule.

Those hearings that are technically open to public view are in practice obscure. Hearings are often scheduled by conference call or orders tucked away in dockets, and court clerks do not publicize schedules. Plea and sentencing hearings are usually mere formalities that rubber-stamp bargains struck in secret and based on unexplained factors. Many victims desperately want information about their cases but are extremely frustrated by how little they have. Though many states have victims' bills of rights that promise notice of plea, sentencing, and parole hearings, many victims nevertheless do not receive notice.[9] In other words, fine-sounding victims' rights are woefully underenforced in practice.

Even when they do attend hearings, outsiders have difficulty understanding them. Legalese, jargon, euphemism, and procedural complexities garble court proceedings. Charge bargaining divorces convictions from actual crimes so that, in court, murder becomes manslaughter and burglary becomes breaking and entering. To outsiders, then, the system seems at best mysterious, at worst frustrating and dishonest. As a result, victims and the public may lose confidence in and respect for the system. Likewise, criminal defendants think they have either cheated justice or gotten bad deals for mysterious reasons, which breeds cynicism.[10]

The public is hungry to see and understand criminal justice, as shown by its insatiable appetite for crime dramas, news stories, and even reality-television courtroom coverage. Unfortunately, the information that the general public does have is often inaccurate, distorted, or outdated. Unlike insiders, outsiders do not have a large, representative sample from which they can draw average or typical cases. Because the justice system is opaque, and most of the general public has little direct experience with crime or criminal justice, they must fall back on memorable, unrepresentative, sensationalistic media accounts. Increased media coverage of crime may make crime seem more frequent, salient, and important, even though crime has fallen in recent years. News media report violent crime and unusually lenient sentences, instead of more prevalent minor crimes and average sentences. Even patently fictional crime dramas influence viewers. Many citizens' impressions of the criminal justice system come from movies or television shows that build open-and-shut cases on forensic evidence and end with swift jury trials.[11] That portrait is anachronistic and ignores the dominance of plea bargaining today.

Like crime dramas, news stories focus on atypical cases that go to trial, such as the trials of the Washington snipers (John Muhammad and

Lee Boyd Malvo), Timothy McVeigh, and O. J. Simpson. A viewer who watched only these trials might conclude that most defendants proceed to trial and are convicted there, unless perhaps they are celebrities who can afford great lawyers. Media coverage of the Columbine school shooting was enough to create the impression of a wave of school shootings. Politicians likewise publicize and exploit anecdotes as if they were symptomatic of trends: Recall the sudden explosion of crack-cocaine penalties in response to basketball player Len Bias's fatal cocaine overdose.[12] Collectively, these news and fictional stories leave outsiders with a memorable but misleading picture of the kinds of crimes and cases that dominate criminal justice. The image is one of glamorous, sensational trials in major cases, not the reality of endless, rapid plea bargaining in myriad minor cases.

Based on these media accounts, the public forms generalized opinions ex ante about crime and punishment in the abstract. Because the general public no longer participates in criminal justice, it does not see the aggravating and mitigating facts of individual real cases. When people receive too simple a description of a crime, they mentally fill in the blanks and base their sentencing recommendations on stereotypes or on memorable or recent examples. When people consider the actual details as jurors ex post, their perspectives change dramatically. For instance, even though 88% of survey respondents favored a mandatory three-strikes statute in the abstract, most favored one or more exceptions when presented with specific cases. A set of four Canadian surveys had some respondents read newspaper accounts of a sentencing and others read court transcripts and the defendant's criminal record in the same case. Readers of the newspaper accounts consistently rated the sentences as more lenient than did readers of the court transcripts.[13]

Because ordinary citizens have very poor information about how the criminal justice system actually works, they suffer from misperceptions. In polls, the public says in the abstract that it thinks judges sentence too leniently. The general public, however, regularly underestimates penalties. For instance, most Vermonters in one survey thought that rapists who wield knives often are not imprisoned. Criminal justice insiders in Vermont, however, maintain that such rapists definitely go to prison, almost certainly for at least fifteen years. South Carolina, Georgia, and Virginia jurors greatly underestimated how long capital murderers would have to be imprisoned before being paroled. Perhaps as a result, they returned death sentences.[14]

In fact, sentences are often as tough as or tougher than the general public would want. For example, in one empirical study, roughly two-thirds of Illinois residents thought that Illinois judges sentenced burglars too leniently. Yet when given a concrete burglary scenario, 89% of them preferred penalties below two years' imprisonment, the effective statutory minimum. Another Illinois study, involving four hypothetical scenarios, found that judges' sentences were as severe as, if not more severe than, laymen's sentences. In a California survey that briefly described six crimes, respondents preferred sentences as low as or lower than the typical punishments prescribed by statute. Another study found "remarkable agreement between average respondent sentences and [federal] guideline sentences." Many other studies found that, when asked to sentence detailed cases, the public is no harsher and may indeed be more lenient than judges.[15]

On the contrary, some liability and sentencing rules raise sentences far above what the public thinks defendants deserve. Paul Robinson and his coauthors studied seven modern rules, most of which are based expressly on the need to prevent crime: three-strikes laws, drug penalties, adult prosecution of juveniles, abolition or narrowing of the insanity defense, strict liability, felony murder, and criminalization of regulatory violations. For each of them, the authors of the study picked one or two real examples. They asked a cross-section of survey respondents to rank the sentences these defendants deserved and compared those with the sentences actually imposed. The results were striking. For each of them, the crime-control rules prescribed sentences higher, often much higher, than respondents thought were fair. A regulatory crime (using plastic rather than cardboard lobster containers) that deserved less than a year in prison in fact got at least fifteen. Having sex with an underage girl who was reasonably believed to be of age earned not three years, but forty to sixty, in prison. And transporting 2/3 of a kilogram of cocaine in the trunk of a car got, not four years' imprisonment, but life without parole.[16] In short, unless prosecutors choose to undercut these laws, many sentences far exceed what the public thinks is deserved in particular cases.

Even where the public agrees with insiders about average sentences, these averages conceal troubling variations and disparities. Prosecutors sometimes raise sentences above the statutory or guideline minimum by stacking charges or adding enhancements. In other cases, they use charge or sentence bargaining to lower real sentences below the nominal minimum or guideline sentences that the public thinks appropriate. Outsiders have little way to review or check these hidden charging and plea-bargaining decisions. A particularly lenient plea bargain in one case may mislead outsiders into thinking sentences are too light across the board. They may thus push for higher nominal penalties, not realizing that insiders will apply them inconsistently and use them as bargaining chips. The result may be that arbitrary sentence dispersion increases, as some defendants receive freakishly high sentences and others much lower ones.

In short, misperceptions about average sentences fuel spiraling sentences and discontent with criminal justice. Because voters are badly misinformed, they clamor for tougher sentences, three-strikes laws, and mandatory minima across the board. This pressure is an artifact of poor information and ex ante consideration; voters are not as reflexively punitive as one might think. The average voter, if fully informed, would likely think the sentences on the books are tough enough in particular cases. The problem is not with the authorized sentences, which outsiders focus on, but with the hidden ways insiders manipulate and subvert them.

Many outsiders also want to participate in criminal justice and benefit from participating, though they do not want to take charge of the process. More than three-quarters of victims surveyed thought it very important to be heard or involved in charge dismissals, plea negotiations, sentencings, and parole proceedings. Participating makes victims feel empowered and helps them to heal emotionally. More generally, while some citizens try to avoid jury service, those who serve report that participating increases their respect for the system and empowers them. Even citizens who do not want a role may feel they have to get involved, because otherwise insiders will serve not the public's interests but their own.[17]

Unfortunately, victims, affected locals, and ordinary citizens rarely take active part in criminal proceedings. In theory, citizens run grand juries, but in practice they are dominated by prosecutors. As Chief Judge Sol Wachtler famously put it, a grand jury would "indict a ham sandwich" if a prosecutor asked it to do so. Similarly, citizens run petit juries, but in practice most cases never make it to jury trials. In many states, victims and citizens have no say in decisions to arrest, charge, and plea bargain. Even at sentencing, a large majority of felony victims are absent. When they are present, many victims merely read prepared victim-impact statements or, more commonly, submit written statements before sentencing.[18] They do not face defendants and, unlike judges, cannot engage in colloquies with them or with the lawyers. Affected locals and ordinary citizens do not enjoy even this much participation.

Moreover, outsiders do not fully share insiders' self-interests and pragmatic concerns. For the most part, victims care only about their own cases, and they often care passionately. Victims and ordinary citizens do not care much about maximizing judges' and lawyers' win-loss records, case-processing statistics, profits, or leisure time. To outsiders, many of these insider concerns may seem illegitimate and selfish. Outsiders base punishment judgments primarily on their intuitions about retributive justice. Their retributive intuitions are often far broader than lawyers', incorporating many factors that to lawyers and philosophers seem irrelevant. For instance, many laymen attach great weight to whether defendants apologize and whether victims forgive them or want to show compassion.[19]

In addition, outsiders are much less jaded and cynical than insiders and loath to surrender justice as an overriding goal. They only dimly glimpse the caseload pressures, funding limitations, and risks of acquittal that induce plea bargains, in part because criminal justice is so opaque. If they had better information, they might acknowledge these practical constraints and the need to trade off some severity for the certainty of punishing more wrongdoers. But even if they were fully informed, outsiders probably would not give self-interest and other practical constraints as much weight as insiders do. For example, outsiders are probably less risk averse than prosecutors, who fear that acquittals will result in personal embarrassment, so outsiders often would not settle as easily.[20]

Also, outsiders do not mellow or become jaded as time goes by, as they do not see the repetitive cycle of cases that desensitize insiders. Insiders may come to see defendants and victims as statistics, but outsiders taking a fresh look see complex, flawed, real people. "[T]he horrible thing about all legal officials, even the best, . . . is not that they are wicked . . . , not that they are stupid . . . , it is simply that they have got used to it," as G. K. Chesterton observed. "Strictly they do not see the prisoner in the dock; all they see is the usual man in the usual place. They do not see the awful court of judgment; they only see their own workshop."[21] Juries existed to bring in a steady rotation of outsiders, whose fresh eyes could see the wounded victim and "the prisoner in the dock" in all their complexity before "the awful court of judgment."

Finally, outsiders are laymen, not lawyers. As noted earlier, insider lawyers tend to focus on bottom-line sentence outcomes. But laymen take into account much more than bottom-line outcomes when evaluating settlements. They care about a much wider array of justice concerns than do lawyers, including their own status, the other side's blameworthiness, and apologies. They want to hold wrongdoers publicly accountable and to make them pay the debts they owe to victims and their own families. (What at first appears to be the public's raw punitive sentiment is at least in part, upon closer inspection, dissatisfaction with idle imprisonment and a desire to hold wrongdoers accountable by making them work.) Outsiders' approach makes sense, and it suggests that insiders may take too narrow a view when evaluating what factors matter to outsiders.[22] Outsiders care about sentences, but they also care about a host of process benefits that come from transparency and participation. Efficiency-minded insiders, however, do little to deliver these process goods.

I do not want to romanticize outsiders, who have plenty of flaws. Voters are often ignorant of policy details and costs and benefits. Their attention is selective and easily overwhelmed by information overload. They may have difficulty empathizing with or may be biased against poor, minority defendants. Critics of voters, however, must also appreciate the public-choice and agency problems that beset insiders, who suffer many of the same cognitive limitations and biases. Moreover, there are many reasons to include outsiders beyond insiders' agency problems in making fact- and value-based decisions. As just discussed, public satisfaction is valuable independent of the substantive details of policy. Public participation is likewise overlooked, both as a way of increasing public satisfaction and as a requirement of democratic legitimacy. And public participation gives criminal-justice policy an expressive value independent of any fact-based, expert policy decisions. All four of these strands—agency costs, public satisfaction, public participation, and expressive values—are distinct yet woven together in the account that follows.

B. THE PLAY OF THE GAME

In many countries, political elites set criminal justice policy and have ample wiggle room to ignore the public's wishes. Many European countries, for example, abolished the death penalty despite public opinion rather than because of it. European political elites are evidently better able to resist popular pressure to change criminal justice policies than their American counterparts.[23] America's political economy is more responsive to popular pressure, giving organized groups of voters tools with which to challenge or regulate insiders' policies. These tools include not only direct elections, but also ballot initiatives, referenda, and recall petitions, to pass laws directly and discipline politicians.

Because the players have such different information, powers, outlooks, and interests, it is no surprise that insiders often do not behave as outsiders would like. The gulf between the two sides is so large that the agency costs are naturally large as well. Because insiders are powerful and knowledgeable, but outsiders can exercise sporadic political pressure, a game of tug-of-war ensues. This part sketches that game schematically, though in real life the tug-of-war continually recurs without always following a neat sequence. Proving causation in history and politics is all but impossible; all I can do is to illustrate how these agency problems appear to create or worsen the pathologies of criminal justice. Insiders use their procedural discretion to apply the laws on the books selectively to suit their own interests and goals. After a lead or lag time, outsiders episodically learn of these maneuvers and react by pushing for new substantive and procedural laws. Insiders then use their procedural powers to twist the new laws, provoking outsiders to push for tougher substantive laws and mandatory procedural strictures. Insiders, however, continue to find new procedural ways to subvert even mandatory laws. The game never ends, though insiders usually maintain the upper hand.

1. Round One: Insiders' Procedural Discretion Shapes the Rules in Action

We start with a system of criminal laws and punishments on the books. In America, however, the law on the books is often tenuously related to the law in action because insiders enforce the law only as far as they see fit. Criminal laws do not create binding obligations but rather a menu of options for insiders.[24] For example, police need not arrest suspects at all and, if they do arrest, need not file charges. They can let suspects off with warnings, as when they return young vandals to their parents so the parents can punish them. Sometimes, the point of the arrest is to inflict quick, discretionary punishment without judicial safeguards: police may arrest drunks briefly to sober them up in the tank, or release domestic abusers after their rage and intoxication subside.

Prosecutors enjoy even more discretion. They may decide not to charge at all or to defer prosecution pending successful drug treatment or restitution. Even after filing charges, they may divert cases for drug treatment, which may lead to suspended charges or suspended or probationary sentences. When prosecutors do charge, they can often choose from a variety of possible felonies and misdemeanors. North Carolina prosecutors, for example, can choose among eight grades of assault-related crimes and six grades of kidnapping-related crimes. Those who rob homes can easily face charges of robbery (armed or unarmed), burglary, breaking and entering, various grades of assault, grand or petit larceny, false imprisonment, weapons possession, possession of burglars' tools, and conspiracy to commit any of these crimes. Prosecutors decide which of these charges to file, which to omit, and which to bargain away. And when prosecutors are not satisfied with the existing rules, they persuade legislatures to enact more rules giving them more substantive and procedural options. For example, when prosecutors found it too hard to prove criminal attempt, legislatures made their jobs easier by criminalizing solicitation. And when prosecutors found it too hard to prove burglary, legislatures made their jobs easier by criminalizing possession of burglars' tools.[25]

Other insiders share in this discretionary power too. Prosecutors and defense counsel can agree to bargain around most rules. For example, they can agree to forfeitures, restitution, or cooperation against other defendants as full or partial substitutes for criminal punishment.[26] Judges have flexibility to dismiss cases, to suggest settlement, and to hint at light or heavy sentences if the parties go along or refuse to do so. Finally, parole and good-time credits create flexible gaps between nominal and real sentences. They allow insider prosecutors, judges, and prison and parole officials to set real prison sentences far below nominal ones. These tools are often obscure or hidden from public view. Even when the public hears about them, it may not grasp their significance.

Unsurprisingly, insiders use these hidden tools in part to serve their self-interests and pragmatic concerns. Police avoid making arrests, and prosecutors avoid bringing and pursuing charges, in cases that are troublesome and not easy to win. For a long time, that was their traditional attitude towards domestic-violence cases, because victims are often scared, ambivalent, and reluctant to testify. Prosecutors may decline cases entirely or divert some defendants to drug treatment in part to limit their workloads. They may file multiple initial charges to give themselves plea-bargaining chips. They may avoid charging troublesome cases to spare themselves effort, headaches, and possible acquittals. They may use plea bargaining to help rack up relatively easy convictions and avoid risking embarrassing acquittals, at the expense of sentence severity. They reward speedy pleas to deter time-consuming motions, extensive discovery, and protracted negotiations. They may be tempted to push a few strong cases to trial to gain marketable experience while bargaining away weak ones. On the other side, defense lawyers may recommend plea agreements to their clients in part to lighten their workloads, dispose of cases easily, and earn quick fees. They may even use pessimistic forecasts and slanted assessments to push their clients towards pleas. Judges use their leverage over sentences to encourage prompt guilty pleas, in effect penalizing those who exercise their rights to trial. By doing so, judges improve their case-processing statistics and avoid time-consuming jury trials and possible appellate reversal.[27]

2. Round Two: Outsiders Try to Check Insiders

In a few respects, some outsiders' concerns shape insiders' self-interests and their exercises of discretion. For example, most district attorneys are elected. Because they face electoral pressure to maximize convictions, they push their unelected subordinates to increase conviction rates.[28]

Three things are noteworthy about this influence. First, it works because voters have access to minimal information (mostly in the form of conviction statistics) and can participate at the ballot box. Second, it is candidates for office who publicize this information, as district attorneys or their opponents seize on a few statistics to bring them to voters' attention. Third, the influence is imperfect because the information is imperfect. Because outsiders no longer see jury trials and town-square punishments, their information is second- or third-hand and manipulable. District attorneys can create the misleading impression of toughness by touting 99.5% conviction rates, when in fact most of those convictions come from lenient pleas. Unlike conviction statistics, sentencing statistics usually are not readily available to the public, so the public cannot check the bargains being struck. District attorneys who push a few high-profile cases to trial and lose may lose their jobs as a result. At the very least, visible trial losses give fodder to electoral opponents and encourage them to run against incumbents.[29] The upshot is that risk-averse prosecutors plea bargain more than fully informed voters would like, because voters see only conviction statistics and not charging or sentencing statistics.

Occasionally, an anecdote will capture the public's attention and lead to reform. The story of Megan Kanka's rape and murder by a recidivist child molester led to a grass-roots push to register sex offenders, for example. Sometimes, politicians exploit or exacerbate these concerns. The Willie Horton advertisement in the 1988 presidential campaign played on public fears that violent criminals were being released into their communities too soon. Partly in response, many states restricted or abolished parole.[30]

Media coverage also fans readers' and viewers' fears of crime, provoking public reactions. For example, extensive media coverage of a 1992 carjacking and murder misleadingly suggested that a carjacking wave was sweeping America.[31] Existing laws already criminalized carjacking as armed robbery and grand theft of an automobile, but the public wanted new action. Thus, the public clamored for politicians and prosecutors to create new crimes and penalties.

To take a different example, the 1972 book *Criminal Sentences: Law Without Order* exposed the lawlessness of sentencing discretion and sparked the sentencing-reform movement. Liberals worried about racial and class disparities at sentencing, and conservatives inveighed against lenient sentences by soft-on-crime judges. There was little hard evidence of the size of the problem, but these concerns resonated with voters. Thus, many states, as well as the federal government, created sentencing commissions and procedures to make sentencing more uniform and predictable.[32]

3. Round Three: Insiders' Procedural Discretion Undercuts Reforms

The result of this sporadic public oversight may be new substantive crimes or penalties, pressure for increased enforcement, or a sentencing commission. The public's attention then fades, and insiders finish drafting, implementing, and administering these new rules. Sometimes, they implement the rules faithfully. Often, however, instead of simply being constrained by them, insiders use their procedural knowledge or power to shape and implement these rules in unexpected ways.

Some police departments, for example, tout their declining crime statistics and even use incentive pay to reward officers for reducing crime. In response, some police officers exaggerate their performance by reporting burglaries as larcenies and underestimating the value of the stolen property.[33]

To give another example of how insiders use procedure, the drafters of the Federal Sentencing Guidelines tried to reduce unwarranted sentence disparity and raised penalties for some kinds of crimes. They also specified fixed discounts for acceptance of responsibility as almost the only permissible reward for guilty pleas in most cases. Some defendants, however, are reluctant to plead guilty and accept long sentences, so insiders find additional discounts to induce pleas. Prosecutors and defense counsel agree to conceal or not disclose aggravating facts to sentencing judges. They use cooperation agreements to get around guidelines, even in cases where the proposed cooperation is marginally useful or a fig leaf for a sentence reduction. Prosecutors create new fast-track departures to plead out large volumes of immigration and drug cases leniently in exchange for waivers of discovery and other rights. Some judges use downward departures to undercut sentences they think are too harsh.[34] At the same time, by hinting that departures are likely or accepting plea agreements that provide for them, judges can induce quick pleas and clear their dockets.

Because insiders apply the rules unevenly, the result is renewed sentencing disparity as women, whites, citizens, the well-off, and the educated receive lighter sentences. In short, expert insiders learn the complexities of sentencing reforms and exploit their inside knowledge and procedural discretion. They pursue their own senses of justice and their self-interests in fast, certain dispositions, at the expense of the reformers' goals of severity and equal treatment.

4. Round Four: Outsiders, Egged On by Politicians, Take Matters into Their Own Hands

Occasionally, outsiders hear about these maneuvers and react by creating new, rigid rules in an effort to bind insiders or at least limit their discretion. Sometimes these reactions result in procedural restrictions on practices such as plea bargaining and sentencing departures. At other times, they give rise to substantive sentencing statutes, such as three-strikes laws and mandatory minima, or new substantive crimes.

When the public learns of charge bargaining, for example, it expresses outrage at the sale of justice and the cheapening of crimes and punishments. Sometimes, politicians capitalize on and highlight an issue, such as downward departures from sentencing guidelines. They may, for example, please the public by blaming insider judges and restricting downward departures, as exemplified by the Feeney Amendment to the PROTECT Act. Legislatures do the same thing by passing mandatory-minimum sentencing laws for drug trafficking, gun crimes, and other high-profile crimes.[35] As the next section describes, these apparent outsider victories often leave insiders plenty of wiggle room.

Occasionally, however, legislatures genuinely side with outsiders in restricting prosecutorial discretion. In New York State, the 1973 Rockefeller drug laws greatly restricted prosecutors' ability to plea bargain away mandatory drug sentences. Legislatures also restrict police and prosecutorial leniency when politically salient crimes are involved. In domestic abuse cases, for example, legislatures passed shall-arrest and no-drop policies to change police and prosecutors' traditional reluctance to arrest and willingness to drop charges. Candidates for office may also raise these issues by campaigning as outsiders against the abuses of insiders. For example, in New Orleans, Harry Connick, Sr. unseated District Attorney Jim Garrison by criticizing and promising to clamp down on rampant plea bargaining.[36]

Outsiders sometimes take matters into their own hands and use direct democracy to circumvent legislatures. In California, for example, voters used a ballot initiative to pass a law generally banning plea bargaining in cases in which indictments or informations charge specified serious crimes. Also in California, voters put a tough three-strikes-and-you're-out initiative on the ballot, mandating twenty-five-year minimum sentences for three-time felons. The legislature had buried the bill in committee, but then twelve-year-old Polly Klaas was kidnapped, molested, and murdered. In the wake of this heinous crime, a total of 840,000 people signed petitions to put the initiative on the ballot. Bowing to this pressure, the legislature passed the law.[37]

Many commentators criticize mandatory-sentencing laws as expressing the public's bloodthirsty desire for ever more punishment. Some denigrate these laws as no more than sound-bite sentencing slogans. These laws do express voters' concerns about the decay of social and moral cohesion. Yet there is another, more charitable way to understand mandatory laws, particularly initiatives and referenda. The public is frustrated by the criminal justice system. The system seems opaque, tangled, insulated, and impervious to outside scrutiny and change. Even though voters dislike plea bargaining and revolving-door justice, it seems to happen all the time. Recidivists, in particular, seem to be thumbing their noses at the law's authority and getting away with it. The solution may seem to be bumper-sticker policies, which are clear and simple enough that voters and prospective wrongdoers can understand them.[38] Clarity and simplicity help to deter and to express condemnation, two prominent justifications for punishment. And by tying insiders' hands, these policies promise to produce greater consistency and make monitoring easier. In short, voters may try to turn flexible, discretionary standards and options into firm rules in the hopes of binding insiders.

5. Round Five: Insiders Circumvent Even "Mandatory" Reforms

Outsiders may pass mandatory bumper-sticker laws, but insiders still get to enforce them. Because monitoring remains imperfect and agency costs exert their pull, insiders find new ways to turn rules back into discretionary options or standards. Sometimes they create or exploit inevitable wiggle room in statutes and discretionary procedures; at other times they simply flout the law. Either way, insiders' procedural powers trump, or at least soften, outsiders' substantive and procedural strictures.

First, prosecutors do not always charge supposedly mandatory crimes or penalties. Even under the mandatory California laws, prosecutors can plea bargain by claiming that the evidence was insufficient. Also, despite the three-strikes law's ban on plea bargaining, California judges and prosecutors can and do strike or dismiss felony counts or downgrade them to misdemeanors. In particular, prosecutors have discretion to charge certain "wobbler" offenses as either misdemeanors or felonies. Only the latter charges trigger the three-strikes law, so prosecutors offer plea bargains that charge misdemeanors instead. In other words, prosecutors turn three-strikes strictures into tools, using them to extract tougher but still discounted plea bargains. One study tracked federal cases that initially included gun charges under 18 U.S.C. § 924(c), which carry mandatory five-year consecutive sentences. In more than half of the cases studied, § 924(c) charges were later dropped. Prosecutors seemed to be using these charge reductions to reward guilty pleas and to soften tough sentences. Another study found that in up to 40% of cases in which mandatory minima for drug crimes would otherwise apply, defendants pleaded guilty to lesser offenses. Whites and women were more likely than minorities and men to avoid minima this way. Finally, while shall-arrest and no-drop policies may stiffen police and prosecutors' spines, the policies leave enough discretion that in practice they are far from mandatory.[39]

Legislatures collude with prosecutors, a powerful insider constituency, to structure supposedly mandatory provisions as bargaining chips. For instance, the Feeney Amendment tilted the Federal Sentencing Guidelines toward prosecutors by binding judges. It left most prosecutor-initiated departures alone; approved, but capped, fast-track departures; and gave prosecutors extra bargaining chips.[40]

Since dropping charges creates a record that is at least potentially open to oversight by supervisors or others, insiders also engage in less visible pre-charge bargaining. Before a grand jury indicts a defendant, the insiders may agree to plead to a lesser offense. For instance, defense counsel may suggest a plea to using a telephone in the course of drug trafficking instead of a substantive drug-trafficking offense. By doing so, they cap the sentence at four years and avoid a minimum sentence of five or ten years. Because the heavier charges are never filed, supervisors and outsiders find it very difficult to detect the bargains. Similarly, in the case of the California ban on plea bargaining indicted cases, insiders evaded the ban by striking bargains before indictment. And New York prosecutors circumvented bargaining restrictions by offering misdemeanor pleas and allowing drug defendants to avoid indictment.[41]

Finally, even after indictment, insiders undercut supposedly mandatory sentences. The most popular way to do so is by using cooperation agreements. Cooperating with police and prosecutors' investigations unlocks otherwise mandatory sentencing laws, providing one of the few ways to avoid minimum sentences. When insiders are determined to strike bargains, sometimes they can enter cooperation agreements despite thin evidence of cooperation. Many judges gladly go along, using even flimsy cooperation motions as an opportunity to reduce sentences. Another way to undercut sentencing guidelines is by plea agreement. In some jurisdictions, stipulated-sentence plea agreements can likewise evade mandatory guideline penalties.[42]

* * * * *

The tale just told interweaves substantive and procedural maneuvers and dissatisfactions. Low-visibility procedures such as charge bargaining and declination frustrate outsiders both because they seem procedurally unfair or dishonest and because they seem to produce bad substantive outcomes. Outsiders respond by pushing for new procedures, such as shall-arrest laws, plea-bargaining bans, and sentencing guidelines, as well as new substantive crimes and sentences. The traditional law-school divorce of substantive criminal law from criminal procedure, however, obscures this interplay.

The moral of the story is that outsiders rarely win enduring victories. For a very few crimes, notably domestic violence and drunk driving, outsider pressure groups have spearheaded legislation and sustained media attention to change law-enforcement culture and priorities. But these crimes may be atypical, with sympathetic victims and well-organized advocacy groups. By and large, outsiders lack the knowledge, the power, and the enduring desire to keep monitoring low-visibility procedural decisions. Politicians and the media play entrepreneurial roles, periodically seizing on gripping (and sometimes unrepresentative) anecdotes to excite popular outrage and pressure for their own ends. This dynamic is a spiral. If it were a simple circle, we would wind up right back where we started. But, as the next part explains, the spiral warps the system, taking a serious toll on criminal justice.

C. COSTS OF THE GAME

Insiders see their policy choices as benefitting criminal justice. They have taken it upon themselves to soften the worst excesses of outsiders' overreactions. They have also sped up the machinery and the processing of cases. Increasing efficiency and speed and lowering costs are of course good things if all other considerations are equal. Ours is an era of quantity, and so we focus on the visible, easily quantifiable benefits, ones we can count in dollars and cents. But we rarely pause to consider the tradeoffs. The persistent game of tug-of-war between insiders and outsiders shows, however, that the agency costs are real and quite significant.

Outsiders' evident dissatisfaction should make us pause and reflect on the costs of the tug-of-war game.

Those costs are considerable. The game wastes prison resources by unjustly and unduly lengthening some sentences. It distracts public and legislative attention from other criminal justice problems and reforms. It gives insiders vast power to apply the new rules selectively to further their own interests or biases. The unchecked discretion makes possible sentencing disparities that disproportionately harm poor, male, and minority defendants. It disempowers outsiders, denying them anything like their day in court or healing, and leaving them frustrated. Moreover, it is an ad hoc, low-visibility, low-accountability way to shape policy in a democracy.

The game, and the insider-outsider gulf from which it springs, also have three other costly side effects: They cloud the substantive criminal law's message and effectiveness; they impair trust in and legitimacy of the law; and they obstruct the public's preferences and its ability to monitor its agents. The next three sections explore each of these problems in turn.

1. Clouding the Criminal Law's Substantive Message and Effectiveness

The traditional Benthamite view holds that criminals commit crimes because they gain more pleasure than pain from them. On this view, the purpose of the criminal law is to deter would-be wrongdoers by making the expected punishment for the crime exceed the expected benefit. Thus, the law must be clear and straightforward enough that prospective wrong-doers will understand the expected punishment. Criminal procedure's opacity and unpredictability undercut this aim of the substantive criminal law. If the expected punishment is unknown, it may not deter the potential or neophyte criminal. Even if some recidivists know expected sentences, first- and second-time offenders and potential offenders do not. This misunderstanding is especially likely because wrongdoers are over-optimistic and prone to underestimate and take risks. As a result, in the face of criminal procedure's opacity and complexity, neophytes are likely to underestimate expected sentences and to take chances on not being punished heavily.[43]

Substantive criminal law also seeks to inculcate and reinforce social and moral norms. By threatening and inflicting proportionate punishment, the law proclaims the badness of the crime and vindicates the victim's worth. It can thus help to heal victims. The law also expresses the community's condemnation and, by doing so, reaffirms society's norms.[44] For criminal punishment to communicate consistently and effectively, criminal procedure must be transparent. Otherwise, current and prospective wrongdoers, victims, and the public neither see justice done nor hear the law's message. As I explained earlier in this chapter, criminal justice is far from transparent to outsiders. In particular, over the last few centuries victims have lost their day in court and do not see justice firsthand, so they feel frustrated and they long for vindication and healing. In sum, criminal procedure's shortcomings obstruct the substantive criminal law's goals of deterring crime, educating the public, vindicating victims, and expressing condemnation.

In recent years, public shaming of convicted criminals has returned. Some judges, for example, have sentenced defendants to wear T-shirts or display bumper stickers proclaiming their crimes. Some scholars and the public embrace shaming as a way to express condemnation of crimes. One point, however, often gets lost in the shaming-punishment debate: Shaming punishments are expressively satisfying precisely because the rest of criminal justice is so opaque. While other punishments seem uncertain, beset by fears that parole will undercut them, and hidden behind prison walls, shaming punishments communicate brashly and unequivocally. They have clear meaning and visible bite. Perhaps one reason some voters support shaming punishments is that they are almost the only ways that outsiders can see justice being done. If criminal procedure were not so opaque, we might have less need and demand for such humiliating punishments.[45]

2. Undermining Legitimacy and Trust

People respect the law more when it is visibly fair and when they have some voice or control over its procedures. Procedural fairness, process control, and trust in insiders' motives contribute greatly to the criminal justice system's legitimacy. Individual experiences with an insider's procedural fairness and trustworthy motives spill over into broader attitudes about the criminal justice system's legitimacy. As Tom Tyler and Yuen Huo explain, "[P]eople generalize from their personal experiences with police officers and judges to form their broader views about the law and about their community." Increased legitimacy increases compliance with the law. Most citizens obey the law not only because they fear punishment, but also because the law seems fair and therefore legitimate.[46] Conversely, perceived unfairness or lack of trust can erode the system's legitimacy and compliance.

Just as citizens must see the criminal law as procedurally fair, they must also see substantive justice being done. When citizens see that the law reaches substantively just outcomes, the law earns moral credibility that persuades citizens to obey the law in other cases. Conversely, when the law reaches outcomes that seem substantively unjust, or at least not visibly just, citizens view the law's judgments as less credible and less worthy of respect. The likely result, empirical research confirms, is decreased respect for and compliance with the criminal law.[47]

At one time, public jury trials not only educated ordinary citizens and let them see and influence justice being done, but also contributed to the law's democratic legitimacy. Yet today, now that jury trials are uncommon, outsiders seldom see, understand, or participate in criminal justice. The system is too opaque and remote to educate the public well. Outsiders lack much of a voice, a stake, or a sense of inclusion. Moreover, many criminal-justice decisions result from secret or low-visibility exercises of discretion and are not constrained by rules or standards. Citizens see very little of the system's workings, except when politicians or the media expose some outrageous anecdote. Secrecy and opacity weaken citizens' trust in the law and may also make them feel distant and alienated. Victims and defendants who experience plea bargaining may see it as procedurally unjust because they lack a voice, respectful treatment, a neutral decision-maker, and trustworthy authorities.[48] Secrecy and opacity also mean that citizens do not see run-of-the-mill, substantively just results. Instead, they see only the aberrantly harsh or lenient sentences that the media or politicians highlight. These visible injustices undermine the law's substantive moral credibility.

Perhaps because of these factors, nearly three-quarters of Americans lack much confidence and trust in the criminal justice system. Two-thirds of Americans see plea bargaining, the most opaque and insider-dominated part of the system, as problematic. Victims have similar reactions. Victims in states with weak victims' rights laws are much less likely to receive notice or participate meaningfully in various stages of the criminal process. Perhaps as a result, they are more likely to come away dissatisfied and doubt the criminal justice system's fairness and thoroughness.[49] In short, criminal procedure's failings may undermine the criminal justice system's legitimacy and efficacy.

Of course, simply exposing injustices is not enough. If citizens see injustices but remain powerless to fix them, they will grow jaded and cynical. But transparency and participation should have dynamic effects. Transparency is a means to inform and empower people to reform perceived abuses, so that they will see the system as legitimate and worthy of respect.

3. Hindering Public Monitoring and Preferences

One reason for the Sixth Amendment's guarantee of public jury trials was to make criminal justice "fundamentally populist and majoritarian." In a related vein, grand juries used to publicize prosecutorial declinations and other hidden executive actions, which increased accountability and checked agency costs.[50] These procedures used transparency and participation to keep criminal justice in line with the public's sense of justice. Now that juries are an endangered species, however, criminal justice is more opaque and dominated by insiders. These barriers obstruct outsiders' ability to monitor insiders and to influence them. Insiders now have more room to indulge their self-interests in lenient, hurried dispositions. As a result, agency costs warp processes and substantive outcomes, causing them to diverge at times from the public's sense of justice.

The agency-cost problem is especially acute because insiders and outsiders increasingly come from different worlds. As Bill Stuntz argued powerfully, in the nineteenth and early twentieth centuries, criminal justice was still local. Policemen and district attorneys came from and were chosen by the urban neighborhoods that grappled with crime. Their constituents balanced fear and sympathy for local victims against empathy for local defendants and their families. Voters would reward local officials who succeeded in serving their concerns and punish those who ignored or failed them. Thus, crime policy never lurched too far towards harshness or leniency. But since the mid-twentieth century, crime politics have moved increasingly to the state and national levels. Insiders have increasingly become removed from the outsiders they should serve. A suburban state legislator or appellate judge need not live near or know victims, defendants, or their families. Federal prosecutors and judges can live even further away and face no electoral check. Though insiders may want to do justice for a community, the ideas of justice and community have become too diffuse. Justice used to mean serving a concrete neighborhood's shared sense and needs. Now, however, the ideas of community and justice are abstract theories. The outsiders most affected by crimes thus have much less say or sway over insiders, who are freer to follow their own priorities.[51]

Without jury participation, outsiders can intervene only crudely. Citizens and victims cannot influence individual cases in the face of prosecutors' monopoly. At best, they can paint with a broad brush by voting and influencing legislatures. At worst, they must resort to ballot initiatives, such as three-strikes laws and mandatory minima, because they have lost faith in insiders and lack subtler tools. What should have been a cooperative relationship has degenerated into a competitive one, as outsiders wield these sledgehammers and insiders feel it necessary to evade these crude blows.

D. DEFENSE LAWYERS AND DEFENDANTS' DISTRUST

Until now, I have focused on the gulf that separates law-enforcement insiders from victim and citizen outsiders whom they supposedly represent. Here I want to focus on a different gulf, the one that separates defense lawyers from their clients. The insider/outsider divide still applies, though in different ways, and there is not the same back-and-forth game.

1. Insider Defense Counsel's Interests and Pressures

Savvy repeat players who know how to work the levers of power defend the bulk of criminal cases, though there is a spectrum. Some defense lawyers are newcomers; some handle criminal cases occasionally; many regularly juggle criminal and non-criminal cases; and public defenders and some private lawyers handle exclusively criminal cases in a single court.

Like prosecutors, defense attorneys are not ideal, perfectly selfless, perfectly faithful agents of their clients or of justice. They too are human and subject to similar failings and temptations. They may want the fame and fortune that come from high-profile trials, and they may fear that embarrassing losses at trial could hurt their reputations.

Defense lawyers face particular temptations that prosecutors do not because of the way we pay them. Many defense lawyers are public defenders, who receive fixed salaries to represent large numbers of poor clients. Others are private lawyers, whom courts appoint and to whom courts pay fixed fees or low hourly rates subject to caps.[52] Still others are privately retained counsel, who may receive flat fees, retainers plus hourly rates, or simply hourly rates. Many clients of private lawyers have modest means and cannot afford to pay more than a certain amount. This financial constraint may operate as a cap on representation unless the client then qualifies for and seeks court-appointed counsel.

This patchwork quilt of funding creates powerful economic pressures to plead cases out quickly. Though not all lawyers are slaves to their pocketbooks, financial incentives influence many. A lawyer who receives a fixed salary or a flat fee per case has no financial incentive to try cases. On the contrary, flat fees create financial incentives to plead cases out quickly in order to handle larger volumes. A lawyer who receives a low hourly rate or an hourly rate subject to a low cap also has little financial incentive to try cases. Financial incentives, combined with a heavy caseload, may incline that lawyer toward plea bargaining. Involuntarily appointed private lawyers are especially unlikely to push cases to trial, particularly because courts often compensate poorly. To put it bluntly, appointed or flat-fee defense lawyers can make more money with less time and effort by pushing clients to plead. Pushing pleas out of financial self-interest is part of what Abraham Blumberg famously called "the practice of law as confidence game."[53] Conversely, some young private-firm attorneys may volunteer for court appointments to gain marketable trial experience. These inexperienced lawyers may be too unyielding in plea bargaining because they want trials.

Another problem is that many public defenders are overburdened. They handle hundreds of cases per year, far more than privately retained attorneys do. Financial incentives may lead some private attorneys to take on more cases than they can handle.[54] In either case, the result is that the caseload burden pushes lawyers to invest little work and press their clients to plead guilty right away.

Insider relationships influence not only prosecutors but also defense counsel. Public defenders work closely with prosecutors and judges, developing close relationships. Judges and clerks put pressure on defense counsel, especially public defenders, to be pliable in plea bargaining. Repeat defense counsel often must yield to this pressure in order to avoid judicial reprisals against clients and perhaps to keep receiving court appointments. Public defenders must choose their battles wisely, which may require implicit tradeoffs of some clients against others. There are even occasional anecdotes in which a defense lawyer agrees to trade a concession in case *A* for a harsher sentence in case *B*. The inequity is particularly troubling when a private defense lawyer cashes in favors that he is owed in order to benefit paying clients but not court-appointed clients.[55]

2. Defendants' Overoptimism and Risk-Taking

Criminal defendants share many outsider characteristics but are an assorted bunch. Innocent, young, and first-time defendants look like classic outsiders. They know and understand little of what is going on, and they may carry expectations from glamorous television trials. Recidivists are more knowledgeable, though they may overestimate how much they know. Both neophytes and veterans, however, are overwhelmingly poor and poorly educated. Many abuse drugs and alcohol, and some suffer mental illnesses or impairments. Most felons and accused felons have little political appeal or clout, particularly because felons lose the right to vote.

Defendants also are too optimistic. People in general tend to be over-confident about their own luck and ability to control events. Defendants are particularly likely to be young, male, and less intelligent, and these groups (as well as first offenders) are especially likely to be overoptimistic. Some groups of defendants, especially sex offenders, are in denial about their guilt or minimize their responsibility, not only to others but even to themselves. And most defendants, especially youths, males, and the unmarried, are prone to take risks and gamble on lucky outcomes.[56] They are far from law-school-trained, cautious, clear-eyed, rational actors.

3. Miscommunication, Mistrust, and Muting

Defendants and defense lawyers tend to come from very different backgrounds. Defendants may come from worlds of poverty, drugs, and crime. They may not be native English speakers. Their lawyers are more likely than they are to be women, well educated, white, and from more prosperous backgrounds. These economic, educational, experiential, and linguistic differences set the stage for poor communication and mistrust.[57]

Defendants are laymen. Most have seen fewer criminal cases than their lawyers. They may see themselves as sympathetic and may overgeneralize from the few criminal cases they have seen or heard about. While some are jaded or indifferent, others are emotionally invested in blaming victims and avoiding blame themselves, or conversely are burdened with shame. In addition to minimizing their punishment, they also may want to tell their side of the story, vent their anger or sorrow, and excuse or apologize for their actions.[58]

Defense lawyers have broader experiences and more accurate senses of going rates. They are less personally and emotionally invested in their clients. And they are trained to evaluate outcomes quantitatively to minimize the chance of conviction and punishment, not to weigh intangible, qualitative factors such as blame and shame. Thus, while defendants may speak of moral blame, lawyers reply in the amoral language of probabilities and sentences. The differing vocabularies reinforce each side's sense that the other does not understand.

The circumstances of criminal representation only exacerbate the communication problems. Overburdened defense lawyers, seeking to dispose of their caseloads, have little time to meet with their clients. They may talk for ten minutes in the courthouse hallway. Particularly if the clients are not free on bail, it can be difficult and time-consuming to go all the way to the jail holding cells and clear security to meet with clients. Meetings in jail may occur in crowded, noisy, uncomfortable surroundings through a partition or screen, hardly the ideal way to communicate and develop trust. In some places, the lawyer may show up on the morning of trial, introduce himself to his client for the first time, lay out the deal he has already negotiated with the prosecutor, and ask the client to take it.[59] There is hardly a chance to get to know each other by talking and listening.

Defense lawyers also try to counterbalance their clients' overoptimism, denial, and recklessness. It is their job to be coldly clear-eyed and realistic, puncturing inflated hopes. Lawyers may go too far towards pessimism, however, in a calculated effort to push clients towards plea bargains that serve lawyers' self-interests. Economic incentives, pressures from judges and opposing counsel, and risk-averse desires to avoid humiliating losses at trial all give defense lawyers incentives to peddle pleas. Lawyers' optimistic forecasts risk being proven disastrously wrong at trial, while clients will never know if a plea rested on too pessimistic a forecast. To persuade their clients to settle, lawyers sometimes underestimate the prospects at trial, misrepresent the course of negotiations, and slant their presentation of settlement offers.[60]

For these and other reasons, defendants often distrust their appointed lawyers. In part, they distrust them because they are not paying for them, and free advice seems to be worth what they paid for it. In part, they see defense counsel as shills for prosecutors' deals. They sense that defense lawyers and prosecutors know one another and work together closely, perhaps too closely. Also, overburdened defense lawyers press their clients to plead guilty more quickly, and defendants suspect that their lawyers do not care to fight for them. To inspire them to fight harder, defendants falsely deny guilt to their lawyers, and lawyers come to distrust most of what their clients say. This mistrust poisons the defense counsel relationship. Because they trust appointed counsel less, defendants are less likely to heed their advice.[61]

Perhaps the biggest shift over the last two centuries has been the silencing of criminal defendants. Since defense lawyers entered the picture, they have steadily displaced defendants, talking for them.

Today, of the few defendants who still go to trial, almost half do not testify, leaving it to their lawyers to challenge the prosecution's case. By doing so, they avoid extra punishment for perjury and obstruction of justice, as well as impeachment based on their criminal records or prior bad acts. Ninety-five percent of defendants plead guilty in scripted colloquies, according to bargains negotiated by their lawyers. They bargain away their day in court entirely. At sentencing, defense lawyers prompt and script their clients. They even write pleas for mercy that clients read to judges, or press them to say nothing at all.[62]

From the defense lawyer's point of view, she is doing her job by doing all the talking. She has a better sense of what the prosecutor and judge are looking for, and can target her pitch to lower her client's sentence. After all, she sees her job as lightening her client's likely sentence in this case. In doing so, the defense lawyer edits her client's story, suppresses his voice and narrative, and puts more palatable words into his mouth. But from the defendant's point of view, his lawyer is manipulating and silencing him, leaving him without a day in court to express himself. He may see the lawyer as usurping his dignity and freedom to make himself heard. He may take umbrage if his lawyer defends him as a helpless victim of circumstance, which lowers legal punishment but humiliates and belittles the client. First offenders who expect the process to seem fair and legitimate and expect insiders to listen to them sometimes come away frustrated and cynical.[63]

Here, no political game erupts. Defendants lack voters' electoral power, and most lack the money to hire new lawyers or change their lawyers' behavior. The rifts between defense-lawyer insiders and defendant outsiders are nevertheless deep, though for a different set of reasons. Differences in background, outlook, interests, and values separate the two. They impair trust and communication. Defense lawyers speak for their clients and greatly influence what they say or do not say and how they choose to proceed. But defense lawyers' interests in quick pleas, and their instrumental outlook, are sometimes in tension with what their clients want. Some clients care about shame, blame, and having some control and voice. The plea bargaining factory's assembly line speeds by, rather than taking the time to listen to defendants' social, emotional, and moral needs. And it disempowers defendants, transferring control to a hidden bureaucracy of self-interested insiders. Defendants thus have grievances similar to those of victims and voters. In some ways, the true adversaries in our adversarial system are not prosecution against defense, but insiders against outsiders.

So far, my account of the insider/outsider game has been fairly general. The next chapter focuses on a case study of how insiders have minimized a set of goods that matter greatly to outsiders: denial, remorse, apology, forgiveness, and reintegration. The exclusion of these goods is troubling for many reasons. In part, insiders have overlooked the factual advantages of admissions of guilt in reinforcing deterrence and fostering reformation. In part, insiders have undervalued the public satisfaction and expressive values that come from confessions, apologies, and forgiveness. And in part, insiders have excluded outsiders from the public participation, especially the day in court, that victims, defendants, and citizens crave.

CHAPTER III

cᴧɔ

Denial, Remorse, Apology, and Forgiveness

Admissions of guilt, remorse, apologies, and forgiveness not only help defendants to reform themselves, but also help victims to release their anger and sorrow, feel vindicated, and find closure. Unfortunately, American criminal procedure does little to promote full admissions, remorse, and apologies. Criminal justice insiders care more about quick dispositions than about airing the truth and healing and reconciling the parties. Many defendants equivocate or have their lawyers speak for them, and many victims never speak or are not heard.

The professionalized machinery reflects the impersonal state's exclusive control of criminal justice. By running criminal procedure as an efficient machine, insiders dispose of their own large caseloads quickly but at the cost of many other criminal-justice values. Most notably, plea-bargaining and sentencing decisions are swift and impersonal. To the extent that they reflect the underlying merits at all, they are tied to the individual defendant's badness and need for retribution, deterrence, and incapacitation. They tend to be static, backward-looking assessments of blame and dangerousness that fit neatly into mechanical compartments.

This chapter explores a prime example of insiders' blinders: criminal procedure's limited concern with denial, remorse, apology, and forgiveness. This limitation slights defendants and all but ignores victims, who come away dissatisfied with the whole process. I begin with equivocal pleas as the tip of the iceberg, a symptom of criminal procedure's more general indifference to relationships, dialogue, and healing. A criminal defendant who is in denial about his guilt may still be able to plead guilty and receive a guilty-plea discount; at most he need admit guilt only grudgingly. These guilty-but-not-guilty pleas dispose of troublesome cases efficiently, but they also leave defendants in denial, which impedes their reform and increases their chance of recidivism. If our system cared more about justice and outsiders' need for clarity, it would abolish or at least severely restrict guilty-but-not-guilty pleas. The rest of this chapter reflects more generally on why remorse, apology, and forgiveness deserve larger roles in criminal justice than they play today.

As chapter VI will discuss, the law could do more to promote this healing process. It could, for example, encourage victim-offender mediation and restorative justice conferences and include more dialogue in plea and sentencing hearings. Doing so would restore more of a moral component to criminal procedure.

A. DENIAL AND EQUIVOCATION

1. The Use of Pleas by Defendants in Denial

To study the problem of denial, I interviewed thirty-four veteran prosecutors, judges, and public and private defense lawyers in seven states. I asked them a series of unstructured narrative questions about their knowledge and experience with pleas in which the defendant does not admit guilt. These impressionistic findings flesh out the dry statistics and psychological literature, explaining when and why these pleas are so popular.[1]

As these interviewees explained, many if not most defendants are initially reluctant to admit guilt to others and even to themselves. Psychological denial is particularly powerful in sex-offense cases, where defendants fear shame, rejection by families and girlfriends, and violence by other prisoners. While plenty of other wrongdoers are in denial too, let us start with a case study of sex offenders.

Denying and minimizing culpability are the norm among sex offenders, according to psychologists. They deny the facts of the crime. They deny their own acts. They deny awareness of or responsibility for what they have done, and they minimize the wrongfulness or impact of their behavior. They deny guilt to their families, friends, employers, and society at large to avoid shame and embarrassment. They are also "afraid to admit the truth, even to themselves. The thought of being a sexual deviate can be so frightening or repugnant to them that they hide from themselves for years."[2]

In many cases, these lies and explanations are not simply excuses for public consumption. Rather, they reveal underlying attitudes and cognitive distortions that may lead to more sexual offenses in the future.

Wrongdoers who lie to others begin to lie to themselves and distort their memories and interpretations of events. For example, a molester might say that there is nothing wrong with having sex with a child, or a rapist might say and believe that the victim asked for it.[3]

When defense lawyers start representing clients who initially deny guilt, they work with them, confront them with the evidence, and bring most around to admitting guilt. A minority of clients remains unwilling to admit guilt even when doing so could earn a favorable plea bargain and lower sentence.[4] Some of these defendants go to trial, but others enter various types of what I call guilty-but-not-guilty pleas.

The first type of guilty-but-not-guilty plea is a guilty plea that barely admits legal guilt, with or without moral guilt. The defendant may hem and haw at the plea allocution or at sentencing. For example, he may admit that he punched the victim but blame the victim for provoking the fight and disagree with the victim's version of events.[5] Or the defendant may admit that he ignored the rape victim's protests, but only after she had led him on with seductive clothing, looks, and kisses. I will set aside these grudging guilty pleas for now and return to them later.

A second type of guilty-but-not-guilty plea is a nolo contendere plea, also called a no-contest plea. It is technically not a guilty plea. By pleading no contest, the defendant neither admits nor denies guilt and lets the court convict and sentence him as if he were guilty. The defendant stands mute and avoids the shame of admitting guilt. In addition, the plea creates no estoppel, which means that the defendant can later plead not guilty or contest civil lawsuits on the same facts. For example, a driver could plead no contest to drunk driving while still disputing a crash victim's tort suit for reckless driving.

The third and most extreme kind of guilty-but-not-guilty plea is an *Alford* plea, sometimes called a best-interests plea. In an *Alford* plea, unlike a no-contest plea, the defendant pleads guilty but at the same time protests his innocence. Henry Alford was charged with first-degree murder, a capital crime. Two witnesses testified that Alford had left his house with a gun saying he would kill the victim and had returned saying he had killed the victim. Rather than go to trial, he pleaded guilty to second-degree murder while protesting his innocence, to avoid the death penalty. The Supreme Court held that defendants may knowingly and voluntarily plead guilty even while protesting their innocence if the judge finds "strong evidence of [the defendant's] actual guilt." The Court compared Alford's plea to a no-contest plea and approved his reasonable tactical choice to cap his maximum sentence. The Court's guiding principle was the defendant's autonomy, his individual freedom to choose whatever seems best to him.

While the Constitution thus permits *Alford* pleas, it does not require them. States and judges may refuse to allow them.[6]

Though guilty-but-not-guilty pleas hedge or claim innocence, most defendants who use them are actually guilty but in denial. Almost all of the defense lawyers, prosecutors, and judges whom I interviewed agreed that innocent defendants rarely use these pleas. Most guilty-but-not-guilty pleas, they said, are fig leaves for defendants who are ashamed, in denial, and trying to save face.[7]

Criminal justice insiders use these pleas to grease the machinery. Defense lawyers prefer classic guilty pleas, as judges and prosecutors are more amenable to them and may reward them with larger sentence discounts. But every defense lawyer whom I interviewed approved of guilty-but-not-guilty pleas. They say they use them as a last resort, a tool for difficult defendants who simply will not admit guilt. Most prosecutors and many judges will accept guilty-but-not-guilty pleas. They value them as efficient ways to dispose of troublesome cases and reduce their staggering dockets. On the other hand, insiders do have practical concerns that guilty-but-not-guilty pleas are more vulnerable to appeal or collateral attack, undercutting their finality.

Some prosecutors, and more judges, told me that they dislike guilty-but-not-guilty pleas for reasons unrelated to finality—they dislike the messages that they send. Pleas without confessions leave victims unvindicated and defendants defiant and resistant to treatment. Thus, two defense lawyers suggested, victims or their families sometimes press prosecutors to oppose *Alford* pleas because they want admissions of guilt and apologies. Moreover, some prosecutors and judges worry that equivocal guilty pleas undermine public confidence, leading defendants' family, friends, and the public to suspect injustice.

Nevertheless, these qualms have not seriously hindered the spread of *Alford* and no-contest pleas. The federal system and more than three-quarters of the states allow no-contest pleas, while all but two states authorize *Alford* pleas. Judges and lawyers use these pleas with some frequency, especially in state courts. Roughly 2% of federal and 10.5% of state defendants plead no contest, while about 3% of federal and 6.5% of state defendants enter *Alford* pleas.[8] We have no good numbers on how many more defendants enter classic guilty pleas while hedging their words, but in my experience many do. In practice, then, insiders' desire to process cases quickly and efficiently trumps outsiders' moralistic concerns for truth, vindication, and healing. Outsiders occasionally make their voices heard, but they have too little clout to end an efficient practice favored by insiders.

2. The Danger of Convicting the Innocent

The most obvious objection to guilty-but-not-guilty pleas is that it is wrong to convict the innocent. Believe it or not, many academics prefer to give innocent defendants an easier way to plead guilty. Frank Easterbrook, Josh Bowers, and others argue that innocent defendants may be trapped by circumstances. Trials are imperfect and innocent defendants are occasionally convicted, so they may rationally prefer to get minor cases over with by pleading guilty. Even Albert Alschuler, a leading critic of plea bargaining generally, reluctantly endorses *Alford* pleas for the innocent. So long as innocent defendants face pressure to plead, he argues, they should be able to take attractive deals openly, without lying.[9] Easterbrook, Bowers, and others assume that the goal of criminal procedure is to maximize free choice: Each actor is a buyer in a utilitarian marketplace who should be able to serve his own understanding of his self-interest.

This market metaphor mistakenly treats innocent defendants as fully informed, autonomous, rational actors. As chapter II discussed, many defendants receive poor advice from overburdened appointed counsel of varying quality whose caseloads and incentives lead them to push guilty pleas. In addition, criminal discovery is not nearly as extensive as civil discovery, which hampers defendants' accurate assessments of their prospects at trial. Thus, innocent defendants who want to enter *Alford* or no-contest pleas are likely overestimating their risk of conviction at trial. Innocent defendants may also plead guilty because of pressure or misinformation; thus their pleas may not be fully intelligent and voluntary.[10] Defendants poor enough to qualify for overburdened appointed counsel and those of low intelligence are most likely to make these mistakes. The result may well be troubling disparities based on wealth, mental capacity, and education. Criminal justice is not a market full of sophisticated, rational, informed parties.

There is also a deeper moral objection to Easterbrook's purely utilitarian argument. One should recoil at the thought of convicting innocent defendants. It is all the more troubling to trumpet this risk as an advantage. Not all of ethics boils down to weighing consequences and maximizing the actors' preferences. Knowingly facilitating injustice is much more troubling than simply allowing it to happen inadvertently. Our system should discourage innocent defendants from pleading guilty and steel their resolve to vindicate themselves at trial.[11]

The moral objection reveals a profound defect in Easterbrook's market metaphor for criminal justice. In a free market, the only people who are affected are the buyer and seller. A grocer who sells a sack of potatoes imposes no harm or externalities on third parties and is not responsible to them. The whole point of the market is to satisfy the preferences of the two private individuals who are doing business. But criminal justice is a public ritual, not a private market. It is about giving defendants not what they want, but what they deserve. It is not about maximizing the preferences of the insiders who run the system, but about doing justice and satisfying outsiders that justice has been done. Justice constrains not only substantive outcomes, but also procedures needed to protect defendants and satisfy victims and the public. Pervasive agency costs make it far too easy for insiders to abuse market options to satisfy their own desires rather than their principals' interests. True, criminal justice sometimes calls for hard tradeoffs. Sometimes prosecutors must cut deals with unsavory small fry so that they will testify against the big fish. Frequently, they must offer plea discounts so that they can handle heavy caseloads. But even these tradeoffs should trouble us more than they do. They are necessary evils, but the market metaphor glosses them as positive goods.

The justice system must consider not only what the parties want, but also public perceptions of accuracy and fairness. Justice and punishment are classic public goods. Allowing innocent defendants to plead guilty creates "serious negative externalities" because society has a strong interest in ensuring that criminal convictions are both just and perceived as just. Some innocent defendants might plead guilty even without guilty-but-not-guilty pleas, but these pleas facilitate and encourage more to do so. Guilty-but-not-guilty pleas send mixed messages, breeding public doubt, uncertainty, and lack of respect for the criminal justice system. The justice system should forestall cynicism by forbidding practices that openly promote injustice or public doubts about guilt. As the Supreme Court noted in *Winship*, the law goes to great lengths to minimize the risk of erroneous convictions. The perception of accuracy is needed "to command the respect and confidence of the community. . . . It is critical that the moral force of the criminal law not be diluted by a standard of proof that leaves people in doubt whether innocent men are being condemned."[12]

Public confidence and faith in the justice system are essential to the law's democratic legitimacy and moral force. When citizens learn that defendants are pleading and being punished while refusing to admit guilt and even protesting their innocence, they may well suspect coercion and injustice. The public may be shocked to learn that innocent defendants are known to have pleaded guilty because, for example, their lawyers were bad and they feared the death penalty. They may also conclude that our system does not care enough about separating guilty from innocent defendants. Some may believe that the defendant is guilty but refuses to admit it, while others may doubt the defendant's guilt and blame the system's callousness. A system less obsessed with efficiency would slow down to take a closer look at these cases. As a result, the inefficient safeguards of trial might catch some of these injustices. But our obsession with efficiency and autonomy has led our system to downplay the importance of justice and the public's perception of justice. This may partially explain why only one-quarter of the American public expresses confidence in the criminal justice system and why two-thirds think plea bargaining is a problem.[13] Proving a causal link between particular pleas and the justice system's reputation is largely impossible. But prudence counsels erring on the side of caution and abolishing guilty-but-not-guilty pleas.

3. The Costs of False Denial and the Value of Confession

The bigger problem here is not with innocent defendants but with guilty ones. As noted earlier, most defendants who enter guilty-but-not-guilty pleas are guilty despite their denials and evasions. Even if we could make these pleas perfectly accurate and fully informed, so that they did not trap any innocent defendants, they would undercut important values of the substantive criminal law. Equivocal guilty pleas interfere with defendants' contrition, education, and reform, which hinders catharsis and vindication and obscures responsibility for one's actions. True, classic guilty pleas erode these values by allowing grudging admissions of guilt to preempt trials, but equivocal guilty pleas are worse. Instead of confessions that can humble wrongdoers and vindicate victims, equivocal guilty pleas are transparently insincere tactical maneuvers.

Criminal punishment serves a variety of functions. It tries to deter crime by making the expected pain of punishment exceed the likely benefits of committing crime. But it is also far more morally laden than that. In Kant's words, it is a powerful "*symbol*" of moral blameworthiness that is "medicinal for the criminal and [sets] an example for others." Punishment teaches the wrongdoer and others that the crime is forbidden because it is morally and legally wrong. It is also a strong tool for penetrating callous hearts. In C. S. Lewis' words, it shatters our illusions and "plants the flag of truth within the fortress of a rebel soul." Punishment seeks to teach by triggering and developing the wrongdoer's sense of guilt. It tries to induce contrition and repentance so that the wrongdoer will repudiate his past wrongful act and avoid committing it again. In a similar vein, punishment should strive to be a secular version of atonement, a way of reconciling wrongdoers with victims and reintegrating them into the community. Before wrongdoers can atone and be reconciled, however, they must first accept responsibility, learn their lessons, and resolve to mend their ways.[14] The external bite of condemnation and pain will, we hope, induce internal remorse, reform, and amends. Of course, some will learn these lessons only in part and some not at all. Nevertheless, the law tries to teach them the errors of their ways, to increase the chance that they will repent and change their ways.

Regardless of whether wrongdoers learn their lessons and repent, their punishment has moral value for others. For example, crimes demean victims by disregarding and trampling on their moral worth. Punishing wrongdoers vindicates their victims' worth and humbles wrongdoers by asserting that they are not entitled to abuse others. Punishment thus serves a cathartic function for victims and brings them closure. If wrongdoers confess or better yet repent and apologize, victims can more easily forgive, surrender resentments, and find peace. This symbolic moral significance of punishment extends beyond the victim to society at large. Punishment denounces the wrong and reaffirms society's moral teachings. Our criminal procedures thus let the community vent its outrage, satisfying the public's sense of justice by bringing catharsis and closure.[15]

To achieve these goals of punishment, the criminal law seeks to lead wrongdoers to repent by humbling them, to exact moral sanctions, and then to return them to the community as equals. Wrongdoers cannot accept responsibility and repent until they admit their actions. Admitting wrongdoing to oneself and others is not easy, however, particularly because so many are in denial. Cognitive distortions and denials impede treatment. Admitting one's wrongdoing is the first step toward moving beyond it. In twelve-step programs such as Alcoholics Anonymous, for example, admitting that one has a problem is an essential step to recovery. Confessed wrongdoers can no longer rest complacent in the illusions that they are good people. In addition, confessing forces wrongdoers to reveal details of their offenses, which therapists need to frame their responses. Denial keeps therapists from examining cognitive distortions, detecting warning signs, and nurturing empathy for victims. Thus, most sex-offender treatment programs refuse to admit offenders who deny any sexual conduct. Denial, in short, obstructs treatment, which in turn greatly increases the risk of recidivism.[16]

When wrongdoers do not admit responsibility, many therapists find it helpful to confront them with the facts to force them to come to terms with their behavior. Firmly challenging these denials and distortions is a "very effective" way of overcoming them. Therapists must actively confront and challenge sex offenders because supportive, passive therapy usually fails. These challenges can be direct or indirect. Either the therapist or the wrongdoers' loved ones can lead it, and they can couple challenges with empathy. The challenges can consist of asking for explanations and details, questioning inconsistencies, or encouraging the wrongdoer to challenge himself. By confronting wrongdoers about their excuses and rationalizations, therapists can trigger feelings of guilt and harness this guilt to induce change. Even external pressures, such as the threat of imprisonment, can induce wrongdoers to overcome their denial.[17]

Confessions and denials within the legal system may have effects similar to confessions and denials within therapy. Confessions in open court, even if induced by external pressure, may begin to breach wrongdoers' denial. If wrongdoers who confess later try to recant during treatment, therapists may confront them with the details of their initial confessions. In contrast, repeated unchallenged denials in the legal system only exacerbate wrongdoers' denial reflex, making later treatment even harder. Thus, wrongdoers who enter *Alford* or no-contest pleas may resist successful treatment and are much more likely to reoffend. For example, one small Minnesota study found that seven out of eight sex offenders who had entered no-contest pleas reoffended within five years of release. This percentage is two to five times the recidivism rate of sex offenders in general.[18]

Two of my anecdotal interviews of judges indicate that defendants' statements in court affect their own and others' perceptions of their guilt. One long-time judge reported that he used to allow defendants to plead no contest. He found that a defendant would say nothing in court, but upon reporting to a probation officer for a presentence interview would deny guilt. The defendant would also tell his family that he was innocent but that his lawyer had forced him to plead guilty. As a result, family members would write angry letters to the judge, complaining that convicting an innocent man was a travesty of justice. They would say, for example, that a rape victim was a tramp who consented to sex. At sentencing, the defendant and his family would continue to deny guilt and, at least implicitly, blame the victim. Thus, victims would be visibly frustrated when making statements at sentencing, feeling that they had to justify themselves. These convicted defendants would continue to deny guilt after sentencing, thus impeding therapy or treatment. Once this judge stopped permitting most no-contest pleas, however, defense lawyers confronted clients and made them admit guilt, and almost none insisted on going to trial.

Defendants and families no longer denied guilt at sentencing or afterwards; the letters from defendants' families stopped; and defendants seemed less defiant, more contrite, and less openly hostile and angry. Victims felt vindicated and expressed healthy outrage instead of frustration at sentencing. Finally, the judge, having heard a detailed plea colloquy, was better able to confront defendants with the details and wrongfulness of their acts.[19] Another judge confirmed these conclusions. He noted that some defendants are agitated and balk at admitting guilt, but they plead guilty when told that trial is the only alternative. These defendants seem calmer and more accepting of responsibility after their guilty-plea allocutions and are less likely to protest innocence and injustice later on.

An analogous dynamic may be at work in insanity cases. Several case studies show that defendants who are found not guilty by reason of insanity resist discussing their thoughts, feelings, and actions. Instead, they externalize their feelings of blame. They may show no remorse, saying "The judge said I was not guilty" or "I have not committed a crime." In contrast, persons with mental illnesses who are convicted of crimes may react more positively. Society's pronouncement of guilt may spur and reinforce the defendant's introspection, acceptance of responsibility, and treatment prospects. In short, when the judicial system ascribes blame, defendants are more likely to accept emotional responsibility for acts they committed while mentally ill, which in turn may aid treatment and reform.[20]

True, this evidence comes primarily from the psychological literature on sex offenders, substance abusers, and mentally ill defendants. Nevertheless, guilt, psychological blocks, and confessions seem to play similar roles in treating other kinds of wrongdoers. Perhaps it is dangerous to generalize from my small set of interviews. One might nonetheless extrapolate that other wrongdoers who enter *Alford* and no-contest pleas, or who barely admit guilt, are doing so in part because they face similar psychological blocks. The idea is intuitively plausible. Wrongdoers who are not reluctant to confess enter straight guilty pleas and admit guilt frankly to increase their chances of getting large sentencing discounts. In contrast, those whose psychological barriers impede confession, to others or even to themselves, are the primary users of *Alford* and no-contest pleas.[21] They are also presumably those in the deepest denials, and thus those who most need to come clean.

Some defendants are willing to confess and plead guilty. As Alschuler rightly notes, most guilty pleas are not the fruit of genuine repentance. Instead, defendants fake repentance to earn sentence reductions. But even feigned or induced repentance may teach lessons to some wrongdoers.

The very act of confessing and pleading guilty in open court heightens the defendant's awareness of the victim's injury, the norm violated, and the community's condemnation. Indeed, the ordeal of feigning repentance, even if initially done for the wrong reasons, can sometimes lead to genuine repentance.[22]

The point should be clear to anyone whose parent ever told him to apologize for hitting a sibling or stealing a toy. Even though the child's apology is grudging at first, over time apologizing inculcates the norms that hitting and stealing are wrong and that the child should feel guilty and ashamed of these wrongs. Cognitive psychology teaches the same point. According to cognitive dissonance theory, persons who publicly take positions that they do not believe are likely to change their attitudes to bring them into line with their public statements.[23] Thus, defendants who publicly accept responsibility for their crimes, even if they do so insincerely, are more likely to internalize that responsibility than those who persist in denying guilt.

For many, confessing is difficult because it requires admitting shameful deeds, putting aside excuses, and taking responsibility for one's actions. As my interviews indicated, defense lawyers often have to work with defendants before they admit guilt. The hard work of admitting guilt and repenting may impress upon the defendant the wrongfulness and gravity of his crime. By admitting guilt, however insincerely, defendants let down their denial mechanisms, begin the process of reform, and bring closure to the community.[24]

Perhaps many defendants plead guilty cavalierly, confessing the words without confronting their significance. But this description is least true of those defendants who balk most at pleading guilty, namely those who want *Alford* and no-contest pleas and those who hedge their admissions of guilt. These defendants are in the deepest denial and would have to struggle the most to admit guilt. The bigger the struggle, the bigger the wrongdoer's breakthrough when he finally confesses. Indeed, it is a catharsis, literally a cleansing, which is why we often speak of confession as coming clean.

4. The Value of Trials as Morality Plays

Whatever their other flaws, plea bargains induce guilty defendants to confess and perhaps start repenting. Some defendants, however, cannot or will not admit guilt. For these guilty defendants, as well as for innocent defendants, the law provides jury trials. Trials not only seek fairness, efficiency, and accuracy, but also further the criminal law's substantive moral aims and norms. The jury, as the conscience of the community, applies and reinforces the community's moral code in the face of its transgression. The parade of live witnesses and the solemn pronouncement of guilt confront the criminal at length with his wrongful deeds. This litany of accusation, evidence, and condemnation may break through the defendant's denial mechanisms, driving home in undeniable detail the wrongfulness of the crime. These morality plays hold out hope for reforming guilty defendants and healing society. As we saw in chapter I, colonial Americans prized trials as opportunities to reclaim lost sheep, encourage repentance, and reintegrate them into the flock. Outsiders, still steeped in this colonial mythos, expect this morality play.

For those wrongdoers who refuse to confess or repent, trials still bring catharsis and closure to victims and the community. As one court noted, "[j]ury trials have historically served to vent community pressures and passions. As the lid of a tea kettle releases steam, jury trials in criminal cases allow peaceful expression of community outrage at arbitrary government or vicious criminal acts." Trials express respect for the law, communicate values, justify punishment, and encourage wrongdoers to critically examine their acts. Moreover, convictions at trial vindicate victims and the community by denouncing wrongdoers and reaffirming moral norms in the face of their transgression. This is true regardless of how wrongdoers respond. Conversely, acquittals at trial vindicate innocent defendants and the moral norms on which they acted. Consider, for example, the prosecution of John Peter Zenger for seditious libel in colonial America. The jury's celebrated acquittal proclaimed to all eternity Zenger's right to criticize the government.[25]

Alford and no-contest pleas subvert the substantive moral messages that unambiguous trial verdicts send. *Alford,* and to a lesser extent no-contest and hedged guilty pleas, are ambiguous on their faces. Guilty-but-not-guilty pleas muddy the moral message by implying that the law does not care enough to insist on clear, honest resolutions and vindications. Truth, justice, and respect for others take a back seat to procedural efficiency and defendants' freedom of choice. By failing to challenge wrongdoers who falsely deny guilt, criminal procedure undermines the criminal law's basic norms of honesty and responsibility for one's actions. Wrongdoers have abused their autonomy at the expense of victims by renouncing compliance with the law. Punishment seeks to "humbl[e] the [defendant's] will," "to bring him low."[26] Jury trials and unequivocal guilty pleas can communicate this lesson, but quick guilty-but-not-guilty pleas short-circuit this process and leave defendants in denial. In other words, amoral procedure undercuts the substantive aims it is supposed to serve.

Some scholars favor *Alford* and no-contest pleas as ways to ease the strain on defendants' relationship with their lawyers. Defense lawyers can avoid friction with clients in denial by letting them enter *Alford* pleas instead of pressing them to admit guilt.[27] This argument fits with the dominant view of lawyering as gamesmanship, in which the defense lawyer's job is to prevent conviction, minimize punishment, and further the client's wishes.

At least in the context of defendants who are in denial, however, the gamesmanship model is misguided. It ignores the constructive role that defense lawyers can play in educating and transforming defendants' misperceptions and short-term desires. Instead, it takes short-term desires as a given, even for clients suffering from psychological blocks that cloud their long-term interests and values. Lawyers can recognize that substance abuse, mental illness, psychological blind spots and denial, or simple shortsightedness impedes their clients' rationality. More importantly, they can persuade clients to face up to patterns of behavior that, if left unchecked, will lead to more crimes and punishment. As suggested by the psychological literature cited earlier, lawyers can confront their clients with the overwhelming evidence of guilt and break down their denials. Furthermore, lawyers can provide moral as well as legal counsel, advising clients that it is right to admit their crime, apologize to victims, and move forward.[28]

Some, but not all, defense attorneys do challenge their clients. Other lawyers say, "Yes, you are innocent, but a jury would probably convict you at trial, so enter an *Alford* or no-contest plea." As one psychologist notes, defense lawyers exacerbate the problem by failing to challenge their clients' denials. The dominant client-centered approach to legal counseling discourages painful confession. Indeed, some defense lawyers purposely avoid learning all the facts about guilt, so they remain free to make arguments that run counter to the undiscovered facts. This see-no-evil approach not only leaves clients' illusions and denials in place but also compounds them. Clients interpret this failure to challenge as confirmation and become even more resistant to the challenges required during therapy and rehabilitation.[29] Instead of repenting and moving forward, clients may continue to pity themselves, focusing their energies on challenging their convictions instead of making amends. The criminal process should focus on teaching the client and opening his eyes during his journey to prison. Letting defense counsel take the easier way out impedes the learning process and disserves the clients' long-term interests. Judges and prosecutors should likewise focus more on healing, teaching, and vindicating than on serving their own shortsighted self-interests in clearing their dockets.

Even if guilty-but-not-guilty pleas do not impair the wrongdoer's own education and reform, they hurt victims and the community by preventing victims' vindication. Without receiving even an admission of wrongdoing or an apology, victims lose their day in court, their chance to vent their sorrows and ask for justice. Molestation victims, for example, can suffer more harm when courts appear to accept the molesters' denials, because this judicial acceptance seems to suggest that the victims are liars.[30] Traumatized victims seeking closure may be more reluctant to pursue these claims at all, and thus society cannot authoritatively vindicate its norms and repudiate the wrong. Instead of communicating that punishment is moral denunciation based on true desert, society treats it as a marketable good, undermining its moral authority. Of course, many pleas are not well publicized, but to the extent that victims and the public do learn of guilty-but-not-guilty pleas, they take away the wrong message. Simply put, these pleas undermine the community's catharsis, its condemnation of the crime, and its vindication of its norms.

B. REMORSE, APOLOGY, AND FORGIVENESS

Guilty-but-not-guilty pleas are the most extreme example of criminal procedure's lack of concern for expressive values and the public's hunger for a morality play. I have focused on them at length because they are one of the worst parts of a flawed system; they epitomize its dishonesty. But denial is not the only blind spot in criminal justice. More often, criminal defendants admit guilt, at least half-heartedly, as part of plea bargains. Wrongdoers, victims, and the public often want more, to hear the defendant express remorse and apologize and the victim forgive. But the criminal-justice machine processes cases quickly and cheaply, to maximize deterrence and incapacitation at minimal cost. Its emphasis on quantity leaves little room for these softer, qualitative goals.

1. The Irrelevance of Remorse and Apology in Contemporary Criminal Justice

At least until sentencing, criminal justice cares little about remorse, apology, or forgiveness. Consider a typical wrongdoer—a vandal, maybe, or a low-level drug dealer, or a thief—in a typical small criminal case. From the time of arrest to sentencing, criminal procedure pays little heed to his expressions of contrition. The two lawyers quickly take over and usually seek to negotiate deals on charges, pleas, and sentences. In the few cases headed toward trial, the two sides investigate, plan pretrial and trial strategy, and deal with motions, trial dates, and the like. In either situation, much negotiation is informal and takes place between the two repeat players, out of the defendant's and victim's presence. The insiders are at best unconcerned with, at worst irritated by, outsiders' intrusions. The insiders, the prosecutor and defense lawyer, strive to balance adversarial processes, efficient and accurate outcomes, and individual rights. They do not emphasize mining the possible value of remorse, apology, or repentance.

Throughout this process, the defendant has little chance to interact with anyone other than his own lawyer. At their first meeting, his lawyer tells him to say nothing to anyone except the lawyer himself. Their few later conversations overwhelmingly concern facts and legal niceties. Until it is time for the presentence report, any expressions of contrition or remorse make it only as far as the defense lawyer or, on rare occasions, the prosecutor. Defense lawyers and prosecutors usually view these expressions as relevant only to the defendant's willingness to fight, plead, or perhaps cooperate. The genuinely remorseful defendant who wishes to apologize to his victim and make amends usually has no readily available way to do so. Indeed, from the time of arrest until trial (if there is one) and sentencing, victims are almost never in sight of defendants.[31]

Procedurally, remorse and apology factor in most significantly at sentencing. Even here, however, these expressions are largely perfunctory. In many cases, the sentencing allocution inhibits meaningful remorse and apology. By the time of sentencing, criminal procedures have done little to encourage repentance, apology to victims, or coming to terms with one's guilt. For defendants who pleaded guilty-but-not-guilty or denied guilt at trial, cognitive dissonance and continued denials make it hard to express remorse and apologize.[32]

Defendants who have fully admitted their guilt and pleaded guilty also face significant psychological and contextual barriers. Courtrooms are public settings, where defendants' families and friends are often present. Criminal defendants understandably fear embarrassment and shame. Sentencing allocutions, moreover, are tightly scheduled, hurried, vague, and often in front of a judge who did not preside over the guilty plea. For most defendants, this is their first real chance to apologize for their crime to victims or the community. It is no wonder that, when apologies do occur at sentencing, they often are stilted, forced, or just not enough. Many defendants simply read from a piece of paper.[33]

Nonetheless, judges heed expressions of remorse and apology and weigh them heavily at sentencing. As Judge Leventhal put it, "There is a natural, and I believe sound, disposition to adjust sanctions when an offender admits his responsibility. . . . I dare say that many judges, possibly the overwhelming majority, respond in this way. . . ." Expressions of remorse can reduce prison sentences by more than a third, and they significantly reduce the odds that a jury will return a death sentence, especially for less vicious murders. But judges seem to view remorse solely as a gauge of an individual defendant's badness, a sign that he is not yet lost and can still change. They may speak of the remorseful defendant's character, his prospects for rehabilitation, how hardened he is, or what he deserves. Though the terms vary, the reasoning is the same: Someone who knows he has done wrong and is genuinely sorry is on the road to disciplining himself to avoid committing more crimes in the future.[34] As chapter V will discuss, the emphasis is on the individual defendant's badness and likelihood of future crime—the quantifiable benefits prized by insiders.

Even at sentencing, where criminal law carves out a procedural space for remorse and apology, the law focuses almost entirely on the criminal defendant and his dangerousness. The sentencing allocution is often the first opportunity a defendant has to apologize to victims of his crime. All too often, however, this opportunity is more theoretical than real. Despite recent and dramatic increases in victims' rights, victims play minimal roles at sentencing. Allocution occurs between the defendant and the sentencer, usually a judge. In many instances, victims are absent from the courtroom; when they are present, defendants do not face them. Even for defendants who are genuinely remorseful and wish to apologize to their victims, the colloquy is between the defendant and the judge. Victims usually sit silently with the public behind the defendant while the judge evaluates the defendant's words and demeanor.[35] There is no victim-offender dialogue and no opportunity for face-to-face apology or expression of contrition, let alone forgiveness.

Defendants likewise have few opportunities to express sorrow and apologize to community representatives. The paradigmatic symbol of the community in the criminal law—a jury of the defendant's peers—usually has no role at sentencing, except at capital trials. Trial judges dominate the sentencing process. Furthermore, the prevalence of guilty pleas means that, before sentencing, most defendants never see a jury. They thus bypass the traditional arbiter of community values, which in times past encouraged repentance and apology. In those few cases that go to trial or give jurors a role at sentencing, defendants can address the jury as the community's conscience. Even here, however, jurors' role is far from interactive—they cannot for example question the defendant, and the defendant rarely addresses them directly.[36] Defendants determined to express remorse and to apologize may have to resort to the news media to circumvent criminal procedure's barrier of silence. What should have been a solemn healing ritual risks becoming a media sensation or circus.

If defendants are muted, victims are silenced. Victims lack structured opportunities to speak directly to defendants, to vent their grievances, to understand what happened to them, and to seek apologies. If victims speak at all at sentencing, at most they read brief victim-impact statements directed to judges, not defendants. More commonly, they submit written statements before sentencing, which judges rarely read aloud.[37] With so little support for remorse and apology, many victims cannot forgive, and certainly cannot communicate forgiveness. Granted, many defendants are reluctant to express remorse and apologize, and many victims never want to see or speak with their assailants again. But for the many who want to do so, opportunities and support are scarce.

Context and procedure, in short, discourage the expressions on which the criminal law bases sentences. This tension leaves criminal law in the uneasy position of judging defendants based on expressions it has done little to elicit or probe. It also denies victims, defendants, and their communities any real opportunity to reap the substantial social, psychological, and moral benefits of these expressions. Frustration and alienation replace the potential for closure, relief, and reconciliation.

2. Crime as a Relational Concept

In short, criminal-justice insiders ignore remorse and apology except perhaps when they bear on individual defendants' badness or dangerousness. By putting on these blinders, insiders ignore the broader impact of crime. Crime and punishment are about more than simply controlling wrongdoers as individuals. As any crime victim can tell you, crime also disrupts status relationships among wrongdoers, victims, and communities. If you are mugged or your car is broken into, you are distressed not just because you lose the money in your wallet or must pay to replace your radio. You probably feel violated and belittled by the perpetrator and his act. Likewise, the crime distresses other members of the community not simply because they fear losing money or property. The crime also carries a symbolic message from the wrongdoer that the community's norms do not apply to him and that he is superior to the victim and others like him.

In other words, crime and punishment are as much about social norms, social influence, and relations among persons as about individual blame and state-imposed punishment. Dan Kahan has espoused a similar, expressive view of crime. As he puts it, "The distinctive meaning of criminal wrongdoing is its denial of some important value, such as the victim's moral worth." In Kahan's view, theft differs from competition in part because "against the background of social norms theft expresses disrespect for the injured party's worth, whereas competition (at least ordinarily) does not." Along the same lines, Jean Hampton's expressive theory of retribution focuses on the messages that wrongful behavior and sanctions send to victims, wrongdoers, and the community. Wrongdoing, Hampton explains, sends a "false message" that the victim is worth less than the wrongdoer. The crime announces that the victim does not deserve respect and that the wrongdoer can instead use him as a means to an end.[38]

Social psychologists, especially equity theorists, emphasize this relational aspect of wrongdoing. Equity theorists, in discussing both criminal and civil wrongdoing, emphasize that a wrong "creates a moral imbalance" between the wrongdoer and the injured party. This moral imbalance extends beyond the specific victims to the moral and social community whose norms the wrongdoer has flouted. Through his transgression, the wrongdoer sets himself off from that community and sends a symbolic message to it and the victim: He is not part of the group and does not have to play by its rules. According to equity theory, punishment seeks to "set the balance right" by mending the breach caused by the wrongdoer and reaffirming social and community norms. An emerging body of empirical evidence supports this theoretical account. The evidence suggests that jurors, litigants, victims, and even wrongdoers in both criminal and civil cases consider this relational aspect of wrongdoing extremely important.[39]

Just as crime is about far more than influencing individual behavior, so too expressions of remorse and apology are about more than predicting future dangerousness or determining just deserts. To be sure, these expressions could offer some insight into an individual wrongdoer's moral orientation—the focus of the individual-badness model. But they also function as essentially social mechanisms of healing, reconciliation, moral education, and reintegration.

Apology, expressions of remorse, and other mea culpas are secular remedial rituals. They both teach and reconcile by reaffirming societal norms and vindicating victims. As such, they are concerned not just with individual dispositions but also with membership in a particular moral community. In Nicholas Tavuchis' words, an apology "is [a] quintessentially social, that is, a *relational* symbolic gesture occurring in a complex interpersonal field." To apologize and repent for one's wrongdoing is to expiate, to make amends. It is also to commit visibly and morally to the norms that govern group affiliation and determine group membership. Genuine apologies and expressions of remorse, in other words, dissociate oneself from one's wrongful past and make a plea for reconciliation. They are fundamentally relational. Traditional criminal law scholars, blinded by the individual-badness model, too often overlook this interpersonal dimension of remorse and apology.[40]

In contrast, sociologists and social psychologists explore how remorse and apology build social norms, educate, and repair breaches in communities and relationships caused by wrongdoing. A broad consensus now supports Tavuchis' central point: Because expressions of remorse and apology are fundamentally relational, any apologetic discourse must be "dyadic," reflecting "an interaction between the primordial social categories of Offender and Offended." Contrite wrongdoers, in other words, do not just apologize *for* something. They also apologize *to* someone—their victims, their community, their families, and their friends. Only by doing so can the remorseful wrongdoer reaffirm the community values that he has flouted and renew his membership in the moral community.[41] And only in this way can victims experience healing.

For this reason, many scholars see face-to-face interaction between offender and offended as essential to effective apologies and remorse. In person, body language and facial expressions communicate with nuance and put the crime and harm in context. A wrongdoer "cannot simply rationalize the crime as being minor or harmless when a real person stands in front of him describing the physical and emotional pain directly flowing from his behavior." By humanizing the wrong and its consequences, face-to-face interaction can break down pride, fear, pain, anxiety, and other barriers to accepting responsibility and thus pave the way for genuine repentance. Wrongdoers can come to see that their crimes had real-world consequences and that their victims want and need to understand why the crime happened. Victims, likewise, can learn why the crime happened, receive needed assurance that it was not their fault, overcome their resentment, and see wrongdoers as redeemable human beings. Even neighborhood residents can stand in as victims to listen and vent their frustrations at drug dealers and prostitutes who harm their neighborhoods. The entire process can provide a starting point for forgiveness and reintegration.[42]

When wrongdoers express genuine remorse in person to those whom they have wronged, the effects can be profound. The news media and popular press are full of stories about the transformative effect of such meetings. Empirical studies and anecdotal evidence from restorative justice programs confirm that face-to-face expressions of remorse and apology matter immensely to wrongdoers and victims. Four empirical studies involving 550 wrongdoers found that 74% of them apologized when given the opportunity to do so in restorative justice conferences. By contrast, only 29% apologized when they had no opportunity to do so except in court. According to these studies, wrongdoers who took part in restorative justice conferences were 6.9 times more likely to apologize than those who went to court, and victims were 2.6 times more likely to forgive them.[43]

Wrongdoers who have the opportunity to meet with victims often apologize even when they start off vowing not to. In return, many victims accept the apologies and forgive. Many studies show that a substantial percentage of victims want to meet with those who have wronged them. The studies suggest that victims value emotional healing much more highly than financial compensation. According to one study, the more that victims are emotionally upset by a crime, the more they want to meet with the wrongdoers.[44]

Wrongdoers' expressions of remorse and apology set the stage for victims' forgiveness. Until they forgive, victims are likely to bottle up sorrow, shame, and even rage. As Jeffrie Murphy notes, "feelings of hatred can, in many cases, consume one's entire self. Thus it might be seen as a blessing—perhaps even divine grace—to have the burden of hatred lifted from one's mind. For this reason forgiveness can bless the forgiver as much as or more than it blesses the one forgiven."[45] Forgiveness means letting go, separating the wrongdoer from the wrong, and recognizing that the crime is past and the time for healing is at hand. In other words, it involves catharsis, a cleansing of anger and hate. With forgiveness may also come understanding, which may lessen fear of the wrongdoer.

Forgiveness likewise benefits wrongdoers. Judges and juries are likely to impose lower sentences if victims are ready to forgive, but heavier sentences if victims remain angry. Parole and clemency boards likewise receive victims' input and may take it into account. Victims' forgiveness may also counteract the infamy of crime, leading friends, neighbors, and employers to stop shunning wrongdoers and reintegrate them into society. And forgiveness brings psychic benefits, lightening the burden of guilt and making it easier for wrongdoers to move on with their lives.[46] Finally, the desire for forgiveness can lead wrongdoers to come out of denial. As noted earlier, twelve-step programs such as Alcoholics Anonymous emphasize admitting guilt as an essential step down the road to reform. Forgiveness and the desire to earn it, in other words, can catalyze healthy change.

Victims, wrongdoers, and community members who have met and engaged in apologetic discourse overwhelmingly feel satisfied and relieved. Wrongdoers who were interviewed, for example, reported feeling "happy, because all my feelings were out." They "liked being able to apologize" "[t]o let [the victim] know that we are not bad." They felt it was important to explain their behavior, apologize, release their guilt, and tell victims that their crimes were not personal. Victims likewise valued the chance to share information, rebuild relationships, heal, and "get over [their] sense of loss."[47]

While preliminary studies are encouraging, it is still too early to be sure precisely how these opportunities affect long-term recidivism rates. But empirical studies of restorative justice programs show that they control crime at least as well as, if not better than, traditional criminal justice.[48] And they bring the added benefits of vindicating victims, healing and reconciling victims and wrongdoers, reaffirming social norms, and morally educating wrongdoers and citizens. Though criminal procedure often overlooks these values, they are fundamentally important to the criminal law.

Of course, remorse, apology, and forgiveness are not panaceas for the problems of crime control and the distress, pain, disrupted relationships, and other effects of crime. Expressing remorse and apologizing can be very hard for wrongdoers, and forgiving can be very hard for victims, for many reasons. Apologizing can be excruciatingly painful. Apologies can go wrong. Not all wrongdoers are remorseful or willing to turn toward genuine repentance. Not all victims or community members want to hear apologies, meet wrongdoers face to face, or consider forgiving. In most cases, as I will discuss, victims do not see apologies as substitutes for punishment. Some apologies and forgiveness are half-hearted or insincere. And when parties do meet, some invariably come away feeling dissatisfied.[49] Nonetheless, remorse and apology are more than mere evidence of a wrongdoer's true character and dangerousness, or reasons for a sentence reduction, or even creative punishments. Ideally, they should be integral parts of criminal procedure, serving relational values and not just deterrence and retribution. In fact, even feigned expressions of remorse and apology can serve many of these values, as chapter VI will discuss. Viewing remorse and apology through the individual-badness lens, judges and scholars have been too slow to see how the social value of remorse and apology can further the criminal law's core aims.

3. Lessons from Noncriminal Contexts: Civil Mediation

Unlike the criminal law, other areas of law have begun to use remorse, apology, and sometimes forgiveness in reconciliation rituals. Though caseloads have pushed civil as well as criminal justice toward nontrial dispositions, civil mediation has better incorporated some classical trial values into the nontrial process. Civil mediation scholarship emphasizes that expressions of remorse and apology can be valuable ways to resolve disputes. Scholars and commentators in this area stress the need for corresponding legal reforms to facilitate the social and relational benefits of remorse, apology, and forgiveness. For example, the rules of evidence may need to exclude some apology-related statements from evidence, and legal education should train law students and lawyers in successful mediation.[50]

Empirical findings support the usefulness of this approach. Victims frequently value genuine expressions of sorrow and contrition more than monetary compensation, as noted earlier, and will often forgo money in the face of such expressions. For example, in one study published in the *Journal of the American Medical Association*, nearly a quarter of families who sued their doctors after prenatal injuries reported doing so mainly because their doctors had not been fully honest about what had occurred. Denial, and the absence of apology, made it hard for victims to find closure and forgive. Similarly, researchers have found that most sexual assault victims who filed civil lawsuits were doing so not for money but as therapy. They felt it important to be heard, to be empowered, to publicly affirm the wrongs they had suffered, and to receive apologies. And many plaintiffs who sue for libel or slander care more about apologies than money. This is partly because retractions counteract reputational harm, but also partly because refusals to apologize antagonize victims and obstruct forgiveness. Many pursue lawsuits only after publishers rebuff their requests for retractions and apologies.[51]

Developments in mediation practice reflect the trend toward apology. Remorse and apology are increasingly seen as central elements in successful mediation. The sessions focus not on legal rights but on peoples' interests. All persons involved can express their needs, their stories, and their feelings. The discourse is designed to foster discussion of moral and interpersonal obligations as well as legal ones. Mediation gives the parties a chance to interact face to face beyond simply fighting as adversaries. Thus, the parties can confront the core values underlying their relationship and have a chance to apologize and forgive. In other words, mediation encourages the parties to express themselves emotionally and morally. This encouragement, glaringly absent from modern adversarial litigation, is intensely important in overcoming psychological barriers, letting wrongdoers take legal and moral responsibility, and giving victims needed moral recompense.[52]

The contrast between civil mediation and criminal litigation could not be more stark. Clearly, these two fields differ significantly, and the parallels are not perfect. Nonetheless, civil mediation's current direction is very different from criminal justice's emphasis on wrongdoers as individuals and its focus on procedural values to the exclusion of substantive concerns. Because routine civil cases are much less about individual blame, retribution, and procedural rights, civil law has found it easier to mine the substantive social value of remorse, apology, and forgiveness.

CHAPTER IV

᷒

Whose Voices Belong
in Criminal Justice?

As we have just seen, victims, defendants, and members of the public
often want admissions of guilt, expressions of remorse, apologies,
and forgiveness. Nevertheless, the impersonal state's machinery has little
interest in individual people's interests or needs. It sees real human beings
as "annoying sources of inefficiency in a system built to incapacitate the
greatest number of source[s of danger] for the longest possible time with
the least effort." Thus, "[i]n the war on crime, offenders and victims alike
are irrelevant nuisances, grains of sand in the great machine of state risk
management."[1] Real human beings need much from criminal justice, ranging from vindication and denunciation to healing of wounds and relationships. They need emotional messages and dialogue, not simply a speedy
bureaucracy or haggling over years in prison. They could benefit from
criminal justice's dynamic potential to vindicate and heal.

The state's criminal-justice monopoly focuses on efficiency to the
exclusion of human emotions. While the state has good reasons to limit
vengeance and inequality, its monopoly slights victims', defendants', and the
public's legitimate need to take part. We misconceive of criminal justice as
the state's exclusive prerogative, an amoral exercise of social control.
Justice demands more of a communal morality play in which victims,
defendants, and members of the public have a stake and deserve a role.

In response to these concerns, three recent reform movements—
victims' rights, restorative justice, and therapeutic jurisprudence—have
attacked the state's impersonal monopoly. Each movement is imperfect
and unbalanced, yet each has something to teach cold, mechanical state-
centered criminal justice.

A. THE STATE'S MONOPOLY ON CRIMINAL JUSTICE

In the last chapter, I suggested that criminal litigation could learn from civil mediation's emphasis on remorse and apology. But, one may ask, aren't civil law and criminal law fundamentally different? In contract and tort suits, an individual plaintiff usually seeks money damages for a private wrong he has suffered. Because the wrong is purely private, rules of proof and procedure do not tip the scales either way. For example, the preponderance-of-the-evidence standard of proof allows whichever side has slightly stronger evidence to prevail. And the parties can compromise or settle their purely private dispute however they wish, with little government interference.

We understand criminal justice very differently. Today, the right to punish belongs exclusively to the state, not the victim. Crimes violate the state's laws and its interest in maintaining public order and social cohesion. Public prosecutors bring criminal cases in the name of the people, and judges rather than victims must approve any settlements. The requirement of proof beyond a reasonable doubt and other criminal procedures tilt the scales to protect defendants from state coercion. The state imprisons and even executes wrongdoers, instead of settling for restitution and fines. It exacts its justice quickly and impersonally to incapacitate the dangerous criminal and to deter him and others. All that seems to matter to the state is the bottom-line number of years in prison and, to an extent, accuracy in discerning guilt.[2]

From the state's point of view, there is little reason to give remorse, apology, and forgiveness much of a role even in gauging the defendant's badness. Wrongdoers who express remorse and apologize may need less punishment to deter them from committing more crimes, but the evidence is hardly conclusive.[3] Moreover, sentence discounts for apologies and forgiveness can undercut general deterrence of other potential wrongdoers. They may assume that, if they do get caught, they can lower their sentences by acting remorseful, apologizing, and perhaps receiving forgiveness.

State-centered retributivism runs into similar problems. Under classical, grievance retributivism, the objective moral seriousness of the crime and the actor's culpability determine the punishment, not any later remorse, apology, or forgiveness. In most cases, these expressions neither lessen the wrongfulness of the crime nor mitigate the victim's physical or monetary harm. Thus, many grievance retributivists leave no room for mercy because it treats similar crimes and wrongdoers differently. Some retributivists emphasize the wrongdoer's character, but even here remorse and apology play unclear roles. On the one hand, the remorseful and apologetic wrongdoer seems to reveal a better character, but on the other hand he reveals a moral nature that he must have suppressed to commit the crime. A wrongdoer who should have known better may perhaps be worse than a thoughtless thug. He may certainly be worse than one who suffers from psychosis or another mental illness for which lack of remorse is a known symptom. Indeed, the insanity and diminished-capacity defenses reflect this intuition: wrongdoers who do not fully appreciate the wrongfulness of their crimes—and so are less likely to express remorse and apologize—are generally less blameworthy than those who do.[4] From the state's perspective, then, denial, remorse, apology, and forgiveness are irrelevant to the state's mechanical exercise of control.

The state-centered model assumes that cold reason should dominate criminal-justice decisions and exclude human emotions. But the cool logic of state-monopolized justice, to the exclusion of victims, conflicts with many people's moral intuitions. Why should the right to punish belong *exclusively* to the state? Disputes are not simply impersonal occasions for the government to control dangerous threats. They wrong both the state and the victims. Crime has a human face, and that face deserves standing and a say in the matter. The victim or his representative seems naturally to deserve at least a partial right to pay back the wrongdoer. "To a victim, the notion that crimes are committed against society, making the community the injured party, can seem both bizarre and insulting; it can make them feel invisible, unavenged, and unprotected." Victims' rights laws are extremely popular because many if not most voters think victims deserve larger roles in their own cases. Empirical evidence confirms this intuition. When surveyed about concrete punishment scenarios, many people give great weight to the victim's attitude and wishes, particularly for crimes involving property or personal injury.[5] A democracy ought to do more to incorporate this widespread lay intuition about justice.

Focusing on victims' stakes fits naturally with Jean Hampton's retributive idea of punishment as defeating crime and protecting victims. By committing crimes, wrongdoers have exalted themselves and humiliated their victims. By their actions, wrongdoers falsely claim that they are superior to their victims and can trample on their rights. In other words, crimes communicate false social messages that can leave victims feeling ashamed, vulnerable, defensive, and powerless. Criminal justice must restore the equilibrium by defeating the wrong and annulling the wrongdoer's false assertion of superiority. By inflicting suffering on wrongdoers, the law not only solemnly condemns crimes, but also vindicates and restores victims.[6] Hampton focuses on vindicating victims by punishing wrongdoers, not by granting victims rights, but one can easily extend her argument to that conclusion. The perfect way to restore powerless victims is to empower them, giving them greater roles in resolving their own criminal conflicts.

Far from being evils or distractions, conflicts are important opportunities for the parties and their community to explain, express, argue, listen, teach, and learn. As Nils Christie famously argued, conflicts belong to the lay participants. The parties have suffered personally and belong at the center of the dispute. Friends, relatives, and a public audience witness and take part but do not take over. For many centuries, and in most cultures, victims brought criminal cases in their own names. Thus, criminal law used to resemble private law, in which tort victims may prosecute, settle, or waive their shares of claims.[7]

Professionalization has stolen conflicts from the parties, muted the clash of interests, and disempowered them. Taking conflicts away not only robs laymen of power and active participation, leaving them helpless. It also deprives society of opportunities to teach its norms and reinforce its social solidarity, as Durkheim would say.[8] Lawyers bargain away disagreements instead of asking citizens to confront whether a drunken brawler or teenage drug dealer poses a threat or deserves prison. If the wrongdoer was a stranger, victims and community members never get to know him, remaining angry and often sequestered from trial. If the wrongdoer was a friend, relative, coworker, or neighbor, lawyers further estrange victims and community members from him and keep them from talking. Wrongdoers may have reasons or excuses for their actions, or they may want to apologize, but they do not speak directly to their accusers. At plea allocutions, trials, and sentencing, lawyers script wrongdoers' statements within a narrow range of admissions and legally recognized defenses. By silencing, scripting, and excluding them, lawyers rob the parties of the emotional and moral teaching and healing that they may crave.

The law could surrender its monopoly on criminal justice by once again making room for the parties' interests and voices. Breaking the state's monopoly does not mean transferring that monopoly to victims. Public prosecutors must retain a leading role, to ensure accuracy, proportionality, equality, and fairness to other victims, defendants, and the public. Victims deserve a voice but not an unregulated and exclusive one that trumps all others. Likewise, defendants should be encouraged to speak more, both in court and in mediation. Judges and juries must filter victims' views by serving as impartial public spectators. On the one hand, judges and juries must empathize and identify with victims' and defendants' feelings and sufferings, to include the human dimension in moral judgment. Yet on the other hand they must reflect upon and keep critical distance from participants' blinding grief and self-interested vindictiveness.[9] That critical distance can prevent retribution from collapsing into unchecked vengeance and keep victims from drowning out defendants.

Even if the state alone has the right to punish, it should take victims' and defendants' interests into account by giving weight to remorse, apology, and forgiveness. Mercy (based on compassion) is a value that competes with retribution, and a world that balances both values is better than a world of strict, merciless retribution. First, remorse, apology, and forgiveness provide bases for mercy. Forgiveness may remit the victim's claim for punishment, and the state should heed the claim of the most interested party. Second, expressing remorse and apologizing help wrongdoers to atone, cleanse their guilt, and learn lessons. Third, as Hampton argued, an important function of punishment is to vindicate victims. Wrongdoers have exalted themselves at victims' expense and violated their autonomy. Punishment evens the scales, vindicating victims by humbling wrongdoers and teaching them lessons. By doing so, it heals victims' psyches and statuses. By accepting apologies and forgiving, victims show that they are already recovering from their wounds and so may need less vindication. In the process, remorse and apology vindicate the violated norm, partly substituting for punishment's role in vindicating norms. Fourth, victims have a psychological need not only to express their feelings about crimes, but also to feel that they are being heard. The power to forgive and dispense mercy places the victim above the wrongdoer, at least partly fixing the power imbalance and empowering the disempowered victim.[10] In those senses, remorse, apology, and forgiveness can partly undo the crime. Thus, even if the state holds the exclusive right to punish, it should heed victims' wishes at least in part.

The exclusion of any victim's right is especially puzzling when the victim wishes to forgive and show mercy. The state may cap punishment to prevent the victim's bloodthirstiness from exceeding proper bounds. The state has much less reason, however, to impose symmetrical limits on leniency. So long as the punishment imposed is sufficient to deter, incapacitate, educate, and condemn the seriousness of the crime, the state's interests are satisfied. Any margin of retribution above that needed to fulfill those goals should be the victim's to forgive. We need to take seriously the metaphor of a debt wrongdoers owe to society and also to victims. As the victim suffered the direct loss and holds a share of the wrongdoer's debt, he may insist upon payment or forgive his share.[11]

The underlying theme here is that, even if the state runs the process, human emotion deserves a seat at the table. Emotion is not some raw, blind passion wholly divorced from and antithetical to reason. It is in part cognitive and evaluative and can be educated. Recent scholarship has impressively defended the importance of giving emotion a role in substantive criminal law alongside reason.[12] Emotions are an important part of what makes us human and how we understand and evaluate our fellow humans' actions. Crime excites fear and anger, empathy and indignation, sorrow and forgiveness. Victims need our solidarity; wrongdoers merit our anger but also empathy for their plight and reasons for breaking the law. This rainbow of emotions is central to appreciating and responding to all the parties' stakes in crime. While the parties have emotional stakes, they must not be judges in their own causes; neutral arbiters must reflect upon and filter the competing emotional claims in order to distill justice. It is time to extend the same emotional logic to criminal procedures. Laymen care whether criminal justice is emotionally sensitive or tone-deaf, and taking these concerns into account should bolster the law's legitimacy. As I will discuss in connection with victims' rights and restorative justice, however, too often lawyers hijack emotional discourse to serve particular political ends.

In short, criminal cases of course differ from civil ones. The state's interests are stronger in seeing justice done, ensuring equality, and deterring and incapacitating future crime. But the state-monopoly model masks the legitimate interests and emotions of real human beings: the victims, wrongdoers, and citizens who have personal stakes. A more humane, human-focused criminal justice system would leave more room to learn from mediation of emotionally charged civil cases. The state's indifference to these personal stakes reflects insiders' mechanical mindset, which ignores outsiders' needs to express themselves and heal.

B. INCOMPLETE ALTERNATIVES TO THE STATE'S MACHINERY

Scholars and policy advocates increasingly recognize that the amoral, state-dominated machinery disserves the emotional needs of victims, wrongdoers, and the public. In recent years, advocates of victims' rights, restorative justice, and therapeutic jurisprudence have proposed alternatives to reform the impersonal, lawyer-run machine. Victims' rights advocates want to give victims more information and a voice in their own cases, to level the playing field. Restorative justice seeks to substitute out-of-court mediation and restitution for criminal punishment. And therapeutic jurisprudence tries to use court procedures as psychotherapy to treat wrongdoers' disorders, such as addiction. Each of these approaches grapples more directly with the problems of denial, remorse, and apology.

Unfortunately, each approach is often unbalanced and captures only a part of the morality play for which outsiders thirst. In America, the victims' rights movement has gone astray because many advocates want more and more punishment; it lacks a goal, forgetting that the end is reconciliation or atonement. The restorative justice movement errs because it forgets that reconciliation or atonement requires some punishment. Much the same goes for therapeutic jurisprudence and especially problem-solving courts, which sometimes forget that most wrongdoers are responsible agents who deserve punishment, not just diseased agents who need treatment. We should take the best from each approach while rejecting its excesses.

1. Victims' Rights

One important development is the victims' rights movement. During the eighteenth and nineteenth centuries, as chapter I noted, public prosecutors steadily displaced victims. This shift reflected Beccaria's (and Bentham's) Enlightenment emphasis on rational deterrence, impersonal equality, and maximizing society's utility. Prosecutors thus gained the power to plea bargain and set sentences, and victims lost their say or even notice of what prosecutors were doing. Even when trials did occur, victims were no longer litigants but mere witnesses, who were often excluded from courtrooms to avoid tainting their testimony.[13] To counterbalance the state's awesome power, the Warren Court expanded criminal defendants' procedural rights in the 1950s and 1960s. Defendants received rights to free appointed lawyers, *Miranda* warnings, exclusion of illegally seized evidence, broad habeas corpus challenges to criminal convictions, and the like. Other trends in criminal justice, including liberal parole policies and an emphasis on rehabilitation instead of harsh punishment, tilted the playing field more toward defendants.

Victims' advocates in America saw these reforms as too soft on wrongdoers and deaf to victims' needs. They complained that victims and witnesses received none of the special rights and solicitude that defendants enjoyed. Thus, since the 1970s, victims' groups have tried at least to level the playing field. Some of their proposals offer victims support by counseling them, encouraging them to testify, offering social services, and compensating them for injuries. Some reforms protect victims' privacy, such as rape-shield laws that restrict use of victims' sexual histories at rape trials. Some provide victims with notice and information about upcoming court proceedings, proposed charges and dispositions, and court rulings. Some laws give victims greater rights to consult with prosecutors and to address the court, orally or in writing. Few go so far as to give victims a veto; prosecutors and courts can decide how much weight their views deserve. And, supposedly in the name of protecting victims, other laws restrict plea bargaining, raise sentences, and abolish parole and exclusionary rules of evidence.[14]

Yet these laws collide with an entrenched prosecutorial culture and mindset that views victims as peripheral if not irrelevant nuisances. Though the federal government and every state has victims' rights laws on the books, enforcement is wildly uneven. For almost every stage except arrest and trial, many victims fail to receive notice. Because victims cannot participate unless they first know of a proceeding, even fewer exercise their rights to take part.[15] In other words, victims' rights often exist on paper but have not been incorporated well into criminal practice.

The victims' rights movement hopes to restore much of the human focus that the machine has lost. It views criminal procedures not just as abstract rights or bargaining chips, but as important ways to vindicate and heal victims. And it restores a crucial focus on victims, who often get lost in lawyer-dominated criminal procedure brought in the name of the state. Many of the more minor measures are uncontroversial. Few can quibble with counseling traumatized rape victims, sheltering battered women, awarding assault victims restitution, or notifying victims of a defendant's bail or conviction. These measures are uncontroversial precisely because they in no way threaten the state's monopoly and are feel-good accessories to the punishment factory. They may make us, and victims, feel better about ourselves. But they are a far cry from including and empowering victims.

Giving victims a voice is more controversial because it intrudes upon the state's bipolar contest with the defendant. Many scholars attack victim-impact statements at sentencing because they fear that victims will cloud justice with emotion and play on sentencers' biases. Others complain that giving victims the right to consult distorts prosecutors' neutral evaluation of justice. Robert Mosteller even complains that victims' mere presence at trial may perhaps sway juries with emotional displays. Tellingly, he objects that emotion is illegitimate at jury trials, which misses the original point of public jury trials as morality plays. These criticisms slight the role a victim deserves as the most interested party, the bearer of the grievance. Though many philosophers deride it as moral luck, harm to victims is undeniably central to popular intuitions of justice. Gauging the harm to a unique human being, not a faceless abstraction, requires evidence of how that particular victim suffered. A victim's expressed feelings and wishes are powerful evidence of the psychological harm that he has suffered or from which he has recovered. As discussed earlier in this chapter, lay intuitions of justice place significant weight on victims' wishes; they implicitly recognize that victims own a share of the right to punish. And if victims share in the right to punish, judges and juries should hear their views on whether wrongdoers desire full punishment or mercy. If victims want trials, or are too scared to go to trial, prosecutors and judges ought at least to listen. Victims who want to watch their trials should have front-row seats as long as they are willing to testify first and not disrupt court proceedings with outbursts.[16] As I will discuss in chapter VI.C, victims do not deserve unfettered power to bring their own prosecutions or veto plea bargains, for otherwise they could do so arbitrarily. Prosecutors, however, ought to justify publicly why they dropped charges or struck plea bargains over victims' objections. While defendants have strong interests in fair trials, victims likewise have strong personal interests in being listened to and taken seriously.

Contrary to what one might expect, victims are not reflexively punitive. Empirical studies find that participation by victims does not lead to harsher sentences.[17] Thus, giving victims voices in the process need not produce widely varying outcomes, particularly because plenty of safeguards would remain. A neutral judge or jury would have to authorize any conviction or punishment and would weigh the victim's input against the defendant's and all the other evidence. A prosecutor would still be able to override a victim's vengeful, selfish, or otherwise unbalanced requests.

One may legitimately worry that judges and juries may favor attractive, white, young, female victims. But sentencing guidelines, rules of evidence, and cautionary jury instructions can limit discrimination. Moreover, despite decades of regulations, scholars still find sentence disparities based on the race, sex, and socioeconomic status of victims.[18] Rich, powerful victims already find ways to influence prosecutors and make their voices heard; poorer victims need formal ways to participate to achieve an equal footing. And efforts to treat like cases alike, such as mandating charging and minimum sentences, often wind up treating unlike cases alike. That is the lesson of chapter II: rules meant to ensure substantive equality often become plea-bargaining chips that turn on insiders' interests rather than blameworthiness or harm. Perhaps, then, it is worth relaxing our fruitless quest for perfect equality in favor of the other values of victim participation.

Indeed, perhaps local participation by victims and the public may be even better at promoting equality than top-down judicial rules have proven to be. Local democracy might perhaps defuse the insider-outsider tension of chapter II, instead of driving outsiders to jack up sentences while insiders covertly and inconsistently undercut them. This is the lesson that William Stuntz drew from his study of the criminal-justice politics of the Gilded Age: "Make criminal justice more locally democratic, and justice will be both more moderate and more egalitarian." In several areas recently, governors, legislatures, and commissions have pushed for more criminal-justice equality where judges have failed. Examples include the backlashes against racial profiling in highway stops, racial disparities in capital punishment, and sentence disparities for crack versus powder cocaine.[19] In other words, judges have failed to regulate police and prosecutors, who feel too little pressure to ensure equality. Political actors, responsive to voters' concern for equality, have had more success. Thus, a better way to equalize outcomes might be to open up participation to victims, defendants, and the public, who are often more receptive to equality concerns.

Critics of victims' rights also overlook prosecutors' flaws. As chapter II argued, prosecutors are far from perfect guardians of the public's and defendants' interests. They have plenty of agency costs and self-interests of their own, which can make them too harsh in some cases and too lenient in others. Other areas of law counterbalance governmental inaction by creating private rights of action and *qui tam* suits, so private parties can pursue civil wrongs. These suits can limit inertia and agency costs, while often letting government lawyers keep the upper hand.[20] The alternative to a victim's check on prosecutors is effectively no check at all. Prosecutors can check victims' excesses, but likewise we need victims to check prosecutors' excesses.

Unfortunately, while the victims' rights movement has much to teach us, it has become confused with law-and-order rhetoric. In Europe, victims' rights movements often emphasize supporting victims. And American academic supporters often focus on procedural rights of victims to receive information and participate. But particularly in America, politicians use victim rhetoric to dress up generic tough-on-crime measures. Put another way, politicians have hijacked outsider rhetoric to advance insiders' pet schemes. For example, three-strikes laws and attacks on parole and exclusionary rules of evidence are touted in the name of victims. These measures appeal to voters' fears and sympathies with victims, and they target defendants as a class. Many of these laws are cynical political ploys by insiders, with only the pretense of concern for outsiders. For example, the Doris Tate Crime Victims' Bureau was a leading proponent of California's three-strikes law. That organization, however, was a mouthpiece for prison guards: it received more than three-quarters of its funding from the state prison guards' union.[21] The real interest at work was not concern for victims, but insiders' self-interest in generating more jobs for themselves.

Often, prosecutors are the insiders guilty of manipulating victims' rights. For instance, the Feeney Amendment to the PROTECT Act purported to rein in prosecutors and judges as part of a bill to protect sexually abused children. Indeed, the acronym PROTECT stands for "Prosecutorial Remedies and Other Tools To End the Exploitation of Children Today." In fact, however, the U.S. Department of Justice was the moving force behind the bill, as part of its ongoing efforts to rein in lenient judges and line prosecutors. Thus, while it greatly limited most downward sentencing departures, it carved out gaping exceptions for prosecutor-approved departures for cooperating witnesses, fast-track programs, and acceptance of responsibility. Far from reining in prosecutors to protect victims, the bill centralized control by reining in judges and line prosecutors, while leaving head prosecutors plenty of wiggle room.[22]

Recall another example from chapter II. In 1982, California's Proposition 8, titled "Victims' Bill of Rights," was the work of tough-on-crime conservative politicians. It contained a grab-bag of proposals, many of which had nothing to do with victims. For example, it limited exclusionary rules and juvenile jurisdiction and allowed more evidence of defendants' prior convictions. It was sold to the public as a ban on plea bargaining designed to protect victims. Prosecutors, however, had blocked an earlier version of the bill that would truly have banned plea bargaining. The version that prosecutors and voters approved forbade plea bargaining only after indictment. In reality, then, the measure served prosecutors by pressuring defendants to plead guilty more quickly, before indictment or much discovery.[23] The rhetoric of protecting outsider victims by banning bargaining masked the creation of a new bargaining tool for insider prosecutors. Victims were dummies for the prosecutor ventriloquists.

What victims really want and need, these laws suggest, is more convictions and ever-harsher punishments. On this view, criminal justice is a zero-sum game, as if the only way to make victims happier is to punish defendants more. The metaphor of leveling the playing field rightly suggests that defendants' rights have turned into a legal game rather than a morality play. The vision is of two hostile groups of football hooligans, each cheering for its own team and booing if not brawling with the other side's supporters. The remedy, however, is not simply to tilt the field the other way. There are of course plenty of tradeoffs in criminal cases, and victims and defendants may desire quite different outcomes. But to reduce it all to a zero-sum contest over the amount of punishment ignores criminal justice's positive ability to heal.[24] Remorse, apology, forgiveness, and reintegration offer more reasons to be optimistic than victims' rights rhetoric would suggest. The appropriate procedures can help to make both victims and defendants better off.

Perhaps in reaction to this pro-victim conservatism, many scholars are reflexively hostile to victims' rights. Often this hostility proceeds from a politically liberal or progressive commitment to the rights of defendants. For example, many liberal scholars ordinarily favor storytelling to particularize concrete, complex harms and thus promote empathetic understanding. Paul Gewirtz has accused them of inconsistency in opposing victim-impact statements, because they selectively favor storytelling only when it serves to lower sentences. In response, Susan Bandes, perhaps the leading scholar of the role of emotion in law, embraces Gewirtz's charge of hypocrisy. She acknowledges that storytelling is simply a tool for advancing liberal, pro-defendant goals.[25] Sadly, this agenda cheapens profound human emotions into footballs and grieving parties into political pawns. If emotion is central to identifying with and understanding the parties' conflict and grievances, it belongs on both sides. Victim information can help defendants, judges, and juries empathize with victims, just as defendant information can help them empathize with defendants. Unfortunately, the conservative victims' rights agenda provokes a liberal reaction that obscures the merits. Both sides embrace the zero-sum approach, treating criminal justice as a game rather than an opportunity to reconcile and heal all the parties.

2. Restorative Justice

Restorative justice is an even more ambitious reform movement that many hope will replace state-centered criminal justice. While its many supporters espouse different versions, most seek to change both criminal justice's substantive aims and its procedures. Substantively, most restorativist scholars reject retribution as a cruel, backward expression of anger. The leading restorativist, John Braithwaite, denounces "retribution [as] in the same category as greed or gluttony," a vice that "corro[des] human health and relationships." To most academic restorativists, retribution is pure vengefulness, returning hurt for hurt and simply increasing the wounds of crime. Criminal justice is wrong to focus on who is criminally responsible and what punishment he deserves, because blaming distracts the blamer from mending harms and preventing recurrence. Speaking for many restorativists, Braithwaite dreams of "A Future Where Punishment Is Marginalized." In these scholars' ideal world, punishment would at most be a last resort, used sparingly only to prevent future crime and not to pay back wrongs.[26]

On this account, the point of criminal justice should be not retribution but restoration. Crime is not primarily an offense against the state but a wrong to a particular human victim and community. It wounds a victim's body, property, psyche, and relationships. Wrongdoers and victims often started out as relatives or friends, but crime estranges wrongdoers from their victims and communities. In response, restorative justice seeks to heal rather than hurt. Victims benefit not from punishment at wrongdoers' expense, restorativists argue, but rather from receiving restitution, expressions of remorse, and apologies. Most restorativists eschew prison as pointless and seek to use shame constructively. The goal is not to stigmatize the wrongdoer but to condemn the offense, have the wrongdoer repudiate it, and reintegrate him back into society. In Braithwaite's terminology, it promotes reintegrative shaming while rejecting disintegrative shaming.[27]

This substantive vision of restoration goes hand-in-hand with distinctive procedures. Because crime is about harm to individuals and not the state, restorativists reject abstruse, impersonal, lawyer-run procedures and the need for formal equality. Instead, they favor lay-run substitutes such as victim-offender mediation, community reparative boards, family group conferences, and sentencing circles. While the people who run these procedures are not lawyers, they are hardly amateurs; often they belong to a professional, trained cadre of facilitators who mediate and promote restorative dialogue. While each model differs slightly, each one lets victims explain how crimes affected them, ask questions, develop restitution plans, seek apologies, air their sorrows, and perhaps forgive. In turn, wrongdoers learn about their victims' sufferings, ideally apologize and commit to make amends, and heal the guilt that might otherwise plague their consciences. The informal, flexible procedures can empower parties to speak for themselves and to tailor remedies to particular people's needs and circumstances. Victim-offender mediation is often limited to the parties themselves. Other restorative justice processes, however, also incorporate victims' and wrongdoers' families and friends, to provide support, encouragement, and oversight as wrongdoers commit to change. Victims can more easily express their pain and anger with loved ones at their sides. Wrongdoers are skilled at denying or minimizing their crimes, but the tears of their parents or siblings may pierce these denials and drive home the need for change.[28]

Restorative justice appears to work as promised. Victims and wrongdoers who choose to take part in restorative justice are on average more satisfied as a result. A review of seven empirical studies found restorative justice performed better than traditional criminal justice on all dimensions studied: Victims and wrongdoers were more likely to think that the system, their judges or mediators, and the outcomes were fair. They were more likely to be satisfied with the handling and outcomes of their cases. They were more likely to believe that they had been able to tell their stories and that their opinions had received enough consideration. They were more likely to believe the wrongdoer had been held accountable, to think more highly of the other party's behavior, and to apologize or forgive. And victims were less likely to remain upset about the crime and afraid of revictimization.[29]

Much of the restorative-justice agenda fits well with my argument. Substantively, restorative justice rightly tries to transcend a one-dimensional, zero-sum struggle between prosecutor and defense counsel. Crime is much more than an abstract offense against an impersonal state. It also wounds human relationships and emotions; where possible, criminal procedure should help restore them. Thus, abstract equality is less important than addressing the particular wrongdoer and the wounds of the particular victim and his family and neighbors. It does help to hear the wrongdoer's story, to understand why he broke the law, and to consider factors that increase or reduce his blame. Making restitution for a victim's monetary losses is also a constructive step. For minor crimes such as vandalism and shoplifting, these steps may suffice to pay the wrongdoer's monetary and moral debts to the victim and others. Youths are especially promising candidates, as they may be less blameworthy and more correctable by their parents' anger and shame. The very process of listening to the victim, apologizing, and making amends may have enough bite to denounce minor crimes and teach lessons. In other words, even retributivists may agree that going through restorative justice inflicts enough retribution for minor crimes. Reintegrative shaming is a sensible way to make the wrongdoer visibly pay his debt and then return to the community, instead of remaining estranged.

Procedurally, restorative justice is also right to re-empower victims, wrongdoers, and their friends and families. Since crime can wound their relationships and psyches, they often need opportunities to actively repair these harms if they are willing to take part. Rather than passively and silently submitting to punishment, the wrongdoer may actively admit his wrong, apologize, and try to repair the harm he has caused. Victims and neighbors can then choose to reciprocate by forgiving and moving on. These procedures logically support the substantive aim of restoring the lay parties by involving them. Conversely, it also makes sense to deemphasize lawyers and move away from technical legalese and procedures that silence laymen. Plain English, with fewer technicalities of procedure and evidence, is far more effective at communicating moral messages. Finally, restorative justice admirably reunites criminal procedure with the aims of substantive criminal law, consciously tailoring its procedures to serve its substantive ends.

Unfortunately, many advocates of restorative justice go too far. Substantively, most academic restorativists leave no room for retribution. Just as victims' rights can be a tool of the right to get tough, so too restorative justice can be a tool of the left to undermine punishment and blame. Most deride retribution as returning hurt for hurt and thus needlessly multiplying suffering, and Braithwaite and Strang downplay deterrence and incapacitation as at best occasional fallbacks. But restorativists are too optimistic about human nature and too quick to separate the wrongdoer from his crime and blame. Right now, restorative justice is most commonly used for minor crimes, especially ones by juveniles. Because of the low stakes and lesser blameworthiness, restorative justice may sufficiently deter and impose retribution along the way.[30]

But many restorativists overreach by seeking to supplant traditional criminal justice in more serious cases. For moderately serious offenses, especially by adults, restoration is no substitute for punishment. It does nothing to incapacitate dangerous wrongdoers. Its mildness undercuts deterrence of more serious crimes, particularly if the penalty is simply paying back the money taken and apologizing. And it sacrifices the retribution that undergirds the public's moral intuitions and its thirst to see justice done. Victims and the public are often justifiably angry and want some payback that goes beyond money. They need not demand the wrongdoer's scalp, but they do want to see him suffer somewhat. The wrongdoer has often exalted himself at the expense of the humiliated, disempowered victim. To turn the tables, criminal justice should empower the victim and lay the wrongdoer low, at least temporarily, before restoring him. The public is willing to accept lower punishments when restorative justice conferences succeed. Studies find, however, that in the public's eyes restorative justice is far from a complete substitute for punishing moderate and severe crimes. But classic restorative justice skips over taking the wrongdoer down a peg, often leaping too quickly to award cheap grace. By itself monetary restitution, or even a fine, does not unequivocally condemn, but rather belittles the crime and the harm. It sends the wrong message that a wrongdoer can simply buy off his victim. Wrongdoers, victims, and society can misread the failure to punish as belittling the crime and leaving the wrongdoer free to keep doing it. The pain and stigma of punishment are needed to right the imbalanced scales, and their bite underscores society's condemnation of the crime. As Stephen Garvey cogently argues, restorative justice short-circuits this process:

> Missing from the restorativist agenda . . . is the idea of punishment as moral condemnation. . . . Restorativism cannot achieve the victim's restoration if it refuses to vindicate the victim's worth through punishment. Nor can it restore the offender, who can only atone for his wrong if he willingly submits to punishment. And if neither the victim nor the wrongdoer is restored, then neither is the community of which they are a part.[31]

Restoration is a laudable goal. But, as the colonists in chapter I recognized, it should be the fruit of the morality play. Denunciation and punishment have their time and place; usually, they must precede forgiveness and reintegration. Having denounced and punished the wrongdoer, neighbors, friends, and society see that he has paid his debt to society and the victim. Only then are they ready to forgive and reintegrate him. The need to condemn and punish crimes before forgiving "is missed by 'restorative justice' advocates who want us to focus on harm and its repair rather than wrongs and their punishment, or to think of 'conflicts' rather than 'crimes.'"[32] Remorse, apology, and restitution may lessen the punishment and speed the process, but for moderately serious crimes cannot supplant it entirely.

Moreover, restorative dreams can be "culpably sentimental and dangerously naive" about both wrongdoers and victims. Some wrongdoers can critically reflect on their actions, emotionally appreciate their wrongdoing, vow to change, and exercise enough self-discipline to make amends and change their ways. But many cannot or will not. Some adolescents may be more malleable, but adults are often set in their ways. Many are impulsive, self-centered, undisciplined, and impaired in their foresight and empathy for the needs of others. Indeed, criminologists identify these traits as hallmarks of wrongdoers. Sometimes restorative justice, apologies, and forgiveness may work magic in transforming people. But the dangers of fakery are enormous, though insincerity is sometimes transparent. Even when wrongdoers sincerely weep and vow to turn over new leaves, their habitual lack of self-discipline makes them very likely to backslide. Drugs and alcohol further undercut self-control and vows to change.[33] It may be worth taking a chance on restorative justice with a first- or second-time wrongdoer whose crime was not very serious. But naïve hope must not triumph over experience when dealing with recidivists.

Restorative justice can likewise be sentimental about victims. While victims are not as bloodthirsty or vengeful as we often assume, many restorativists lurch to the other extreme. They expect them to forgive and be healed by a cathartic conference, apology, and restitution. As I have argued, remorse, apology, and forgiveness have remarkable healing power if the parties are willing. But sometimes they are not, perhaps because victims are understandably frightened and angry. Restorative justice's very softness may sometimes increase fears, as when a victim realizes that a violent wrongdoer will not be safely behind bars for a while. It can also belittle, disregard, or shut down victims' and the public's justified anger as out of bounds. In one restorative conference, when a burglary victim "'let that punk know' how angry" he was by expressing his fury with the burglar's "crap," the wrongdoer and then mediators intervened to stop the angry words. By saying that they needed another ten minutes to work out a settlement, the mediators implicitly sided with the wrongdoer and cut the victim short. Mediators are supposed to interrupt and deflect displays of anger and moral indignation; by doing that, they implicitly condemn victims' outbursts as aggressive and disrespectful. In other words, mediators see it as their job to protect wrongdoers' dignity from being condemned even in words, the kind of verbal fusillade many victims long to discharge before they can forgive. Emotions are important, but angry and judgmental emotions are at best briefly tolerated, at worst off limits. In their zeal to restore without offending offenders, mediators may pressure victims to suppress their natural bitterness and anger instead of venting it.[34]

As the previous example shows, restorativist professionals sometimes skew their processes where the lay participants might veer toward retribution. They have rejected legal professionals only to replace them with a different professional elite with its own agenda. So, for example, in one conference a young wrongdoer's mother and the victim agreed that her son ought to learn a lesson by wearing a T-shirt bearing the words "I am a thief." John Braithwaite began publicly to denounce that outcome as cruel and degrading. That response, however, conflicts with restorativists' focus on the particular participants' needs and the consensus that emerges from their discussions. Braithwaite had not been at the conference and so could not know whether the T-shirt punishment might teach this particular wrongdoer a valuable lesson. In his zeal to avoid any stigma for the wrongdoer, he stigmatized the mother and victim who had agreed on the punishment.[35] In other words, many restorativists' substantive prejudice against retribution undercuts the power of their procedures to achieve moral consensus and particularize punishments to crimes and wrongdoers. Despite all the talk of respecting victims and communities, it can disregard their moral intuitions when they conflict with the anti-punishment agenda.

Another problem with restorative justice is that it sometimes focuses so greatly on the immediate parties that it can exclude the public's legitimate concerns. For example, private restorative justice conferences, somewhat like plea bargains, bypass the public morality play of a trial. They keep the public from seeing the victim vindicated and justice done. The lack of publicity is especially acute in victim-offender mediation, which need not include friends, family, neighbors, or community representatives. Likewise, restorative justice effectively denies that the state has any interest in doing justice. By encouraging victims to settle cases as entirely private matters, and taking substantial punishment off the table, it slights future victims' and the public's interests in seeing some justice done. The same problem hampers restorative justice for so-called victimless crimes. While restorativists sometimes substitute police officers or victims of other drunk-driving crashes, there is no real victim to confront the wrongdoer in many cases of drunk driving, drug dealing, or creation of other risks.

Thankfully, some restorativists have begun to reject the false dichotomy between retribution and restoration. For example, Howard Zehr, who had helped to popularize this dichotomy, has admitted that he was wrong to oppose the two. In this vein, the practice of restorative justice is often much better than what its academic boosters espouse. Many restorative processes inflict deserved punishment in the course of restoring the parties and communities. In practice, restorative conferences contain many retributive elements, such as censuring the wrongdoer, which may be prerequisites for reconciliation. The same is true of indigenous punishment practices on which restorativism draws, such as ritual spearing and other physical reprisals. (Comically, some restorativist scholars contort themselves to deny that this blatant violence involves retribution.) As some restorativists acknowledge, the public would not be likely to accept restorative justice if it did not see retributive aspects in it.[36]

Shorn of its reflexive hostility to punishment, restorative processes have much to offer criminal justice. Restorative justice could supplement criminal justice without supplanting it for crimes serious enough to require punishment. For example, the University of Wisconsin Law School has begun a restorative justice project that arranges mediation in prison between wrongdoers and victims or their relatives. During one mediation session, an attempted murderer accepted responsibility, broke down in tears, and hugged his victim, who in turn forgave him. In another, the mother of a rape and stabbing victim asked to meet with the rapist, who had steadfastly claimed innocence during and after his trial. In the prison-based mediation, he broke down and admitted guilt. Likewise, the Iowa and Minnesota Departments of Corrections have begun prison-based victim-offender mediation, circles of support and accountability, family team meetings, and victim-impact classes for incarcerated wrongdoers. Victims can ask wrongdoers why the crime happened, give voice to their wounds, and heal. So long as the parties are truly free to participate or not, there is every reason to offer these kinds of restorative processes more broadly before and after trial or plea. And justice can easily set boundaries for restorative processes, limiting harshness and leniency. Similarly, restorative processes can help to heal nations in the wake of mass atrocities, particularly if they do not substitute for punishment.[37]

It is telling that left-wing restorativists and right-wing victims' rights advocates make fundamentally the same complaint about criminal justice: Our current system is too opaque and dominated by lawyer insiders. As a result, it excludes the legitimate needs and voices of the outsiders who once were and should again be the parties. Legalese, procedural technicalities, and unfettered back-room deals, they agree, should give way to more transparent and participatory procedures. This political convergence suggests that the broader public would support reforms shorn of their polarized excesses.

3. Therapeutic Jurisprudence and Problem-Solving Courts

A third criminal-justice reform movement is not an effort to add new speakers' voices to criminal justice, but to have existing speakers speak in a different tone. Therapeutic jurisprudence is an amorphous movement of the last two decades led by David Wexler and Bruce Winick. Though it shares themes with restorative justice and is sometimes confused with it, therapeutic jurisprudence originated in mental-health law and extends far beyond criminal justice. It focuses on how the legal system can promote or hinder the psychological well-being of those it affects, such as victims and defendants. It is forward-looking, using social science to evaluate and reform legal rules.[38] It is also holistic, looking at a person's full range of needs and not just his desire to achieve a narrow legal judgment.

Importantly, therapeutic jurisprudence looks not only at substantive legal rules, but also legal procedures, rhetoric, and judges' and lawyers' roles. For example, advocates criticize substantive insanity law's verdict of not guilty by reason of insanity. The label "not guilty," they argue, encourages wrongdoers to believe they have done nothing wrong and need no treatment. Others criticize the Federal Sentencing Guidelines for rewarding snitching and using uncharged, dismissed, or acquitted crimes to raise sentences for other crimes of conviction. These measures arguably conflict with popular morality and so may undermine legitimacy and respect for the law.[39]

Procedurally, the law ought to make the parties feel the law has listened to them and treated them fairly. Procedures ought to respect the parties' emotions and give them space to express them. For example, procedures can let victims tell their stories and can encourage defendants to accept responsibility and apologize at guilty plea hearings and sentencing. Therapeutically minded lawyers should take into account their clients' long-term psychological needs in counseling them. For example, a lawyer for a drunk driver can confront his client's denials and encourage him to admit guilt and enter Alcoholics Anonymous. Doing so serves the client's long-term interest in kicking his addiction and avoiding future injury and crime. The lawyer can then use this evidence of constructive change to fashion a favorable plea deal.[40]

Judges can likewise tailor their rhetoric to the needs of their audience. They can take pains to decode their legalese for their listeners. For example, sentencing judges can speak plainly about the wrong and the harm instead of retreating into mathematical sentencing-guidelines gobbledy-gook. And an appellate court, instead of uttering the single word "affirmed," can explain in a few sentences that while it has listened to the appellant's contention, it has decided that the trial judge did not abuse his broad discretion.[41]

Though it did not give birth to them, therapeutic jurisprudence has welcomed the recent development of problem-solving courts, which apply many therapeutic jurisprudence ideas. The most common and widespread of these are drug courts. Drug courts, like other problem-solving courts, eschew the formal, adversarial language and procedures of traditional courts. Defendants whose cases and records are not too serious are diverted in large numbers, usually before trial, to these specialized courts. Literally and figuratively, drug-court judges come down from their benches to serve as super-probation officers. Prosecutors and defense lawyers are supposed to become members of the treatment team instead of adversaries. Instead of focusing on criminal ascription of blame, judges often speak as counselors and cheerleaders for their "clients." They warn clients who violate program rules, by for example testing positive for drugs. Repeated violations of rules may lead to short jail terms or eventually to traditional incarceration. Conversely, eventual success in staying drug-free and looking for work may lead to dismissal of the criminal case. Judges hold graduation ceremonies and express emotions, even hugging their clients to celebrate successes. It is all staged as "therapeutic theater." Much controversy has swirled around drug courts in particular. Critics accuse them of widening the net of drug arrests, punishing addicts while freeing those not addicted, and effectively decriminalizing drugs through a back door.[42] Rather than wading into these drug-specific issues, let us focus on common therapeutic jurisprudence issues that can affect crimes with identifiable victims.

Several of the themes of therapeutic jurisprudence resonate strongly with my approach. Most notably, therapeutic jurisprudence is right to emphasize the messages and effects of legal procedures and rhetoric. Too often, lawyers focus only on the bottom-line number of dollars or years in prison that a court will impose. Substantive law should pay more attention to procedure, particularly the meanings that procedures convey. For example, therapeutic jurisprudence echoes my concern in chapter III with how procedures can promote healing apologies or conversely harden defendants' denials, hindering reform. It also dovetails nicely with Tom Tyler's work on how fair procedures increase trust and make parties more willing to respect legal outcomes.[43] Hearing all the parties and treating them respectfully reinforces the law's moral credibility regardless of the outcome. Publishing reasoned opinions helps to explain and justify court decisions, increasing transparency and legitimacy. Even simple steps, such as translating legalese into plain English, can help to make legal decisions intelligible and respected. These measures are not zero-sum tradeoffs, but ways to make all parties more satisfied.

Another valuable aspect of therapeutic jurisprudence is its attention to the consequences of lawyers' and judges' roles. Lawyers should not focus solely on their interactions with other insiders. Their advice and actions translate into real-world consequences for the outsider laymen whom they are supposed to serve. Focusing too narrowly on winning a particular case can overlook the longer-term needs and interests of a victim or defendant. For instance, simply minimizing punishment for an alcoholic or a sex offender in denial may leave the underlying problem to fester and grow worse. A lawyer should care not only about winning a criminal case but also, in appropriate cases, about referring his client for job-training, drug-treatment, educational, medical, and counseling services. Indeed, even in

narrowly legal terms these social services often matter in structuring pretrial diversion, plea bargains, prison sentences, probation, and parole.[44]
Like restorative justice, therapeutic jurisprudence is a useful effort to
integrate substantive law, procedures, and practices to serve common
ends. It steps back from the machinery to ask what broader purposes and
human needs the law should serve.

Like restorative justice, therapeutic jurisprudence is right to question
the machinery's extreme emphasis on equalizing outcomes. Equality, as
one of the few quantifiable metrics of success, gets over-emphasized by
the machine. The result has been Procrustean Federal Sentencing
Guidelines and mandatory-minimum penalties. Yet these measures
never work as outsiders hope; as chapter II explained, insider prosecutors
use them as plea-bargaining chips based not on justice but on case-
processing efficiency. Even when they are consistently applied, broad
mandatory rules treat unlike cases alike. And this fruitless quest for
perfect formal equality has hardly eliminated race, wealth, and sex disparities from American criminal justice. While we should not surrender
equality as a goal, we should loosen its strictures and allow more tailoring
of procedures and outcomes to the particular needs of individual victims,
defendants, and communities. Unfortunately, some restorative-justice
and therapeutic-jurisprudence enthusiasts have gone too far in the
other direction, jettisoning even a pretense of measures to equalize
treatment.[45]

Finally, therapeutic jurisprudence tries to respect the place of emotions
in criminal justice. As chapter II suggested, a great gulf separates insiders'
perspectives from those of outsiders. Too often, law comes across as cold,
hard, and inhumane in its logic. Lawyers are typically aggressive, rights-
oriented, and concerned only with bottom-line outcomes such as dollars
and cents or years in prison. They are not always good at listening to and
truly understanding their clients and their needs. They should do more to
cultivate their emotional intelligence, so they can understand and serve
their clients' needs. Clients may feel better knowing that an attorney has
listened to them, empathized with them, and tried to help, regardless of
the outcome.[46]

Unfortunately, therapeutic jurisprudence is flawed in several ways. For
one, it is too enamored of experts. Judges are not trained as therapists, yet
they are expected to diagnose and treat defendants as if they were patients.
The dominance of experts undercuts therapeutic jurisprudence's emphasis on procedural legitimacy. But, as chapter II discussed, the problem
with our system is not a lack of professionals but a surfeit of them, squeez-
ing out juries and community sentiment. It is thus far too easy for the law

to drift away from the public's sense of justice toward the agenda of a professional elite.

This expert-worship raises legitimate concerns of paternalism in practice. Though theorists disavow it, and many deny it, some judges admit candidly that they lean very hard on their clients by threatening added punishment or other consequences. Of course, the state may legitimately threaten punishment for crime. It is troubling enough when the state threatens extra punishment simply for failing to cooperate in plea bargaining. But when the judge sees himself as a benevolent therapist, few proportionality limits constrain him from applying ever more pressure to force the client to improve. In practice, one critic notes, therapeutic jurisprudence is neo-rehabilitationism, so it suffers from rehabilitation's lack of proportion to deserved punishment. Therapists can even redefine justice to require whatever is needed to treat the diseased client. Professionals' views of what clients need often diverge markedly from what clients themselves think they need.[47]

Another problem with expertise is its divorce from popular moral judgment. Therapeutic rhetoric has a clinical ring. It speaks in a psychological vocabulary that, especially in problem-solving courts, can degenerate into psychobabble. Notably, judges speak of their charges not as wrongdoers, nor defendants, nor even offenders, but clients.[48] The language of treatment suggests that crime is not about succumbing to evil or weakness of will, but a disease to treat or fix. Disease rhetoric risks undercutting clients' sense of responsibility free will, and need to change themselves. Therapeutic jurisprudence is right that rhetoric matters, but its particular choice of rhetoric is somewhat off.

When judges in problem-solving courts are not speaking like therapists, they sometimes imitate talk-show hosts. This behavior is most obvious and extreme in many drug courts. Problem-solving judges descend from their formal distance and height of authority to mingle with their clients, empathizing, hugging, and celebrating. This extreme informality undermines judges' air of authority, solemnity, and neutral justice. Empathy per se is not a problem; as I have argued, it is an important ingredient in moral judgment. The problem is that problem-solving courts can indulge in emotionalism, a psychobabble of feelings adrift without a moral compass. Some reject retribution and shame as "inappropriate jurisprudential theories"; blame and free will are inconsistent with the disease model of crime. Hence, many cases are diverted to problem-solving courts before any plea or adjudication of guilt.[49] Avoiding the issue of guilt is debatable at best for actions that do not deserve moral censure and so should not be crimes at all. But even if one wants to decriminalize drugs, one certainly cannot extend this amoral approach to crimes that are inherently wrong (*mala in se*). Particularly for crimes involving force or fraud against persons or property, a talk show is no substitute for a morality play.

Here, as with restorative justice, the reluctance to speak moral language leaves therapeutic jurisprudence incomplete. Crime is not primarily a problem of disease and pathology, but of free will and bad or even evil choices. Moderately serious crimes require blame and punishment before atonement, forgiveness, and healing. Courts need solemn rituals to underscore the gravity of crimes and communicate moral messages. Our nation has plenty of talk-show hosts already; it needs authority figures to serve different, timeless roles.[50] The full range of emotional language must inform criminal judgments, including anger, indignation, sorrow, remorse, empathy, and pity. Unfortunately, while therapeutic jurisprudence has laudable elements, it does not emphasize the morality-play aspect. Its psychological language can obscure moral blame and censure. Therapeutic theater is talk-show drama of a sort, but not a morality play.

Last but not least, in practice therapeutic jurisprudence sometimes sacrifices the most basic safeguard built into a morality play. By removing their robes and coming down from their benches, judges literally dethrone justice. That symbolic descent reflects a real shift. Particularly in problem-solving courts, judges may abandon any pretense of neutrality and impartiality to become cheerleaders. By embracing their new role as super-probation officers, judges abandon the fundamental requirement of due process. Neutrality and impartiality guarantee that rich and poor, black and white, educated and illiterate defendants and victims all enjoy equal justice before the law. Granted, plea bargaining had already cut neutral judges and juries out of the picture, but that is hardly a reason to extend and celebrate that worrying trend. Judges and juries should use their emotions in judging, but using emotions thoughtfully is quite different from sacrificing neutrality. Therapy must not supersede impartial justice. Indeed, doing justice through a morality play is the kind of healing therapy for which victims, defendants, and their communities hunger.

* * * * *

Though all three of these reform movements are flawed, they share many valuable insights. All three reject the zero-sum idea that criminal justice can make victims happy only at the expense of defendants and vice versa. All three recognize that mechanical criminal justice has become too impersonal and unconcerned with laymen's interests and needs. All three sense that assembly-line rhetoric is deeply unsatisfying and inadequate. All three emphasize the needs of particular parties and de-emphasize abstract, formal equality of outcomes. All three try to listen to the parties, to respect their human emotions, and to let them have their say. All three reflect some frustration with lawyers as hired guns who speak in legalese and obstruct or obscure the truth. All three take seriously how procedures and rhetoric affect the parties' satisfaction with outcomes. And the three approaches span the political spectrum, suggesting that the appropriate reforms would enjoy broad public support. The time is ripe for reform that gleans the best from each approach while leaving behind each one's peculiar baggage.

CHAPTER V

✧

Popular Moral Discourse Versus Mechanical Efficiency

Today, criminal procedure strives to be a cheap, fast punishment factory, to the exclusion of most other values. The punishment factory maximizes efficiency, but lawyers rarely pause to consider what exactly they are supposed to be doing efficiently. It emphasizes quantity with little regard for quality. And it stresses following procedures and defendants' individual rights to the exclusion of outsiders' social and moral needs. It has a tin ear for the rhetoric of justice and mercy, sometimes dismissing rhetoric as mere words and irrelevant ideals.

This chapter argues that criminal justice has gone astray because it has embraced efficiency precisely as a way of avoiding popular moral judgment. The efficiency mindset focuses on quantifiable criteria, procedures, and rights as seemingly neutral ways to avoid disagreement. At least four factors are largely to blame for this trend. One factor lies in law schools' artificial divorce of substantive criminal law from procedure. A second is the criminal justice bureaucracy, which has its own incentives and quantifiable measures of success as well as its own administrative ideal of equality. A third factor is nonjudgmentalism, as scholars fear that moral judgments are arbitrary or intolerant. A fourth is elitism, which leads some scholars and lawyers to fear popular moral input by the passionate crowd.

Each of these barriers to moral discourse is unjustified. First, law school curricula are historical accidents that need to be revised. Second, criminal justice bureaucracies are captured by insiders, develop tunnel vision, and lose touch with their nominal constituencies. They need to become less insulated and less enamored of relying on rules to advance equality. Third, scholars and insiders must not dismiss moral judgments as arbitrary or intolerant, especially in the realm of criminal justice. It is not judgmental to condemn those who inflict harm and violate others' rights. On the contrary, people's intuitions show striking agreements in judging both substantive punishments and fair criminal procedures. Bringing these issues out into the open would thus be less divisive and more legitimate than skeptics fear. Finally, elitism is an illegitimate basis for criminal justice policy in a democracy. As a matter of political theory, popular moral discourse is essential to give the system the democratic legitimacy it needs. And criminal justice should reject the dichotomy between justice and mercy; a balanced justice system needs both.

A. EFFICIENCY INSTEAD OF MORAL JUDGMENT

When judges and scholars evaluate criminal procedure, they tend to focus on efficiency. Criminal-justice efficiency seeks to maximize speed and volume and minimize cost within the constraints of accuracy and procedural fairness. These neutral, amoral criteria rightly matter a great deal, but they are incomplete. Chief among these criteria is speed. The Sixth Amendment guarantees defendants the right to a speedy trial, and the Speedy Trial Act further requires federal trials to begin within 70 days of the formal criminal charge.[1] The old adage "justice delayed is justice denied" captures the importance of speed. It is valuable to many parties: defendants want to clear their names or get their cases over with; victims and the public want to see justice done; and courts want to hear evidence before witnesses forget or die. Speedier convictions should in theory increase deterrence by connecting the punishment to the crime. Speeding cases along also makes room for more of them to enter the system.

Related to the speed of cases is their volume. Overwhelmed police cannot investigate and prosecutors cannot prosecute every suspected crime, but ideally they would handle more cases. Case-processing statistics tally the numbers of defendants arrested, charged, convicted, and sentenced. Increasing arrests, convictions, and sentences should deter and incapacitate more wrongdoers. Like speed, the volume of cases is a neutral, quantifiable measure of success.

The volume of cases depends on the cost of each one. Police, prosecutors, and judges have fixed budgets of time, manpower, and money. Given those budgets, they feel pressures to maximize arrests, convictions, and sentences. To maximize these statistics, they must drive down the cost of each case, prosecuting as quickly and cheaply as possible. That is the economic logic of mass production on an assembly line.

Two important procedural values constrain speed, volume, and cost. One is accuracy. Accurate procedures must both punish the guilty and protect the innocent. Thus, the justice system needs to gather and consider as much relevant evidence as it can, screen out irrelevant distractions, and weigh carefully the evidence on either side.

The other important constraint is procedural fairness. To most lawyers, fairness (also called due process) is a relatively narrow concept. Primarily, it means that the government must level the playing field and give the defense a sporting chance in adversarial combat. Before imprisoning a defendant, the government must give him a lawyer, notify him of the criminal charges, turn over favorable evidence, and prove guilt beyond a reasonable doubt to a neutral judge or jury. Lawyers think of these requirements as the defendant's due process rights against the government. Another component of fairness is equality. Governments must take pains to treat like cases alike, regardless of race, sex, wealth, or other irrelevant factors.

These criteria fit within Herbert Packer's classic, stylized portrait of two opposing models of criminal procedure, which exemplifies the scholarly debate of the past half-century. At one end of the spectrum, the Crime Control Model's overriding goal is to prevent as much crime as possible given limited criminal justice budgets. It seeks to maximize speed, volume, and finality while minimizing cost. To be efficient, procedures must be routine and stripped down. "The process must not be cluttered up with ceremonious rituals that do not advance the progress of a case." Instead, it should be like an assembly line, hurrying large volumes of cases along to guilty pleas.[2]

At the other end of the spectrum, the Due Process Model emphasizes procedural fairness and perceived fairness to defendants as limits on efficiency. It sees criminal justice as an obstacle course, requiring the prosecution to clear more hurdles. Both models value accuracy, though the Due Process Model is less tolerant of error and prefers more second-guessing of police and prosecutors' factual judgments. That model also seeks to limit abuse of official power, even at the cost of freeing some factually guilty defendants. Thus, it denies the government legal power to punish where it has no jurisdiction or venue, or where a statute of limitations or double jeopardy bars prosecution. It supports excluding illegally obtained evidence as a way to deter police and prosecutorial misconduct. It emphasizes equality of outcomes, so that poor and minority defendants suffer no disadvantage. And it is uneasy about criminal punishment's morality and efficacy; it doubts whether the government should exert its power and whether poor defendants ought to suffer.[3]

The two models differ in obvious ways but share many important assumptions. Though the Crime Control Model tilts toward prosecutors and police and the Due Process Model tilts toward defense lawyers, both see criminal justice as an adversarial duel between experts. Both models entrust power to criminal-justice professionals. Both reflect the bottom-line concerns of insiders and ignore the broader moral interests of outsiders.

Both models are particularly narrow in defining efficiency. Speed, volume, cost, accuracy, and fairness are procedural values not directly tied to most of the criminal law's substantive goals. The Crime Control Model rests on the substantive goal of minimizing crime. Speed, volume, cost, and to an extent accuracy are ways to maximize incapacitation and deterrence. But these few goals are mechanistic and incomplete. Neither model shows any direct concern for retribution. Neither one cares about criminal law's communicative functions: denouncing wrongs, vindicating victims, and educating the public. Neither one sees deterrence as a broader process of reinforcing social norms and earning public legitimacy. Neither one emphasizes teaching or reforming defendants. Neither one tries to empower outsiders or give them their day in court. And neither one seeks to heal wounded relationships or reconcile torn communities.

This last point bears emphasis. Both models view criminal justice as a zero-sum contest rather than a multi-faceted morality play. Both are bipolar, pitting an individual defendant against a faceless, unitary government. Methodologically, both are individualistic. The Due Process Model emphasizes the defendant's individual legal rights against the state. It tends to sympathize with defendants and doubt how much punishment they need. It is suspicious of criminal justice generally and lacks an affirmative vision of what good criminal justice can accomplish. Its language is of legal rights, not morality or healing.

Conversely, the Crime Control Model views criminal punishment as simply a way to further the state's impersonal interest in stopping crime. It cares about the state, not the community. It is reflexively hostile to criminal defendants, focusing on how much of a threat each one poses. Both models, in other words, fight on the terrain of individual badness: how much punishment does this particular defendant need?

As chapter III argued, focusing on individual defendants' rights and badness excludes criminal justice's social, relational, and moral goals. The public expects criminal justice to vindicate the innocent defendant, vindicate the wronged victim, and denounce the guilty wrongdoer. The machinery, however, speeds past the dramatic public rituals that used to reinforce social solidarity in the face of crime. Its very efficiency is counterproductive, as in the long run it costs the system its democratic legitimacy and public respect. And it wastes precious opportunities to heal wrongdoers' relationships with victims and their communities. Wrongdoers remain ostracized, victims wounded, and communities torn and fearful when they do not *see* justice done and take part in doing it.

My alternative to Packer's two models is the Morality Play Model. Like the other two models, it is an ideal, one end of a spectrum that in practice will compromise with the other models. On this account, criminal justice ideally should be neither an assembly line nor an obstacle course but an educational public theater. Instead of being bipolar, it should respect and include a wide range of parties: defendants, victims, their friends and families, neighbors, and the public at large. Instead of silencing and excluding these outsiders, it should give them plenty of opportunities to speak and listen. Instead of isolating the parties, it should focus on encouraging face-to-face dialogue and healing relationships. Instead of being amoral, it should openly engage in communal, collective moral judgment of alleged crimes. Instead of just haggling over the bottom line, it should also strive to make the parties feel respected and well treated. Instead of satisfying itself with mechanistic deterrence and incapacitation, it should also emphasize law's ability to teach, denounce, and heal. Instead of being drab and functional, it should exploit criminal justice's dramatic rituals and heritage. In short, instead of resenting outsiders as inefficient distractions, the Morality Play Model would respect their human needs and moral concerns.

The Morality Play Model takes a much broader vision of the role of legal rules and the importance of criminal procedures to democratic self-government. Justice requires both consistent rules and wise, contextual application of those rules. Legal rules embody moral and policy judgment. While judges and juries are not free to reweigh morality and policy anew in each case, they must use judgment in applying them wisely, particularly in novel or close cases. They must see not just "the usual man in the usual place" but "the prisoner in the dock . . . [before] the awful court of judgment." And yet, in judging individual cases, the morality play can reaffirm, refine, or question the justice of the broader rules. Jurors check overbroad legislation, overzealous prosecutors, and jaded judges. Moreover, all outsiders who take part in criminal justice play a role in self-government. Participation "teaches men to practice equity; every man learns to judge his neighbor as he would himself be judged," Tocqueville observed. Thus he praised the jury as "a gratuitous public school, ever open, in which every juror learns his rights . . . and becomes practically acquainted with the laws." Entrusting outsiders with this civic responsibility, he wrote, "rubs off that private selfishness which is the rust of society."[4] The morality play is not a means to efficient results in cookie-cutter cases; rather, it does justice to and by unique human beings. And it teaches justice by empowering citizens to do justice themselves. Criminal procedures, in short, should have rich moral and political goals.

B. WHY NOT ADDRESS SUBSTANTIVE MORAL GOALS?

Lawyers might offer four reasons why criminal procedure emphasizes narrow efficiency instead of pursuing broader moral goals: academics, bureaucracy, nonjudgmentalism, and elitism. First, academics see criminal procedure and substantive criminal law as separate fields. In law school, first-year students studying criminal law learn various justifications for punishment in the context of common-law cases and the Model Penal Code. Likewise, many substantive criminal law scholars address the moral justifications for punishment. In contrast, upper-level students who choose to study criminal procedure learn about the U.S. Constitution and defendants' individual rights.[5] The two courses are quite separate. Criminal procedure courses and scholars rarely return to the criminal law's substantive justifications for punishment. Scholars tend to write about one field or the other, rarely integrating the two siblings.

Law school quirks may help to explain why the two fields do not talk, but that explanation hardly justifies the rift. The academic emphasis on defendants' individual rights is ahistorical and undercut by recent academic scholarship. As Akhil Amar has argued, the Bill of Rights is not primarily a series of individual rights against the majority, but rather a guarantee of self-government. Most of its rights are populist and majoritarian. For example, the Sixth Amendment guarantees public, local jury trials precisely so that the local community can sit in moral judgment and see justice done. Local, public jury trials checked arbitrary laws and applied them common-sensically, to suit the "conscience of the community."[6] Criminal procedures should apply substantive criminal laws in morally appropriate ways, to earn the criminal law public legitimacy and trust. Procedure and substance have been thus intertwined for centuries. History is far from infallible, but it is at least relevant to understanding what citizens expect and what is possible.

Seen against this historical backdrop, the modern academic divorce of the two fields is arbitrary. Procedures are supposed to serve and implement the criminal law's substantive goals. The two fields need to work together as they once did.

Second, bureaucratic pressures push insiders to maximize efficiency and quantity. Understandably, many lawyers "plea bargai[n] to ease their crushing workloads" and dispose of cases any way they can; judges accept and sometimes encourage plea bargains for the same reasons. Even when workloads are not crushing, however, lawyers seek to handle cases ever more efficiently. Prosecutors evaluate themselves on how quickly they dispose of their cases and how many defendants they convict. Prosecutors running for (re)election often make campaign issues out of case-processing speed, backlogs, conviction rates, and overall sentence severity. Police officers are evaluated on the numbers of their open cases, arrests, and charges filed. Bureaucracies may reward police and prosecutors' quantifiable successes with incentive pay, raises, and promotions.[7]

Even judges evaluate themselves based on case-processing statistics. Although they have secure jobs, judges praise or blame themselves and their colleagues based on how fast they move the court's business and close pending cases. Chief judges and administrators circulate memoranda summarizing each judge's numbers of pending cases and dispositions. Judges thus feel peer pressure based on how well they move their business along. Even in low-volume courts with minimal case backlogs, judges feel few cases are worthy of full-blown trial. As a result, judges push most cases to plead out, by imposing lower sentences for guilty pleas and higher ones after trial, to improve judicial efficiency.[8] More efficiency means that fewer parties can enjoy their day in court and their chance to have their say.

In other words, the criminal-justice machinery takes on a life of its own. As chapter II discussed, insiders have distinctive outlooks and incentives. They care about particular bureaucratic measures of success. They define efficiency in terms of quantity and bottom-line outcomes: dollars, convictions, and years in prison. Because they are hidden and insulated from outsiders' scrutiny, insiders care much less about outsiders' broader moral concerns. The machinery's relentless efficiency undermines the criminal law's broader moral goals. Efficient case processing and crime reduction are important goods, but not the only ones that matter. Insiders' obsession with quantity blinds them to outsiders' concern for quality.

Quality should not always trump quantity. Today, however, the situation is almost exactly the reverse. Quantity automatically trumps quality, without much discussion or thought about the appropriate tradeoff between the two. More is always treated as better because quantity is concrete and tangible and requires no evaluation. But that logic is confused.

Economics and its concept of efficiency are tools, means to maximize exogenous ends based on other principles. But efficiency-speak tempts us to treat whatever is quantifiable as the only end simply because it is all we can measure. (Recall the joke about the drunk who looks for his keys under the lamppost, rather than by the front door where he dropped them, because that is where the light is best.) Procedures may be efficient in terms of dollars and speed, but nonetheless counterproductive because they betray fairness, legitimacy, and other moral principles. Efficiency does not equal effectiveness.

The premises of the morality play conflict with those of the modern administrative state. The colonial morality plays described in chapter I.A were human and particularistic. Each one was about an individual victim, an individual defendant, their friends and neighbors, and the local community sitting in moral judgment. Nonlawyers were central to the drama, which was solemn, public, and participatory. The parties spoke directly to each other and to the public in the language of justice and mercy. Public trials were about who did what and who deserved what. Less detailed laws left judges and juries much discretion to do justice based on common sense and the community's shared moral intuitions. Jury trials and public punishments brought public, dramatic closure and reconciliation.

The bureaucratic ideal of justice, in contrast, depends on expertise and rules. It trusts lawyers to run a system too complex for laymen to operate. It develops rules too technical for laymen to understand. It does not value opening bureaucratic decisions to public scrutiny and input. Its vision of justice is neutral and impersonal, focusing on the bottom line. Far from emphasizing particularity, it stresses equality and predictability to grease the plea-bargaining machinery for repeat players. The bureaucracy is threatened by discretion and mercy, which its insiders view as undermining equality. Thus, as Rachel Barkow has argued perceptively, the administrative state has steadily reduced the discretion of juries and executive clemency. In contrast, it has left prosecutorial discretion alone, in part because it is less visible and in part because bureaucrats trust prosecutors as insider experts.[9] Unpredictable outsiders have lost their power, while the least accountable, least representative actors have kept as much discretion as ever. The insiders have squeezed out the outsiders, substituting bureaucratic equality and expertise for individualized popular morality.

In their rush to treat like cases alike, however, insiders may not slow down to individualize and treat unlike cases unlike. In their emphasis on predictable results, they leave little room for mercy. In their suspicion of outsiders, insiders put too much faith in themselves. And in pursuing bottom-line outcomes, they neglect outsiders' process values, such as their desire to see justice done and take part. Mass-produced, impersonal, bureaucratic justice is a mediocre substitute for traditional criminal justice.

True, modern caseloads and our heterogeneous society stand in the way of the village ideal. Even if one must shoehorn criminal justice into modern rules, there must be better ways to measure and promote success. Qualitative surveys, for example, could try to measure any number of dimensions. They could ask outsiders whether insiders had treated them respectfully and fairly. Surveys could inquire whether outsiders understood the progress of their cases and received timely notice. They could measure how well they were able to express their views at various points. They could ask whether outsiders were able to heal and reconcile with one another. They could even try to assess forgiveness and reintegration into society, tracking how wrongdoers fared in returning to their families, neighborhoods, and careers. Broader measures would at least reduce over-reliance upon speed, volume, crime rates, and recidivism as the only measures of success. The next chapter will suggest ways to implement these suggestions in our heterogeneous society amidst staggering caseloads.

After academics and bureaucracy comes a third explanation for embracing efficiency at the expense of popular morality: nonjudgmentalism. Many modern intellectuals fear that moral judgments are at best contentious, at worst arbitrary. Judge Richard Posner, for example, insists that moral judgments lack solid foundations and that moral arguments cannot resolve disputes. Scholars see only deep disagreements about the scope of the criminal law, so one cannot build a consensus on appeals to morality. Criminal defendants sometimes raise and even prevail with cultural defenses, arguing that American law conflicts with their own moral values.[10] The message is that there are no clear standards of right and wrong that the law should communicate and enforce across the board.

Many intellectuals who are not true relativists nevertheless worry that moral language is divisive and intolerant. Following John Rawls, liberals strive to remain neutral among competing conceptions of the good. Overt appeals to morality seem illiberal, unsuitable for a pluralistic democracy. Here I mean liberal in the classical sense of those who prize individual freedom and autonomy, not just those on the political left. Many liberals seem uncomfortable with having the government declare that some actions are wrong. Thus, scholars such as David Garland denounce "explicit expressions of punitiveness . . . as taboo in the official discourse of civilized society." Though politicians now speak in explicitly punitive terms, these scholars argue for restoring the taboo against punitive rhetoric.[11]

In other words, even the rhetoric of punishment and just deserts threatens society's neutral calm.

In contrast, efficiency seems to be a neutral concept from economics, not moral philosophy or religion. Some liberals would at most resort to utilitarianism, a moral theory that speaks the language of efficiency and maximizing quantifiable happiness. Equality seems to be an uncontroversial, almost mathematical principle of justice. And deterrence seems mechanical, not moral; it speaks in a scientific idiom of preventing harms rather than judging and punishing wrongs. Popular morality seems too slippery and subjective, unlike solid, neutral mathematics and science. Nonjudgmentalism is a shibboleth in respectable intellectual company. If one rejects the traditional moral order, there seems to be little basis for discretion, grace, and mercy. Following Beccaria and Bentham, some academics and judges see equality, efficiency, and crime control as the main if not the only objective principles to guide criminal justice.[12]

Intellectual skepticism has filtered down to many ordinary people. Many Americans eschew moral language, lest they seem bigoted and intolerant. "Thou shalt not judge" has, in the words of one sociologist, become the Eleventh Commandment.[13] Among some insiders, skepticism has fermented into cynicism. Some lawyers who run the plea-bargaining mill, with its guilty-but-not-guilty pleas and abstruse language, may make no pretense of doing justice. A few of the lawyers whom I interviewed for chapter III shared that attitude: that the criminal justice system is misnamed because it has nothing to do with justice.

Neutral justifications paper over contentious moral debates. In our society, many people justify their positions on capital punishment, gun control, and other hot-button issues in terms of deterrence. As Dan Kahan argues, this deterrence-speak is a façade, a neutral idiom that cloaks the contentious moral disagreements that actually drive criminal justice policy. Talking in neutral terms seems practical, as it promotes acceptance and legitimacy in the eyes of those with widely varying moral beliefs. It also respects the autonomy of citizens who remain free to hold their own moral beliefs; society need not disrespect them by overtly rejecting their views. It pretends that deterrence-speak offers a neutral answer for all questions, even though it cannot tell us what is worth deterring. For example, how important is it to prevent a cuckold from killing his unfaithful wife? Is that more important than preventing a mother from killing her child's molester? The rhetoric of efficiency, equality, and deterrence hides these value choices instead of offering truly neutral answers.[14] It delegates these crucial yet hidden value choices to insiders, such as prosecutors who exercise discretion in charging and plea bargaining these cases away.

Despite academic skepticism, popular morality is an enduring foundation for criminal justice. Descriptively, it is what drives criminal justice policy. Even though survey respondents justify their views on capital punishment and gun control in terms of deterrence, new evidence for or against deterrence does not sway their answers. The driving forces behind their intuitions are value-laden moral judgments. Deterrence-speak is merely a seemingly neutral façade for the expressive moral judgments that seethe beneath it.[15]

Empirically, these moral judgments are hardly arbitrary or unpredictable. Ordinary citizens share a robust consensus about the substantive wrongfulness of various crimes. In an important series of works, Paul Robinson and his coauthors have surveyed Americans and foreigners about the wrongfulness of various crimes, defenses, and aggravating or mitigating factors. They present survey participants with detailed factual scenarios of arguable wrongdoing and ask them to assign liability and punishments. They consistently find an astonishing degree of consensus about which acts are wrongful and how wrongful they are relative to other crimes. For classic crimes involving force, theft, or fraud against persons or property, diverse people's judgments show a Kendall's W correlation of 0.95. In other words, people agree as much on the relative wrongfulness of crimes against victims as they do on which images are brightest on a page. Even when asked about more controversial crimes, such as prostitution, buying or dealing in drugs, drunk driving, late-term abortion, bestiality, and date rape, people's rankings correlate at a rate of 0.55. They agree more about these crimes than travel-magazine readers agree on the risk of terrorism across eight travel destinations from Israel to New York to Canada. Thus, the basic principles of criminal blame and responsibility are hardly arbitrary theories that risk provoking unbounded strife. On the contrary, though there remain pockets of disagreement, there is enormous consensus on a wide range of core cases. That is particularly true of the crimes involving harms to person or property that are at the core of American criminal justice. If anything, vindicating these widely shared principles should bring citizens closer together. Conversely, neglecting or ignoring these principles risks frustrating citizens and driving them apart. That is Emile Durkheim's insight: Denouncing crimes reaffirms society's shared norms and thus its cohesion.[16]

Moreover, popular moral judgments are not tied to narrow notions of efficiency based on deterrence or incapacitation. When ordinary people assign punishments to particular cases, they base their judgments primarily on the retribution a wrongdoer deserves. One empirical study found that ordinary people assigned punishments based on the seriousness of the crime and the existence of mitigating factors, which matter for retribution. In contrast, they paid little attention to the chance of detection and the amount of publicity, factors that matter for deterring future crime. Another empirical study varied the moral seriousness of the crime and the chance that the wrongdoer would commit similar crimes in the future. People assigned punishment to wrongdoers based on the wrongfulness of and moral outrage at the crime, not on the danger of future crime.[17]

Much of the apparent disagreement on crime and punishment is an artifact of our abstract, politicized process, as chapter II suggested. People show remarkable agreement on most crimes when given detailed, concrete factual scenarios. That is how they used to approach cases as jurors, looking at each case up close and coming to consensus. But abstract scenarios, in television soundbites or campaign advertisements, allow listeners' minds to fill in widely varying details.[18] Politicians and the media eagerly exploit these abstractions, fanning the flames of fear and disagreement. But that abstract, politicized disagreement cloaks underlying agreement on substantive right and wrong in most concrete cases.

People likewise agree on fair procedures. As Tom Tyler's work confirms, people agree on many elements that make procedures fair irrespective of the outcomes. People want to have a voice: to have the ability to present arguments, be heard, and have their views considered. They want procedures to be consistent. They want authorities to be impartial, meaning that they are unbiased, honest, and strive to be fair. They want authorities to treat them politely and with concern for their rights. They also want authorities to base decisions on the necessary information and to bring problems out into the open to solve them.[19]

Surprisingly, fair procedures matter much more than favorable outcomes, and the interpersonal aspects of procedures matter more than those directly tied to outcomes.[20] People who do not get their way may be gravely dissatisfied if they feel ignored. Conversely, if the system has treated them respectfully, listened to them, and given them roles in the process, they are likely to come away satisfied regardless of the outcome.

The robust popular consensus about the wrongfulness of crimes and the fairness of procedures means the pessimists' fear is unfounded. Open discussion of criminal justice need not mire the public in bitter trench warfare. On the contrary, in most areas, discussion would likely produce policies that enjoy greater democratic legitimacy and respect. We should worry not about moral discourse per se but about letting a few unrepresentative, vengeful outsiders engage in *idiosyncratic* moralizing. To combat this fear, criminal justice should make deliberating groups large and representative enough to reflect the local community's consensus. The next chapter discusses what these deliberative policies might look like.

Moreover, moralizing in criminal justice need not be not intolerant or bigoted. On the contrary, it is quite tolerant in the classic sense of that word. Tolerance, to John Locke and the Enlightenment, meant that different religious groups would not kill or persecute one another. It did not mean that those being killed, beaten, or robbed had to remain non-judgmental about the wrongs they had suffered. People who respect the laws and the rights of others need fear no intrusion into their values or deeds. Criminal law intrudes only after someone has committed a wrong, usually by harming the person or property of another through force or deception. Even a libertarian criminal law committed to John Stuart Mill's harm principle must punish those who wrong others, to teach them and others lessons.[21] Teaching these lessons is essential self-defense for citizens and society.

America is built on the Enlightenment notion of individualism and tolerance undergirded by virtue. As Alexis de Tocqueville keenly observed, America's primary creed is that of individual rights. But religious faith and civic virtue undergird that individualism, tempering self-interest with moral traditions and habits.[22] The languages of individual freedom and morality live in constant but productive tension. Morality teaches people to respect one another's rights and to sustain social order without a police state. Skepticism and relativism threaten to unfetter individualism from the morality that counterbalances it. They lurch away from self-restraint toward unbridled self-interest, which would force the state to rely upon constant totalitarian enforcement. Far from contradicting individual freedom, the morality of the criminal law undergirds and sustains freedom.

Finally, even supposed relativists do not believe their own arguments. If there were no right and wrong, there would be no basis for objecting to any conceivable criminal justice policy. But most supposed skeptics and relativists vehemently oppose genocide, racism, torture, and poverty.[23] At root, they do not believe morality is a matter of whim or taste; they oppose these evils because they are wrong. Their objection is not to morality but to popular morality.

The root problem, then, is not nonjudgmentalism but elitism. Academic elites object to public moralizing because they fear the public's alleged vengefulness, inconsistency, and bigotry. Michael Tonry, for example, decries America's punitive policies as partly driven by a benighted, emotional public and advocates insulating elites from democratic pressures. James Whitman laments America's penal populism because it robs power from more merciful penal professionals. David Garland regrets that public vengeance, emotion, and populism have displaced expert judgment. To his mind, those who speak the popular language of punishment are illiberal and anti-modern, as they simplistically blame wrongdoers' wickedness. Likewise, British liberal elites fear "untutored public sentiment" and emotion.[24]

These scholars are often hostile to overt negative moral sentiments, such as disgust, disdain, indignation, and shame. Thus, many academics vehemently condemn proposals to shame wrongdoers, as if communal shame were a barbaric throwback to the Dark Ages. James Whitman specifically attacks shame sanctions because they stir up fickle, lawless mob outrage; he paints the darkest possible portrait of public involvement. Likewise, Martha Nussbaum has argued at length that disgust deserves no place in the law because it is inherently hierarchical and regressive.[25] To many academics, denunciation, condemnation, and informal social sanctions or pressures such as ostracism seem backward and judgmental. Academics prefer bureaucratic criminal justice because they trust their own merciful inclinations more. Moral discourse frames criminal justice as an issue for popular deliberation. Many American intellectuals would prefer to avoid that kind of popular moral input and instead follow Europe's lead, leaving crime policy to insider lawyers and judges.

Academics and lawyers also legitimately worry about inequality and bias. Our country has a sorry history of mistreating minorities, especially blacks. Racist juries often refused to convict whites accused of victimizing blacks, and racist mobs lynched or railroaded many a black defendant. Racial disparities remain an acute injustice plaguing modern criminal justice.[26] The public may agree on crimes and punishments when asked hypothetical questions about faceless defendants. But giving citizens more of a discretionary moral role in individual cases would open the door to latent biases based on race, sex, and wealth. The Fourteenth Amendment's Equal Protection Clause guarantees citizens the right to be free of intentional discrimination, regardless of what the majority wants. Thus, in the civil rights era, the Supreme Court did much to regulate local criminal justice in order to thwart community biases.

Many readers, trained as lawyers, may not be too troubled by criminal justice elitism at first. They may applaud insiders' expert dominance and prefer to squelch outsiders' benighted interventions. That simplistic attitude, however, fails to take seriously outsiders' perspectives and pressures. Descriptively, America is not Europe. We lack the professionalized civil service and tradition of deference to experts that makes countermajoritarian criminal justice possible. Instead, our cultural memories of jury trials and our issue-oriented election campaigns, initiatives, referenda, and recalls bring direct popular forces to bear. Squelching the older, healthier outlets for the voice of the people has created hydraulic pressures that erupt in crude policies, as chapter II lamented. Popular pressure is a fact of life in America, and criminal justice ignores it at its peril.

Moreover, outsiders are not as benighted as elites fear. As chapter II explained, when presented with detailed cases, the public is on average no more punitive than judges and sometimes a good deal less punitive than legislators. Excessive punitiveness comes not from outsiders' contextual moral intuitions, but from a warped political process. Outsiders no longer handle retail justice. At the wholesale level of legislation and referenda, they have a skewed sense of which cases are typical. Much of the blame rests not on outsiders but on insiders, who exclude the outsiders from seeing and taking part. And insiders' self-interests in plea bargaining sometimes lead to freakishly high sentences (for defendants who dare to go to trial) or low ones (for those rich and well-connected enough to hire the best lawyers). Outsiders can check insiders' self-interests and their jadedness, reducing agency costs.

Academics and lawyers understandably fear that, in today's polarized criminal justice politics, outsider pressure tilts towards justice without mercy. That is Whitman's fear of the irrational mob. And they rightly fear that modern criminal justice exiles felons to a political underclass, degrading them permanently with no hope of redemption or restoration. That is Nussbaum's and to some extent Markel's fear of hierarchical, degrading punishments. Convicts remain our brothers and sisters, sharing our common humanity and deserving our love as well as our condemnation. That is a fair reason to temper justice with opportunities for mercy, forgiveness, and redemption, as colonial Americans did. Indeed, that is the message of contemporary faith-based prison programs, such as Charles Colson's Prison Fellowship.[27] It is heartening to see the left and the religious right converge on forgiveness and mercy.

Tempering justice, however, is quite different from discarding the public rhetoric and principle of moral justice. Unfortunately, many academic elites are too tempted in that direction. Many favor warm emotions such as empathy and mercy, but are much more critical of negative emotions such as outrage, anger, and disgust. Their vision of dignity is so egalitarian that some are uncomfortable even temporarily humbling, blaming, and shaming wrongdoers. As chapter IV pointed out, Susan Bandes openly admits that "storytelling is political" and one-sided, part of a zero-sum sacrifice of justice for mercy. Defendants should be able to tell their stories in moral and emotional language, but she thinks victims should not, because she sympathizes with defendants. Robert Solomon decried this prevalent academic opposition to condign punishment as a "suffocating . . . case of 'political correctness.' . . . To even consider the brutal opinions of hoi pol[l]oi is to place oneself out of bounds. And so we dismiss as beneath contempt and unworthy of discussion those powerful negative feelings that in fact move most people and help form their political views. . . ."[28]

The elite bias in favor of mercy tries to pick apart one side of a two-sided coin. Mercy cannot be meaningful as an exception without justice as a rule, or else mercy swallows justice.[29] Kindness and empathy require anger and outrage toward those who abuse the objects of our empathy. Both victims and defendants deserve empathy for their blameless suffering as well as fitting censure for any blameworthy acts. Both sets of emotions, positive and negative, flow from our identifying with our fellow humans as brothers and sisters who deserve our respect. Our hearts go out to those who are wrongfully accused or victimized, because they are members of our moral community. They have been treated in ways that they do not deserve.

As for the academic fear that most punishment permanently stigmatizes and degrades, that need not be so. On the contrary, punishment is usually supposed to be temporary. Robert Solomon deftly unpacks four related metaphors that underlie traditional ideas of vengeance and retributive justice. First, just punishments must be proportionate. The biblical *lex talionis*, an eye for an eye, means that punishment must be commensurate to the wrong, no more severe than the wrongdoer deserves. Second, a wrong creates a debt, so that retribution is payback of one's debts to society and to the victim. Third, wrongs disrupt the balance of the scales of justice, exalting the wrongdoer and humiliating the victim. Just punishment restores the balance by restoring the victim and humbling the wrongdoer, as Jean Hampton argued. Fourth, crime creates a kind of pollution or blood guilt, and punishment washes away the stain. All four of these metaphors recognize that a wrong is temporary, a discrete disruption, but that punishment can to an extent restore the world and undo the wrong.[30]

In other words, punishment should not be permanent. Criminal justice should punish proportionately, satisfy the debt, restore the balance, and wash away the stain. At bottom, we punish an act, not simply an actor; we punish people for what they do and not simply who they are. A sliver of heinous crimes merit permanent punishment, whether by execution, life imprisonment, or banishment. These punishments are most often inflicted on incorrigible recidivists on whom we have given up. But at some point, most actors pay their debts; ideally they express remorse, apologize, and are forgiven along the way. After that, they deserve a second chance. Punishment may involve temporary exile from law-abiding society, but ultimately it should bring wrongdoers back into the fold, as the colonists did. To use Braithwaite's restorative justice terminology from chapter IV, it should be reintegrative, not disintegrative. (The best argument against modern shaming sanctions is that in practice, some are disintegrative, making reintegration that much harder.) At its best, punishment is a dynamic opportunity to heal and educate, not a zero-sum tradeoff between victims and defendants.

Yes, I am giving an optimistic account of a frequently cynical system. But the cynic's objection is hardly a reason not to aspire to the ideal, and the rhetoric of justice can help to improve criminal justice. True, modern American prosecutions and prisons do not live up to this ideal, and the next chapter will suggest possible solutions to this problem. But the failings of modern criminal justice are reasons to reform punishment, not to jettison the language and reasoning of justice. The point is that temporary blame and condemnation are steps along the road to permanent restoration and reintegration. Criminal punishment should not create a permanent underclass of felons, of the sort that offends elites' egalitarian sensibilities. But neither should it reject even temporary blame and condemnation, because without moral judgment and justice there can be no restoration. That is the lesson of chapter IV's critique of restorative justice. Temporary blame, shame, and dishonor should pave the way to restore and reconcile the parties as much as humanly possible. But one cannot have mercy and restoration without justice and punishment, any more than one should have rigid justice without mercy. Justice and mercy are two sides of the same coin; they can coexist and did so in our nation's past.

Equality concerns likewise do not justify wholesale elitism and excluding outsiders. First, we should not fixate on bias in cross-racial stranger crimes, such as the black stranger accused of raping a white woman. While these cases are significant, they are hardly paradigmatic. Most crimes are intra-racial, intra-neighborhood, even intra-familial.[31] Rather than excluding communities from all cases, we could target racial solutions at the fraction of cross-racial cases. Second, insider domination is hardly a guarantee of equality. The current criminal justice system, dominated by insiders, is widely criticized for racial disparities. Elitism's racial track record in America is hardly enviable.

Third, there is a huge difference between making criminal justice policy wholesale and making it retail. The public may be scared by a television advertisement showing a menacing mug shot of Willie Horton. Voters vividly imagine predators rather than the ordinary wrongdoer in a particular case, and their imaginations lead them astray. Sound bites and stereotypes can play on voters' fears, leading them to push for legislation and referenda. But the calculus changes when jurors look at flesh-and-blood victims and defendants up close. Good lawyers can humanize their clients so that jurors and others see a real person rather than a racial stereotype. Racial biases appear to be much less powerful when one gets to know people as individuals rather than simply as members of a race. Likewise, explicitly facing the issue of race may bring some self-awareness and reduce the influence of bias.[32]

Fourth, in the civil rights era the criminal justice system often oppressed minority communities. That polarized way of thinking is increasingly outmoded. As Dan Kahan and Tracey Meares have argued, minority communities now have much more political power. Far-off, unelected judges should not shackle them, but instead empower them within the criminal justice system. Indeed, as William Stuntz has argued, the problem may be over-legalization of the system by insiders too far removed from the community. Making criminal justice more local and democratic may make it more egalitarian as well. Whites, many of whom proudly voted for Barack Obama, care about racial equality. While judges have failed to stamp out racial disparities in the death penalty, traffic stops, and drug policy, elected officials have recently begun to address each of these problems.[33] Populism, in short, need not mean racism.

The final, fatal flaw with elitism is one of political theory. Normatively, insiders should not ignore outsiders even if they could. Ours is a representative democracy, and our representatives derive their legitimacy from the consent of the governed. The public has a right to set criminal justice policy, and unelected elites ought not thwart it. The Equal Protection Clause has a role to play in regulating intentional bias, but we should not just assume that outsiders are bigots while insiders are not. Moreover, outsiders have important contributions to make. Criminal justice can inform, empower, hear, and heal outsiders, but insulated insiders are deaf to these process goods. Outsiders can also check and temper insiders' self-interests and their jadedness, reducing agency costs. The problem is not outsider influence per se, but an unhealthy political dynamic that creates chapter II's crude, costly tug-of-war.

*   *   *   *   *

In short, criminal justice is much more than Herbert Packer's assembly line or obstacle course. It is not simply a bipolar contest between an individual defendant's rights and an impersonal state, but a morality play.

A morality play must speak in moral language, not just dollars and years in prison. Rhetoric and process matter, not just bottom-line results. The academic divorce of morality from criminal procedure is an arbitrary historical oversight. The bureaucratic blinders that exclude morality from procedure are far too narrow, confusing means with ends and people with statistics. Nonjudgmentalism ignores the popular consensus on the moral issues of crime and fair procedures. Finally, elitism ought to yield to the popular democratic consensus and its insistence that justice and mercy go hand in hand.

My call for a more moral, populist, participatory criminal justice system is a ringing ideal. Skeptics will question its practicality and relevance. It is far easier to sketch out abstract ideals than to implement them in the messy real world, where caseloads are staggering and budgets are tight. The next chapter takes up that challenge, suggesting concrete policies that could better include outsiders and their points of view.

CHAPTER VI

༄

Returning Power to the Public
in a Lawyer-Driven System

The preceding chapters have woven together a variety of strands. Lawyers (and their allies in legislatures) have shunted aside laymen. Lawyers' bottom-line, cost-benefit approach has brought many undoubted benefits, including efficient case processing and thus crime control. Those goods do indeed matter greatly to ordinary citizens. But criminal justice ought to serve more than this single goal to which it has been boiled down. The machinery's relentless pursuit of mechanistic efficiency has slighted the downsides: It disempowers victims, defendants, and the public. It cheapens justice into a marketable commodity, a fungible widget to be mass-produced. It eschews the rhetoric of moral judgment in favor of legalese and mathematical gobbledygook. It hides the workings of the system, leaving outsiders frustrated and mistrustful and insiders free to indulge their self-interests or idiosyncratic preferences. It exacerbates the cycle of pathological politics of crime legislation, helping to provoke draconian referenda in response and later dishonest subversion of those populist measures. It neglects remorse, apology, forgiveness, healing of relationships, reintegration, and reentry. It creates a semi-permanent underclass of prisoners and ex-cons in exile. It hollows out large swaths of minority neighborhoods. And it deprives countless children of their fathers and women of their husbands and boyfriends, with little hope that these men will return to lives of lawful work and responsible fatherhood.

It defies belief to characterize this system as reasonably reflecting the public's will. Chapters I and II drove a stake through the heart of that myth. The machinery of plea-bargaining grew up, jerry-built, and serves the interest of the insiders. A democracy need not slavishly follow every blip of opinion polls; Burkean representatives may legitimately serve the public's interests rather than their short-term wishes, particularly when momentary passions cloud longer-term reflection. But American criminal justice is much too far out of alignment with outsiders' needs and views to derive robust legitimacy from the consent of the governed. The foundations of liability and punishment, as well as the processes that implement those punitive judgments, ought to reflect the public's enduring sense of what defendants and victims deserve. As chapter II showed, the public is not knee-jerk punitive as intellectuals assume. Indeed, in the context of individual cases the public would often prefer less punishment than draconian laws require. But victims and the public do want to play roles in the process and see wrongdoers held accountable before they are satisfied, willing to forgive, and move on.

Our modern society is centuries removed from the colonial era, and wistful nostalgia cannot bring back colonial criminal justice. Our communities are too large and far-flung, our society too complex, and our standards of due process too high to rely on volunteer night watchmen and minutes-long jury trials. Nor would we want to go back to brutal, often racist whippings in the town square. But we can learn from the good things that we have lost, in particular colonial criminal justice's transparency and participation. Professionals must continue to run the system, but laymen could see and take part much more than they do now. We could do much more to revive elements of the morality play.

A transparent, participatory morality play should pursue two goals. First, it should strive to reduce the negative procedural side effects of our secretive, insular criminal process. These include outsider cynicism, frustration, and loss of faith and trust. Second, it could achieve better substantive outcomes. It would better heal and vindicate victims and encourage more of them to come forward. It would reduce agency costs and align arrest, charging, plea, and sentencing patterns more closely with public preferences. It might perhaps even reduce reliance on simplistic punishment slogans such as three-strikes-and-you're-out.

One could attempt reforms at three levels. First, there is the macro-level of state and national governments. Sections A.1 and A.2 suggest changing the modes of punishments and collateral consequences of convictions, to emphasize public accountability, work, and reintegration. Wrongdoers would have to receive education, job training, and mandatory drug treatment. They would have to work to pay at least a fraction of their debts to society, their families, and their victims. Nonviolent inmates might even have to serve in the military. Some work might be open to the public, or at least to reality television cameras; citizens could easily visualize the prisoners laboring to pay their debts instead of idly lounging. And when inmates were done, they would emerge with job skills and without housing and job restrictions that would otherwise prevent them from becoming law-abiding, productive citizens.

Unfortunately, big, central changes are far easier to dream about than to implement. These macro-level reforms would collide with entrenched institutional barriers, such as opposition from the military, unions, and businesses. And the diverse pathologies require more than a single national law or Supreme Court decision, or even a single centrally planned reform agenda. They need diverse grass-roots pressures to reform criminal justice at the levels of counties, cities, neighborhoods, and even individual cases.

At the mid-level of counties, towns, and neighborhoods, one may hope for more public involvement. Section B considers a range of mid-level reforms that could make criminal procedures and substantive outcomes better reflect local public involvement and views. Community policing and community prosecution, more honored in theory than in practice, could better align government policy with the needs of local voters. Satisfaction surveys of victims, defendants, witnesses, and other lawyers, akin to eBay's feedback surveys, would make insiders more accountable and responsive to outsiders. That might lead to a welcome shift in enforcement away from truly victimless crimes towards crimes with direct victims or spillover effects on neighbors. One could experiment with a variety of ways for citizens to participate, as rotating advocates in prosecutors' offices, or on neighborhood grand juries, or on advisory plea or sentencing juries. Particularly in big cities, however, I am not optimistic about educating large swaths of the public through jury service, because it is hard to mass produce.

Finally, Section C evaluates micro-level solutions that would help individual victims, defendants, and their families. Victims could receive far more in the way of information, support, and consultation, as well as a voice in punishment. Defendants and their families could have more opportunities to speak and apologize and not be penalized for doing so. For example, whether their rap sheets are admissible should not depend on whether they decide to testify, as it does now; they should be either completely inadmissible or completely admissible. And restorative conferences, divorced from restorative justice's substantive hostility to punishment, would help victims, defendants, and their families to express themselves, reconcile, and get on with their lives.

I envision a system that would blend restorative-justice conferences with neighborhood juries, which would play a role in punishment decisions.

Sentencing law should allow the public's sense of justice to set the minimum and maximum punishment, and then empower victims to influence where within the range juries set the final sentence. Restorative juries could reflect the neighborhood's views while tailoring punishment ranges to individual cases. These reforms would work better in small towns and small cohesive neighborhoods, possibly diffusing some of the benefits of jury service across the public. But even where that is not feasible, these measures would at least help the public's views to influence outcomes in individual cases.

Finally, we must keep hope alive despite the temptations to inertia, cynicism, and despair. One faces immense difficulty in beginning to reform a system as broken as our punishment factory. Skeptics can dismiss incremental, easy-to-implement reforms as cosmetic, akin to straightening deck chairs on the Titanic. More ambitious reforms get attacked from the other side as unrealistic given the massive caseloads and chronic funding constraints that hobble justice. Still other critics assume that if the public supported any workable reforms, politicians would already have implemented them, so the public must not want or be willing to pay for change.

We must not let these naysayers paralyze us with despair and seduce us away from the struggle to reform. We need both aspirations and realism, both small, quick improvements now and major overhauls in due time. Some reforms would be simple and cheap, such as better informing defendants and victims by using modern technology. More ambitious would be mid-level ones, such as giving outsiders more opportunities to speak, offer feedback, and influence prosecutors and police. Still other, larger changes would nevertheless be popular and likely cost-effective, such as making prisoners work, pay some of their debts, quit drugs, and learn skills. Finally, one can aspire in the long term to the biggest structural changes, ranging from easing prisoners' reentry into society to organizing neighborhood restorative juries. This sequence of changes cannot happen overnight; some might never prove to be workable at all. But we need ideals as our goals. Even if we are doomed to fall short of our dreams, some improvements are better than none at all.

The time is ripe for change. Though national insider institutions are not about to reform themselves, our decentralized system of government has bred more experimentation at lower levels. Community policing, problem-solving courts, restorative justice, medical marijuana decriminalization, and faith-based prison programs began as local experiments that were copied elsewhere. Norm entrepreneurs for these experiments have publicized their successes and inspired others to copy them, creating trends.

Tight budgets also encourage experimenting with less expensive alternatives to long-term imprisonment.

Moreover, the changing technological landscape has made it far easier for outsiders to organize and push for reform. Information technology, especially social-networking media, have enabled bottom-up populism to topple authoritarian regimes across the globe. Facebook, Twitter, and the like let outsiders fuse their shared grievances into reform movements that can crack insiders' monopoly on power. Now, outsiders can channel diffuse discontent to effect concrete experiments and reforms from the bottom up. These media can usefully supplement democratic electoral processes, fixing the low visibility and infrequency of prosecutorial elections. They can cast more light on how police, prosecutors, and courts operate day to day. Thus, outsiders can better monitor insiders, pressing them to become more responsive to their needs.

In short, it is time to breach the wall that separates insiders from outsiders. Victims, the public, and defendants need not remain outsiders. As stakeholders, they should once again play integral roles in criminal justice alongside insiders.

A. MACRO-LEVEL REFORMS

1. From Idle Imprisonment to Work, Accountability, and Reform

Today, when we convict defendants of moderately serious crimes, we usually imprison them. American prisons, however, are deeply flawed. Some of these flaws are inherent in any prison system; others are artifacts of how poorly our prisons work in practice. Prison severs inmates from their responsibilities, hides their punishment, and does little to train or reform them. Victims and the public do not see wrongdoers being held accountable, paying their debts to society and victims, and learning disciplined work habits. Instead, they visualize lives of idleness, funded by taxpayers. Thus, wrongdoers are unprepared to reenter society. And victims and the public, believing that wrongdoers have neither suffered enough nor learned their lessons, are loath to welcome them back.

The vast majority of prison inmates spend their days in idleness, with endless television and little labor. In the month before their arrests, about three-quarters of inmates were employed, earning the bulk of their income lawfully. Many were not only taking care of their children but helping to pay for rent, groceries, utilities, and health care. But once in prison, only a small minority are employed in prison industries; by the Great Depression, union and small-business opposition had choked off the interstate market for prison labor. The minority of prisoners who do some work in a prison laundry, cafeteria, or license-plate shop rarely cultivate skills that are in demand in the outside world. Even prisoners who are able to work earn far less than the minimum wage, not enough to support a family or repay victims. Not many inmates receive education or vocational training. On the contrary, legislatures have repeatedly cut prison-education programs such as Pell grants. Too few receive drug treatment or similar therapy, as waiting lists are far longer than the number of treatment spaces offered. Nor is life inside most prisons structured to teach good habits such as self-discipline or productivity. On the contrary, prison encourages listless dependence on institutional routine, setting prisoners up for failure upon release. Healthy habits, such as the orderly work envisioned by prison reformers, broke down long ago.[1]

Incarceration also cuts prisoners off from their families, friends, and neighbors. Responsibilities as husbands and fathers are key factors that tame young men's wildness and encourage them to settle down. Thus, prisoners who do not maintain family relationships are much more likely to reoffend. Careful empirical studies confirm that marriage and father-hood appear to inhibit crime after release; one longitudinal study found that marriage may reduce reoffending by 35%. But instead of working to support their own families and their victims, most prisoners are forced to remain idle. Instead of having to learn vocational skills, they have too much free time to hone criminal skills and connections. And instead of removing wrongdoers from criminogenic environments, prison clusters together neophytes and experienced recidivists, breeding more crime. Once prisoners could easily mingle and talk, prison became a prime place to join gangs, network with potential partners in future crime, and learn exactly the wrong lessons.[2]

Perhaps the most troubling aspect of imprisonment is its hiddenness. It is out of sight behind high prison walls and thus out of mind. It is too easy for the public to forget about it, to overlook the sporadic prison stabbings and rapes, or simply to discount the terrible soul-destroying, idle monotony. Because the punishments are invisible and idle, the public never *sees* justice done. Voters may clamor for higher sentences to express outrage at crimes. But, because they do not see and appreciate the punishment, they have less sense of how much is enough and when inmates have paid their debts to society and to victims. Sunlight is the best disinfectant in a democracy, but prisons are shrouded in gloom.[3]

Public dissatisfaction, according to conventional wisdom, reflects the public's knee-jerk punitiveness and desire to ratchet sentences ever upward.

But that account gives the public too little credit. Donald Braman argues convincingly that the public wants not so much more punishment as more accountability. The antidote for antisocial crimes is enforced prosocial behavior and responsibility. That means quitting drug habits, learning skills, getting a job, supporting one's family, and paying one's debts to victims.

The public cares not only about the quantity of punishment but also about the message that it sends and the values that it inculcates. Thus, the public has shown renewed interest in shaming sanctions, forced labor, restitution, and victim compensation. Polls show overwhelming (87%) support for requiring prisoners to work. Even many opponents of prison work in general favor work if inmates must use their wages to compensate their victims and the state. Public support for mandatory job training and mandatory literacy programs is even stronger, at 92%. And almost as many respondents support drug treatment. Interestingly, support for these measures is strong across the political spectrum, from liberals to conservatives and from Democrats to Republicans. Liberals embrace these programs as ways to reform inmates and offer them social welfare benefits, while conservatives endorse them as punitive obligations. Inmates' own families complain that inmates remain idle and shirk their duties, instead of working to support their families.[4] By overwhelming margins, everyone agrees that inmates ought to be held accountable.

Prisons must change from dens of idleness and crime to places of public accountability, mandatory work, and sustained reform. First and foremost, prisons must force all able-bodied prisoners to work. That does not mean chain gangs. While polls show substantial public support for chain gangs, the idea is deeply polarizing. A plurality or even a majority is not enough; broad punishment policies need near-consensus support. Chain gangs, like public whippings, have a sorry racist history in America. The spectacle of a line of black men, shackled together and guarded by white overseers, could sap minority communities' fragile faith in equal justice. Returning to chain gangs, corporal punishment, or similar hallmarks of slavery would deeply divide public opinion.

There are plenty of other ways to require work without echoes of slavery. Governments could abolish restrictions on trade in prison-made goods and prevailing-wage requirements, relying on competitive bidding to raise wages. Wages below prevailing civilian rates could compensate for greater security costs and unskilled prisoners' greater need for training, encouraging more employers to enter the market. These submarket wages would still be substantially higher than the dollar per hour or less currently paid by state-run industries and farms.[5] Outside monitors and inspectors could police worksites to prevent abusive conditions. Inmates at medium and maximum security facilities would have to work in prison for security reasons. But minimum-security inmates and those near the ends of their sentences could transition back into the outside world by working outside prison walls, as many already do in halfway houses, supervised by trained volunteers. Inmates might even be able to prove themselves to employers and so have jobs waiting for them upon release.

Prison work should be demanding, but at the same time it would give inmates a focus, a purpose, a goal that most now lack. In *One Day in the Life of Ivan Denisovich*, Alexander Solzhenitsyn memorably described life in a Siberian prison camp. One would have expected the inmates, many of them unjustly confined, to sullenly shirk and slack at their assigned jobs. But when assigned to build a wall, they pushed themselves far beyond what they had to do, exhilarated by accomplishing something concrete.[6] Work made them feel human. It gave meaning and purpose to their days. It also gives inmates a productive outlet for their energies instead of leaving them idle to fight or plot crimes. Ideally it would even develop a taste for work, a virtuous habit. Of course not every inmate will throw himself into his job, but work may move and encourage many in that direction.

To make their work prosocial and accountable, inmates should have to use their wages to pay at least a portion of their moral and monetary debts. Perhaps a quarter of the wages could go to the government to defray the costs of investigation, conviction, and imprisonment. Perhaps a quarter could go to victims to make restitution and pay for medical care. Perhaps a quarter could go to inmates' families, requiring inmates to support their spouses and children. And the remaining quarter might go to inmates themselves, to encourage their efforts. The message would be that inmates are no longer idle, irresponsible wards of the state. On the contrary, they would be making amends to victims and the state while supporting themselves and their families. These earnings might never fully repay the state or victims of serious crimes, and we would not imprison them longer just to exact full repayment,[7] but even partial repayment would be materially and symbolically important.

Ideally, many jobs would be visibly demanding, satisfying the public that inmates were enduring the hard treatment they had earned. The public might have controlled access and prison tours to watch prisoners at work, and could see non-dangerous inmates out on work-release programs cleaning highways, repaving roads, and the like. Jailers would avoid the shackles and trappings of chain gangs, perhaps using electronic ankle bracelets instead of chains. Prisoners would not be marked not as composing a permanent underclass but as enduring temporary shame before they earn reintegration. At the very least, the press and reality-television programs could broadcast images of prisoners toiling instead of watching soap operas. Just possibly, victims and the public might accept shorter terms of imprisonment if they were visibly more intense, as a tradeoff. If so, shorter, more intense imprisonment would save strapped state budgets substantial money while reducing the spillover suffering of inmates' families and neighborhoods.[8]

My proposal for prison work will face no shortage of practical hurdles. First, most prisoners have few skills and many have disciplinary problems, so their unskilled labor would not be especially lucrative. Second, many law-abiding businesses and workers will oppose having to compete against prison labor, fearing that it will undercut their wages and cost them jobs. Though this argument rests on the economic fallacy that there is a fixed pie of work to be done, it has undeniable intuitive and political appeal. Several substantial forces could combine to push through this reform: the government's need to offset prison costs, victims' clamor for restitution, and the religious right's support of prison ministries. One can only hope that these forces may someday counterbalance or buy off opposition, particularly as organized labor continues to weaken. Another obvious hurdle is that even if inmates work and acquire job skills, they will face difficulty finding jobs on the outside afterwards. Some inmates may demonstrate to their prison employers that they are good enough to be hired once they finish their sentences. And, as discussed below, prison ministries and affiliated churches may view it as their mission to find jobs and housing, helping to ease the transition. But there is no denying that the political and practical hurdles are substantial enough to make this proposal a long-term hope rather than a realistic short term goal.

Even more controversial and tricky would be drafting convicts into the military (except for those with serious violent tendencies or major disabilities). Throughout history, many societies have sentenced convicts to military service, offering them a concrete way to work off their debts and earn freedom. Currently, however, most of the American military services military forbid enlistment as an alternative to criminal prosecution or as a form of punishment.[9] The rigors of military service are vivid and easy to visualize: think of boot camps, with bugles at dawn, shouting drill sergeants, and strenuous calisthenics. The public sees military service as rigorous, demanding labor. Yet these rigors would be productive and prosocial, inculcating work habits and discipline that wrongdoers often lack.

Now, readers from both sides of the political spectrum will doubtless object. Those on the left may complain that military service would put

defendants in harm's way and degrade them. Those on the right may fear
that using military service as punishment would demean the honorable
service of law-abiding men and women who choose to serve their country.
Military leaders might well resist the change, both for reasons of honor
and for concerns about administering unruly convicts. But a properly
crafted program could allay all three sets of concerns. To satisfy those on
the right, prisoners would be compelled to join, not free to choose. They
would come in at lower ranks and lower wages than ordinary enlistees.
Garnishment and restitution would further reduce their take-home pay,
and GI Bill benefits would not vest for some time. They would not enjoy the
free handouts and taxpayer-supported idleness that they currently do.
They could wear different uniforms and enjoy fewer privileges than ordinary soldiers and sailors, by for example being confined to base. They
would have to endure the lowliest of jobs, even cleaning latrines, and
suffer push-ups and other punishments for the smallest infractions. In
other words, prisoners would not start out equal with law-abiding service
members. Nor would prisoners crowd out military opportunities for
law-abiding citizens, given the steady decline in enlistments and the
military's need for more manpower.

On the other hand, those on the left might note that the military has
one of the best records of racial equality and meritocratic advancement
in America.[10] Integrating minority prisoners into the military, full of
minority officers, would be far less vulnerable to charges of racism than
exiling them to prisons. Integrating prisoners into barracks would also
reduce the criminogenic clumping and self-segregation that prisons
breed. Any harms faced would be prosocial, in the service of their country
and as payment of their debts to society. Requiring inmates to risk
harm in serving their country would offset the harms they threatened or
caused to others. (Alternatively, one could limit combat roles to inmates
who volunteered for them.) Any humbling would be productive and temporary. Inmates could prove themselves and in time earn promotions and
restoration to full equality with their law-abiding fellow citizens and soldiers, including equal rank, pay, and benefits. After a time, their families
could come to live with them on military bases, helping to reintegrate
them. The military teaches service members productive, marketable skills
that could lead to jobs after discharge. And employers view military service as a valuable credential that bespeaks dependable, disciplined work
habits. In other words, the military would pave the way for prisoners'
reentry far better than current programs do.

Military leaders might note that military service in lieu of criminal
punishment has a long history and has hardly dishonored the law-abiding

soldiers who served alongside wrongdoers. At least if one screens out problem candidates, the disciplinary problems have historically been manageable and may have been improved by the structure, rigor, and sense of purpose in military life. Inmates paroled to serve in the Army in World War II appear to have served well, with lower recidivism rates and better behavior than those who remained in prison.[11] We cannot know whether the same would hold true today, particularly in peacetime, but the idea is at least worth trying.

Nevertheless, the military almost certainly will resist being asked to take on a social purpose in addition to fighting wars and defending against attacks. Moreover, the current all-volunteer ethos of the American military may conflict with effectively drafting convicts. If military opposition proves insurmountable, the military could at least repeal its bans and selectively admit convicts who are most compatible with military life. Or one could experiment with creating a civilian analogue to the military, something like the Civilian Conservation Corps, with uniforms, hierarchical ranks, strict discipline, and a mission. Its job would be not only to build and rebuild public works, but to build convicts' character and skills.

In addition to (perhaps before) work, prisons should mandate education and vocational training. Every inmate who has not finished high school and is not mentally disabled should have to complete a GED program to earn the equivalent of a high-school diploma. Unskilled inmates should have to receive vocational training, at first in classes and then where possible on the job. Intensive drug treatment, with frequent urinalysis, could likewise be mandatory.[12] Prisons could even consider marriage and parenting classes, though it is not clear how much of that is teachable. Education would not only enable inmates to earn and pay restitution, but also encourage self-reliance, the chance to take responsibility and care of their families.

These programs must impose obligations, instead of simply conferring special benefits, lest the public resent giving prisoners better treatment than law-abiding citizens. The social message must be that these are prosocial punishments, making wrongdoers into good citizens. These programs could also turn out to be expensive, though perhaps faith-based prison charities could donate materials and volunteer labor. Given the expense, these training programs may not be practical immediately but can at least be long-term aspirations.

Our expectations must be realistic. Drug dealers will not become model citizens overnight. Many will resist and relapse no matter how much opportunity and training they are offered. But nevertheless they ought to be held accountable and made to work, learn, and train. While I hope these programs would also reduce recidivism and save money, those are fringe benefits. The costs of education, job training, and drug treatment could easily consume any earnings. The primary goals are to hold wrong-doers accountable in a way people can visualize, to try to teach them lessons, and to make them pay their debts at least in part. The most that we can hope for is that some fraction will make the most of the opportunity and responsibility, learning better habits and turning their backs on lives of crime.

2. Collateral Consequences and Reentry

Making inmates quit drugs, learn, and work can better prepare them to reenter society. But even after they have supposedly paid their debts to society and victims, our laws are remarkably unwilling to give them a second chance. Ex-cons face a web of laws and prejudices. Some exclude them from the polity symbolically, by forbidding them to vote, serve on juries, or hold public office. Others harm them more tangibly by limiting where they can live and how they can work. After conviction, inmates are often shipped off to distant prisons at the other end of the state, impeding family visits and straining or breaking family bonds. Even after they are released from prison, sex offenders and others are often forbidden to live within 500 to 2000 feet of schools, day-care centers, playgrounds, churches, and hospitals. In many urban areas, these residency restrictions rule out most of the city, in effect exiling or banishing ex-cons entirely. Likewise, licensing laws limit felons' employment not only as police or schoolteachers, but also as embalmers and septic tank cleaners. The net these laws cast is quite broad: sex offenders include not only child molesters but also flashers, public urinators, or teenage lovers.[13] And the effects are often perverse: Ex-cons may not be able to live with their families and neighbors, who might keep an eye on them. Instead, they may have to crowd into the same motels on the wrong side of the tracks and build new criminal networks. Likewise, when we deny felons the right to work in the profession for which they have trained, we may be consigning them to unemployment or crime.

There is little evidence that these laws make us safer. Predators on the prowl can easily travel a mile or two to commit their crimes. On the contrary, residency restrictions probably make us less safe, by clustering ex-cons and preventing them from reintegrating into their families. Thus, even one prosecutor's group has vocally opposed a residency law as ineffective and distracting from the core mission of preventing crime.[14]

Punishment must condemn the crime without giving up on the criminal. The actor is not reducible to his worst act; except for the most heinous recidivists, we should be slow to give up hope and throw away the key. Imprisonment should not mean exile; inmates should be incarcerated close to home whenever possible. Once inmates are acknowledged to have paid their debts to society, society must stand ready to forgive them and offer a second chance. Dismantling this web of collateral consequences, which reflect hysteria and trade protectionism rather than effective crime prevention, is an important first step. As the colonists understood, there is a time to punish and a time to forgive.[15]

This approach resembles what John Braithwaite calls reintegrative shaming.[16] The point of punishment is not to ostracize wrongdoers into a permanent underclass, embittered and tempted to revicitimize a society that shuns them. The point is to exact appropriate retribution and prepare, wrongdoers to return to the fold. Shame, embarrassment, even modest degradation are fitting so long as they are temporary. They must last just long enough for the wrongdoer to be seen repudiating his wrong and discharging at least his moral debt by suffering punishment. The public must see, or at least be able to visualize, some suffering or hard treatment or shame, for a limited time. To keep shame from hardening into permanent stigma, prisons should avoid broadcasting prisoners' names, as discussed below. The point is to punish the wrong for a limited time, not to brand the wrongdoer permanently.

Forgiving and reintegrating wrongdoers, especially remorseful ones, are valuable both symbolically and practically. Forgiveness and reintegration hold out incentives for prisoners to reform themselves and earn these rewards, which should not be automatic. They hold out hope for prisoners that after suffering abasement, they will be symbolically lifted up again and start afresh. They highlight a law-abiding, respectable alternative way of life to the cycle of recidivism and reincarceration that snares far too many ex-convicts. Most of all, they reflect the humaneness of a society that, having denounced and punished, can rejoice over the return of its prodigal sons. As Winston Churchill, who was no softie, said: "The mood and temper of the public in regard to the treatment of crime and criminals is one of the most unfailing tests of the civilisation of any country. . . . [This civilized attitude includes] unfaltering faith that there is a treasure, if you can only find it, in the heart of every man. . . ."[17]

The left and the right ought to be able to unite behind a combination of restorative punishment followed by forgiveness. Indeed, one prominent group associated with the religious right has already come out against many collateral consequences on just this ground. The Prison Fellowship, founded by Chuck Colson, draws on Biblical language of forgiveness to support a dramatic narrowing of collateral consequences. Governments, they argue, should abolish all restrictions that are not related to the crime of conviction and not needed to protect the public.[18] Though a powerful political ratchet keeps toughening collateral consequences, conservative groups such as the Prison Fellowship can give politicians cover for ameliorating them.

With the help of these groups, animated by faith, hope, and love, outsiders must relearn how to forgive as they did in the colonial era. Sometimes fear is prudent, but sometimes hope must tame fear. As Abraham Lincoln did in closing his First Inaugural Address, we must hold out hope for quenching anger and reconciling a riven people, which includes even victims of wrongdoing. Even incensed citizens, embittered by fratricidal war, can be reminded to forgive "when again touched, as they surely will be, by the better angels of our nature."[19]

Now, forgiving does not require forgetting. One can legitimately worry about the sincerity of a wrongdoer's remorse or a sincerely repentant wrongdoer's ability to resist future temptations. It is one thing to restore a pedophile's right to work as a bartender or plumber; it is another to license him as an elementary-school teacher. A convicted drug dealer and user should not quickly return to work as a pharmacist with access to prescription narcotics. A defendant convicted of fraud or embezzlement probably should not reenter financial or legal services right away. Restoring rights requires difficult judgment calls about how severe the wrongdoer's crimes were, how trustworthy he has become, and how sensitive the right in question is. On the other hand, we should not be so afraid that we refuse to take any chances at all. Voting rights, jury rights, and rights to live in most areas and hold less sensitive jobs are probably suitable for rapid restoration. Rights to hold office and practice more sensitive professions might deserve slower restoration. Timetables could vary depending on the profession, the crime of conviction, and the wrongdoer's remaining drug-free for a period of time. Wrongdoers who need medication to control mental illnesses could likewise be required to show that they had been taking their medications continually for a period of time.

As I have just suggested, this area requires a difficult weighing of interests and the chances we are willing to take. To some, it seems safest always to err on the side of tough and inflexible punishment. The benefits of maximum incapacitation are immediate, certain, and concrete, while the payoffs from forgiveness and mercy are longer-term, squishier, and more speculative. In striking a balance, we must decide what kinds of persons we wish to be. Are we ruled exclusively by fear, or will we also make judicious room for hope and humaneness? Many readers, I hope, will see the intuitive value of taking a chance on reconciling at least the most promising wrongdoers.

Offender registries and stigmatizing publicity require similar judgment calls. Sex-offender registries, for example, have a protective and regulatory function when viewed by schools, day-care centers, and probably parents who make particular inquiries. On the other hand, registries are proliferating and becoming so publicized that many are designed simply to stigmatize and shame. Other forms of publicity, besides registries, have the same problem. Once a prostitute or her customer has served a sentence, there seems to be little protective or regulatory reason to keep publicizing that person's name. Continued publicity is simply punishment without end. Ideally, governments could limit registry access to those with some need to know and would remove stigmatizing publicity after a time. In practice, because search engines cache web pages long after they have been removed, posting a name on the Internet once may amount to a life sentence. In light of this problem, governments should be more restrained in deciding what to post in the first place. They need to be more sparing in broadcasting convicts' names and addresses to the public at large through registries, media, and the like.

Perhaps governments could even put out positive information to reward law-abiding behavior and to end ex-cons' stigma. They could, for example, issue certificates praising them for remaining crime- and drug-free over the preceding six months, year, two years, and so on. Positive reinforcement would complement the negative reinforcement of probation officers' keeping tabs on ex-cons. Similar graduation ceremonies and certificates can be important parts of drug- and alcohol-treatment programs.

Finally, public-private partnerships can promote successful reentry. Public reentry programs remain woefully inadequate; many inmates are released from prison with no support other than a bus ticket and a few dollars. In response, some private groups such as Prison Fellowship's InnerChange Freedom Initiative run reentry programs. Volunteers, often from local church congregations, mentor inmates and help to arrange for housing and jobs upon release. Though more study is needed, empirical evidence suggests that participating inmates are much less likely to recidivate. Contact with mentors and congregations, it turns out, are crucial in holding ex-cons accountable and keeping them on a lawful path. There are of course serious Establishment Clause problems with giving inmates preferential treatment only if they choose to enroll in a religious program. But these problems are manageable: Prisons must remain open to secular alternative reentry programs, state dollars must not directly fund specifically religious activities, and religious programs should receive no better facilities or perquisites.[20] Secular alternatives could include a Teach-for-America-style corps of young graduates who would spend a couple of years working with prisoners as they prepare to reenter society. Governments should try harder, but public reentry programs are woefully underfunded and unprepared to help the masses of released inmates. As long as there is no religious coercion, we should welcome all manner of private assistance to bring inmates home and give them the mentoring, accountability, and community reintegration they need.

B. MID-LEVEL REFORMS TO INCLUDE THE PUBLIC

Federal and state governments typically control prison systems, prisoner reentry, and the collateral consequences of convictions. Prosecution and policing, in contrast, are usually handled at the county and town level and could be broken down further by neighborhood. The lower the level of government, the greater hope there is for meaningfully including the public in policy choices and oversight. Technology helps, too: discussion boards, chat rooms, Facebook groups, and Twitter feeds have made it easier for locals interested in criminal justice to organize themselves. Local citizens can thus join forces to press local police and prosecutors to offer more information and public participation. This section explores what reforms they might seek.

1. Greater Transparency

Improving information holds some hope at the county level, the level at which most Americans elect their district attorneys. Electoral candidates can do much of the work of bringing statistics to voters' attention. In the status quo, incumbent district attorneys simply brag about astronomical conviction rates or cherry-pick juicy anecdotes. If, however, government offices published more good data, challengers could stress high rates of charge reductions and deflated sentences in their campaign advertisements. Data gathering in New Orleans has gone hand-in-hand with this kind of change in district attorney election rhetoric, and voters there have taken note.[21] Better statistics would help electoral rivals to fight statistics with statistics, painting a somewhat more balanced picture. The prognosis is not bright, however, since anecdotes tend to trump dry statistics.

Other, more limited reforms are more likely to succeed. For example, some types of plea bargaining are especially opaque. As Ronald Wright and Marc Miller argue, charge bargaining and fact bargaining are more opaque and dishonest than trials, open pleas without plea bargains, and sentence bargains. Charge and fact bargains lie about the crime that actually happened and the facts surrounding it, breeding public cynicism. Historically, prosecutors have discouraged sentence bargaining more than charge bargaining, but this focus is backwards. Though plea bargaining will persist for the foreseeable future, judges and head prosecutors can at least clamp down on charge and fact bargaining. They can, for example, make prosecutors document and explain why they downgraded a murder to manslaughter, enabling voters and the press to check charge bargaining. Turning charge bargains into sentence bargains or open pleas will make them more honest, transparent, and accessible to public scrutiny.[22] The public may thus regain some faith in the criminal justice system and view its message as more legitimate and worthy of obedience.

One might also consider publishing prosecutors' procedural and substantive policies governing plea bargaining and sentencing. A few prosecutors' offices have already done so. Repeat defense counsel already know the going rates for particular crimes. Providing this information would level the playing field for novice defense counsel, help inform the public, and discipline prosecutors. One might not want to publish policies on when to arrest or what charges to decline. If for example policies exempted thefts of less than $40 from arrest or charging, potential criminals might be emboldened to steal amounts below the threshold. But plea and sentencing policies would not encourage potential criminals much, because certainty of punishment is a much greater factor than severity in deterring wrongdoers.[23] Besides, recidivist offenders may know the going rates anyway.

Transparency could also illuminate local policing. Better, publicized data could be an important part of increasing local oversight of police. Many jurisdictions do not even keep data on police shootings, though many must do so for traffic stops in order to expose racial profiling. Laws should require collecting, recording, and publishing data on everything from stops and frisks to types of arrests to enforcement priorities. Citizen review boards could then publicize these data and pressure errant police departments to change. One could likewise create comparable citizen review boards to oversee prosecutors' offices and publicize data. As Bill Stuntz argued persuasively, these optimistic-sounding transparent solutions may actually work, just as disclosures effectively reduce lending discrimination and pollution. More open community review boards could restore public trust in the police. Videotaping police interrogations and searches, as well as mandatory record-keeping, could improve monitoring and credibility. Sharing crime maps with the community could facilitate reciprocal sharing of information, neighborhood watch groups, and the like. Information sharing also helps to explain police resource allocation decisions to minority neighborhoods and lets neighbors respond with their concerns. This increased transparency may help allay minorities' fears that police targeting decisions are racially biased.[24]

Transparency would work in both directions. It would not only inform neighborhood residents, but also illuminate police decision-making by eliciting and addressing local concerns. This approach is known as community policing, widely praised in theory but inconsistently implemented in practice. Police and prosecutors could divide counties and precincts into smaller geographic beats, focusing their efforts on each neighborhood's pressing problems. Officers could have longer-term assignments to these beats, knock on doors, and listen to residents at community meetings. Collaborative, open decision-making, in consultation with local residents, can reflect neighborhood priorities and accommodate outsiders' concerns. Electronic discussions could supplement physical meetings for residents who cannot attend but want to offer feedback. Community policing emphasizes proactive responses to nascent problems identified by local residents, instead of waiting to react to 911 calls. Pay and promotion criteria could be changed to encourage listening to and serving the neighborhood's expressed needs, not just maximizing arrests. And, as Erik Luna suggests, public administrative rulemaking could develop rules or standards to guide the use of force, vice enforcement patterns, and other practices.[25]

In that vein, local residents could consult with neighborhood police about proposed police tactics. These may include curfews, gang-loitering laws, anti-nuisance injunctions, and order-maintenance policing. As Tracey Meares and Dan Kahan have argued, these approaches are more democratically legitimate when adopted in consultation with community members. This consultation and legitimacy may help reassure members of minority groups, who have historically distrusted law enforcement. Local residents would choose how to govern themselves, instead of having white officials from outside the neighborhood impose their own will on minority neighborhoods. That would insulate police somewhat against the charge that they discriminate against poor minorities; those minorities may in fact ask for police help to clean up their neighborhoods.[26] As a matter of procedural justice, eliciting their views makes residents feel they were treated fairly and taken seriously. In addition, police tactics are far more likely to succeed with community support. People are more likely to cooperate with the law when they perceive it to be procedurally fair and respectful and substantively just.

Community meetings are instrumentally valuable in explaining police actions and eliciting local citizens' information and views. But police meetings can also bring together local groups, such as churches and parent-teacher associations. By building social networks of trust, police can help neighbors to help themselves.[27] Each group learns to trust the others' willingness to cooperate. As a result, different neighborhood groups may jointly contribute to neighborhood watches and similar private crime-fighting measures. They may also cooperate to hold police and prosecutors accountable and make their views known to them.

This room for bottom-up as well as top-down policymaking would lead to a welcome shift in enforcement priorities. Many arrests and prosecutions involve so-called victimless crimes, such as drug crimes and prostitution. But not all victimless crimes are alike. Crack houses and street-corner drug dealers breed neighborhood violence and crowds of addicts, while discreet sales may have little spillover effect on others. Streetwalkers blight corners and draw curb-crawling cars, while Internet escort services impose much less harm on others. Though they may not want to legalize drugs or prostitution, neighbors will press police and prosecutors to focus on the crimes that harm the neighborhood. That would shift enforcement away from truly victimless crimes toward violent and property crimes, as well as drug crimes that harm others. Local pressure would counteract police and prosecutors' temptation to rack up easy vice conviction statistics. The upshot would be that police would enforce vice laws more narrowly, in ways tailored to local needs and priorities. In response, vice offenders would be more discreet and less likely to create public nuisances.

2. Increasing Public Participation

While community-policing and -prosecution programs let local citizens consult and voice views, there are more systematic, direct ways to include them. Today, "the public interest" is an amorphous nominal client onto which police and prosecutors can project their own ideas. Letting a cross-section of local citizens participate more actively would discipline insiders' freedom, injecting the public's views into concrete cases. Insiders would have to grapple with the public's sense of justice, just as outsiders would see the caseloads and tradeoffs that temper insider justice.

Another benefit of public participation is that it would legitimate insiders' exercises of discretion. Scholars fret that official discretion risks being lawless and arbitrary. The common response is to suggest fettering discretion with more rules.[28] But, as chapter II explained, the quest for perfect rules is doomed to failure. Insiders' low-visibility decisions consistently subvert supposedly mandatory rules and turn them into bargaining chips. Outsiders respond episodically, leaving criminal justice in an unhealthy spiral.

Instead of seeking perfect rules, we should give public participation a greater role in guiding and tempering official discretion. Aggregated, decentralized input and feedback from a wide range of stakeholders should better reflect the public's shared sense of justice than a single prosecutor's position.[29] That would depend on the eBay-style reputational feedback loops that I propose below. Similar feedback could rate and review police and public defenders' performance. Aggregation should rein in outliers and reduce inequality of like cases, while letting results vary for atypical, unlike cases.

Scholars have proposed various ways to involve the local community more thoroughly even in cases that are plea bargained. Kevin Washburn suggests using neighborhood grand juries for each zip code, so neighbors play a role in charging decisions. Jason Mazzone proposes lay plea panels to review the voluntariness and fairness of individual plea bargains. Josh Bowers suggests using lay panels at the charging stage. Laura Appleman, Richard Bierschbach, and I have endorsed plea juries—lay tribunals that would inject community notions of retribution, expression, and fairness into pleas and sentences.[30] Jurors would be drawn from a cross-section of the community, to inject community values and check excessive harshness or leniency in plea bargaining.

Likewise, citizen advocates, drawn from a cross-section of the community, could rotate through police departments and prosecutors' offices for a few weeks at a time. They would review enforcement priorities, indictments, plea agreements, and sentence recommendations. They need not receive vetoes. Simply giving them voices would force insiders to reckon with outsiders' perspectives, needs, and desires. Having to articulate reasons for decisions, even orally and briefly, would discipline prosecutors, much as having to write reasoned opinions disciplines judges. Faced with concerned citizens, prosecutors might find it harder to indulge possible risk aversion or sloth.

Ideally, these measures would help to educate the public, let it express itself, and help voters to see justice being done. Unfortunately, these Tocquevillean educative benefits are hard to mass produce. Now that grand and petit juries are rarities, it is hard to re-create their roles effectively. Plea and sentencing juries would likely prove too cumbersome to replicate widely in our mechanical, efficiency-obsessed system. Citizen advocates who rotated through police and prosecutors' offices would probably lack enough expertise and knowledge of cases to serve as effective voices. There is also the fear that general public participation might not check insiders effectively, as laymen may routinely defer to insider experts.[31] Nevertheless, elected insiders, worried about reelection, might err on the side of caution and solicitude toward lay views, lest persistent callousness erupt into a scandal.

So, as to the broad educative effects of jury service, I am skeptical that we can recover them wholesale, at least in large cities and suburbs. But jury service is good not only for the broad public, but also for the particular cases and parties that juries hear. As the next section argues, one could blend restorative-justice conferences with neighborhood juries. Doing so would not only let the parties express themselves and heal, but satisfy locals that justice had been done.

Finally, the system must actively solicit insiders' and outsiders' feedback to encourage insiders to serve their principals' interests. Just as eBay routinely solicits members' feedback to build reputation scores, so victims, defendants, defense counsel, judges, and fellow prosecutors could leave routine post-case feedback about the various insiders by email or automated telephone survey. Aggregating a range of views would create a subtler and more complete metric of success than simply numbers of arrests or convictions, reflecting qualitative judgments as well as quantitative ones. Algorithms could weed out vindictive or otherwise unrepresentative outliers. These feedback loops would draw on the Internet habit of commenting on or reviewing just about everything, and taking this feedback seriously would reinforce that habit, creating a virtuous cycle. Feedback could influence promotion and salary decisions for line prosecutors as well as reelection for district attorneys. Likewise, the feedback of defendants and others could assess defense lawyers' performance, influencing their promotions and salaries. Feedback would shift insiders' mindset from insisting that they know best to addressing customer service, much as successful private firms value customer service. Even judges could benefit from litigants,' lawyers,' and jurors' feedback, much as tenured professors sometimes learn from their students' course evaluations. Conscientious public servants may heed evaluations, much as many tenured professors do, even if evaluations have little influence on pay or promotion.

These and other forms of participation would help to discipline insiders much better than the general public can, at least in cases with identifiable victims. Victims, and to a lesser extent affected local citizens, are a discrete, identifiable group who already know about the crimes they have endured and are motivated to take part. Because of their background knowledge, they do not need to be brought up to speed, can speak with authority, and will not automatically defer to insiders' assessments. They also have palpable interests in the process and outcomes, which can counterbalance insiders' own stakes and preferences. Precisely because they are not repeat players, they can counteract insiders' jading and mellowing as well as their (over)emphasis on pragmatic concerns. At the same time, victims and locals will see some practical constraints and aggravating and mitigating factors ex post, helping them to understand outcomes better. In short, insiders will have to address outsiders' moralism, and outsiders will have to see insiders' ex post perspective and pragmatism. Though they will not always see eye to eye, the perspectives of the two sides may converge.[32]

C. MICRO-LEVEL SOLUTIONS

1. Victim Information and Consultation

Informing victims about their cases should be relatively easy. Victims are a discrete, identifiable group with whom police and often prosecutors must make contact in any event. While most states have some form of victims' rights law on the books, enforcement is uneven and many victims fail to receive notice.[33] States should redouble their efforts to provide victims with timely advance notice of all key stages, from arrest through charging to plea and sentence. A dedicated official, such as a victim/witness coordinator, could help to increase contact with victims and keep tabs on the progress of cases. With the advent of email, notifying victims and defendants is even easier. The district attorney's or clerk of the court's computer system should email victims and defendants automated updates every time an arraignment, bail, plea, trial, or sentencing hearing is scheduled or rescheduled, and again two days before the hearing. For victims or defendants without email access, an automated telephone reminder system could do the same job. These communications should include directions to the courthouse and courtroom, as well as contact telephone numbers, to make it easier for victims and defendants to attend proceedings and see justice done. Emails after each hearing could summarize what had happened at each stage. Internet access could permit simplified access to online docket sheets, summarizing what had happened and what was scheduled to happen next when.

The performance feedback loops just discussed would give police and prosecutors greater incentives to provide this information consistently. These simple measures would increase victim information, satisfaction, and healing.

Empowering victims is a bit harder but still manageable. There will always be some participation gap between insiders and victims because victims will not supplant prosecutors. As long as victims are not in charge, police, prosecutors, and judges will make some decisions that upset them. But even though "victims' desire is to be included in the criminal justice process, they have no desire to take control over the outcome of the case." Interestingly, most victims are not angry and vengeful, and many do not demand harsher punishments. It is simple participation that helps to empower and heal victims. Participants see the law as more fair and legitimate when they have some control over the process and feel they have been heard, whether or not they control ultimate outcomes. A participatory role and fair and respectful treatment would go a long way toward addressing victims' grievances, regardless of the outcomes.[34] Thus, criminal justice can make victims better off by better informing and including them. The same is probably true of crime bystanders and locals who live near the crime scene, though it would be harder logistically to identify and include them all.

As chapter IV argued, victims deserve a stake and a voice in criminal justice, provided that neutral arbiters retain the final word. The state's monopoly is too cold and goes too far in ignoring victims' interests and desires. Some readers will balk at this claim, viewing criminal justice's purpose as exclusively public. But readers who are persuaded that victims deserve more voice should consider a range of options to increase victims' participation.

Restorative-justice mediation and conferences make both parties better off when both are willing to take part, as chapter IV.B.2 explained. Victims who participate in mediation are more likely to believe that the system is fair, that their cases were handled satisfactorily, that they were able to tell their stories, that the outcome was satisfactory, and that the wrongdoer was held accountable. They are also more likely to receive apologies and to forgive, and they are less likely to fear revictimization or stay upset.[35]

Victims could participate in other ways as well. At a minimum, they could allocute orally at sentencing, instead of simply submitting perfunctory written victim-impact statements. They could also speak with, question, and respond to defendants and lawyers at trials and at plea and sentencing hearings. If trial judges refused to let them speak, they could file interlocutory appeals to protect their rights to participate. One could even imagine giving violent-felony victims the right to appeal sentences and interlocutorily appeal plea bargains, at least with permission of the court of appeals. Appeals, however, might be too cumbersome if widely used. And plea appeals would have to be restricted to narrow procedural grounds, though sentence appeals could more broadly check substantive reasonableness. It may make more sense to give victims a voice in prosecutors' internal decisions whether to strike plea bargains and appeal sentences.

The most interesting and difficult set of questions involves what kind of voice victims should have over the course of the prosecution. Prosecutors could be required to consult with victims before dropping charges, entering into plea bargains, or recommending sentences. But there are many different ways to implement consultation. At one extreme, prosecutors would simply inform victims, giving them only a perfunctory opportunity to speak after prosecutors had made up their minds. A purely nominal right to consult would come off as callous and deaf, not empowering. At the other end of the spectrum, victims could have a veto over prosecutorial decisions. The danger there is that a vengeful or unreasonable victim could hold the system hostage, heedless of the public interest or justice.

The trick to making victim consultation meaningful yet just is striking some middle path between those extremes. The public has an interest in following the community's shared sense of justice. At the same time, victims provide important information about the unique harms they have suffered, and harm is central to public intuitions about what punishment wrongdoers deserve. Moreover, as chapter IV discussed, many people give significant weight to the victims' expressed wishes in deciding how much punishment defendants deserve. In other words, the public wants to hear what victims have to say but also wants to check that reaction with its own sense of justice.

So, prosecutors should not be beholden to victims, but neither should they be deaf to their pleas. The first step to ensuring meaningful participation is providing timely notice of upcoming decisions, as discussed above.

Second, prosecutors need to affirmatively solicit victims' views. Third, they should do so in plenty of time to influence decisions. Participation is a meaningless charade if it comes after the die is cast.[36]

Fourth, prosecutors should have to articulate reasons for their decisions, much as judges do. For routine and minor decisions they could give those reasons orally or on a checklist form. For major decisions, particularly where prosecutors disagree with victims in felony cases, they should justify their decisions in writing.

Fifth, victims ought to have the time and opportunity to appeal major felony decisions to a prosecutor's supervisor. Appeals need not be formal; simply the opportunity to meet for ten minutes, talk on the phone, or email an explanation of disagreement could be enough to ensure that victims feel heard. Victims could point out errors or inconsistencies in prosecutors' statements of reasons, and supervisors could review those reasons and objections. This summary, informal procedure would be far more practicable than judicial appeals of prosecutorial decisions. Supervisors would be less risk averse than line prosecutors about going to trial, since they are not personally invested in the outcome, so they could discipline line prosecutors who were too hasty in getting rid of cases. Knowing of this right of appeal, line prosecutors would listen more respectfully to victims and be careful to justify any contrary decisions.

Sixth, victims should have avenues to leave feedback on police and prosecutors' performance. As discussed above, feedback from victims and others would illuminate and check police and prosecutors' decisions. But it would also empower victims and make them feel heard, which might promote their healing. Soliciting victims' feedback would send the message that the system takes them seriously and cares about their views.

Of course, victim involvement works only where one can identify a victim. Just under a quarter of arrests are for violent crimes and more than a quarter are for property crimes. In these cases, it is usually clear who the victim is. More than a third of arrests, however, are for drug crimes, and one-ninth are for public-order offenses, such as weapons and driving-related offenses.[37] Where there is no clear victim, victim information, input, and participation in restorative justice cannot work. But not all drug and public-order offenses are truly victimless. Sometimes, a victim is injured or threatened by a gun or a drunk or reckless driver. Often a crack house blights an entire neighborhood, scaring residents and forcing them to flee gunfire and addicts. Where so-called victimless crime has these spillover effects, police and prosecutors should make efforts to identify and include the victims in criminal justice proceedings. If it proves impossible to give all victims these rights, insiders should at least make special efforts to include the direct victims of violent or other serious crimes. Conversely, where even indirect victims are absent, that very absence should weigh against aggressive enforcement.

2. Defendants' Information and Participation

As chapter II noted, defendants as well as victims feel shut out and kept in the dark. Many defendants feel that they are not informed, not listened to, and simply told to take quick pleas. Like victims, defendants have little and often inaccurate information about the criminal justice system, and have much less say than one might expect.

Many of the informational solutions suggested for victims could work for defendants as well. Automated email and telephone systems could keep them abreast of their cases, as could simplified Internet access to on-line docket sheets. Plain-English explanations of charges and sentences would help too.

There is no substitute, however, for one-on-one conversations with defense lawyers. Unfortunately, just as managed care has pushed primary-care physicians toward six-minute appointments and pill-pushing, the plea-bargaining machinery has pushed defense lawyers toward plea-pushing. The problem is so bad that one chief public defender had to issue a policy prohibiting his lawyers from advising clients to plead guilty at arraignment, until they had had "meaningful contact" ahead of time with their clients.[38] Defendants should not be pressured to plead guilty immediately upon meeting their lawyers, often in the holding cells minutes before an initial court appearance, except in trivial cases. Particularly in felony cases, they should meet privately with their lawyers, for at least fifteen minutes, to discuss the charges and defenses in advance of any decision to plead guilty. Serious cases should require in-person meetings; less-serious ones could use videoconferencing to avoid the difficulties of visiting incarcerated defendants. Before defendants decide to plead, prosecutors should disclose, and defense lawyers should relay, any classic exculpatory evidence, such as eyewitness or physical evidence incriminating a different suspect. And as patients get second opinions before undergoing major surgery, defendants should have a right to a second opinion before a major felony plea.

Many of the problems stem from chronic underfunding and conflicts of interest inherent in court-appointed defender systems. Defense lawyers often have so little time that they feel they can do nothing but tell their clients to plead guilty right away. A comprehensive solution would require much better training and funding of defense counsel, which is unlikely any time soon. Even with existing resources, however, we can do better. Some systems are worse than others. Some appointed lawyers receive flat fees, or low hourly rates subject to a cap, so they make more money if clients plead quickly and lose money if they go to trial. Others are public defenders, who receive flat salaries and so face no financial pressures to induce pleas. Public-defender systems are preferable because they may reduce temptations to pressure defendants. Even public defenders, however, feel caseload pressure to shrink their dockets by encouraging pleas.

Ultimately, indigent defense requires much more funding so that lawyers need not juggle hundreds of cases at once (though I will not hold my breath awaiting that needed reform).

More generally, defense lawyers need to listen to their clients' stories and goals. Many clients undoubtedly just want to minimize their punishment and get their cases over with. But often they also want to be treated respectfully, taken seriously, tell their stories to their lawyers and victims, and have some kind of day in court. Defendants may legitimately balk at plea deals that excuse them as imbeciles incapable of more serious crimes. And defendants may benefit when encouraged to take responsibility, seek drug and alcohol treatment, make restitution, and apologize. Defense lawyers may have to firmly challenge defendants' incredible stories in the face of overwhelming evidence, to make them confront what they have done. Many wrongdoers have wounded their friends and families, and accepting responsibility can be a painful but important step toward rebuilding their lives.

So that they can learn from the process, defendants need more opportunities and encouragement to speak. They can tell their stories and engage in dialogue with their defense lawyers. But they also need opportunities to have their day in court and in conferences with victims, their families, and neighbors. Encouragement to speak, express remorse, and apologize should start at the beginning of the criminal process. Police and prosecutors could use their existing discretion with more of an eye towards encouraging remorse and apology. For minor property crimes, for example, police could forgo arrest or delay it pending restitution and amends, encouraging wrongdoers to interact face-to-face with their victims. Even after arrest, prosecutors may decline to prosecute low-level wrongdoers if they apologize and agree to make restitution. (Prosecutors can use the same rhetoric of remorse to encourage more serious wrongdoers to cooperate with the government, partially undoing the harm by bringing other wrongdoers to justice.) And by bringing in parents or other authority figures to bear witness, the law can reinforce the moral authority of its pronouncements and the need for remorse, reform, and apology.

Guilty-plea hearings also need to change, particularly in more serious cases, to elicit defendants' stories and apologies. These plea hearings could do much more than simply allowing participants to recite rights, facts, and a scripted admission of guilt written by a defense lawyer. Judges could use their existing authority to truly judge. They could take the time to observe and evaluate defendants. Defendants often deny or minimize their behavior or offer excuses. Judges could keep them honest by questioning them closely, probing their excuses, and refusing to accept pleas if defendants denied or evaded guilt. For example, they could ask about defendants' statements during the crime, how victims appeared, the harm inflicted, and the use of force or weapons. These questions could elicit spontaneous responses, breaking away from lawyers' scripted statements, and draw attention to the impact on the victim. Judges could encourage remorse, apology, and dialogue, by asking defendants if they wish to say anything to victims in the courtroom. If defendants chose to express remorse or apologize, the result might be catharsis and reconciliation.

Defendants should likewise find it easier to tell their stories at trial. For instance, they should not be penalized for testifying unless they willfully perjure themselves. Right now, defendants' criminal records are usually inadmissible if they do not testify at trial but admissible to impeach their testimony if they do.[39] That rule perversely discourages them from telling their side of the story. Instead, rap sheets should either be completely inadmissible or completely admissible, so defendants face no penalty for speaking. (They could, for example, be completely inadmissible at trial unless the previous conviction was for perjury or was similar to the current one, but admissible at sentencing.) The next section suggests other ways that both victims and defendants could play larger speaking roles.

Of course, most defendants will behave strategically. Many will apologize insincerely just to minimize their punishment. But, as chapter III suggested, the process of admitting guilt and apologizing can still overcome denial, teach lessons, and even begin the process of reform. We teach our children to say "I'm sorry," even when they do not yet mean it, in the hopes that they will learn their lessons and learn to feel sorry. We should hold out some of the same hope for defendants.

3. Restorative Sentencing Juries

This book has highlighted a series of competing demands that criminal procedure must accommodate. We need to create procedures that blend the old and the new, the historical ideal with the modern reality. We need both fair rules and wise contextual discretion to temper those rules. We need both laws and local community voices addressing how to implement those laws. We need ways to recover some of the benefits of local juries within the framework of plea bargaining. We need both retribution and restoration, both blaming and forgiveness. We need the private parties' views and wants tempered by the public's sense of justice.

Most of all, we need to empower laymen to have their day in court, express themselves, and reconcile within a lawyer-driven system.

Lawyers are good at putting cases into legal boxes and at processing them efficiently. But their legal training and repeated exposure can numb them to the equities of individual cases, much as emergency-room physicians grow numb to the anguish and grief surrounding them.[40] Lawyers check boxes to determine whether defendants are legally guilty, slighting how morally guilty they are and what they and victims deserve. The press of business and the ideal of formal equality can lead lawyers to treat like and unlike cases alike, rather than slowing down to individualize. Laymen need not only equitable substantive justice, but also fair, respectful procedures. Real victims and defendants need to speak and be heard, to forgive and be forgiven. We need to inject fresh lay voices to empower them and to counterbalance insiders' cold, mechanistic case processing.

We can no longer give every victim and defendant a full-blown jury trial. Criminal trials have grown expensive, cumbersome, and protracted, and we cannot hire twenty times as many lawyers, judges, bailiffs, and court reporters. But there ought to be ways to hold much shorter jury proceedings, free of technicalities and staffed largely by the parties and their neighbors. The parties could blame, apologize, and heal face to face, while their community sat in judgment. What we need are restorative juries at sentencing in at least the most serious cases, blending the best of restorative justice procedures with the expression and retribution of traditional trials. Victims, wrongdoers, their families, and their friends ought to *see* justice done by doing justice themselves. In essence, we would re-create short, intelligible, lawyer-free colonial trials at sentencing instead.

The basic insight comes from chapter IV's discussion of restorative justice. While restorative procedures have much to offer and often help to satisfy all the parties, restorative justice's substantive hostility to punishment is deeply at odds with popular intuitions of justice. The idea would be to sever the useful procedures from the substantive anti-punishment philosophy. Restorative procedures could empower the parties to express themselves and heal in the course of having local lay juries gauge and impose deserved punishment. Restoration need not be at odds with retribution, but could complement it.

The first challenge is to blend individual litigants' say with publicly shared senses of justice. On the one hand, victims and wrongdoers have their own distinctive voices that deserve substantial weight. On the other hand, the public has a strong interest in seeing justice done that must not be hijacked by idiosyncratic or extreme preferences. The jury must be large and heterogeneous enough to represent the neighborhood community. A large, heterogeneous group will reflect a range of opinions and will limit polarization toward extremes. Traditionally, petit juries comprise twelve jurors, who must vote unanimously to convict. Grand juries comprise twenty-three jurors, of whom a majority (twelve) must vote to charge a defendant. Sentencing juries could fall somewhere within this range. For misdemeanors, sentencing juries could comprise six jurors, of whom a majority would have to agree on a sentence. For lesser felonies, the number could be the traditional twelve. For more serious felonies, sentencing juries could be larger and require two-thirds or three-quarters agreement to impose heavier sentences.[41]

Heterogeneity would be built into the jury's composition. A handful of jurors, at most a quarter, would represent victims, perhaps their family members or close friends. An equal handful would represent defendants. The balance of power, at least half of the jury, would rest with a random range of neighbors not related to either party or directly harmed by the crime. Jurors would pledge to deliberate not as partisans but as citizens, setting an atmosphere of respectful discourse about justice. Mediators and fellow jurors could remind one another of their pledge. They would listen to the victims' and defendants' statements, as well as videotapes of plea allocutions, before reaching their own punishment decisions. Proceedings could be open to the public, and neighborhood residents could receive notice and submit comments online.

Advisory sentencing guidelines would set broad punishment ranges for different types of crimes based on the public's sense of justice and the sentences imposed in similar cases. These guidelines would turn on the common-sense factors that influence the public's punishment intuitions, eschewing the mathematical gobbledygook of the U.S. Sentencing Guidelines. Even advisory guidelines serve as mental anchors, helping to equalize outcomes across a range of cases while leaving flexibility for truly unusual cases and permitting appellate review. Within the guideline ranges, victims could argue for heavier sentences or forgive and ask for lighter ones, subject to the jury's veto. The ranges would set outer bounds on the parties' wishes, ensuring some equality and limiting the impact of idiosyncratically vengeful or merciful victims. Maximum sentences and appellate review could check extremes as well. Victims would have substantial say over their share in punishment, because victims' desires carry significant weight with many jurors. But the public's sense of justice would still set upper and lower bounds to reflect what defendants deserve.

Importantly, both guidelines and the jury's case-specific sense of justice would check insiders. Prosecutors sometimes stack charges and minimum sentences as plea-bargaining chips, thus greatly penalizing defendants who go to trial. Conversely, they sometimes lower sentences markedly for defendants who cooperate. They may thus seek much heavier punishment than they otherwise think is needed in some cases, while acquiescing in substantially lighter punishment in others. The effect is most extreme in cases in which prosecutors charge and pursue recidivists or regulatory crimes that require little mental or moral blameworthiness. A prosecutor could still charge those crimes but would have to convince a jury that this defendant in this particular case deserved this particular punishment. No longer could prosecutors lock up recidivists for decades for minor crimes, such as a $120 fraud or shooting one's own television screen in frustration.[42] Nor could they arbitrarily fragment one drug-dealing conspiracy into hundreds of individual sales to raise sentences, or ignore those sales to lower them. Juries could scrutinize these charging decisions at sentencing.

Nor could prosecutors use mandatory minimum sentences to punish uncooperative minor drug dealers just as much as major ringleaders. Minima would no longer be mandatory. Juries, not just prosecutors, would have to decide whether the minimum punishment fit the crime. Conversely, prosecutors would have to justify what juries might see as sweetheart deals. Sentencing juries would thus restore checks and balances to our system, counterbalancing what had become unilateral prosecutorial power to plea bargain. They would restore a measure of sanity and common sense to offset overcriminalization.

Right now, politicians sell minima as essential to rein in soft-on-crime judges. But that justification does not apply where a local jury, or better yet the victim, agrees to a lower sentence. The victim in particular has moral standing to forgive and lower the sentence without being accused of insensitivity to the victim's suffering. Thus, the public might be more willing to turn mandatory penalties into presumptive or benchmark sentences.

In sentencing-jury hearings, parties would be free to vent, discuss, apologize, and forgive, but could not be forced to do so. Free of rules of evidence and procedure, jury sentencing would be much shorter than trials, spanning several hours rather than days or weeks. A mediator could try to coax the parties and their friends and families into talking but would not bring an anti-punishment agenda to the table. Mediators would give the most basic jury instructions on applying the advisory sentencing guidelines and provide verdict forms. Lawyers would play no role, apart from explaining (either orally or in writing) why a sentence bargain or cooperation agreement merited a discount. Ideally, the parties would often express themselves, engage in restorative dialogue, and agree to make amends, as they do in restorative conferences. They would speak in plain English, not legalese. The jury, seeing both parties visibly satisfied, might be more comfortable sentencing toward the lower end of the range. The local public would see justice done at sentencing and later in public work and restitution; neighborhood residents could be notified and invited to attend. Wrongdoers would thus pay their debts to society and hopefully be welcomed back by their neighbors, particularly when victims had expressed satisfaction at seeing justice done.

In other words, restoration would be one important strand in criminal justice. But it would not displace the legitimate roles of denunciation and retribution. Restoration, as I have argued, can valuably supplement traditional retributive justice as long as it does not supplant it. And the process would be guided and deliberative rather than determined by mob rule. Mediators would focus dialogue and, as discussed below, benchmarks and advisory sentencing guidelines would constrain arbitrariness.

Giving juries a meaningful sentencing role might seem to collide with plea bargaining. After all, if juries are to sentence, how can prosecutors and defense counsel credibly promise any particular outcomes? Conversely, if plea bargains carry force, must jury sentencing be a sham?

My vision of restorative sentencing would go hand in hand with a shift in the working of plea bargains. Currently, plea bargains work through brute force. Defendants promise to give prosecutors their pleas, and prosecutors in turn trade bargaining chips as a matter of unreviewable executive grace. They need not explain their actions nor have any particularly good reasons for doing so.

Plea bargaining needs to become less an exercise of power and more a discourse of reason. The dishonest forms of plea bargaining, such as charge and fact bargaining as well as *Alford* and no-contest pleas, must end. Jurors would also frown upon hedged or equivocal guilty pleas, discouraging defendants from evading responsibility. Sentence bargaining would be transformed from a raw quid pro quo to a process of explaining why a wrongdoer deserves a particular sentence. If he agrees to plead guilty, the prosecutor can explain to the sentencing jury, resources are freed up to pursue other wrongdoers. (Suggested discounts for simply pleading guilty would be a more standardized range, perhaps 10% to 15%, reducing the fear that well-connected defendants get better deals than poor ones.) If he pleads guilty quickly and admits guilt completely, his actions may reflect remorse and acceptance of responsibility, earning a larger discount. If he turns on his former criminal associates and takes risks to bring them to justice, he may deserve still more credit. In each case, however, prosecutors should make these decisions not unilaterally, but subject to the sentencing jury's review. As agents of the public, prosecutors should ordinarily convince the relevant public that their plea bargaining decisions are just. Juries would decide for themselves how remorseful and sympathetic defendants were and how much of a break they deserved. Suggested percentage discounts for pleas and for cooperation would serve as mental benchmarks, while leaving juries flexibility to gauge each individual's remorse, apologies, and healing.

Sentencing juries would check prosecutors as well as victims from getting out of line. In other words, outsiders would check insiders, requiring them to justify their decisions with publicly accessible reasons and reviewing those reasons. For instance, they could check prosecutors' understandable temptation to overbuy cooperating-witness testimony, probing whether cooperating witnesses were essential to make this particular case. This checking would take place not in the abstract, but with flesh-and-blood victims and defendants who defy cartoonish stereotypes. As chapter II argued, juries are far more nuanced ex post than voters are ex ante, because jurors must confront complex real people face to face. Prosecutors would exercise less coercive leverage by threatening harsh charges and then promising to drop them. They might thus fear that defendants will have less incentive to cooperate. But jurors would predictably reward valuable cooperation, much as federal judges predictably award cooperation discounts. The rewards might be less iron-clad, but they would be more legitimate and better justified. The upside is that juries would check prosecutorial abuse of what is now unilateral leverage.

Stripped of their dishonesty, hiddenness, and brute force, plea bargains would begin local conversations instead of hiding and ending them. Insiders would no longer dictate outcomes to outsiders, but would have to persuade or convince them. Outsiders could defer to insiders' expertise when their justifications seemed considered but not when they seemed unreasonably harsh or lenient. Sentencing would once again become a public moral conversation, as well as a chance for the parties to express themselves and heal. (These proceedings might not be so public in the sliver of terrorism, organized-crime, and violent-gang cases, to protect cooperating witnesses from reprisals. Even in other cases, confidentiality rules, akin to those governing grand juries, might let juries but not the public hear the most sensitive pieces of evidence, such as parts of presentence reports.) Plea bargaining would become part of a neo-colonial morality play, offering a way to both punish wrongdoers and reintegrate them into the fold.

The same restorative-jury idea could revive clemency. Currently, presidents and governors fear pardoning convicts or commuting their sentences, lest they be accused of softness on crime. Executives could insulate themselves against this criticism by delegating clemency decisions whole-sale to restorative clemency juries, constituted much like the restorative sentencing juries discussed above. Clemency would be the province not just of executives but of juries, acting independently. These juries could represent the public's sense of justice and take the heat for clemency grants. They would not undercut restorative sentencing juries but rather complement them. Their job would be to focus on facts that had changed since sentencing, such as wrongdoers' moral reform, amends, and apologies and victims' and communities' forgiveness. Particularly where victims recommend or acquiesce in clemency, critics would find it harder to attack juries' decisions as too soft and could not threaten political repercussions. One can cautiously hope that this measure would restart the stalled clemency process, restoring it to its historic role as a reflection of the public's mercy.

Critics will complain that many places in America no longer have any meaningful sense of community on which criminal justice can draw. That argument is too pessimistic. My vision of local community seeks to draw upon shared culture and experiences, as well as participatory deliberation.[43] Community is not static but dynamic and can be cultivated; jury service and deliberation can draw upon and strengthen communal bonds. Moreover, while only a fraction of Americans live in small towns, suburbs and cities comprise their own neighborhood communities. Even in the largest cities, neighborhood residents interact repeatedly, both informally and formally in neighborhood meetings, parent-teacher associations, and the like. And the empirical evidence confirms that Americans share far more criminal-justice intuitions than we might think. As chapter V discussed, Paul Robinson, Tom Tyler, and others have found a healthy consensus of popular criminal-justice intuitions. Neighbors already share fundamental intuitions about desert and fairness and can build deliberation on that foundation.

There are nevertheless serious practical barriers to implementing such sweeping changes. Restorative sentencing juries would not cost nearly as much as trials, but they would still be costlier than rubber-stamp sentencing hearings. They would also take much more time of more participants, albeit a more diffuse set of lay participants. Providing restorative sentencing juries in a million cases a year would still require a staggering number of mediators, conference rooms, and prosecutors. One could start smaller, with the most serious violent and property felonies, but even those would require tens or hundreds of thousands of juries. Some savings could come from prosecuting fewer crimes with no aggrieved victims, but those savings would fund restorative sentencing only partially. This visionary change could take decades and billions of dollars to implement fully. But it may be an ideal worth striving towards, even if we can implement it only partially. Empowerment, apologies, and healing are not cheap but may nevertheless be worth the price. Sometimes, it makes sense to trade off some quantity for quality. At the very least, we need to discuss these tradeoffs openly instead of blindly processing the largest quantity of cases at the lowest possible price.

Critics will also complain that giving sentencing juries discretion to individualize sentences will undercut equality. Fans of mandatory sentencing likewise worry about undermining deterrence, by blurring the clear penalties needed to deter crime. These worries are understandable but manageable. As I hope I have shown, the bigger problem in our system is too much mechanization, not too little. In our fruitless pursuit of treating like cases alike, we treat unlike ones alike too, forcing them all onto a Procrustean bed. As a result, chapter II showed, sentences are often driven not by morally relevant considerations, but by prosecutors' and defense counsel's preferences and administrative considerations. Mechanization has hardly reduced racial and other disparities in the system, while breeding suspicion and mistrust in both minority and non-minority communities. The punishment factory forces crimes into static bureaucratic categories, ignoring dynamic factors such as remorse, apology, and forgiveness that many people consider relevant. And overoptimistic defendants can always hope that they will be the ones to receive sweetheart plea bargains, so the seeming arbitrariness of plea bargaining undercuts deterrence in its own way. It is time to try new solutions, pursuing equality through inclusive, decentralized deliberations rather than through a failed centralized administration. As chapter IV.B.1 argued (following Bill Stuntz's lead), local criminal justice might well be milder and more egalitarian than the machinery we have now. Frankly, we have little good evidence about whether noncapital jury sentencing exhibits greater racial disparities than judicial sentencing.[44] Benchmarks, such as advisory sentencing guidelines, could guide juries to focus on the specifics of the crime and so less on irrelevant facts such as race.

At the root of the equality objection is the assumption that insiders care more about and are better at ensuring equality than outsiders on juries. At the end of chapter V, however, I disputed this common assumption. Judges and other professionals, psychological studies show, are not immune from the racial attitudes and assumptions that pervade our society. Likewise, capital punishment scholars find that "white-victim disparities are principally the result of prosecutorial charging decisions rather than jury or judicial sentencing decisions."[45] Decades of top-down efforts to stamp out racial disparities in criminal justice have not come close to solving the problem. In recent years, the political branches have taken the lead in attacking racial disparities in capital punishment and traffic stops, while courts have been largely ineffective. And there is plenty of reason to think that local juries, drawn from the neighborhood and roughly reflecting its racial composition, will be at least as sensitive to issues of race and class as insiders. Conversely, countywide prosecutors and judges who live some distance away may be less representative and less sensitive to local issues of race and class. Certainly, neighborhood juries are not perfect, but there is little reason to mistrust them as systematically more biased than insiders. Moreover, careful jury instructions and advisory sentencing guidelines can help to guide juries and make them reflect on their thought processes, and appellate review can moderate extreme decisions. The solution is not to exclude outsiders but to trust them, particularly when they see defendants up close as jurors instead of hearing news accounts that evoke stereotypes. At the very least, one could experiment with restorative sentencing juries and monitor whether they appeared to increase racial disparities.

If restorative sentencing juries prove impossible to implement, or lead to intolerable expense, delay, and inconsistency, there are less radical though less effective ways to temper prosecutors' unilateral power. Judges could be allowed to participate openly in plea bargaining and have the power to offer deals more moderate than those offered by prosecutors. Judges could solicit victims' views both in plea bargaining and at sentencing and pay them due heed. They could also strive to make sentence discounts track more closely the wrongfulness of the crime, the likelihood of conviction, and the post-trial sentence. Though these measures could somewhat counterbalance prosecutors' unilateral power, they would not restore the outsider perspective that we have lost. They might improve the machinery but would not inject the needed fresh air from outside.

*****

The gap between historical ideals and criminal-justice reality has never been starker. Expectations are high and disappointments great. Reforming a system so broken seems hopeless, but we must keep hope alive. We must recall, as Abraham Lincoln memorably said in the Gettysburg Address, that ours should be a "government of the people, by the people, for the people." Insiders and their agency costs have pulled criminal justice far from its morality-play moorings, sometimes consciously, sometimes instinctively. Insiders and professionals are not malicious, benighted, or bad people. As a former prosecutor, I have great respect for the many judges, defense counsel, prosecutors, and law enforcement agents with whom I worked. But professionals' tunnel vision, and their distance from popular expectations and desires, can only sap a criminal justice system that depends on the people for its legitimacy and respect.

Populist, democratic aspirations for criminal justice risk seeming unsophisticated, quaint, even naïve. There certainly is danger in romanticizing the people, who at their worst can behave like bigoted mobs. Juries are sometimes unpredictable and biased; victims are sometimes vengeful; citizens are sometimes apathetic. Today, however, the danger seems stronger in the other direction. Too often elites pooh-pooh the masses and their benighted retributive instincts, instead of engaging in dialogue and finding common ground. And too often professionals are blind to their own shortcomings and how their own views and self-interests need checking too. Insiders need to check outsiders, but outsiders likewise need to check insiders.

The reforms I have suggested are just that, suggestions. Some may seem too modest, others too bold and impractical. I come neither to bury plea bargaining nor to praise it, but to reconceive it and reintroduce outsiders' voices and perspectives. But I hope my suggestions can shatter our mental blinders and fatalism. Our procedures are too hidden, too insular, and too deaf to the range of needs people have. Both procedures and punishments need to be more public and participatory; social-networking technology can now enable outsiders to push for these changes. I can only hope that, by taking part, outsiders can reclaim their role as stakeholders and remain outsiders no longer. Stakeholders will better appreciate insiders' realism, and insiders will better appreciate stakeholders' idealism. That process will not be quick or easy, but it may eventually soften our cold plea-bargaining machinery by bringing back the best features of the public, redemptive morality play. Professionals can live up to their job as public servants. The public can once again play an active role in its own local dramas. And victims and defendants alike can once again hope to be treated with respect, as active participants in a cathartic morality play.

NOTES

INTRODUCTION, OVERVIEW, & THEMES

1. The first quotation in the paragraph is from Thurman Arnold, *The Criminal Trial as a Symbol of Public Morality*, *in* CRIMINAL JUSTICE IN OUR TIME 137, 143 (A. E. Dick Howard ed. 1965); *see also* William J. Stuntz, *Self-Defeating Crimes*, 86 VA. L. REV. 1871, 1882 (2000) ("Criminal trials are morality plays. Their public nature, and the rituals that surround them, seem designed for sending messages, both about the system's care not to punish the undeserving and about the deserved nature of the punishment the system imposes.").

   The second quotation is from Abraham S. Goldstein, *Converging Criminal Justice Systems: Guilty Pleas and the Public Interest*, 49 SMU L. REV. 567, 569 (1996).

   The third quotation is from *Witherspoon v. Illinois*, 391 U.S. 510, 519 & n.15 (1968) (explaining also that juries are desirable because they inject "contemporary community values" into the punishment decision); *accord* AKHIL REED AMAR, THE CONSTITUTION AND CRIMINAL PROCEDURE: FIRST PRINCIPLES 122–23 (1997) ("Criminal trials are unavoidably morality plays, focusing on the defendant's moral blameworthiness or lack thereof. And the assessment of his moral culpability is, under the Sixth Amendment, a task for the community, via the jury, and not the judge. . . ."); Kyron Huigens, *Virtue and Inculpation*, 108 HARV. L. REV. 1423, 1462–66 (1995) (justifying the criminal jury as an institution that applies the community's moral sense and sound practical judgment to the context of a particular crime).

2. The concept of street-level bureaucrats making policy by exercising low-level, hidden discretion is from MICHAEL LIPSKY, STREET-LEVEL BUREAUCRACY: DILEMMAS OF THE INDIVIDUAL IN PUBLIC SERVICES 3–25 (updated ed. 2010). On rational apathy and deference to experts, see JOHN R. HIBBING & ELIZABETH THEISS-MORSE, STEALTH DEMOCRACY: AMERICANS' BELIEFS ABOUT HOW GOVERNMENT SHOULD WORK 130–32 (2002) (arguing that citizens neither care nor want to get involved in most governmental decisions and would prefer to defer to neutral experts, but feel pressure to do so only because it seems like the only way to stop "greedy politicians and special interests" from taking self-serving measures at odds with what the public wants).

3. *Cf.* LIPSKY, *supra* note 2, at 54–70 (offering a model of how "relations with clients" constrain and shape street-level bureaucrats' behavior, including those in criminal justice).

4. The best and most recent general history of plea bargaining is GEORGE FISHER, PLEA BARGAINING'S TRIUMPH: A HISTORY OF PLEA BARGAINING IN AMERICA (2003). Other works with substantial historical components, most of which focus

on specific jurisdictions, include THEODORE FERDINAND, BOSTON'S LOWER CRIMINAL COURTS, 1814–1850 (1992); LAWRENCE M. FRIEDMAN & ROBERT V. PERCIVAL, THE ROOTS OF JUSTICE: CRIME AND PUNISHMENT IN ALAMEDA COUNTY, CALIFORNIA 1870–1910, at 173–81 (1981); ALLEN STEINBERG, THE TRANSFORMATION OF CRIMINAL JUSTICE: PHILADELPHIA, 1800–1880 (1989); MARY E. VOGEL, COERCION TO COMPROMISE: PLEA BARGAINING, THE COURTS AND THE MAKING OF POLITICAL AUTHORITY (2007); Mike McConville & Chester Mirsky, *The Rise of Guilty Pleas: New York, 1800–1865*, 22 J.L. & SOC'Y 443 (1995); Raymond Moley, *The Vanishing Jury*, 2 S. CAL. L. REV. 97 (1928); Mary E. Vogel, *The Social Origins of Plea Bargaining: Conflict and the Law in the Process of State Formation, 1830–1860*, 33 LAW & SOC'Y REV. 161 (1999); *Special Issue on Plea Bargaining*, 13 LAW & SOC'Y REV. 185 (1979) (includes important historical articles by Albert W. Alschuler, Lawrence M. Friedman, John H. Langbein, Mark H. Haller, and Lynn M. Mather).

On the role of the Warren Court, see HAROLD J. ROTHWAX, GUILTY: THE COLLAPSE OF CRIMINAL JUSTICE (1996); *see also* Peter Arenella, *Rethinking the Functions of Criminal Procedure: The Warren and Burger Courts' Competing Ideologies*, 72 GEO. L.J. 185, 192 (1983) (reporting that, in the late 1960s, the public believed that the Warren Court had mandated technicalities that prevented the police from stopping crime).

5. *See* Darryl K. Brown, *Democracy and Decriminalization*, 86 TEX. L. REV. 223, 270–71 (2007) (arguing that caseload increases, among other factors, drive plea bargaining); *see also* Malcolm M. Feeley, *Legal Complexity and the Transformation of the Criminal Process: The Origins of Plea Bargaining*, 31 ISRAEL L. REV. 183, 183 (1997) (describing this position as the dominant view in plea-bargaining scholarship).

6. The leading recent history of plea bargaining adroitly explores how prosecutors' and judges' self-interests interacted with the need to dispose of rising civil caseloads. FISHER, *supra* note 4, at 19–58, 111–36.

7. *See infra* chapter V note 24 and accompanying text.

8. For an explanation of how empirical desert differs from more traditional deontological conceptions of desert, see Paul H. Robinson, *Competing Conceptions of Modern Desert: Vengeful, Deontological, and Empirical*, 67 CAMBRIDGE L.J. 145, 148–50 (2008). For the importance of procedural justice, see, for example, TOM R. TYLER, WHY PEOPLE OBEY THE LAW 115–57 (1990).

9. HERBERT L. PACKER, THE LIMITS OF THE CRIMINAL SANCTION 158–73 (1968).

CHAPTER I

1. Where direct evidence of colonial practice is thin, I will cautiously supplement it with evidence about what was going on in England around the same time, on the tentative assumption that colonial practice is likely to have mirrored much of what went on in the mother country. I do so primarily in chapter I.A.2 and secondarily in chapter I.A.3. The former covers the relative lack of professionalization and stiffness in colonial criminal proceedings, while the latter discusses the room colonial justice left for discretion and mercy. Given that the colonies had no law schools and no law books of their own until the very end of the colonial period, the roles for laymen in the colonies must *a fortiori* have been at least as large and flexible as in the mother country.

2. Douglas Greenberg, *Crime, Law Enforcement, and Social Control in Colonial America*, 26 AM. J. LEGAL HIST. 293, 296 (1982) (noting "substantial differences" across and within colonies and that any generalizations about colonial criminal justice are "almost inevitably subject to challenge and exceptions").

3. Lawrence Friedman calls the colonies "tight little islands." LAWRENCE M. FRIEDMAN, CRIME AND PUNISHMENT IN AMERICAN HISTORY 17 (1993). On the homogeneity of colonists' backgrounds and values, see SAMUEL WALKER, POPULAR JUSTICE: A HISTORY OF AMERICAN CRIMINAL JUSTICE 15–17 (2d ed. 1998). New York was exceptional in its "extraordinary heterogeneity." DOUGLAS GREENBERG, CRIME AND LAW ENFORCEMENT IN THE COLONY OF NEW YORK, 1691–1776, at 55–56, 215 (1974).

4. Even well into the eighteenth century in Massachusetts, "nearly all members of society shared common ethical values and imposed those values on the occasional individual who refused to abide by them voluntarily." WILLIAM E. NELSON, AMERICANIZATION OF THE COMMON LAW: THE IMPACT OF LEGAL CHANGE ON MASSACHUSETTS SOCIETY, 1760–1830, at 4 (1975). Popular morality and understandings of sinfulness likewise suffused the administration of criminal justice in England. *See* CYNTHIA B. HERRUP, THE COMMON PEACE: PARTICIPATION AND THE CRIMINAL LAW IN SEVENTEENTH-CENTURY ENGLAND 3, 7 (1987).

    On morals crimes in the colonies, see FRIEDMAN, CRIME AND PUNISHMENT IN AMERICAN HISTORY, *supra* note 3, at 32–36.

5. NATHANIEL HAWTHORNE, THE SCARLET LETTER (Bantam Classic 2003) (1850).

6. On the universality of human weakness, see Eli Faber, *Puritan Criminals: The Economic, Social, and Intellectual Background to Crime in Seventeenth-Century Massachusetts, in* XI PERSPECTIVES IN AMERICAN HISTORY 83, 85–87 (Donald Fleming ed. 1978) (citing Cotton Mather and others); *see also* 4 WILLIAM BLACKSTONE, COMMENTARIES *2; HERRUP, *supra* note 4, at 191 (England).

    As for gallows sermons, of course most audience members had not committed the very crime for which the wrongdoer faced execution. Nevertheless, ministers preaching from the scaffold stressed, for example, that common fornication often led to infanticide, or that common drunkenness caused murders. STUART BANNER, THE DEATH PENALTY: AN AMERICAN HISTORY 33–34 (2002).

    On criminal justice's mission to reintegrate errant sheep, see FRIEDMAN, CRIME AND PUNISHMENT IN AMERICAN HISTORY, *supra* note 3, at 31, 37; NELSON, *supra* note 4, at 39–40.

    Even men condemned to die were still valued as children of God, who could at least symbolically achieve reintegration into society. Thus, colonists made a point of offering condemned prisoner the opportunity to repent and earn God's forgiveness, and if he did, they were likely to empathize and forgive him. BANNER, *supra*, at 32.

7. FRIEDMAN, CRIME AND PUNISHMENT IN AMERICAN HISTORY, *supra* note 3, at 28–29.

8. On the informality of colonial legal training, see LAWRENCE M. FRIEDMAN, A HISTORY OF AMERICAN LAW 81, 83–87 (1973); *see also* WALKER, *supra* note 3, at 31 (noting that, by the time of the Revolution, Massachusetts had fewer than 100 lawyers for its population of 200,000 and that few defendants could afford them).

On Virginia in particular, see A. G. Roeber, *Authority, Law, and Custom: The Rituals of Court Day in Tidewater Virginia, 1720 to 1750*, 37 WM. & MARY Q. (3d Ser.) 29, 34 (1980).

9. On procedural flexibility, see WALKER, *supra* note 3, at 28–29. On the atmospherics of colonial judicial proceedings, see Roeber, *supra* note 8, at 31–32, 35–37, 51 (discussing the Tidewater area of Virginia between 1720 and 1750).

10. On the lack of counsel in English criminal trials, see JOHN H. LANGBEIN, THE ORIGINS OF ADVERSARY CRIMINAL TRIAL 11–12 (2003). On the slow advent of professional prosecution in America, see, for example, FISHER, *supra* Introduction note 4, at 19 & 246 n.1 (noting that Middlesex County, Massachusetts did not receive its first county prosecutor until the early nineteenth century); STEINBERG, *supra* Introduction note 4, at 38 ("During the first half of the nineteenth century, private prosecution dominated criminal justice in Philadelphia. . . . [M]ost criminal prosecutions were initiated by private citizens.").

    On the lack of a systematic criminal-justice bureaucracy, see, for example, McConville & Mirsky, *supra* Introduction note 4, at 448–49, 453 (noting that in New York until 1847, "the District Attorney did not resemble a state agent concerned with orchestrating case outcomes to further social control objectives. Rather, the District Attorney's principal function was to receive the case file assembled by the magistrate and to guide the case to conclusion often representing the private prosecutor at trial, when the prosecutor was not represented by privately retained lawyers").

    On the limited powers exercised by public prosecutors in the early nineteenth century, see McConville & Mirsky, *supra* Introduction note 4, at 447, 465; *e.g.,* JULIUS GOEBEL JR. & T. RAYMOND NAUGHTON, LAW ENFORCEMENT IN COLONIAL NEW YORK: A STUDY IN CRIMINAL PROCEDURE (1664–1776), at 340–41, 347–48, 368 (1944); STEINBERG, *supra* Introduction note 4, at 7.

    Likewise, in England victims played pervasive roles and exercised discretion in initiating criminal cases. *See* HERRUP, *supra* note 4, at 7, 67–92 (seventeenth-century England); PETER KING, CRIME, JUSTICE, AND DISCRETION IN ENGLAND: 1740–1820, at 17–46 (2000).

11. On the original understanding of the Sixth Amendment as limited to the right to hire one's own lawyer: In 1963, the Supreme Court overturned this understanding and broadly guaranteed defense lawyers appointed at the State's expense. Gideon v. Wainwright, 372 U.S. 335 (1963). Earlier, in the 1930s, the Court had begun to create limited rights to appointed counsel, especially in capital cases. *See, e.g.,* Powell v. Alabama, 287 U.S. 45, 71 (1932).

    On colonial defendants' inability to afford their own lawyers, see FRIEDMAN, CRIME AND PUNISHMENT IN AMERICAN HISTORY, *supra* note 3, at 57.

    On representation rates in Maryland, see James D. Rice, *The Criminal Trial Before and After the Lawyers: Authority, Law, and Culture in Maryland Jury Trials, 1681–1837*, 40 AM. J. LEGAL HIST. 455, 457 & tbl. 1 (1996) (noting that between 1767 and 1771 only 27.5% of felony defendants in Frederick County, Maryland retained defense attorneys; between 1818 and 1825, 92.1% had counsel).

    On low representation rates in London and Massachusetts, see FISHER, *supra* Introduction note 4, at 96 & 286 n.14 (citing Charles Lester & Malcolm M. Feeley, *Legal Complexity and the Transformation of the Criminal Process, in* SUBJEKTIVIERUNG DES JUSTIZIELLEN BEWEISVERFAHRENS 355 (André Gouron et al. eds.

1994)). Fisher acknowledges that he has no solid evidence of representation rates in Middlesex County, Massachusetts before 1844 but plausibly infers a sharp rise in representation around 1832. *Id.* at 96–97 & tbl. 4.1.

12. On the speed of English trials, see LANGBEIN, *supra* note 10, at 16–22. On trial speed in the colonies, see Rice, *supra* note 11, at 463 (noting that trials in colonial Maryland lasted less than half an hour, from arraignment through sentencing, and that by 1817 their length had risen to forty to forty-five minutes).

13. On the altercation between the parties, see LANGBEIN, *supra* note 10, at 13–14. On the role of trials in weighing leniency, see *id.* at 57–59; *see also* J. M. BEATTIE, CRIME AND THE COURTS IN ENGLAND, 1660–1800, at 429 (1986); 4 WILLIAM BLACKSTONE, COMMENTARIES *238–*239 (describing juries' frequent reduction of the value of stolen goods below twelve pence, the threshold for hanging, as "pious perjury").

14. FRIEDMAN, CRIME AND PUNISHMENT IN AMERICAN HISTORY, *supra* note 3, at 31, 37, 39–40.

15. On the simplicity of jury instructions, see GOEBEL & NAUGHTON, *supra* note 10, at 666–69; LANGBEIN, *supra* note 10, at 14. Judges' instructions turned from case-specific opinions to abstract, legalistic verbiage over the course of the eighteenth and early nineteenth centuries, as judges increasingly feared appellate reversal. FRIEDMAN, CRIME AND PUNISHMENT IN AMERICAN HISTORY, *supra* note 3, at 246–47.

    On judicial comment on the testimony, see Vicksburg & M. R. Co. v. Putnam, 118 U.S. 545, 553 (1886) (declaring that judges' expressions of their views are unreviewable on appeal so long as they misstate no rule of law, and citing cases back to 1830 to show the long-standing foundations of this rule); FRIEDMAN, CRIME AND PUNISHMENT IN AMERICAN HISTORY, *supra* note 3, at 237, 245–46.

    On judicial involvement in questioning, see LANGBEIN, *supra* note 10, at 15–16, 28–32. On judges' suggestion of lesser, noncapital verdicts, see BEATTIE, *supra* note 13, at 286, 426. On judges' discouragement of guilty pleas, see LANGBEIN, *supra* note 10, at 19–20.

16. On jurors' comments and questions, see LANGBEIN, *supra* note 10, at 319. On juries' power to interpret the law for themselves, see NELSON, *supra* note 4, at 3; Matthew P. Harrington, *The Law-Finding Function of the American Jury*, 1999 WIS. L. REV. 377, 385–404. On juries' political and moral role, see AMAR, THE CONSTITUTION AND CRIMINAL PROCEDURE, *supra* Introduction note 1, at 90, 122–23.

17. On the public nature of trials, see U.S. CONST. amend. VI (guaranteeing the right to a speedy, public trial in the district where the crime had been committed). On trials as public spectacles and topics of gossip, see LAURA F. EDWARDS, THE PEOPLE AND THEIR PEACE: LEGAL CULTURE AND THE TRANSFORMATION OF INEQUALITY IN THE POST-REVOLUTIONARY SOUTH 75–77 (2009) (discussing antebellum South). On trials' role in educating the public and ensuring public confidence in the system, see AKHIL REED AMAR, THE BILL OF RIGHTS: CREATION AND RECONSTRUCTION 113 (2000).

18. AMAR, THE BILL OF RIGHTS, *supra* note 17, at 113–14. True, colonial sheriffs sometimes packed or stacked juries to influence their decisions, to the displeasure of colonists. *See* VALERIE P. HANS & NEIL VIDMAR, JUDGING THE JURY 29, 35–36 (1986); *see also* 1 EDWARD COKE, THE FIRST INSTITUTES OF THE LAWES OF ENGLAND, OR A

COMMENTARY ON LITTLETON *156a (recognizing the sheriff's duty to stack juries in favor of the King in cases to which the King was a party). To the extent that sheriffs did so, they undercut the community's participation and the mirroring of community sentiment. To combat this abuse, the Sixth Amendment guarantees impartial juries drawn from the local vicinage. Courts read this provision as requiring that jury venires represent a fair cross-section of the community. Duren v. Missouri, 439 U.S. 357, 363–67 (1979); Taylor v. Louisiana, 419 U.S. 522, 527–31 (1975).

19. BANNER, *supra* note 6, at 6–8.

20. On slave justice in North Carolina and elsewhere in the south, see BANNER, *supra* note 6, at 9. On Virginia and New York, see FRIEDMAN, CRIME AND PUNISHMENT IN AMERICAN HISTORY, *supra* note 3, at 44.

21. On the rarity of executions for morals crimes, see BANNER, *supra* note 6, at 6–7; *see also* EDGAR J. MCMANUS, LAW AND LIBERTY IN EARLY NEW ENGLAND: CRIMINAL JUSTICE AND DUE PROCESS, 1620–1692, at 173–75 (1993). On Pennsylvania's leniency and the rarity of hangings for burglary, robbery, or theft, see FRIEDMAN, CRIME AND PUNISHMENT IN AMERICAN HISTORY, *supra* note 3, at 41–42.

22. On English juries' differing responses to menacing and more minor property crimes, see LANGBEIN, *supra* note 10, at 58–59 (reporting on a sample of Old Bailey cases from the 1750s); *see also* THOMAS ANDREW GREEN, VERDICT ACCORDING TO CONSCIENCE 276–78 (1985).

    On leniency toward shoplifters and house thieves, and acquittals of sheep stealers, see BEATTIE, *supra* note 13, at 428–29 & tbl. 8.5 (reporting verdicts in capital property offenses at Surrey Assizes between 1660 and 1800). Conversely, once English criminal law authorized manslaughter convictions, which were eligible for noncapital punishment, juries were much more likely to convict and less likely to find self-defense to circumvent the death penalty. GREEN, *supra* note 22, at 121–22.

23. On benefit of clergy in England, see BEATTIE, *supra* note 13, at 141–42, 144; BANNER, *supra* note 6, at 62–64; GREEN, *supra* note 22, at 117–18; LANGBEIN, *supra* note 10, at 192–93. On benefit of clergy in the colonies, see FRIEDMAN, CRIME AND PUNISHMENT IN AMERICAN HISTORY, *supra* note 3, at 43–44. Of course, sparing slaves may have served the economic interest of the individual slave's owner, though it undercut the collective penal control exercised by slaveowners as a class.

24. BEATTIE, *supra* note 13, at 142–43, 452 (discussing English experience); LANGBEIN, *supra* note 10, at 192–93 (discussing English practice).

25. BANNER, *supra* note 6, at 56–58; BEATTIE, *supra* note 13, at 432–35 & tbl. 8.7, 437–39 (discussing jury verdicts in Surrey); GREEN, *supra* note 22, at 282–83; LANGBEIN, *supra* note 10, at 324.

26. BANNER, *supra* note 6, at 55–56; BEATTIE, *supra* note 13, at 440–49; GREEN, *supra* note 22, at 283–84. The humane impulses of public opinion played an important role in securing mercy even for deserving offenders without substantial connections. KING, *supra* note 10, at 326–27.

27. BANNER, *supra* note 6, at 18–20, 58–61 (quoting AN ACCOUNT OF THE ROBBERIES COMMITTED BY JOHN MORRISON (Philadelphia: s.n. 1750–51)); GREEN, *supra* note 22, at 283; HERRUP, *supra* note 4, at 158, 185.

28. BANNER, *supra* note 6, at 65–68; FRIEDMAN, CRIME AND PUNISHMENT IN AMERICAN HISTORY, *supra* note 3, at 37–41, 48; MCMANUS, *supra* note 21, at 164–73, 201–10 (tabulating typical crimes and penalties in seventeenth-century Massachusetts, Connecticut, and Rhode Island).

29. HAWTHORNE, *supra* note 5, at 54.

30. On the greater solemnity of American executions, compare V.A.C. GATRELL, THE HANGING TREE: EXECUTION AND THE ENGLISH PEOPLE 1770–1868, at 56–69 (1994), *with* BANNER, *supra* note 6, at 24, 27–28. The supposed gallows poem is from THE DYING PENITENT; OR, THE AFFECTING SPEECH OF LEVI AMES, TAKEN FROM HIS OWN MOUTH, AS DELIVERED BY HIM AT THE GOAL [*sic*] IN BOSTON THE MORNING OF HIS EXECUTION (Boston: s.n., 1773), *quoted in* BANNER, *supra* note 6, at 11–13.

31. FRIEDMAN, CRIME AND PUNISHMENT IN AMERICAN HISTORY, *supra* note 3, at 37 (quoting PROCEEDINGS OF THE COUNTY COURT OF CHARLES COUNTY, 1658–1666, at 560 (J. Hall Pleasants ed.), *in* 53 ARCHIVES OF MARYLAND (1936)).

32. BANNER, *supra* note 6, at 29–34, 41–43. The extensive pamphlet literature of gallows speeches reflects the social expectation that even condemned men would repent, instruct their hearers, and earn some measure of redemption. "The men and women whose executions we have noted were, for the most part, doing more than just accepting their fates. They were the willing central participants in a theatre of punishment, which offered not merely a spectacle, but also a reinforcement of certain values." J. A. Sharpe, *"Last Dying Speeches": Religion, Ideology and Public Execution in Seventeenth-Century England*, 107 PAST & PRESENT 144, 156 (1985).

33. On spectators' manifesting their disapproval, see BANNER, *supra* note 6, at 32. On punishment as a reinforcer of social solidarity, see EMILE DURKHEIM, THE DIVISION OF LABOR IN SOCIETY 57–60, 62–64 (W.D. Halls trans., The Free Press 1st paperback ed. 1997).

34. FRIEDMAN, CRIME AND PUNISHMENT IN AMERICAN HISTORY, *supra* note 3, at 25–26, 31, 37, 39–40, 47; *see* KAI T. ERICKSON, WAYWARD PURITANS: A STUDY IN THE SOCIOLOGY OF DEVIANCE 194 (1966); GEORGE LEE HASKINS, LAW AND AUTHORITY IN EARLY MASSACHUSETTS: A STUDY IN TRADITION AND DESIGN 206–11 (1960); Gail Sussman Marcus, *"Due Execution of the Generall Rules of Righteousnesse": Criminal Procedure in New Haven Town and Colony, 1638–1658*, *in* SAINTS & REVOLUTIONARIES: ESSAYS ON EARLY AMERICAN HISTORY 130–31 (David H. Hall et al. eds. 1984); John M. Murrin, *Magistrates, Sinners, and a Precarious Liberty: Trial by Jury in Seventeenth-Century New England*, *in id.* at 152, 173–75; *see also* EDWARDS, *supra* note 17, at 83–85 (noting the importance of repentance, forgiveness, and reintegration in antebellum Carolinas and the understanding that crime did not permanently mark someone as a criminal).

    By the same logic, defendants often confessed or pleaded guilty to show their contrition and lack of defiance. Having acknowledged their wrongs and vindicated their victims and society's norms, they hoped to earn lighter sentences. Conversely, going to trial could appear to be an act of defiance that required heavier punishment to humble the unrepentant. *See* Marcus, *supra* at 130–31. Thus, there was some legal pressure to confess and plead guilty, though far less than the plea-bargaining machinery exerts today.

35. On sanctions of restitution, fines, extra damages, and workhouses, see FRIEDMAN, CRIME AND PUNISHMENT IN AMERICAN HISTORY, *supra* note 3, at 38–39,

48–50. The hog thief example is from Raphael Semmes, Crime and Punishment in Early Maryland 67 (1938). On punishment as a means of promoting accountability, see Donald Braman, *Punishment and Accountability: Understanding and Reforming Criminal Sanctions in America*, 53 UCLA L. Rev. 1143, 1167–71 (2006).

36. On paternal punishment of prodigal sons, see Friedman, Crime and Punishment in American History, *supra* note 3, at 52. The biblical reference is to the Parable of the Prodigal Son, found at *Luke* 15:11–32. In that parable, the prodigal son stands ready to admit his profligacy and to say that he deserves to be treated as a servant, not a son. But as soon as the father sees his son from a great distance, he has compassion, runs to kiss him, and rejoices over his return to life. Likewise, in *The Scarlet Letter*, even though Hester must wear the "A" all her life, she redeems herself through her good works and the community eventually forgives her. Hawthorne, *supra* note 5, at 145–47, 234.

   Today, in contrast, ex-cons face a permanent grudge, almost ineradicable resentment, particularly when seeking work or housing. *See* Anthony C. Thompson, Releasing Prisoners, Redeeming Communities: Reentry, Race, and Politics 68–121 (2008) (discussing the collateral consequences of criminal convictions on housing, health care, and employment); Nora Demleitner, *"Collateral Damage": No Re-Entry for Drug Offenders*, 47 Vill. L. Rev. 1027, 1036–39 (2002) (same, for housing and employment); David Thacher, *The Rise of Criminal Background Screening in Rental Housing*, 33 Law & Soc. Inquiry 5, 12 (2008) (same, for housing).

   Perhaps today we are less willing to forgive ex-cons in part because society has never seen them receive their just deserts publicly and in part because imprisonment has estranged them.

37. Faber, *supra* note 6, at 137–44. Faber located 468 known criminals who lived in Middlesex County during this time and was able to trace the later history of 73 of them, of whom 67 were reintegrated. *Id.* at 137. He also noted that the women who went on to marry had not all married men with whom they had been convicted of fornicating. Five fornicators went on to marry other men, and several women had been convicted of other crimes, such as denouncing a minister in church, and also went on to marry. *Id.* at 142–43. William Offutt concluded: "Clearly, the criminal law touched in some way every level of this society; just as clearly such accusations did not ostracize the defendant from further participation in public life." William M. Offutt, Jr., Of "Good Laws" and "Good Men": Law and Society in the Delaware Valley, 1680–1710, at 186 (1995).

38. Offutt, *supra* note 37, at 186–91. Offutt defined recidivists as those charged two or more times during the thirty-year period of his study. *Id.* at 186. Offutt's most striking finding, that recidivists were much more likely to hold high or lesser legal office, was statistically significant with a chi-square probability of 0.001. *Id.* at 190 tbl. 28.

39. Banner, *supra* note 6, at 31–32; *see, e.g.*, Daniel A. Cohen, Pillars of Salt, Monuments of Grace: New England Crime Literature and the Origins of American Popular Culture, 1674–1860, at 59–80 (1993) (describing three conversion narratives of early eighteenth-century New England convicts awaiting execution); Helen Prejean, Dead Man Walking 93 (1993) (describing a condemned man's apology to the father of his murder victim right before being executed).

40. Women of course could not serve on juries. Moreover, some laws and prosecutions targeted women specifically and reinforced patriarchal discipline, ranging from punishments for common scolds to the Salem witchcraft prosecutions. *See* FRIEDMAN, CRIME AND PUNISHMENT IN AMERICAN HISTORY, *supra* note 3, at 38, 45–47, 242–43. For example, the shape of fornication and rape laws, including the marital-rape exception, was designed not to protect women's sexual autonomy but to reinforce men's control over women's chastity. *See* Anne M. Coughlin, *Sex and Guilt*, 84 VA. L. REV. 1 (1998). Also, the older common law had authorized husbands to beat their wives "within reasonable bounds" to correct them and maintain order. More recent law, however, had begun to cast doubt on the husband's right to beat his wife, though "the lower rank of people" clung to the husband's ancient privilege, and courts continued to permit beating of wives who were guilty of "gross misbehaviour." 1 WILLIAM BLACKSTONE, COMMENTARIES *444–45 (bk. I, ch. XV) (citations omitted); *see also* Reva B. Siegel, *"The Rule of Love": Wife Beating as Prerogative and Privacy*, 105 YALE L.J. 2117 (1996).

41. THE DECLARATION OF INDEPENDENCE para. 11, 20; U.S. CONST. art. III, § 2, cl. 3; *id.* amends. V, VI.

42. *See* FRIEDMAN, CRIME AND PUNISHMENT IN AMERICAN HISTORY, *supra* note 3, at 54, 127; ADAM JAY HIRSCH, THE RISE OF THE PENITENTIARY: PRISONS AND PUNISHMENT IN EARLY AMERICA 35–39, 45 (1992).

43. *See* JEREMY BENTHAM, AN INTRODUCTION TO THE PRINCIPLES OF MORALS AND LEGISLATION 1–2, 170–71 & n.1 (Oxford: Clarendon Press 1907) (new corrected ed. 1823) (also noting the role of criminal law in incapacitating and reforming wrongdoers, but rejecting retribution because only a greater future benefit can justify inflicting pain); CESARE BECCARIA, AN ESSAY ON CRIMES AND PUNISHMENTS 21, 47, 93–94, 153, 158–60 (Edward D. Ingraham trans., Philip H. Nicklin 2d Am. ed. 1819). This edition includes a warmly approving commentary by Voltaire, reflecting how well Beccaria's project of rational, predictable, codified, utilitarian punishments fit within the Enlightenment. David Rothman argues that Enlightenment rationalists, especially Beccaria, were instrumental in America's shift from treating crime as sin to addressing it as a problem of social control. DAVID J. ROTHMAN, THE DISCOVERY OF THE ASYLUM: SOCIAL ORDER AND DISORDER IN THE NEW REPUBLIC 58–62 (Aldine de Gruyter rev. ed. 2002). Rothman's argument has proven to be quite influential, though controversial. *But see* HIRSCH, *supra* note 42, at xiii-xiv, 13–31 (disputing Rothman's emphasis on Beccaria and tracing the ideology of imprisonment to sixteenth-century English workhouses, though also acknowledging the influences of eighteenth-century Enlightenment rationalism and eighteenth- and nineteenth-century American religious optimism).

44. CESARE LOMBROSO, CRIMINAL MAN 43, 48–49, 51, 53, 56–57, 91–93, 108–09, 336 (Mary Gibson & Nicole Hahn Rafter trans., Duke Univ. Press 2006) (1876–97).

45. NELSON, *supra* note 4, at 118. By the last decade of the eighteenth century,

> [t]he protection of order and property was becoming an end in itself rather than merely a means to the pursuit of community morality—an end to which men with differing ethical ideals could adhere.... At least in the context of the criminal process, protection of property and hence economic stability was becoming an important value in itself, completely separate from any lingering concern that law may have had for the protection of ethical unity.

Id. at 120–21.

46. FRIEDMAN, CRIME AND PUNISHMENT IN AMERICAN HISTORY, *supra* note 3, at 28.

47. *Id.* at 68–70, 150; McMANUS, *supra* note 21, at 67–70 (discussing the role of neighbors as holy watchers or paid informants who informed on victimless crime in New England); WALKER, *supra* note 3, at 50–56.

48. FRIEDMAN, CRIME AND PUNISHMENT IN AMERICAN HISTORY, *supra* note 3, at 359–60; WALKER, *supra* note 3, at 131–37.

    Lately, the community-policing movement has begun to budge the pendulum back toward local control and interaction. *See generally* MATTHEW J. HICKMAN, BUREAU OF JUSTICE STATISTICS, COMMUNITY POLICING IN LOCAL POLICE DEPARTMENTS, 1997 AND 1999, at 1, 5–10 (2001); Mark Harrison Moore, *Problem-Solving and Community Policing, in* MODERN POLICING 99 (Michael Tonry & Norval Morris eds., 1992); David Alan Sklansky, *Police and Democracy*, 103 MICH. L. REV. 1699 (2005) (linking the move from progressive insulation to community policing to the mid-twentieth-century rise in democratic theory emphasizing community deliberation and participation).

49. *See* NELSON, *supra* note 4, at 2 (noting the explosion of American judicial reports, legal treatises, and legal periodicals between 1760 and 1830); STEINBERG, *supra* Introduction note 4, at 171–232 (discussing how police and police magistrates displaced private prosecutors in Philadelphia in the second half of the nineteenth century); NICHOLAS PARRILLO, AGAINST THE PROFIT MOTIVE: THE TRANSFORMATION OF AMERICAN GOVERNMENT, 1780-1840 ch. 7, at 24-61 (forthcoming Yale Univ. Press; partial manuscript, on file with the author) (noting that in the nineteenth century, legislatures raised conviction fees for prosecuting victimless crimes such as gambling and liquor-law violations to encourage prosecutions, but they ultimately backed away from this model because prosecutors were pursuing too many technically guilty defendants who were only marginally blameworthy).

50. On retained counsel in the nineteenth century, see *supra* note 11 and accompanying text (discussing evidence from England, Maryland, and Massachusetts). On appointed counsel in the nineteenth century, see FRIEDMAN, CRIME AND PUNISHMENT IN AMERICAN HISTORY, *supra* note 3, at 245.

    The quotation of the prominent defense lawyer is from Mayer C. Goldman, *The Need for a Public Defender*, 8 J. CRIM. L. & CRIMINOLOGY 273, 274 (1917); *accord* Mayer C. Goldman, *Public Defenders for the Poor in Criminal Cases*, 26 VA. L. REV. 275, 275 n.*, 280 (1940) ("The harmonious coöperation between the District Attorney and the public defender would necessarily result in a higher approach to justice. The public defender, being a public official, would not be interested in seeking to pervert justice by trying to acquit a guilty defendant, through fair means or foul, as is frequently done by private counsel in what they mistakenly presume is the proper function of counsel."); Michael McConville & Chester L. Mirsky, *Criminal Defense of the Poor in New York City*, 15 N.Y.U. REV. L. & SOC. CHANGE 581, 598–99 (1986–87).

    On the current reading of the Sixth Amendment, see Argersinger v. Hamlin, 407 U.S. 25, 40 (1972) (misdemeanants who face actual imprisonment); Gideon v. Wainwright, 372 U.S. 335 (1963) (felony defendants).

51. On the growth of public prosecutors' roles, see LANGBEIN, *supra* note 10, at 116–36, 145–47 (discussing parallel developments in English prosecution in the

mid-eighteenth century); Juan Cardenas, *The Crime Victim in the Prosecutorial Process*, 9 HARV. J.L. & PUB. POL'Y 357 (1986). On the exclusion of victims, see Douglas E. Beloof & Paul G. Cassell, *The Crime Victim's Right to Attend the Trial: The Reascendent National Consensus*, 9 LEWIS & CLARK L. REV. 481, 484–503 (2005).

52. On defense lawyers' growing roles, see LANGBEIN, *supra* note 10, at 266–73 (discussing parallel development in late eighteenth century English criminal trials); *see also* Rice, *supra* note 11, at 460–62 (noting the differences between a Maryland trial with no defense lawyer in 1681 and one with lawyers in 1831). On the admissibility of defendants' criminal records, see 2 JOHN HENRY WIGMORE, A TREATISE ON THE SYSTEM OF EVIDENCE IN TRIALS AT COMMON LAW §§ 980, 983(4) (1904).

53. *See* LANGBEIN, *supra* note 10, at 136–45, 269–70 (discussing parallel developments in England, as well as the fear of perjury in London circa 1730); Rice, *supra* note 11, at 461–62 (noting the difference that lawyers' detailed questioning and witness coaching made in an 1831 Maryland trial).

54 On the length of jury selection, see FRIEDMAN, CRIME AND PUNISHMENT IN AMERICAN HISTORY, *supra* note 3, at 243–44 (discussing extensive voir dire questioning by lawyers and noting that it took twenty-one days to pick a jury in the infamous Chicago Haymarket case); Rice, *supra* note 11, at 460 (noting that in Maryland, the lawyers' jury selection in an 1831 case took one or two hours but the *pro se* defendant's jury selection in a 1681 case took only five or ten minutes).

On the use of evidentiary rules to hem in juries, see FRIEDMAN, CRIME AND PUNISHMENT IN AMERICAN HISTORY, *supra*, at 248–49 ("In some ways jurors were also positively forbidden to use their common sense. Why else treat so many obviously relevant facts as *legally* irrelevant," such as evidence that the accused had committed prior similar crimes?); *see also* Rice, *supra*, at 462 (noting Maryland defense lawyers' efforts to exclude adverse testimony).

On the lengthening of trials, see FRIEDMAN, CRIME AND PUNISHMENT IN AMERICAN HISTORY, *supra*, at 245; John H. Langbein, *Torture and Plea Bargaining*, 46 U. CHI. L. REV. 3, 10–11 (1978) (noting that in the 1730s, the Old Bailey heard twelve to twenty felony trials per day, whereas in 1968 the average felony jury trial in Los Angeles took 7.2 days). Fisher questions the link between trial lengths and plea bargaining, noting that nineteenth-century Middlesex County, Massachusetts trials stabilized at just under two trials per judge per day, though murder trials lengthened from three or four days to 6.6 days at the end of the century). FISHER, *supra* Introduction note 4, at 118–21. In Maryland, however, trials had crept up from thirty to forty-five minutes by 1818; but when lawyers began to get involved, jury selection alone could take an hour or two. Rice, *supra*, at 460, 463. Even if Fisher is right that trial length was not the driving force behind plea bargaining's rise, Langbein's numbers still show that the introduction of lawyers and their attendant rules and machinations went hand-in-hand with longer, more obscure trials.

55. FRIEDMAN, CRIME AND PUNISHMENT IN AMERICAN HISTORY, *supra* note 3, at 245–47. The leading case that declared that juries must follow the law declared by the court was Sparf v. United States, 156 U.S. 51, 106 (1895). *See generally* Harrington, *supra* note 16 (tracing the diminution of the jury's law-finding function over the course of the nineteenth century).

56. On the trend toward direct local elections of prosecutors, see JOAN JACOBY, THE AMERICAN PROSECUTOR: A SEARCH FOR IDENTITY 24–26 (1980). On the

part-time status of many prosecutors, see FRIEDMAN, CRIME AND PUNISHMENT IN AMERICAN HISTORY, *supra* note 3, at 30 n.*.

On prosecutors' incentives to dispose of their caseloads, see FISHER, *supra* Introduction note 4, at 13, 42–43; *see also* Albert W. Alschuler, *Plea Bargaining and Its History*, 13 LAW & SOC'Y REV. 211, 225, 233–36 (1979) (discussing the historical roles of workloads, time, and expense in encouraging charge bargaining and other forms of plea bargaining).

57. FISHER, *supra* Introduction note 4, at 40–44, 98 (discussing a case study of Middlesex County, Massachusetts).

58. *See id.* at 21–44, 155–74 (focusing on Middlesex County, Massachusetts, but also discussing how the presence or absence of public prosecutors, fixed sentences, gradations of crimes, and the ability to dismiss charges explain the lack of plea bargaining in eighteenth-century London and its presence in nineteenth-century New York and California).

59. *Id.* at 62–90.

60. *Id.* at 121–24, 129–36.

61. A leading sociological study of plea bargaining observed the same forces at work among new prosecutors, defense counsel, and judges, who gradually learn the ropes and come to see the advantages of plea bargaining. MILTON HEUMANN, PLEA BARGAINING: THE EXPERIENCES OF PROSECUTORS, JUDGES, AND DEFENSE ATTORNEYS 53–91, 99–126, 134–52 (1978).

62. In Alameda County in the 1880s and 1890s, 46% of adjudicated defendants pleaded guilty either initially or later, while 54% were convicted or acquitted at jury trials. Between 1900 and 1910, the figures were 57% and 43%, respectively. FRIEDMAN & PERCIVAL, *supra* Introduction note 4, at 173 tbl. 5.11 (1981) (noting also that these percentages exclude judicial dismissals and continuances).

On New York, see McConville & Mirsky, *supra* Introduction note 4, at 466 fig. 3 (showing that by 1890, roughly 75% of New York City criminal cases were resolved by guilty plea, 15% by trial, and 10% by discharge); Moley, *supra* Introduction note 4, at 108 (showing, in a graph, guilty-plea rates in adjudicated cases in 1899 of 80% in New York and Kings Counties (Manhattan and Brooklyn), just over 85% in six rural New York counties, and just over 80% statewide).

On Middlesex County, see FISHER, *supra* Introduction note 4, at 161. On guilty-plea rates today, see BUREAU OF JUSTICE STATISTICS, SOURCEBOOK OF CRIMINAL JUSTICE STATISTICS ONLINE tbls. 5.34.2009 (reflecting a 96.3% guilty-plea rate for adjudicated defendants in federal court in 2007), 5.46.2004 (showing that 95% of state felony convictions resulted from guilty pleas in 2004), *available at* http://www.albany.edu/sourcebook/tost_5.html.

63. FRIEDMAN, CRIME AND PUNISHMENT IN AMERICAN HISTORY, *supra* note 3, at 49.

64. *Id.* at 77.

65. *Id.* at 77–78; HIRSCH, *supra* note 42, at 59. Several colonies, especially Pennsylvania, had already been sentencing convicts to hard labor through much of the preceding century. HIRSCH, *supra*, at 28.

66. Gustave de Beaumont & Alexis de Tocqueville, On the Penitentiary System in the United States and Its Application in France 37–41, 46, 56–57 (S. Ill. Univ. Press 1964) (Francis Lieber trans. 1833); Friedman, Crime and Punishment in American History, *supra* note 3, at 78–79; Hirsch, *supra* note 42, at 29; Andrew Skotnicki, Religion and the Development of the American Penal System 30–36, 39–40 (2000).

67. Friedman, Crime and Punishment in American History, *supra* note 3, at 79–80.

68. Beaumont & Tocqueville, *supra* note 66, at 41–42 (noting that many prisoners at Auburn who were placed in solitary confinement without labor fell into depression, went insane, or tried to commit suicide); Hirsch, *supra* note 42, at 62–64; E.C. Wines & Theodore W. Dwight, Report on the Prisons and Reformatories of the United States and Canada, Made to the Legislature of New York, January, 1867, at 61–62 (1867) (surveying various states' and Canada's prisons and lamenting that not one of them focused primarily on reformation or was effective at reforming inmates).

69. On Zebulon Brockway's views, see James J. Beha II, Note, *Redemption to Reform: The Intellectual Origins of the Prison Reform Movement*, 63 N.Y.U. Ann. Surv. Am. L. 773, 783–97 (2008).
    On the efficacy of rehabilitation: While there is an ongoing debate about the efficacy of rehabilitation, one prominent meta-analysis of 231 studies was widely read as concluding that "nothing works." D. Lipton, R. Martinson & J. Wilks, Effectiveness of Correctional Treatment—A Survey of Treatment Evaluation Studies (1975); Robert Martinson, *What Works? Questions and Answers About Prison Reform*, 35 Pub. Interest 22 (1974). Martinson's 1974 study marked a pendulum shift away from hopes in rehabilitation back toward retributivism.

70. Revolutionary-era reformers hoped that corporal punishment would soon die out. As Benjamin Rush put it in his address to the Society for Promoting Political Enquiries: "I cannot help entertaining a hope, that the time is not very distant, when the gallows, the pillory, the stocks, the whipping-post, and the wheel-barrow (the usual engines of public punishments) will be connected with the history of the rack and the stake, as marks of the barbarity of ages and countries, and as melancholy proofs of the feeble operation of reason and religion, upon the human mind." Benjamin Rush, An Enquiry into the Effects of Public Punishments upon Criminals and upon Society (Philadelphia 1787).
    On reformers' reliance on prison as a substitute for corporal and shaming punishments, see Friedman, Crime and Punishment in American History, *supra* note 3, at 74–75, 77; Myra C. Glenn, Campaigns Against Corporal Punishment: Prisoners, Sailors, Women, and Children in Antebellum America (1984); Michael Stephen Hindus, Prison and Plantation: Crime, Justice, and Authority in Massachusetts and South Carolina, 1767–1878 (1980); Hirsch, *supra* note 42, at 38–39 (1992).
    Dickens' trenchant criticisms of prisons are in Charles Dickens, American Notes for General Circulation 111–13 (Patricia Ingram ed., Penguin Classics 2000) (1842) (also insisting that "because [imprisonment's] ghastly signs and tokens are not so palpable to the eye and sense of touch as scars upon the flesh; because its wounds are not upon the surface, and it extorts few cries that human ears can hear: therefore I the more denounce it, as a secret

punishment which slumbering humanity is not roused up to stay"); *cf.* MICHEL
FOUCAULT, DISCIPLINE AND PUNISH: THE BIRTH OF THE PRISON 7–19, 23, 293–
308 (Alan Sheridan trans., Vintage Books 2d ed. 1995) (1975) (arguing that the
shift from punishing body to soul allowed law to become a more invasive and pervasive tool for social control of disorder, as opposed to simply a response to a discrete crime).

71. The ban on interstate trade in prison-made goods is at 18 U.S.C. § 1761 (2006).
The requirement that prisons pay prevailing wages for prison labor is at 18 U.S.C.
§ 1761(c)(2) (2006). *See generally* Stephen P. Garvey, *Freeing Prisoners' Labor*,
50 STAN. L. REV. 339, 358–67 (1998).

　　Statistics on prison labor today are found in THE 2002 CORRECTIONS YEAR-
BOOK: ADULT CORRECTIONS 118 (Camille Graham Camp ed. 2003).

72. Before the Civil War, a few Northern states abolished the death penalty entirely.
Many more greatly restricted its use, abolishing it for robbery, burglary, and sometimes sodomy, rape, and arson. Some states that retained the death penalty for homicide limited it to murder. Many divided murder into degrees and retained the death
penalty only for first-degree murder and treason. Southern states retained the death
penalty on paper for a wider range of crimes for whites, and in practice for free blacks
and slaves. BANNER, *supra* note 6, at 131–43; FRIEDMAN, CRIME AND PUNISHMENT
IN AMERICAN HISTORY, *supra* note 3, at 73–74. Capital punishment kept declining
in the North in the century after the Civil War, with more states abolishing it and
others using it much less frequently. BANNER, *supra*, at 220–30. In the last half-century, the Supreme Court has restricted the death penalty to homicide and treason,
abolishing it for rape and briefly halting it entirely. Furman v. Georgia, 408 U.S. 232
(1972) (invalidating existing death-penalty laws because they did not limit arbitrary,
random, or discriminatory application of the penalty, and thus halting executions
across America); Gregg v. Georgia, 428 U.S. 153 (1976) (approving Georgia's revised
post-*Furman* death penalty statute and thus allowing executions to resume); Coker
v. Georgia, 433 U.S. 584 (1977) (striking down the death penalty for rape of an adult
woman); Kennedy v. Louisiana, 554 U.S. 407 (2008) (invalidating the death penalty
for the rape of a child). Of course, the Court has imposed many other procedural and
substantive limits on capital punishment too numerous to summarize here.

　　On the roles of disgust and elitism in the decline of public executions, see
BANNER, *supra* note 6, at 148–53; FRIEDMAN, CRIME AND PUNISHMENT IN AMERI-
CAN HISTORY, *supra* note 3, at 75–76.

73. BANNER, *supra* note 6, at 154–63, 193–94, 197–99, 206.

74. FRIEDMAN, CRIME AND PUNISHMENT IN AMERICAN HISTORY, *supra* note 3, at
179–92.

75. JAMES MEASE, OBSERVATIONS ON THE PENITENTIARY SYSTEM, AND PENAL CODE
OF PENNSYLVANIA: WITH SUGGESTIONS FOR THEIR IMPROVEMENT 71 App. (Philadelphia: Clark & Raser 1828) (reprinting an essay originally published in Philadelphia newspapers in 1820); CHRISTEN JENSEN, THE PARDONING POWER IN THE
AMERICAN STATE 26 (1922).

76. JENSEN, *supra* note 75, at 26–28.

77. *Id.* at 29–64; Rachel E. Barkow, *The Ascent of the Administrative State and the
Demise of Mercy*, 121 HARV. L. REV. 1332 (2008).

78. *See id.*; Michael Heise, *Mercy by the Numbers: An Empirical Analysis of Clemency and Its Structure*, 89 VA. L. REV. 239, 251–52 (2003) (finding that the use of executive clemency in capital cases has steadily declined since 1973); *see also* MARGARET COLGATE LOVE, RELIEF FROM THE COLLATERAL CONSEQUENCES OF A CRIMINAL CONVICTION: A STATE-BY-STATE RESOURCE GUIDE App. B (2006).

79. FISHER, *supra* Introduction note 4, at 186–94; *Legislation—Indeterminate Sentencing Laws—The Adolescence of Peno-correctional Legislation*, 50 HARV. L. REV. 677, 683 (1937) ("The correctional benefits which should result from imprisonment under an indeterminate sentence have often been lost by the mechanical application of parole"); *State Board Tells of Parole System*, N.Y. TIMES, June 12, 1926, at 7 (reporting parole board members' testimony that they were obligated to parole inmates after the minimum sentence unless the inmates had broken prison rules); *see also* JENSEN, *supra* note 75, at 88–96 (discussing the standardization of parole and automatic parole eligibility upon completion of a minimum term, as well as consideration of behavior in prison).

80. The federal Sentencing Reform Act of 1984 is Pub. L. No. 98–473, tit. II, ch. II, § 218(a)(5), 98 Stat. 1837, 2027 (repealing 18 U.S.C. § 4201 et seq. (1988) and thus abolishing the Parole Commission); 18 U.S.C. § 3624(b) (2006) (authorizing good-time credits of fifty-four days per year in prison); *see also* KATE STITH & JOSÉ A. CABRANES, FEAR OF JUDGING: SENTENCING GUIDELINES IN THE FEDERAL COURTS 40, 42, 63 & tbl. 1 (1998) (noting that federal inmates went from serving 47% to 85% of their nominal sentences after the Federal Sentencing Guidelines took effect).

On state truth-in-sentencing laws, see Office of Justice Programs, Bureau of Justice Statistics, Reentry Trends in the U.S.: Releases From State Prison, http://bjs.ojp.usdoj.gov/content/reentry/releases.cfm (last visited Nov. 30, 2011) (noting that sixteen states have abolished discretionary parole for all offenders, with four of them having narrow exceptions for some homicides or very long sentences); TODD REIMERS, SENATE RESEARCH CTR., PAROLE: THEN AND NOW 1–7 (1999) (noting that by 1999, "14 states had abolished discretionary parole for all offenders, and 21 others had severely limited its use"); Joan Petersilia, *Parole and Prisoner Reentry in the United States*, 26 CRIME & JUST. 479, 480, 496 tbl. 1 (1999).

Even those states that retain discretionary parole have substantially curtailed its use. From 1976 to 1999, the fraction of state prison releases that were by discretionary parole fell from 65% to 24%. Dhammika Dharmapala et al., *Legislatures, Judges, and Parole Boards: The Allocation of Discretion Under Determinate Sentencing*, 62 FLA. L. REV. 1037, 1048 (2009). Even as late as 1999, 42% of adults being paroled were on discretionary parole; by 2008, that figure had fallen to 26.6%. *Compare* DEP'T OF JUSTICE, U.S. CORRECTIONAL POPULATION REACHES 6.3 MILLION MEN AND WOMEN: REPRESENTS 3.1 PERCENT OF THE ADULT U.S. POPULATION tbl. 6 (2000), *available at* http://bjs.ojp.usdoj.gov/content/pub/pdf/pp99pr.pdf *with* LAUREN E. GLAZE & THOMAS P. BONCZAR, U.S. DEP'T OF JUSTICE, NCJ 228230, PROBATION AND PAROLE IN THE UNITED STATES, 2008, at 39 App. tbl. 13 (2009), *available at* http://bjs.ojp.usdoj.gov/content/pub/pdf/ppus08.pdf.

81. On sentencing guidelines, see MARVIN E. FRANKEL, CRIMINAL SENTENCES: LAW WITHOUT ORDER (1973); Richard S. Frase, *State Sentencing Guidelines: Diversity, Consensus, and Unresolved Policy Issues*, 105 COLUM. L. REV. 1190, 1196 (2005);

U.S. Sentencing Guidelines Manual § 3E1.1 (2010) (prescribing a two-level reduction for acceptance of responsibility and a third level upon the prosecutor's motion for crimes of offense level 16 or greater); Michael M. O'Hear, *Remorse, Cooperation, and "Acceptance of Responisbility": The Structure, Implementation, and Reform of Section 3E1.1 of the Federal Sentencing Guidelines*, 91 Nw. U. L. Rev. 1507, 1534–40 (1997) (reporting the results of an empirical study of one district in which acceptance-of-responsibility reduction operated as a nearly automatic plea discount in practice; also reviewing national evidence that 88% of defendants who plead guilty, but only 20% of those who go to trial, receive the discount).

On mandatory minimum penalties, see U.S. Sent'g Comm'n, Mandatory Minimum Penalties in the Federal Criminal Justice System 8–11 (1991); *e.g.*, 18 U.S.C. § 924(c) (2006) (establishing mandatory consecutive penalties for using or carrying a gun during a violent or drug-trafficking crime); 21 U.S.C. §§ 841, 846, 848, 960 (2006) (establishing mandatory minimum penalties for various drug crimes).

Of course, *Apprendi v. New Jersey* and its progeny have swung the pendulum back somewhat, invalidating binding sentencing guidelines operated by judges in the name of restoring jury discretion. 530 U.S. 466 (2000). These cases, however, do not affect mandatory minimum statutes, Harris v. United States, 536 U.S. 545 (2004), and they have hardly returned much power to juries. Only six states give juries the power to sentence noncapital felonies. Nancy J. King & Rosevelt L. Noble, *Felony Jury Sentencing in Practice—A Three-State Study*, 57 Vand. L. Rev. 885, 886 (2004).

82. *See* Ring v. Arizona, 536 U.S. 584 (2002) (requiring that juries find facts that make defendants eligible for capital punishment); Shannon v. United States, 512 U.S. 573, 587 (1994) (reiterating "the rule against informing jurors of the consequences of their verdicts" and rejecting a proposed exception).

83. On prosecutorial use of plea-bargaining chips, see Stephanos Bibas, *Plea Bargaining Outside the Shadow of Trial*, 117 Harv. L. Rev. 2463, 2470–76 (2004). On the opacity of prosecutorial discretion, see Barkow, *supra* note 77, at 1353–54.

CHAPTER II

1. Bibas, *supra* chapter I note 83, at 2481, 2483–85.

2. *Id.* at 2480, 2485; Fisher, *supra* Introduction note 4, at 129, 131, 136, 198–99; Heumann, *supra* chapter I note 61, at 43–46, 61–75, 122–26, 134, 136, 140–43, 150–51; Bureau of Justice Statistics, Sourcebook of Criminal Justice Statistics Online, *supra* chapter I note 62, tbls. 5.46.2004, 5.24.2007 (reflecting that 95% of state and federal convictions result from guilty pleas).

3. Caroline Wolf Harlow, *Defense Counsel in Criminal Cases*, Bureau Just. Stat. Special Rep., Nov. 2000, at 1, 3, http://bjs.ojp.usdoj.gov/content/pub/pdf/dccc.pdf.

4. On insiders' mellowing, see Heumann, *supra* chapter I note 61, at 117–21 (describing how prosecutors undergo this "mellowing process"). It is possible, indeed likely, that insiders differ systematically from outsiders in their race, class, sex, culture, and levels of education. These differences may well exacerbate the gulf between insiders' and outsiders' perspectives. I am not aware, however, of any empirical evidence to confirm this claim.

On insiders' unwritten, shared sense of the factors relevant to plea bargaining: From an objective, external point of view, prosecutors, parole officers, and other criminal-justice actors have broad discretion, as few statutes, cases, or published rules constrain them. Yet these same actors often offer consistent reasons for their actions and report that they exercise little discretion in following consistent office policies and understandings. In other words, from a subjective or internal point of view they feel self-constrained by shared norms, understandings, and practices. For a fascinating study and contrast of these two perspectives, see Marc L. Miller & Ronald F. Wright, *The Black Box*, 94 IOWA L. REV. 125 (2008).

On juries' less cynical perspective, see HARRY KALVEN, JR. & HANS ZEISEL, THE AMERICAN JURY 66–75, 115–16, 164–89 (1966) (finding that in the majority of cases where juries differed from judges, jurors' reasons included issues of evidence, and in these cases they were much more likely to read the evidence as favorable to defendants). On the way in which insiders acclimate to plea bargaining, see HEUMANN, *supra* chapter I note 61, at 49–91, 95–117, 134–55.

On insider cynicism about injustice: When, for example, I interviewed dozens of prosecutors, defense lawyers, and judges for the material in chapter III, I was surprised to hear several drop any pretense of justice. When I questioned a defense lawyer about whether accepting guilty pleas from defendants who maintained their innocence was unjust, he did not respond with a substantive defense of the pleas or of the justice of advocating for a client's interests. Instead, he challenged my premise with cynicism. Our criminal justice system, he maintained, is not and cannot be about justice—justice is simply window dressing. He openly admitted that he saw it simply as a game to get the lowest possible sentence.

5. See HEUMANN, *supra* chapter I note 61, at 110–14, 144–48; Bibas, *Plea Bargaining Outside the Shadow of Trial, supra* chapter I note 83, at 2471–72 & nn.21, 22, 26, 2474, 2476–77, 2479 (discussing risk aversion and prosecutors' and defense counsel's incentives to dispose of their caseloads quickly through plea bargaining, including caseload and conviction statistics); FISHER, *supra* Introduction note 4, at 13, 40–49, 121–24 (discussing how funding and caseload pressures encourage prosecutors and judges to dispose of criminal cases through plea bargaining); *see also* State v. Peart, 621 So. 2d 780, 784, 788–90 (La. 1993) (finding the New Orleans public defender system presumptively ineffective because a defense lawyer handled 70 active felony cases at a time, amounting to 418 defendants in the space of seven months, and had an inadequate support staff, library, and other resources; as a result, that lawyer's clients entered 130 guilty pleas at arraignment during this seven-month period); Frank O. Bowman, III & Michael Heise, *Quiet Rebellion II: An Empirical Analysis of Declining Federal Drug Sentences Including Data from the District Level*, 87 IOWA L. REV. 477, 542–44, 552–53 (2002) (finding statistically significant correlation between federal prosecutors' workloads and declining federal drug sentences, which could suggest that prosecutors use more generous plea bargains to dispose of larger caseloads); Adam M. Gershowitz & Laura R. Killinger, *The State (Never) Rests: How Excessive Prosecutor Caseloads Harm Criminal Defendants*, 105 Nw. U. L. REV. 261, 267–74 (2011) (reporting results of empirical survey finding that prosecutors in most of the twenty-five largest districts in the United States were overworked and handled caseloads that were well above recommended ranges, handling up to 457 felonies and misdemeanors per prosecutor in 2006); Albert W. Alschuler, *The Prosecutor's Role in Plea Bargaining*, 36 U. CHI. L. REV. 50, 106–07 & n.138 (1968).

6. Stephanos Bibas & Richard A. Bierschbach, *Integrating Remorse and Apology into Criminal Procedure*, 114 YALE L.J. 85, 147 (2004); *see also* Russell Korobkin & Chris Guthrie, *Psychological Barriers to Litigation Settlement: An Experimental Approach*, 93 MICH. L. REV. 107, 111–14 (1994) (describing the standard law-and-economics rational-actor approach to modeling settlements); Russell Korobkin & Chris Guthrie, *Psychology, Economics, and Settlement: A New Look at the Role of the Lawyer*, 76 TEX. L. REV. 77, 96–101, 121–22, 124 (1997) (presenting an empirical study that found "that lawyers are more likely [than lay litigants] to explicitly or implicitly employ expected financial value calculations when considering litigation options" and thus are more likely to favor settlement).

7. *See* Barkow, *supra* chapter I note 77, at 1337–51; Dan Markel, *Against Mercy*, 88 MINN. L. REV. 1421 (2004).

8. *See Department of Justice Authorization and Oversight, 1981: Hearings Before the Senate Comm. on the Judiciary*, 96th Cong. 1046 (supplemental statement of Assistant Attorney General Philip Heymann) ("[W]e can't talk very much about our declinations. . . . So the public is often not given any detailed information on the reason for a declination; they simply learn that an investigation of an obvious scoundrel has been closed."). On the invisibility of discovery, grand jury proceedings, and plea bargaining, see HEUMANN, *supra* chapter I note 61, at 36–46; *e.g.*, FED. R. CRIM. P. 6(e), 16.

9. On the hiddenness of plea bargaining, see FISHER, *supra* Introduction note 4, at 131–33; HEUMANN, *supra* chapter I note 61, at 43–46, 134. On victims' lack of information, see Heather Strang & Lawrence W. Sherman, *Repairing the Harm: Victims and Restorative Justice*, 2003 UTAH L. REV. 15, 20–21; PEGGY M. TOBO-LOWSKY, CRIME VICTIM RIGHTS AND REMEDIES 36–39 (2001); Bibas & Bierschbach, *supra* note 6, at 137; *see also* JO-ANNE M. WEMMERS, VICTIMS IN THE CRIMINAL JUSTICE SYSTEM 19–20 (1996). For a discussion of the gap between victims' statutory rights and their implementation in procedural rules and in practice, see U.S. GOV'T ACCOUNTABILITY OFFICE, GAO-09–54, CRIME VICTIMS' RIGHTS ACT: INCREASING AWARENESS, MODIFYING THE COMPLAINT PROCESS, AND ENHANCING COMPLIANCE MONITORING WILL IMPROVE IMPLEMENTATION OF THE ACT (2008); Paul G. Cassell, *Recognizing Victims in the Federal Rules of Criminal Procedure: Proposed Amendments in Light of the Crime Victims' Rights Act*, 2005 BYU L. REV. 835; Paul G. Cassell, *Treating Crime Victims Fairly: Integrating Victims into the Federal Rules of Criminal Procedure*, 2007 UTAH L. REV. 861, 867–68 (quoting statement by Attorney General Janet Reno at the *Victims' Rights Amendment: Hearing on S.J. Res. 6 Before the S. Judiciary Comm.*, 105th Cong. 64 (1997)).

10. *See* Ronald Wright & Marc Miller, *Honesty and Opacity in Charge Bargains*, 55 STAN. L. REV. 1409, 1411–12 (2003); Ronald Wright & Marc Miller, *The Screening/ Bargaining Tradeoff*, 55 STAN. L. REV. 29, 34, 95–96 (2002).

11. On the media's distorted images of criminal justice, see Rachel E. Barkow, *Administering Crime*, 52 UCLA L. REV. 715, 748–50 (2005); Lawrence W. Sherman, *Trust and Confidence in Criminal Justice*, 248 NAT'L INST. JUST. J. 22, 28–29 (2002). Of course, those with direct experience with crime and justice, particularly residents of high-crime neighborhoods, do not need to rely on these accounts as much. The media occasionally report harsh sentences as well, but anecdotes of leniency seem more likely to scare and thus attract viewers.

For thoughtful discussions of the possible direct and indirect linkages between media crime coverage and public opinion, see Sara Sun Beale, *Still Tough on Crime? Prospects for Restorative Justice in the United States*, 2003 UTAH L. REV. 413, 425–28 (discussing how the news media's deluge of crime stories helped to set the political agenda and may have increased the public's fear of crime); Sara Sun Beale, *What's Law Got to Do with It? The Political, Social, Psychological and Other Non-Legal Factors Influencing the Development of (Federal) Criminal Law*, 1 BUFF. CRIM. L. REV. 23, 44–51 (1997) (same); Dennis T. Lowry et al., *Setting the Public Fear Agenda: A Longitudinal Analysis of Network TV Crime Reporting, Public Perceptions of Crime, and FBI Crime Statistics*, 53 J. COMM. 61, 61 (2003); Daniel Romer et al., *Television News and the Cultivation of Fear of Crime*, 53 J. COMM. 88 (2003).

On viewers' expectations of forensic evidence and trials, see, for example, *CSI: Crime Scene Investigation* (CBS television series); *L. A. Law* (NBC television series). Apparently, jurors who have seen *CSI* come to expect air-tight forensic evidence in every case and "are reluctant to convict" in cases that lack forensic evidence. Jamie Stockwell, *Defense, Prosecution Play to New "CSI" Savvy: Juries Expecting TV-Style Forensics*, WASH. POST, May 22, 2005, at A1; *see also* Juror Evaluation Forms, U.S. Dist. Ct., S.D. Ia. (on file with the author) ("Before coming to this court case, I tho't there had to be physical evidence . . . to bring a person to trial. I still think that may be the way it should be."). *Compare* Andrew P. Thomas, *The CSI Effect on Jurors and Judgments*, 115 YALE L.J. POCKET PART 70 (2006), *available at* http://www.thepocketpart.org/2006/02/thomas.html (reporting evidence of the CSI effect based on a survey of Maricopa County, Arizona prosecutors), *with* Tom R. Tyler, Review, *Viewing CSI and the Threshold of Guilt: Managing Truth and Justice in Reality and Fiction*, 115 YALE L.J. 1050 (2006) (expressing doubts about proof of the *CSI* effect). More than 61% of those surveyed regularly or sometimes get their information about the courts from such television dramas, and more than 40% do the same from television reality shows such as *Judge Judy*. NAT'L CENTER FOR STATE CTS., HOW THE PUBLIC VIEWS THE STATE COURTS: A 1999 NATIONAL SURVEY 19 fig. 7 (1999).

12.   Joel Best, *Monster Hype*, EDUC. NEXT, Summer 2002, at 50, *available at* http://www.educationnext.org/monster-hype/ (describing school shootings as a "phantom epidemic" and noting that "[i]n large part, media coverage promoted this distorted view of the problem"). On the penalties for crack cocaine: In 1986, popular publications such as *Time* magazine were abuzz about the advent of crack cocaine. *E.g.*, Jacob V. Lamar Jr. et al., *Crack: A Cheap and Deadly Cocaine Is a Fast-Spreading Menace*, TIME, June 2, 1986, at 16; Evan Thomas, *America's Crusade: What Is Behind the Latest War on Drugs*, TIME, Sept. 15, 1986, at 60 (cover story); *see* William A. Henry III, *Reporting the Drug Problem: Have Journalists Overdosed on Print and TV Coverage?*, TIME, Oct. 6, 1986, at 73, 73 ("Crack has dominated media attention during the recent surge in drug coverage," including many television, magazine, and front-page newspaper articles). That June, Boston Celtics draft pick Len Bias died of a cocaine overdose. Congress then rushed to pass new crack-cocaine penalties in time for the November election. As the bill wended its way through Congress, politicians kept raising the penalties to show how tough they could be toward drug dealers, until the bill provided for 5 grams of crack cocaine to receive the same penalty as 500 grams of powder cocaine. *See* David A. Sklansky, *Cocaine, Race, and Equal Protection*, 47 STAN. L. REV. 1283, 1291–97 (1995).

13. On how media portrayals shape the public's abstract views on criminal justice, see Barkow, *Administering Crime, supra* note 11, at 748–50; *see also* JOHN DOBLE, CRIME AND PUNISHMENT: THE PUBLIC'S VIEW 14, 16 (1987) (reporting that many focus-group participants focused on "recent highly publicized crimes," notably a string of child murders, and exaggerated the incidence of violent crimes); Loretta J. Stalans, *Measuring Attitudes to Sentencing, in* CHANGING ATTITUDES TO PUNISH- MENT: PUBLIC OPINION, CRIME AND JUSTICE 15, 23–24 (Julian V. Roberts & Mike Hough eds., 2002).

    On the role of mental stereotypes and recent examples in the public's views of crime, see James P. Lynch & Mona J.E. Danner, *Offense Seriousness Scaling: An Alternative to Scenario Methods*, 9 J. QUANTITATIVE CRIMINOLOGY 309, 311 (1993); *see also* Paul H. Robinson, *Some Doubts About Argument by Hypothetical*, 88 CAL. L. REV. 813, 819–23 (2000) (explaining that hypothetical crime scenarios are frequently too sketchy and leave respondents to mentally fill in many details relevant to blameworthiness, which makes it dangerous to generalize from the respondents' resulting judgments of blameworthiness); Stalans, *supra*, at 22 (describing a study that found that subjects who were given descriptions of a seri- ous burglary case before determining the sentence in a typical case tended to give a higher sentence to the typical defendant).

    On how differently people evaluate individual cases ex post, see Barkow, *Admin- istering Crime, supra*, at 750–51; Rachel E. Barkow, *Federalism and the Politics of Sentencing*, 105 COLUM. L. REV. 1276, 1283–84 (2005); Edward Zamble & Kerry Lee Kalm, *General and Specific Measures of Public Attitudes Toward Sentencing*, 22 CANADIAN J. BEHAV. SCI. 327, 330–37 & tbl.1 (1990) (finding that when asked general poll questions, most survey subjects say that the criminal justice system is too lenient, but when asked to assign sentences for four specific crimes, respon- dents' sentences are close to actual sentences, though more severe for breaking and entering and, to a lesser extent, for theft).

    On three-strikes laws, see Brandon K. Applegate et al., *Assessing Public Support for Three-Strikes-and-You're-Out Laws: Global Versus Specific Attitudes*, 42 CRIME & DELINQ. 517, 522 tbl.2, 528–30 & tbl.4 (1996).

    On the Canadian surveys, see Anthony N. Doob & Julian Roberts, *Public Punitiveness and Public Knowledge of the Facts: Some Canadian Surveys, in* PUBLIC ATTITUDES TO SENTENCING: SURVEYS FROM FIVE COUNTRIES 111, 126–32 (Nigel Walker & Mike Hough eds., 1988). Indeed, in at least one notorious case, the Canadian newspaper readers rated the actual sentence as too lenient, while the readers of court documents saw the same sentence as too harsh.

14. On the public's perception of lenient sentencing, see, for example, JULIAN V. ROBERTS ET AL., PENAL POPULISM AND PUBLIC OPINION: LESSONS FROM FIVE COUNTRIES 27–28 (2003); Julian V. Roberts & Loretta J. Stalans, *Crime, Criminal Justice, and Public Opinion, in* THE HANDBOOK OF CRIME & PUNISHMENT 31, 33, 49 (Michael Tonry ed. 1998); *see* BUREAU OF JUSTICE STATISTICS, SOURCEBOOK OF CRIMINAL JUSTICE STATISTICS ONLINE, *supra* chapter I note 62, at 140–41 tbl.2.47, *available at* http://www.albany.edu/sourcebook/pdf/t247.pdf.

    On the Vermont survey, see JOHN DOBLE RESEARCH ASSOCIATES, INC. & JUDITH GREENE, ATTITUDES TOWARD CRIME AND PUNISHMENT IN VERMONT: PUBLIC OPINION ABOUT AN EXPERIMENT WITH RESTORATIVE JUSTICE 14–15 & n.5 (2000), *available at* http://www.ncjrs.gov/pdffiles1/nij/grants/182361. pdf.

On capital jurors in South Carolina, Georgia, and Virginia, see Theodore Eisenberg & Martin T. Wells, *Deadly Confusion: Juror Instructions in Capital Cases*, 79 CORNELL L. REV. 1, 7–8 (1993); Anthony Paduano & Clive A. Stafford Smith, *Deathly Errors: Juror Misperceptions Concerning Parole in the Imposition of the Death Penalty*, 18 COLUM. HUM. RTS. L. REV. 211, 220–25 (1987); William W. Hood, III, Note, *The Meaning of "Life" for Virginia Jurors and Its Effect on Reliability in Capital Sentencing*, 75 VA. L. REV. 1605, 1623–27 (1989).

15. On the Illinois studies, see Loretta J. Stalans & Shari Seidman Diamond, *Formation and Change in Lay Evaluations of Criminal Sentencing: Misperception and Discontent*, 14 LAW & HUM. BEHAV. 199, 202 & n.1, 205–07 & tbls. 2, 3 (1990); Shari Seidman Diamond & Loretta J. Stalans, *The Myth of Judicial Leniency in Sentencing*, 7 BEHAV. SCI. & L. 73, 75–81 (1989).

    On the California survey, see William Samuel & Elizabeth Moulds, *The Effect of Crime Severity on Perceptions of Fair Punishment: A California Case Study*, 77 J. CRIM. L. & CRIMINOLOGY 931, 938–40 & tbl.1 (1986). Indeed, the respondents' proposed sentences for five of the six crimes (auto theft, theft of $1000, armed robbery, armed rape, and homicide) appear to be lower than the sentences prescribed by statute as the middle or normal term. *Id.*

    On the public's agreement with federal guideline sentences, see PETER H. ROSSI & RICHARD A. BERK, JUST PUNISHMENTS: FEDERAL GUIDELINES AND PUBLIC VIEWS COMPARED 149 (1997). On other studies, see JULIAN V. ROBERTS & LORETTA J. STALANS, PUBLIC OPINION, CRIME, AND CRIMINAL JUSTICE 210–12 (1997).

16. Paul H. Robinson et al., *The Disutility of Injustice*, 85 NYU L. REV. 1940, 1949–78 (2010).

17. On victims' desires to participate, see Dean G. Kilpatrick et al., *The Rights of Crime Victims—Does Legal Protection Make a Difference?*, NAT'L INST. JUST.: RES. IN BRIEF, Dec. 1998, at 4 (1998) (NCJ 173839), *available at* http://ncjrs.org/pdf-files/173839.pdf; Strang & Sherman, *supra* note 9, at 21.

    On the effects of jury service, see, for example, E. ALLAN LIND & TOM R. TYLER, THE SOCIAL PSYCHOLOGY OF PROCEDURAL JUSTICE 106 (1988) ("The perception that one has had an opportunity to express oneself and to have one's views considered by someone in power plays a critical role in fairness judgments."); TYLER, *supra* Introduction note 8, at 163; Brian L. Cutler & Donna M. Hughes, *Judging Jury Service: Results of the North Carolina Administrative Office of the Courts Juror Survey*, 19 BEHAV. SCI. & L. 305, 311 (2001) (reporting that jury service improved the opinions of the justice system of more than 20% of jurors); Daniel W. Shuman & Jean A. Hamilton, *Jury Service—It May Change Your Mind: Perceptions of Fairness of Jurors and Nonjurors*, 46 SMU L. REV. 449, 468 (1992) (reporting that those with jury experience view the criminal justice system as 11% fairer than nonjurors do); Telephone Interview with the Hon. Robert W. Pratt, U.S. Dist. Judge, S.D. Iowa (July 15, 2005) (reporting, based on empirical data from survey forms returned by ex-jurors, that they consistently gained respect for the system, learned a great deal, and came away impressed with the importance of their service).

    On how citizens feel they must get involved to check insiders, see HIBBING & THEISS-MORSE, *supra* Introduction note 2, at 131 (offering this explanation for why citizens who would rather not get involved in politics nevertheless do so).

18. On the supineness of grand juries, see David Margolick, *Law Professor to Administer Courts in State*, N.Y. Times, Feb. 1, 1985, at B2 (quoting then-Chief Judge Sol Wachtler of the New York Court of Appeals).

    On victims' and citizens' limited roles at arrest, charging, and plea bargaining decisions, see Douglas E. Beloof, Paul G. Cassell & Steven J. Twist, Victims in Criminal Procedure 259–62, 302, 308–10, 476–77 (2d ed. 2006). Victims could instead consult with prosecutors before each of these decisions and have standing to express their views in court or even seek judicial review of prosecutors' decisions. These rights to participate need not rise to the level of vetoes.

    On victims' limited role at sentencing in practice, Tobolowsky, *supra* note 9, at 96–98. Though, as noted earlier, a majority of victims want to take part, many victims may be unaware of sentencing hearings because prosecutors never notify them. Others may decline to attend because the law gives them inadequate rights to participate; if they are consigned to be powerless observers, they may see little reason to attend.

19. On the role of retribution in outsiders' punishment judgments, see Cass R. Sunstein, *On the Psychology of Punishment*, 11 S. Ct. Econ. Rev. 171, 175–76 (2004) ("This study strongly suggests that punishment judgments are retributive in character, not tailored to consequentialist goals. . . . These studies indicate that when assessing punishment, people's judgments are rooted in outrage; they do not focus solely on social consequences, at least not in any simple way."); Cass R. Sunstein et al., *Do People Want Optimal Deterrence?*, 29 J. Legal Stud. 237, 240–41 (2000) ("[T]hese studies strongly suggest that intuitive punishment judgments are not directly tailored to consequentialist goals."); *see also* Dan M. Kahan, *The Secret Ambition of Deterrence*, 113 Harv. L. Rev. 413, 414–19, 472–76 (1999) (arguing that deterrence does not explain people's attitudes toward crime and punishment but instead serves as a rationalization or rhetoric to conceal disagreements rooted in their moral values).

    On the roles of apology and forgiveness in laymen's punishment judgments, see Paul H. Robinson et al., *Extralegal Punishment Factors: A Study of Forgiveness, Hardship, Good-Deeds, Apology, Remorse, and Other Such Discretionary Factors in Assessing Criminal Punishment*, 65 Vand. L. Rev. (forthcoming 2012).

20. Bibas, *Plea Bargaining Outside the Shadow of Trial*, *supra* chapter I note 83, at 2471–72. As I argued in that article, plea bargaining is far from a rational, efficient market in which prosecutors seek only to maximize retribution, deterrence, or some other measure of justice. Many other factors enter into their calculus. Even though fully informed outsiders would likely acknowledge the need for some plea bargaining, they would likely strike different bargains because they lack insiders' self-interests and the years on the job that cause insiders to grow more mellow.

21. G.K. Chesterton, *The Twelve Men*, in Tremendous Trifles 80, 85–86 (1909).

22. On the role of public dissatisfaction with idle imprisonment, see Braman, *supra* chapter I note 35, at 1181–1200. On the broader array of considerations that factor into outsiders' judgments, see Korobkin & Guthrie, *Psychological Barriers to Litigation Settlement: An Experimental Approach*, *supra* note 6, at 148–50; Korobkin & Guthrie, *Psychology, Economics, and Settlement: A New Look at the Role of the Lawyer*, *supra* note 6, at 99–101, 108–12, 121–22, 124, 129–36. Both studies dealt with civil settlements. Richard Bierschbach and I have argued elsewhere

that these concerns are likely to be even more powerful in criminal cases, because crime victims and wrongdoers have powerful needs to heal, reconcile, learn lessons, and reintegrate into society. Bibas & Bierschbach, *supra* note 6, at 109–18.

23. BANNER, *supra* chapter I note 6, at 301 (noting that European governments were able to abolish the death penalty in the face of popular support for it because their elected officials feel less pressure than American politicians to implement the majority's preferred policies); JAMES Q. WHITMAN, HARSH JUSTICE: CRIMINAL PUNISHMENT AND THE WIDENING DIVIDE BETWEEN AMERICA AND EUROPE 13–15, 199–201 (2003) (explaining that the strong culture of deference to bureaucracies in France and Germany "works both to shield the state from the [tough-on-crime] pressures of democratic politics and to manage prisons and other punishments in a sober and disciplined way"); FRANKLIN ZIMRING, THE CONTRADICTIONS OF AMERICAN CAPITAL PUNISHMENT 23 (2003); Joshua Micah Marshall, *Death in Venice*, NEW REPUBLIC, July 31, 2000, at 12, 13 (explaining that European parliamentary government makes it harder for upstarts to seize power and for single-issue politics to rock established party platforms, and noting that political elites dictate these platforms and can defy popular support for the death penalty).

24. William J. Stuntz, *Plea Bargaining and Criminal Law's Disappearing Shadow*, 117 HARV. L. REV. 2548, 2549–58 (2004).

25. For the North Carolina examples, see Ronald F. Wright & Rodney L. Engen, *Charge Movement and Theories of Prosecutors*, 91 MARQ. L. REV. 9, 15–16 (2007). For the other examples of prosecutors' persuading legislators to give them more options by adding new crimes, see William J. Stuntz, *The Pathological Politics of Criminal Law*, 100 MICH. L. REV. 505, 534–35, 537–38 & n.131 (2001).

26. Nancy Jean King, *Priceless Process: Nonnegotiable Features of Criminal Litigation*, 47 UCLA L. REV. 113, 114–15, 118–19 (1999).

Note that this section discusses the first round in the game, before the public catches on and reacts. Once the public learns that insiders pervasively discount sentences, it reacts to this perceived dishonesty by demanding truth-in-sentencing laws and abolishing parole, as discussed later in this chapter. The key point is that the system's opacity creates a lead time or lag between insiders' maneuvers and outsiders' reactions. Thus, insiders used to be able to show leniency without outsiders' knowledge. Now, many citizens still assume that parole will discount sentences, long after many states and the federal government have abolished parole.

27. Police and prosecutors were reluctant to bring domestic-abuse cases, at least until legislatures enacted shall-arrest and pro-prosecution policies. *See, e.g.,* U.S. COMM'N ON CIVIL RIGHTS, UNDER THE RULE OF THUMB: BATTERED WOMEN AND THE ADMINISTRATION OF JUSTICE 12–34 (1982); Cheryl Hanna, *No Right to Choose: Mandated Victim Participation in Domestic Violence Prosecutions*, 109 HARV. L. REV. 1849, 1857–65 (1996); Lawrence W. Sherman & Richard A. Berk, *The Minneapolis Domestic Violence Experiment*, POLICE FOUND. REP., Apr. 1984, at 1–2, *available at* http://www.policefoundation.org/pdf/minneapolisdve.pdf.

For the large plea-bargaining rewards offered for waivers of procedural rights, see, for example, United States v. Ruiz, 536 U.S. 622, 625 (2002); State v.

LaForest, 665 A.2d 1083, 1085 (N.H. 1995). For judges' use of their sentencing leverage to encourage pleas and thereby improve their statistics and avoid reversal, see HEUMANN, *supra* chapter I note 61, at 140–45.

28. Stephen Perry, *Prosecutors in State Courts, 2005*, BUREAU JUST. STATS. BULL., July 2006, app. at 11; Daniel S. Medwed, *The Zeal Deal: Prosecutorial Resistance to Post-Conviction Claims of Innocence*, 84 B.U. L. REV. 125, 182 (2004); Abbe Smith, *Can You Be a Good Person and a Good Prosecutor?*, 14 GEO. J. LEGAL ETHICS 355, 390 (2001).

29. *See, e.g.*, Andrea Ford, *The Simpson Verdicts; The Prosecution: Another Stumble; The D.A.'s Office Adds to Its List of High-Profile Defeats, Which Could Leave Gil Garcetti Vulnerable in Next Year's Election*, L.A. TIMES, Oct. 4, 1995, at A3; Mitchell Landsberg, *Garcetti's Chances Were Slim, Analysts Say*, L.A. TIMES, Nov. 12, 2000, at B1.

    In theory, the public might truly care only about conviction rates and not about sentences (or at least not much, in which case they would vote based on convictions alone). But some district attorneys, such as Harry Connick, Sr. in New Orleans, have run successfully (and repeatedly) for reelection on platforms of restricting plea-bargaining. Connick survived repeated criticism of his low conviction rates by explaining that he screened out weak cases in order to hang tough and not plea-bargain down charges and sentences in cases strong enough to survive at trial. Wright & Miller, *The Screening/Bargaining Tradeoff, supra* note 10, at 65, 113–15.

    Another possibility is that the public prefers incumbents or is simply too apathetic to kick them out of office. *See, e.g.*, Jonathan P. Hicks, *Steady Work, If You Can Get It: District Attorneys Hold Surest Elective Posts in City*, N.Y. TIMES Apr. 17, 2005, § 1, at 33 (explaining that no New York City district attorney has lost a reelection battle in the last fifty years, in part because district attorneys enjoy many opportunities to stage dramatic press conferences announcing arrests or indictments). A significant incumbency advantage of course greatly dampens outsiders' electoral check on insiders' behavior.

30. *See* Megan Nicole Kanka Foundation, Mission, http://www.megannicolekanka-foundation.org/mission.htm (last visited Aug. 26, 2008); *A 30-Second Ad on Crime*, N.Y. TIMES, Nov. 3, 1988, at B20 (Willie Horton ad); Alexandra Marks, *For Prisoners, It's a Nearly No-Parole World*, CHRISTIAN SCI. MONITOR, July 10, 2001, at 1.

31. *See, e.g.*, Alan Farnham & Tricia Walsh, *U.S. Suburbs Are Under Siege*, FORTUNE, Dec. 28, 1992, at 42; Bruce Frankel & Dennis Cauchon, *"Young & The Restless": Crime in 1992 More Violent*, USA TODAY, Dec. 31, 1992, at 7A; Don Terry, *Carjacking: New Name for Old Crime*, N.Y. TIMES, Dec. 9, 1992, at A18.

32. FRANKEL, *supra* chapter I note 81. For the best account of the sentencing-reform movement at the federal level, culminating in the Sentencing Reform Act of 1984, see KATE STITH & JOSÉ A. CABRANES, FEAR OF JUDGING: SENTENCING GUIDELINES IN THE FEDERAL COURTS 29–77 (1998). At least eighteen states plus the District of Columbia and the federal government use sentencing guidelines, and a number of other states are considering enacting them. Richard S. Frase, *State Sentencing Guidelines: Diversity, Consensus, and Unresolved Policy Issues*, 105 COLUM. L. REV. 1190, 1195–96 (2005).

33. *See* David Seidman & Michael Couzens, *Getting the Crime Rate Down: Political Pressure and Crime Reporting*, 8 LAW & SOC'Y REV. 457, 468–83 (1974) (analyzing evidence that police departments in Washington, D.C., Baltimore, and Philadelphia

police did so); Fox Butterfield, *As Crime Falls, Pressure Rises to Alter Data*, N.Y. TIMES, Aug. 3, 1998, at A1 (noting that police departments in New York, Philadelphia, Atlanta, and Boca Raton, Florida had systematically downgraded burglaries and other felonies to misdemeanors to reduce their reported crime rates); Philip Messing et al., *NYPD Stats Were Captain Cooked*, N.Y. POST, Feb. 7, 2010, at 22; Rocco Parascandola, *Brooklyn's 81st Precinct Probed by NYPD for Fudging Stats; Felonies Allegedly Marked as Misdemeanors*, N.Y. DAILY NEWS, Feb. 2, 2010, at 8.

34. On fact bargaining, see Ilene H. Nagel & Stephen J. Schulhofer, *A Tale of Three Cities: An Empirical Study of Charging and Bargaining Practices Under the Federal Sentencing Guidelines*, 66 S. CAL. L. REV. 501, 522, 547 (1992) (discussing cases of fact bargaining); Probation Officers Advisory Group, *Probation Officers' Advisory Group Survey*, 8 FED. SENT'G REP. 305, 306, 310–11 (1996) (citing, as evidence of fact bargaining, federal probation officers' survey responses that indicate that plea agreements frequently omit or misrepresent relevant facts).

On the use of cooperation agreements as a plea-bargaining tool, see Jeffery T. Ulmer, *The Localized Uses of Federal Sentencing Guidelines in Four U.S. District Courts: Evidence of Processual Order*, 28 SYMBOLIC INTERACTION 255, 263–65 & tbl.1 (2005) (reporting that at least one federal prosecutor's office uses "soft" cooperation discounts for "information of questionable value" as a tool for reducing stiff sentences). On fast-track departures, see Stephanos Bibas, *Regulating Local Variations in Federal Sentencing*, 58 STAN. L. REV. 137, 145–48 (2005).

For a judge's remarkably candid admission that he uses downward departures to undercut harsh sentences, see, for example, Jack B. Weinstein, Comment, *A Trial Judge's Second Impression of the Federal Sentencing Guidelines*, 66 S. CAL. L. REV. 357, 365 (1992) ("[T]he Guidelines . . . have made charlatans and dissemblers of us all. We spend our time plotting and scheming, bending and twisting, distorting and ignoring *the law* in an effort to achieve a just result."); *see also* Jack B. Weinstein, *A Trial Judge's Reflections on Departures from the Federal Sentencing Guidelines*, 5 FED. SENT'G REP. 6, 12 (1992) ("One would think that most Americans, judges and legislators, as well as members of the Sentencing Commission would be embarrassed by this implacable urge to incarcerate and by the overwhelming desire to ignore the good that people have done and probably will do. Fortunately, court interpretations of the guidelines are not always so unyielding. Judges must continue to assume their individual responsibility of exercising the discretion to depart if sentencing is to approach the levels of fairness and economy that is required of our criminal justice system.").

35. On public outrage at charge bargaining, see, for example, FISHER, *supra* Introduction note 4, at 148–52; *see also* Laura B. Myers, *Bringing the Offender to Heel: Views of the Criminal Courts*, in AMERICANS VIEW CRIME AND JUSTICE: A NATIONAL PUBLIC OPINION SURVEY 46, 49, 54–55 & tbl.4.2 (Timothy J. Flanagan & Dennis R. Longmire eds., 1996) (reporting multiple surveys that found that the public dislikes plea bargaining); Wright & Miller, *The Screening/Bargaining Tradeoff*, *supra* note 10, at 96 (noting that charge bargaining disappoints the public's expectations and creates a feeling of "learned helplessness").

The PROTECT Act is Pub. L. No. 108–21, § 401, 117 Stat. 650, 667–76 (2003) (codified as amended at scattered sections of 18 U.S.C. & 28 U.S.C.). The Feeney Amendment restricted sentencing judges' ability to lower sentences unilaterally under the federal Sentencing Guidelines. It did so by eliminating or restricting many permissible grounds for downward departures, requiring prosecutorial assent to several downward adjustments, and increasing appellate, executive, and legislative scrutiny of downward departures. *See generally* Stephanos Bibas, *The Feeney Amendment and the Continuing Rise of Prosecutorial Power to Plea Bargain,* 94 J. CRIM. L. & CRIMINOLOGY 295, 296, 299–301 (2004) (explaining these and other provisions).

Prominent examples of federal mandatory-minimum penalties include 18 U.S.C. § 924(c)(1)(a) (2006) (prescribing a mandatory five-year consecutive sentence for anyone who "uses or carries a firearm" "during and in relation to any crime of violence or drug trafficking crime"); 21 U.S.C. § 841(a)(1), (b)(1)(A), (B) (2006) (prescribing five- and ten-year mandatory minimum sentences for trafficking in certain quantities of drugs).

36. The Rockefeller drug laws' restrictions on plea bargaining away mandatory sentences are at N.Y. CRIM. PROC. LAW § 220.10 (McKinney 2005). Examples of shall-arrest and no-drop policies for domestic abuse include FLA. STAT. § 741.2901 (2005) (establishing "a pro-prosecution policy" and special prosecutorial units for domestic abuse and empowering prosecutors to proceed even over the victim's objection); WIS. STAT. § 968.075 (2003–2004) (requiring police officers to arrest domestic abusers whenever a victim has suffered physical injury or is likely to suffer continued abuse, requiring police to adopt written policies encouraging arrest in other domestic abuse cases, and requiring police officers to explain in writing any decisions not to arrest domestic abusers); *see also* Hanna, *supra* note 27, at 1859–65.

For a discussion of New Orleans District Attorney Harry Connick, Sr.'s electoral success, see Wright & Miller, *The Screening/Bargaining Tradeoff, supra* note 10, at 60–61. Connick is the father of the famous singer Harry Connick, Jr.

37. California's plea bargaining ban is at CAL. PENAL CODE ANN. § 1192.7 (West 2011). *See generally* CANDACE MCCOY, POLITICS AND PLEA BARGAINING: VICTIMS' RIGHTS IN CALIFORNIA (1993).

California's three-strikes law is at CAL. PENAL CODE ANN. § 667(e)(2) (West 2011). *See also* Richard Kelly Heft, *Legislating with a Vengeance: Criminals in California Now Face Life Sentences After Their Third Offence Under the "Three Strikes, You're Out" Law,* INDEP. (London), Apr. 26, 1995, at 27.

38. For criticisms of mandatory-sentencing laws, see, for example, Franklin E. Zimring, *Tough Crime Laws Are False Promises,* 7 FED. SENT'G REP. 61, 62 (1994); Symposium, *Juvenile Justice: Reform After One-Hundred Years,* 37 AM. CRIM. L. REV. 1409, 1414–15 (2000) (remarks of Congressman Bobby Scott); *see also* Barkow, *supra* note 11, at 735 (describing the public's views as lacking nuance, but not explicitly criticizing the public's approach).

For the public's anger at rule-flouters, see Julian V. Roberts, *Public Opinion, Criminal Record, and the Sentencing Process,* 39 AM. BEHAV. SCIENTIST 488, 493 (1996) (suggesting that public support for recidivist enhancements might be due to the perception that repeat offenders are flouting the law and showing contempt for the criminal justice system).

For the role of social cohesion in explaining public support for three-strikes laws, see Tom R. Tyler & Robert J. Boeckmann, *Three Strikes and You Are Out, but Why? The Psychology of Public Support for Punishing Rule Breakers,* 31 LAW & SOC'Y REV. 237, 254–55 (1997). Tyler and Boeckmann found that social values and fears about social and moral cohesion are the dominant explanations for three dependent variables: California's three-strikes law, the public's general punitiveness, and the public's willingness to abandon criminal procedural protections. Tyler & Boeckmann, *supra*, at 253–55. They also found significant, though smaller, correlations between judgments about crime and the courts and the public's support for general punitive policies (including mandatory sentencing) and willingness to abandon criminal procedural protections (including discontent with courts' solicitude for defendants and technicalities and courts' disregard for ordinary citizens' rights). *Id.* at 245, 252 tbl.2. They speculated that the latter finding may rest on the public's judgment that current criminal procedures are unfair. *Id.* at 259. They found only an insignificant correlation between judgments about crime and the courts and support for California's three-strikes law. *Id.* at 252 tbl.2. They found strong and significant correlations among all three dependent variables (between .40 and .68 Pearson correlation coefficients). *Id.* at 250 tbl.1. They did not, however, test the causal pathways among these variables because they treated all three as dependent variables. *See id.* at 253–54. Thus, frustration with and willingness to abandon criminal procedures may partially explain California's three-strikes law; Tyler and Boeckmann did not test this hypothesis.

Moreover, the point of their study was to show that symbolic politics and social values, rather than tangible crime risks and court outcomes, were the more important explanations for the three-strikes initiative. *Id.* at 255. That finding supports my argument that outsiders are frustrated with the criminal justice system's opaque procedures and its failure to condemn crime and vindicate victims unequivocally. The court system fails to deliver these softer, qualitative process goods, as it is too focused on quantitative outcomes.

39. The loopholes in California's bans are at CAL. PENAL CODE ANN. § 667(f)–(g) (West 2011) (banning plea bargaining or dismissal of three-strikes allegations except for insufficiency of the evidence or "in the furtherance of justice"); CAL. PENAL CODE ANN. § 1192.7(a) (West 2011) (banning plea bargaining or dismissal of serious crimes charged in indictments or informations except for insufficiency of the evidence, unavailability of material witnesses, or where bargains would make no substantial difference to sentences).

For discussions of how California judges and prosecutors dismiss felonies or downgrade them to misdemeanors, see Erik G. Luna, *Foreword: Three Strikes in a Nutshell*, 20 T. JEFFERSON L. REV. 1, 24–25 (1998); Samara Marion, *Justice by Geography? A Study of San Diego County's Three Strikes Sentencing Practices from July-December 1996*, 11 STAN. L. & POL'Y REV. 29, 37 (1999).

On the use of "wobblers" in plea bargaining, see CAL. PENAL CODE ANN. § 17(b) (4) (West 2011); David Bjerk, *Making the Crime Fit the Penalty: The Role of Prosecutorial Discretion Under Mandatory Minimum Sentencing*, 48 J.L. & ECON. 591, 604–09 (2005); Joshua E. Bowers, Note, *"The Integrity of the Game Is Everything": The Problem of Geographic Disparity in Three Strikes*, 76 N.Y.U. L. REV. 1164, 1178 n.75 (2001); Loren Gordon, *Where to Commit a Crime If You Can Only Spare a Few Days to Serve the Time: The Constitutionality of California's Wobbler Statutes As Applied in the State Today*, 33 SW. U. L. REV. 497, 505–08 (2004).

On how prosecutors circumvent § 924(c) through charge bargains, see Paul J. Hofer, *Federal Sentencing for Violent and Drug Trafficking Crimes Involving Firearms: Recent Changes and Prospects for Improvement*, 37 AM. CRIM. L. REV. 41, 53–59 (2000); United States v. Angelos, 345 F. Supp.2d 1227, 1231–32 (D. Utah.

2004) (recounting that prosecutors offered to let a defendant plead guilty to one § 924(c) gun charge but, after the defendant rejected the plea bargain, penalized him by adding four more § 924(c) counts in superseding indictments).

On how often defendants circumvent mandatory sentences through charge bargaining more generally, see U.S. SENT'G COMM'N, *supra* chapter I note 81, at 90, at 66 tbl.10, 77 tbl.19, 80 tbl.22.

On the discretion left in even supposedly mandatory domestic-abuse policies, see Hanna, *supra* note 27, at 1864; Angela Corsilles, Note, *No-Drop Policies in the Prosecution of Domestic Violence Cases: Guarantee to Action or Dangerous Solution?*, 63 FORDHAM L. REV. 853, 854–55, 857 (1994).

40. *See* Bibas, *The Feeney Amendment*, *supra* note 35, at 299–301.

41. On the use of federal telephone counts, see 21 U.S.C. §§ 841(a)(1), (b)(1)(A-B), 843(b), (d)(1) (2006); Bibas, *Plea Bargaining Outside the Shadow of Trial*, *supra* chapter I note 83, at 2484–85; *see also* Frank O. Bowman, III & Michael Heise, *Quiet Rebellion? Explaining Nearly a Decade of Declining Federal Drug Sentences*, 86 IOWA L. REV. 1043, 1121–22 (2001) (noting that "such [phone charges] are almost always Guidelines-evading plea bargains").

On evasion of the California plea-bargaining ban, see CAL. PENAL CODE ANN. § 1192.7(a) (West 2011); MCCOY, *supra* note 37, at 37–38, 80–84, 97–104. On how New York prosecutors circumvented plea-bargaining restrictions, see JOINT COMM. ON N.Y. DRUG LAW EVALUATION, THE NATION'S TOUGHEST DRUG LAW: EVALUATING THE NEW YORK EXPERIENCE 27–28, 95 (1977).

42. Provisions allowing cooperation to undercut otherwise mandatory minimum sentences include 18 U.S.C. § 3553(e) (2006); U.S. SENTENCING GUIDELINES MANUAL § 5K1.1 (2010); ALA. CODE § 13A-12–232(b) (LexisNexis 2005); COLO. REV. STAT. ANN. § 18–18–409 (2004); N.C. GEN. STAT. ANN. § 90–95(h)(5) (West 2010); VA. CODE ANN. § 18.2–248.H2.5 (2005). Unlike the Federal Guidelines, mandatory minimum statutes and state guidelines were not rendered advisory and non-binding by the Supreme Court's decision in *United States v. Booker*, 543 U.S. 220, 258–65 (2005) (Breyer, J., remedial majority opinion).

On judges' collusion with cooperation motions to reduce sentences, see Ulmer, *supra* note 34, at 263–65; *see also* Weinstein, *A Trial Judge's Reflections on Departures from the Federal Sentencing Guidelines*, *supra* note 34, at 6, 7 (suggesting the same).

Though courts are split, a majority of federal courts let stipulated-sentence plea agreements trump mandatory guideline provisions. *See* Bibas, *The Feeney Amendment*, *supra* note 35, at 305–06 & n.61. Of course, the U.S. Sentencing Guidelines are no longer mandatory, but prosecutors and courts still generally abide by them—except when they circumvent them as described in the text.

43. *See* Bibas, *Plea Bargaining Outside the Shadow of Trial*, *supra* chapter I note 83, at 2498–2502, 2507–10. These and other problems impede deterrence in the real world. *See* Paul H. Robinson & John M. Darley, *Does the Criminal Law Deter? A Behavioural Science Investigation*, 24 OXFORD J. LEGAL STUD. 173 (2004); Paul H. Robinson & John M. Darley, *The Role of Deterrence in the Formulation of Criminal Law Rules: At Its Worst When Doing Its Best*, 91 GEO. L.J. 949, 953–56 (2003).

44. On punishment's role in teaching and reinforcing social norms, see Jean Hampton, *The Moral Education Theory of Punishment*, *in* PUNISHMENT: A PHILOSOPHY &

PUBLIC AFFAIRS READER 112, 116–21 (A. John Simmons et al. eds., 1995); Jean Hampton, *The Retributive Idea, in* JEFFRIE G. MURPHY & JEAN HAMPTON, FORGIVENESS AND MERCY 111, 124–32 (1988).

There are several variations on the idea that punishment should express society's condemnation of crimes. *See, e.g.,* JOEL FEINBERG, *The Expressive Function of Punishment, in* DOING & DESERVING: ESSAYS IN THE THEORY OF RESPONSIBILITY 95, 101–05 (1970); 2 JAMES FITZJAMES STEPHEN, A HISTORY OF THE CRIMINAL LAW OF ENGLAND 80–82 (1996) (London: MacMillan & Co. 1883); Jean Hampton, *An Expressive Theory of Retribution, in* RETRIBUTIVISM AND ITS CRITICS 1, 20–22 (Wesley Cragg ed., 1992). The most prominent recent advocate of this view is Dan Kahan. *See, e.g.,* Dan M. Kahan, *What Do Alternative Sanctions Mean?*, 63 U. CHI. L. REV. 591, 593, 597–601 (1996).

45. The leading proponent of shaming punishments has been Dan Kahan. For Kahan's seminal work in the area, see Kahan, *supra* note 44, at 637–60. Other publications in this vein include Katharine K. Baker, *Sex, Rape, and Shame*, 79 B.U. L. REV. 663, 698–701 (1999); Jayne W. Barnard, *Reintegrative Shaming in Corporate Sentencing*, 72 S. CAL. L. REV. 959, 1001–02 (1999); David A. Skeel, Jr., *Shaming in Corporate Law*, 149 U. PA. L. REV. 1811, 1812 (2001).Kahan has since repudiated his embrace of shaming punishments, not because he thinks they are wrong but because he doubts that egalitarian citizens can be persuaded to support them as a more humane alternative to imprisonment. Dan M. Kahan, *What's* Really *Wrong with Shaming Sanctions*, 84 TEX. L. REV. 2075 (2006).

For criticisms of shaming punishments as cruel and humiliating, see, for example, ANDREW VON HIRSCH, CENSURE AND SANCTIONS 82–83 (1993); Stephen P. Garvey, *Can Shaming Punishments Educate?*, 65 U. CHI. L. REV. 733, 759 (1998); Toni M. Massaro, *Shame, Culture, and American Criminal Law*, 89 MICH. L. REV. 1880, 1942–43 (1991). *Cf.* Dan Markel, *Are Shaming Punishments Beautifully Retributive? Retributivism and the Implications for the Alternative Sanctions Debate*, 54 VAND. L. REV. 2157 (2001) (rejecting shaming punishments as hostile to proper understandings of retributivism and liberalism); James Q. Whitman, *What Is Wrong with Inflicting Shame Sanctions?*, 107 YALE L.J. 1055, 1089–92 (1998) (condemning "shaming as a form of lynch justice" because it stirs up and plays on mob passions).

46. TOM R. TYLER & YUEN J. HUO, TRUST IN THE LAW: ENCOURAGING PUBLIC COOPERATION WITH THE POLICE AND COURTS 101–38 (2002); *see* LIND & TYLER, *supra* note 17, at 76–81, 106, 208, 215 ("Procedures are viewed as fairer when they vest process control or voice in those affected by a decision."); TYLER, *supra* Introduction note 8, at 94–108, 125–34, 146–47, 161–70, 178; Tom R. Tyler, *What Is Procedural Justice?: Criteria Used by Citizens to Assess the Fairness of Legal Procedures*, 22 LAW & SOC'Y REV. 103, 121 (1988); *cf.* ALBERT O. HIRSCHMAN, EXIT, VOICE, AND LOYALTY: RESPONSES TO DECLINE IN FIRMS, ORGANIZATIONS, AND STATES 77–78 (1970) (noting that people who feel they have a voice in an organization tend to develop affection for and loyalty to it); Fred W. Friendly, *On Judging the Judges, in* STATE COURTS: A BLUEPRINT FOR THE FUTURE 70, 72 (Theodore J. Fetter ed., 1978) ("[A] public that is cynical or ignorant about its laws is a lawless one.").

47. Janice Nadler, *Flouting the Law*, 83 TEX. L. REV. 1399, 1410–26 (2005) (finding that survey subjects who read stories of unjust laws were later more willing to violate unrelated laws, and that survey subjects who read accounts of an unjust criminal outcome were later more willing to nullify the law as jurors in an unrelated

criminal case); Paul H. Robinson & John M. Darley, *The Utility of Desert*, 91 Nw. U. L. Rev. 453, 457, 474, 477, 483–85, 488 (1997).

48. On the role jury trials played historically in educating and empowering citizens and legitimating the justice system, see I Alexis de Tocqueville, Democracy in America 280–87 (Phillips Bradley ed., Francis Bowen rev., Henry Reeve trans., Vintage Books 1990) (1835); Amar, The Constitution and Criminal proce-dure, *supra* Introduction note 1, at 93–96, 111–14; *supra* chapter I.A.1.

    For a powerful argument that the secrecy and opacity of police and prosecuto-rial discretion weaken citizens' trust in the law, see Erik Luna, *Transparent Policing*, 85 Iowa L. Rev. 1107, 1156–63 (2000). *See also* Amy Gutmann & Dennis Thomp-son, Democracy and Disagreement 95–101 (1996) (explaining that publicity of information and government officials' reasons for actions not only "help[s to] sustain a sense of legitimacy" but also promotes democratic deliberation).

    On victims' and defendants' perceptions that plea bargaining is procedurally unjust, see Michael M. O'Hear, *Plea Bargaining and Procedural Justice*, 42 Ga. L. Rev. 407, 415–20 (2008).

49. On general lack of confidence in the criminal justice system, see Gallup Poll, June 2009, retrieved June 9, 2010 from the iPOLL Databank, The Roper Center for Public Opinion Research, University of Connecticut. http://ropercenter.uconn.edu/data_access/ipoll/ipoll.htm (last visited July 14, 2010) (reporting that only 11% of poll respondents had "a great deal" of confidence in the American criminal justice system and an additional 17% had "quite a lot" of confidence in it).

    On suspicion of plea bargaining in particular, see Myers, *supra* note 35, at 54–55 & tbl.4.2; Robert F. Rich & Robert J. Sampson, *Public Perceptions of Criminal Justice Policy: Does Victimization Make a Difference?*, 5 Violence & Victims 109, 114 (1990); *see also* Public Agenda Foundation, Polling the Nations, Feb. 10, 2002 (reporting, based on June 2001 telephone survey, that only 14% of respondents support plea bargaining for violent crimes).

    On the implementation of strong and weak victims' rights laws, see Nat'l Ctr. for Victims of Crime, Statutory and Constitutional Protection of Victims' Rights: Implementation and Impact on Crime Victims 31–38, 43–46, 51–63 (1996). That study differentiated strong from weak victims' rights laws using a mathematical formula that averaged the laws' comprehensiveness, enforceability, and specificity. It compared the implementation of victims' rights in states in the top quartile (those with strong laws) with those in the bottom quartile (those with weak laws). *Id.* at 11–16.

50. Amar, The Constitution and Criminal procedure, *supra* Introduction note 1, at 84–88.

51. This is the argument of William J. Stuntz, The Collapse of American Crimi-nal Justice (2011).

52. *See generally* The Spangenberg Group, Rates of Compensation Paid to Court-Appointed Counsel in Non-Capital Felony Cases at Trial: A State by State Overview app. 1–9 (June 2007) (reporting states' hourly rates for appointed defense counsel in noncapital cases, most of which cluster between $40 and $65 per hour, and indicating that almost half of states cap fees in many cases at levels between $445 and $3600, meaning that, in many states, any work invested beyond several dozen hours per case is effectively uncompensated).

53. On the effects of flat fees and salaries, see Jones v. Barnes, 463 U.S. 745, 761 (1983) (Brennan, J., dissenting) (discussing how flat fees encourage fast dispositions); Recorder's Court Bar Ass'n v. Wayne Circuit Court, 503 N.W.2d 885, 887–88 (Mich. 1993) (stating that under a fixed-fee system, "'[t]he incentive, if a lawyer is not paid to spend more time with and for the client, is to put in as little time as possible for the pay allowed. Under the current system, a lawyer can earn $100 an hour for a guilty plea, whereas if he or she goes to trial, the earnings may be $15 an hour or less'" (quoting special master's findings of fact)); RICHARD KLEIN & ROBERT SPANGENBERG, THE INDIGENT DEFENSE CRISIS 6 (1993); Ken Armstrong et al., *Attorney Profited, But His Clients Lost*, SEATTLE TIMES, Apr. 5, 2004, at A1 (reporting that a part-time appointed defense lawyer earned large salaries for disposing of cases after little work, leaving time to earn more money in part-time private practice); Ken Armstrong et al., *For Some, Free Counsel Comes at a High Cost*, SEATTLE TIMES, Apr. 4, 2004, at A1 (reporting that a county's flat-fee system led appointed defense counsel to dispose of staggering caseloads through perfunctory representation, producing the highest guilty-plea rate in Washington State).

On the caseloads and financial pressures that push defense lawyers to plea bargain, see David Luban, *Are Criminal Defenders Different?*, 91 MICH. L. REV. 1729, 1757 (1993); Stephen J. Schulhofer, *Plea Bargaining as Disaster*, 101 YALE L.J. 1979, 1988–90 (1992); *see also* Richard Klein, *The Emperor Gideon Has No Clothes: The Empty Promise of the Constitutional Right to Effective Assistance of Counsel*, 13 HASTINGS CONST. L.Q. 625, 672 (1986).

On the incentives of involuntarily appointed private lawyers, see JAMES EISENSTEIN, COUNSEL FOR THE UNITED STATES: U.S. ATTORNEYS IN THE POLITICAL AND LEGAL SYSTEMS 173 (1978); Albert W. Alschuler, *The Defense Attorney's Role in Plea Bargaining*, 84 YALE L.J. 1179, 1182, 1259 (1975); William J. Stuntz, *The Uneasy Relationship Between Criminal Procedure and Criminal Justice*, 107 YALE L.J. 1, 10–11, 33 (1997); *see also* STATE BAR OF TEX. LEGAL SERVS. TO THE POOR IN CRIMINAL MATTERS COMM., PROSECUTOR SURVEY RESULTS, THE STATUS OF INDIGENT CRIMINAL DEFENSE IN TEXAS questions 18, 31 (n.d.) (unpublished manuscript, on file with the author) (reporting that Texas defense lawyers who handle both retained and appointed cases devote less time to their indigent clients, are less prepared to defend them, and put on less vigorous defenses, and that nearly half of Texas prosecutors believe that compensation rates are inadequate to attract qualified private counsel for court appointments).

The quotation in the text is from Abraham S. Blumberg, *The Practice of Law as Confidence Game: Organizational Cooptation of a Profession*, 1 LAW & SOC'Y REV. 15, 24–31 (1967) (capitalization of initial letters omitted) (describing defense lawyers as players in a game who influence clients' choices to serve their own interests in collecting fees without doing much work and their cooperation with prosecutors and court personnel in moving cases along).

54. On public defenders' dockets, see State v. Peart, 621 So. 2d 780 (La. 1993) (finding New Orleans's public defender system presumptively ineffective because counsel handled 70 active felony cases at a time, which amounted to 418 defendants over a seven-month period); ROBERT BURKE ET AL., NAT'L LEGAL AID & DEFENDER ASS'N, INDIGENT DEFENSE CASELOADS AND COMMON SENSE: AN UPDATE 3–5 (1992); Ken Armstrong & Justin Mayo, *Frustrated Attorney: "You Just Can't Help People,"* SEATTLE TIMES, Apr. 6, 2004, at A1. On private attorneys' incentives to take on too many cases, see Alschuler, *The Defense Attorney's Role, supra* note 53, at 1201.

55. On repeat defense counsel's fears of reprisals, see Alschuler, *The Defense Attorney's Role, supra* note 53, at 1237–38, 1240, 1261–62 & n.225; Darryl K. Brown, *Rationing Criminal Defense Entitlements: An Argument from Institutional Design*, 104 COLUM. L. REV. 801, 812 & n.46 (2004) (explaining that courts lean towards appointing defense lawyers who dispose of cases quickly instead of making extra work for judges by filing motions, investigating, or seeking expert witnesses); *see also* PROSECUTOR SURVEY RESULTS, *supra* note 53, question 3 (noting that an attorney's reputation for moving cases is the single biggest factor in winning court appointments, and so implying that defense attorneys who wish to keep receiving court appointments must dispose of them efficiently). *Cf.* Margareth Etienne, *Remorse, Responsibility, and Regulating Advocacy: Making Defendants Pay for the Sins of Their Lawyers*, 78 N.Y.U. L. REV. 2103, 2171–73 (2003) (arguing that judges have incentives to penalize defendants and their counsel for zealous advocacy, leading defense counsel to tread lightly in their advocacy); Margareth Etienne, *The Declining Utility of the Right to Counsel in Federal Criminal Courts: An Empirical Study on the Role of Defense Attorney Advocacy Under the Sentencing Guidelines*, 92 CAL. L. REV. 425, 429–30 (2004) (same).

On public defenders' triage, see HEUMANN, *supra* chapter I note 61, at 61–66, 69, 72, 74, 123–26; Alschuler, *The Defense Attorney's Role, supra*, at 1210–11, 1222, 1224; *see* Rodney Thaxton, *Professionalism and Life in the Trenches: The Case of the Public Defender*, 8 ST. THOMAS L. REV. 185, 187 (1995) (comparing the work of public defenders to battlefield triage, in which medics must focus their efforts on the most serious cases).

On trading off one client against another, see DAVID A. JONES, CRIME WITHOUT PUNISHMENT 120–21 (1979) (noting that defense counsel will sometimes concede that one defendant who is uncooperative or has committed a very serious crime deserves a heavier sentence in exchange for a lighter sentence for other defendants, and also noting that whites are more likely to benefit from this practice while minorities are more likely to suffer); Alschuler, *The Defense Attorney's Role, supra*, at 1223.

56. Bibas, *Plea Bargaining Outside the Shadow of Trial, supra* chapter I note 83, at 2498–2504, 2511–12.

57. *Cf.* Alexandra Natapoff, *Speechless: The Silencing of Criminal Defendants*, 80 N.Y.U. L. REV. 1449, 1465 (2005) (noting the enormous social, linguistic, and experiential gap between judges and defendants).

58. *Id.* at 1465, 1468.

59. AM. BAR ASS'N, GIDEON'S BROKEN PROMISE: AMERICA'S CONTINUING QUEST FOR EQUAL JUSTICE: A REPORT ON THE AMERICAN BAR ASSOCIATION'S HEARINGS ON THE RIGHT TO COUNSEL IN CRIMINAL PROCEEDINGS 16 (2004) (describing the typical practice in Calcasieu Parish, Louisiana, as related by several witnesses who experienced the "meet 'em and plead 'em" lawyers there); Natapoff, *supra* note 57, at 1462–63, 1474 (describing this "not uncommon . . . 'meet 'em and plead 'em' scenario" as "exacerbated by mistrust").

60. *See* Lisa G. Lerman, *Lying to Clients*, 138 U. PA. L. REV. 659, 700–01 (1990) (discussing the findings of a study on lawyer-client relationships in personal injury cases in DOUGLAS E. ROSENTHAL, LAWYER AND CLIENT: WHO'S IN CHARGE (1974)); *id.* at 734 (discussing lawyers who lowball their valuations of cases so that eventual settlements look favorable); *id.* at 740 (discussing how lawyers who

want to lighten their workloads present settlement offers to their clients in ways that are calculated to induce acceptance).

61. Natapoff, *supra* note 57 at 1474; Bibas, *Plea Bargaining Outside the Shadow of Trial*, *supra* chapter I note 83, at 2482. As a result, defendants lie to their lawyers, so their lawyers disbelieve them. HEUMANN, *supra* chapter I note 61, at 59 (quoting four defense attorneys to the same effect: "the first year you practice law you believe everything your client tells you. The second year you practice, you believe everything that the other side tells you. The third year you don't know who's telling the truth. Most people tend not to believe their clients that much, justifiably." (quoting one of the four defense lawyers)).

On defendants' greater reluctance to follow appointed counsel's advice, see Alschuler, *The Defense Attorney's Role*, *supra* note 53, at 1242; Abbe Smith, *The Difference in Criminal Defense and the Difference It Makes*, 11 WASH. U. J.L. & POL'Y 83, 119 (2003); Daniel W. Stiller, *Guideline Sentencing: Deepening the Distrust Between Federal Defendant and Federal Defender*, 11 FED. SENT'G REP. 304, 304 (1999) (exploring psycho-social factors that cause defendants to distrust their appointed counsel and so hinder defense representation).

62. On how the entry of defense lawyers silenced defendants, see LANGBEIN, *supra* chapter I note 10, at 258–84 (emphasizing "the revolutionary importance of lawyerization of the trial in silencing the accused at trial"). On defendants' refusal to testify to avoid impeachment with their criminal records, see, for example, FED. R. EVID. 404(b), 609; Natapoff, *supra* note 57, at 1459–61. On defense lawyers' scripting of their clients' statements at sentencing, see *id.* at 1462–66.

63. Natapoff, *supra* note 57, at 1470–72, 1476.

CHAPTER III

1. I conducted these telephone interviews in early 2002 with veteran prosecutors, judges, and public and private defense lawyers in Louisiana, Michigan, Missouri, Pennsylvania, and Ohio, all of which appear to use guilty-but-not-guilty pleas frequently, and in Indiana and New Jersey, which forbid them. I followed no scientific method, and of course my sample size was far too small to generate statistically significant results. My methodology was journalistic and impressionistic: It replicated on a much smaller scale the surveys on which Albert Alschuler built his famous articles on plea bargaining.

2. Richard M. Happel & Joseph J. Auffrey, *Sex Offender Assessment: Interrupting the Dance of Denial*, 13 AM. J. FORENSIC PSYCHOL., No. 2 1995, at 5, 6 ("It is rare to find incarcerated sex offenders who are completely honest about their sexual deviance or history of sexual offending. Instead they deny culpability and minimize their behavior. Simply put, they fail to understand the traumatic impact of their sexual aberrance."); *see also* JUDITH LEWIS HERMAN, FATHER-DAUGHTER INCEST 22 (1981) ("Denial has always been the incestuous father's first line of defense"); BARRY M. MALETZKY WITH KEVIN B. MCGOVERN, TREATING THE SEXUAL OFFENDER 27, 164–65, 253–55 (1991) (finding that 87% of sex offenders denied all or part of their crime when first interviewed and that they may give lip service to acceptance of responsibility but rarely appreciate the seriousness or harm caused by their actions); ANNA C. SALTER, TREATING CHILD SEX OFFENDERS AND VICTIMS: A PRACTICAL GUIDE 97 (1988); Howard E. Barbaree, *Denial and*

Minimization Among Sex Offenders: Assessment and Treatment Outcome, 3 F. ON CORRECTIONS RES., no. 4 1991, at 30, 32 tbl.1 (1991) (finding that 54% of rapists denied the existence of an offense and 42% minimized their responsibility, harm to the victim, or the extent of their actions, and also finding that 66% of child molesters denied the offense and 33% minimized it); Nathan L. Pollock & Judith M. Hashmall, *The Excuses of Child Molesters*, 9 BEHAV. SCI. & L. 53, 57 & fig.1 (1991); Diana Scully & Joseph Marolla, *Convicted Rapists' Vocabulary of Motives: Excuses and Justifications*, 31 SOC. PROBS. 530 (1984); Mack E. Winn, *The Strategic and Systematic Management of Denial in Cognitive/Behavioral Treatment of Sexual Offenders*, 8 SEXUAL ABUSE: J. RES. & TREATMENT 25, 27–28 (1996).

3. Gene G. Abel et al., *Sexual Offenders: Results of Assessment and Recommendations for Treatment, in* CLINICAL CRIMINOLOGY: THE ASSESSMENT AND TREATMENT OF CRIMINAL BEHAVIOR 191, 198–200 (Mark H. Ben-Aron et al. eds., 1985); Gene G. Abel et al., *Complications, Consent, and Cognitions in Sex Between Children and Adults*, 7 INT'L J. L. & PSYCHIATRY 89 (1984); Happel & Auffrey, *supra* note 2, at 6; Pollock & Hashmall, *supra* note 2, at 58; John F. Ulrich, A Case Study Comparison of Brief Group Treatment and Brief Individual Treatment in the Modification of Denial Among Child Sexual Abusers 52 (May 1996) (unpublished Ph.D. dissertation, Andrews University School of Education) (on file with the James White Library, Andrews University).

4. *See* Alschuler, *The Defense Attorney's Role, supra* chapter II note 53, at 1280 (quoting one defense lawyer as saying: "the psychological obstacles to confession in [a sex] case are so often overpowering"); *id.* at 1287 (quoting a defense lawyer: "Some clients beg to plead guilty while still asserting their innocence. Their egos are so involved in their initial denials of guilty that it is psychologically impossible for them to change."); *id.* (quoting another defense lawyer as saying: "There are many things people do that they can never bring themselves to admit. Some defendants are literally insane on this point."); *id.* at 1304 (discussing defendants "who are psychologically incapable of admitting their guilt" and those who want "face-saving denials of culpability—'grace notes' that could enable the defendants to pretend to their families, to their friends, or perhaps even to themselves that they were the hapless victims of circumstance").

5. *See, e.g.*, Natapoff, *supra* chapter II note 57, at 1467–68.

6. North Carolina v. Alford, 400 U.S. 25, 26–29, 36–38 & n.11 (1970). Because an *Alford* plea is a guilty plea, it does create an estoppel in future litigation against the defendant, unlike a no-contest plea.

7. Interviewees' descriptions of the frequency with which innocent defendants use guilty-but-not-guilty pleas ranged from "occasionally" to "extremely uncommon" to "[in]significant" to "very rare." For example, one longtime public defender estimated that he had seen no more than five to ten innocent defendants use these pleas over the last sixteen years.

8. FED. R. CRIM. P. 11(b); G. NICHOLAS HERMAN, PLEA BARGAINING §§ 7.12, 8.05, 8.06 (1997). Thirty-eight states plus the District of Columbia permit no-contest pleas. *See* ALASKA R. CRIM. P. 11(a); ARIZ. R. CRIM. P. 17.1(a)(1); ARK. R. CRIM. P. 24.3(a); CAL. PENAL CODE § 1016(3) (West 2011); COLO. REV. STAT. § 16–7–205(1)(c) (2009); CONN. R. SUPER. CT. § 37–7; DEL. SUPER. CT. CRIM. R. 11(b); D.C. SUPT. CT. R. CRIM. P. 11(a); FLA. R. CRIM. P. 3.170(a); GA. R. UNIF. SUPER.

CT. R. 33.1(A); GA. CODE ANN. § 17–7–95 (2010); HAW. R. PENAL P. 11(a)(1); 725 ILL. COMP. STAT. ANN. 5/113–4.1 (West 2010) (specifying their availability for state income tax violations); KAN. STAT. ANN. § 22–3208(1) (West 2010); LA. CODE CRIM. PROC. ANN. art. 552(4) (West 2010); ME. R. CRIM. P. 11(a); MD. CODE ANN., Maryland Rules § 4–242(a) (West 2010); MASS. R. CRIM. P. 12(a)(1); MICH. CT. R. 6.301(A); MISS. UNIF. CIR. & CTY. CT. R. 8.04(A)(1); MONT. CODE ANN. § 46–12–204(1) (2009); NEB. REV. STAT. § 29–1819.01 (2010); NEV. REV. STAT. ANN. § 174.035(1) (2009); N.H. REV. STAT. ANN. § 605:6 (2010); N.M. DIST. CT. R. CRIM. P. 5–304.A(1); N.M. MAGISTRATE CT. R. CRIM. P. 6–302.A; N.M. METRO. CT. R. CRIM. P. 7–302.A; N.C. GEN. STAT. ANN. § 7A-272(c) (West 2009); OKLA. STAT. ANN. tit. 22, § 513 (2010); OR. REV. STAT. ANN. § 135.335(1)(c) (West 2010); PA. R. CRIM. P. 590(A)(2); R.I. SUPER. CT. R. CRIM. P. 11; S.C. CODE ANN. § 17–23–40 (2010) (for misdemeanors); S.D. CODIFIED LAWS § 23A-7–2(4) (2004); TENN. R. CRIM. P. 11(a)(1); TEX. CODE CRIM. PROC. ANN. § 27.02(5) (West 2009); UTAH CODE ANN. § 77–13–1(1)(c) (LexisNexis 2010); VT. R. CRIM. P. 11(a) (1); VA. CODE ANN. § 19.2–254 (West 2010); W. VA. R. CRIM. P. 11(a)(1); W. VA. MAGISTRATE CTS. CRIM. P. R. 10(a); WIS. STAT. ANN. § 971.06(1)(c) (West 2009); WYO. R. CRIM. P. 11(a). South Carolina cases indicate that felony defendants are still entering no-contest pleas even though the South Carolina Supreme Court advised lower courts to refuse such pleas in felony cases. *See* Kibler v. State, 227 S.E.2d 199, 201 (S.C. 1976); *see also* Deal v. State, 527 S.E.2d 112, 112 (S.C. 2000) (indicating that the defendant entered a nolo contendere plea to possession of contraband by a prisoner); State v. Munsch, 338 S.E.2d 329, 329–30 (S.C. 1985) (indicating that the defendant entered a nolo contendere plea to the felony crime of assault and battery of a high and aggravated nature).

Forty-eight states plus the District of Columbia permit *Alford* pleas (sometimes called best-interests pleas). *See* Allison v. State, 495 So. 2d 739, 741 (Ala. Crim. App. 1986); Wike v. State, 623 P.2d 356, 359 (Alaska Ct. App. 1981); State *ex rel.* McDougall v. Nastro, 800 P.2d 974, 975 (Ariz. 1990) (en banc); Harris v. State, 620 S.W.2d 289, 291 (Ark. 1981); *In re* Alvernaz, 830 P.2d 747, 758 n.9 (Cal. 1992) (in bank); People v. Canino, 508 P.2d 1273, 1274–75 (Colo. 1973) (en banc); State v. Amarillo, 503 A.2d 146, 162 n.17 (Conn. 1986); Robinson v. State, 291 A.2d 279, 281 (Del. 1972); *In re* Fogel, 728 A.2d 668, 669–70 (D.C. 1999); Boykin v. Garrison, 658 So. 2d 1090, 1090–91 (Fla. Dist. Ct. App. 1995); Goodman v. Davis, 287 S.E.2d 26, 30 (Ga. 1982); State v. Smith, 606 P.2d 86, 89 (Haw. 1980); Sparrow v. State, 625 P.2d 414, 415 (Idaho 1981); People v. Barker, 415 N.E.2d 404, 410 (Ill. 1980); State v. Hansen, 344 N.W.2d 725, 727 n.1 (Iowa App.1983); State v. Dillon, 748 P.2d 856, 859–60 (Kan. 1988); Commonwealth v. Corey, 826 S.W.2d 319, 321 (Ky. 1992); State v. Blanchard, 786 So. 2d 701, 703 (La. 2001); State v. Malo, 577 A.2d 332, 334 (Me. 1990); Banegura v. Taylor, 541 A.2d 969, 971 n.1 (Md. 1988); Commonwealth v. Lewis, 506 N.E.2d 891, 892 (Mass. 1987); State v. Goulette, 258 N.W.2d 758, 760 (Minn. 1977); Reynolds v. State, 521 So. 2d 914, 916 (Miss. 1988); Brown v. State, 45 S.W.3d 506, 507–08 (Mo. Ct. App. 2001); State v. Cameron, 830 P.2d 1284, 1290 (Mont. 1992), *overruled on other grounds by* Montana v. Deserly, 188 P.3d 1057, 1060 n.1 (Mont. 2008); State v. Rhodes, 445 N.W.2d 622, 624–25 (Neb. 1989); State v. Gomes, 930 P.2d 701, 705 (Nev. 1996); Wellington v. Comm'r, N.H. Dep't of Corr., 666 A.2d 969, 970 (N.H. 1995); State v. Hodge, 882 P.2d 1, 3 n.1 (N.M. 1994); People v. Hicks, 608 N.Y.S.2d 543, 543–44 (N.Y. App. Div. 1994); State v. McClure,185 S.E.2d 693, 696–97 (N.C. 1972); Commonwealth v. Cabrera, 2 N. Mar. I. 311, 316–19 (1991); State v. Padgett, 586 N.E.2d

1194, 1197–98 (Ohio Ct. App. 1990); Ocampo v. State, 778 P.2d 920, 923 (Okla. Crim. App. 1989); State *ex rel.* Juvenile Dep't v. Welch, 501 P.2d 991, 995 (Or. Ct. App. 1972); Commonwealth v. Fluharty, 632 A.2d 312, 315–16 (Pa. Super. Ct. 1993); State v. Fontaine, 559 A.2d 622, 624 (R.I. 1989); Gaines v. State, 517 S.E. 2d 439, 440–41 n.1 (S.C. 1999); State v. Engelmann, 541 N.W. 2d 96, 101 (S.D. 1995); State v. Williams, 851 S.W.2d 828, 830 (Tenn. Crim. App. 1992); Johnson v. State, 478 S.W.2d 954, 955 (Tex. Crim. App. 1972); State v. Stilling, 856 P.2d 666, 671 (Utah Ct. App. 1993); State v. Fisk, 682 A.2d 937, 938 (Vt. 1996); Perry v. Commonwealth, 533 S.E.2d 651, 652 (Va. Ct. App. 2000); State v. Osborne, 684 P.2d 683, 687 (Wash. 1984); Kennedy v. Frazier, 357 S.E. 2d 43, 45 (W. Va. 1987); State v. Garcia, 532 N.W.2d 111, 115–17 (Wis. 1995); Johnston v. State, 829 P.2d 1179, 1181 (Wyo. 1992); *see* People v. Booth, 324 N.W.2d 741, 748 (Mich. 1982); State v. Bates, 726 N.W. 2d 595, 589 & n.1 (N.D. 2007).

The statistics are found in Harlow, *supra* chapter II note 3, at 8 tbl.17 (reporting statistics on the types of pleas entered by state and federal prison inmates in 1997).

9. Josh Bowers, *Punishing the Innocent*, 156 U. Pa. L. Rev. 1117 (2008); Frank H. Easterbrook, *Criminal Procedure as a Market System*, 12 J. Legal Stud. 289, 320 (1983); Steven E. Walburn, *Should the Military Adopt an* Aford [*sic*]*-Type Guilty Plea?*, 44 A.F. L. Rev. 119, 143–44, 160–61 (1998); Curtis J. Shipley, Note, *The Alford Plea: A Necessary but Unpredictable Tool for the Criminal Defendant*, 72 Iowa L. Rev. 1063, 1073, 1089 (1987); Albert W. Alschuler, *Straining at Gnats and Swallowing Camels: The Selective Morality of Professor Bibas*, 88 Cornell L. Rev. 1412, 1422–24 (2003); Albert W. Alschuler, *The Defense Attorney's Role*, *supra* chapter II note 53, at 1296–98.

10. On innocent defendants' overestimating their risk of conviction at trial, see Stephen J. Schulhofer, *Criminal Justice Discretion as a Regulatory System*, 17 J. Legal Stud. 43, 78–79 (1988); Schulhofer, *Plea Bargaining as Disaster*, *supra* chapter II note 53, at 1981–82. On misrepresentations and pressures to plead, see Alschuler, *The Defense Attorney's Role*, *supra* chapter II note 53, at 1191–98, 1287–89 (describing how defense lawyers whom Alschuler interviewed used lies, misrepresentations, interrogation, cajolery, and psychological pressure "'almost to the point of coercion'" to procure confessions and guilty pleas).

11. The very prosecution of innocent people should gravely concern us. We can sympathize with innocent defendants who are sorely tempted to plead guilty in exchange for generous plea bargains, but encouraging these guilty pleas sweeps the underlying problem of innocence under the rug. We must work to reduce the prosecution of innocent defendants by funding better defense counsel, eyewitness-identification and informant procedures, private investigators, DNA testing, and much more.

12. The quotation about externalities is from Schulhofer, *Plea Bargaining as Disaster*, *supra* chapter II note 53, at 1985. The perception of accuracy quotation is from *In re* Winship, 397 U.S. 358, 364 (1970); *accord* Schulhofer, *Plea Bargaining as Disaster*, *supra*, at 1985–86.

13. The wrongful-conviction literature details several dozen cases of defendants who pleaded guilty (whether out of fear of the death penalty, because of mental retardation, or for other reasons) but were later exonerated. *See, e.g.*, Carroll v.

State, 474 S.E.2d 737, 738–40 (Ga. Ct. App. 1996) (noting that the defendant had pleaded guilty to vehicular homicide and vehicular serious injury based on a faulty accident reconstruction, though a later accident-reconstruction expert found no evidence of the defendant's excessive speed and concluded that the new pavement and drop-off shoulder had contributed to the accident); State v. Gardner, 885 P.2d 1144, 1147, 1149–50, 1152 (Idaho Ct. App. 1994) (noting that a defendant who had not remembered an accident had pleaded guilty to vehicular manslaughter, despite an undisclosed witness's statement that a tire blowout rather than driver error had caused the accident); Hugo Adam Bedau & Michael L. Radelet, *Miscarriages of Justice in Potentially Capital Cases*, 40 Stan. L. Rev. 21, 92, 96, 97, 103–05, 111–12, 116, 119, 127, 139, 141, 146, 150 (1987) (detailing twenty-one false guilty pleas); *The Innocence Project—Know the Cases: Browse Profiles*, http://www.innocenceproject.org/know/Browse-Profiles.php (last visited May 12, 2011) (profiling the wrongful guilty pleas of Larry Bostic, Marcellius Bradford, Keith Brown, John Dixon, Anthony Gray, Eugene Henton, Christopher Ochoa, James Ochoa, Jerry Frank Townsend, David Vasquez, and Arthur Lee Whitfield).

On public opinion, see Myers, *supra* chapter II note 35, at 54–55 & tbl. 4.2 (noting that 67% of Americans oppose plea bargaining); Lawrence W. Sherman, *Trust and Confidence in Criminal Justice*, Nat'l Inst. Justice J., Mar. 2002, at 23 exhibit 1 (noting general lack of confidence in the system).

14. Letter from Immanuel Kant to J.B. Erhard (Dec. 21, 1792) *in* Kant: Philosophical Correspondence 1795–99, at 199 (Arnulf Zweig ed. & trans., 1967); C.S. Lewis, The Problem of Pain 95 (1962); *accord id.* at 93–95, 120–22; Hampton, *The Moral Education Theory of Punishment*, *supra* chapter II note 44, at 115–17, 120–21; *see also* 2 Nikolai Velimirović, The Prologue from Ochrid 301 (Mother Maria trans., 1985) (explaining that when a person's spirit and conscience are insensitive, love requires punishing the body to rouse the spirit and conscience from their sleep).

On contrition and repentance, see R.A. Duff, Trials and Punishments 254–62 (1986); *see also* Thomas Hobbes, Leviathan 35 (Michael Oakeshott ed., Basil Blackwell 1960) (1651) (defining "Revengefulness" as "*Desire*, by doing hurt to another, to make him condemn some fact of his own").

On atonement, see Stephen P. Garvey, *Punishment as Atonement*, 46 UCLA L. Rev. 1801, 1804–05 (1999). Indeed, the word "atone" comes from "at one"— atonement makes the wrongdoer at one with the victim and the community. Oxford English Dictionary 754 (2d ed. 1989). Similarly, repentance involves "remorseful[ly] accept[ing] responsibility" for the wrong and harm one has done, "repudiati[ng]" and resolving to change the character traits that led one to misbehave, "and [] resolv[ing] to atone or make amends for the [wrong and] harm that one has done." Murphy, *Repentance, Punishment, and Mercy, in* Repentance: A Comparative Perspective 143, 147 (Amitai Etzioni & David E. Carney eds., 1997).

15. On vindicating victims, see Jean Hampton, *The Retributive Idea, in* Murphy & Hampton, *supra* chapter II note 44, at 111, 124–32, 154 (explaining that "the *retributive* motive for inflicting suffering is to annul or counter the appearance of the wrongdoer's superiority and thus affirm the victim's real value," and that repentance paves the way for forgiveness and an end to alienation); Jeffrie Murphy, *Forgiveness and Resentment, in* Murphy & Hampton, *supra* chapter II note 44, at 14, 24–26 (same); Garvey, *Punishment as Atonement*, *supra* note 14, at 1827–29 (arguing that when wrongdoers repent and, better yet, apologize,

they enable victims to forgive, overcome resentment, and reconcile with the wrongdoers).

On expressing society's condemnation, see FEINBERG, *supra* chapter II note 44, at 101–05; ROBERT NOZICK, PHILOSOPHICAL EXPLANATIONS 370–74 (1981); 2 STEPHEN, *supra* chapter II note 44, 170, at 80–82 ("[T]he sentence of the law is to the moral sentiment of the public in relation to any offence what a seal is to hot wax. It converts into a permanent final judgment what might otherwise be a transient sentiment."); Jean Hampton, *An Expressive Theory of Retribution*, *supra* chapter II note 44, at 20–22; Henry M. Hart, Jr., *The Aims of the Criminal Law*, 23 LAW & CONTEMP. PROBS. 401, 404–05 (1958); Kahan, *What Do Alternative Sanctions Mean?*, *supra* chapter II note 44, at 593, 597–601 (1996); *see also* DURKHEIM, *supra* chapter I note 33, at 63 (noting that the real function of the criminal law is to reinforce social cohesion by denouncing transgressions and thus reaffirming the violated social norms).

16. On the need to admit wrongdoing, see McKune v. Lile, 536 U.S. 24, 33–34 (2002) (Kennedy, J., plurality opinion); Winn, *supra* chapter II note 2, at 26–27. As the Ninth Circuit has noted, it is "almost axiomatic that the first step toward rehabilitation of an offender is the offender's recognition that he was at fault." Gollaher v. United States, 419 F.2d 520, 530 (9th Cir. 1969) (affirming trial court's decision to impose a harsher sentence because of defendant's refusal to admit guilt after he was convicted).

On twelve-step programs, see ALCOHOLICS ANONYMOUS, TWELVE STEPS AND TWELVE TRADITIONS 21–24 (1981) (noting that in Step One, an alcoholic must "humbl[e] himself" and be "rigorously honest" as a prerequisite to change); *id.* at 56–63 (stating that in Step Five, alcoholics must humble themselves by admitting their defects to others, in order to pierce self-delusions, rationalizations, and wishful thinking); *see* Robert A. Moore & Thomas C. Murphy, *Denial of Alcoholism as an Obstacle to Recovery*, 22 Q. J. STUD. ON ALCOHOL 597 (1961).

On the importance of confessed details to therapeutic responses, see Barbaree, *supra* note 2, at 30 ("Therapists depend on offenders' truthful descriptions of events leading to past offences in order to determine which behaviours need to be targetted [*sic*] in therapy"); Diane D. Hildebran & William D. Pithers, *Relapse Prevention: Application and Outcome*, *in* 2 THE SEXUAL ABUSE OF CHILDREN: CLINICAL ISSUES: 365, 367–75 (William O'Donohue & James H. Geer eds., 1992); William O'Donohue & Elizabeth Letourneau, *A Brief Group Treatment for the Modification of Denial in Child Sexual Abusers: Outcome and Follow-Up*, 17 CHILD ABUSE & NEGLECT 299, 300 (1993).

On how denial masks cognitive distortions and warning signs and obstructs development of empathy, see Stefan J. Padfield, Comment, *Self-Incrimination and Acceptance of Responsibility in Prison Sex Offender Treatment Programs*, 49 U. KAN. L. REV. 487, 498 (2001).

On denial as a disqualification for sex-offender treatment, see Randy Green, *Comprehensive Treatment Planning for Sex Offenders*, *in* NAT'L INST. OF CORR., U.S. DEP'T OF JUSTICE, A PRACTITIONER'S GUIDE TO TREATING THE INCARCERATED MALE SEX OFFENDER 71, 72–73 (1988), *reprinted in* 1 THE SEX OFFENDER: CORRECTIONS, TREATMENT AND LEGAL PRACTICE 10–1, 10–4 (1995) ("Most treatment programs only take offenders who admit their guilt. . . . The offender should be able to openly acknowledge guilt. This admission is a basic requirement for meaningful participation. . . . Not only must an offender admit his guilt but he must accept full responsibility for it."); BARBARA E. SMITH ET AL., AM. BAR ASS'N, THE

PROBATION RESPONSE TO CHILD SEXUAL ABUSE OFFENDERS: HOW IS IT WORK- ING? 8 (1990) ("With few exceptions, the therapists interviewed said they would not accept anyone in their program who absolutely denied sexual contact with children. Most firmly believed that individuals who denied the abuse were not amenable to treatment."); O'Donohue & Letourneau, *supra* at 300. According to my interviews, the sex-offender treatment program in Missouri state prison requires admission of guilt as a condition of therapy. Thus, Missouri judges will not allow sex offenders to enter *Alford* pleas.

On denial's link to recidivism, see *McKune*, 536 U.S. at 33 (Kennedy, J., plural- ity opinion) (noting that untreated wrongdoers are more than five times as likely to recidivate as treated wrongdoers (80% versus 15%) and that denial greatly increases the likelihood that wrongdoers will fail treatment (citing MALETZKY & MCGOVERN, *supra* note 2, at 253–55 and NAT'L INST. OF CORR., U.S. DEP'T OF JUSTICE, *supra*, at xiii)); Lucy Berliner, *Sex Offenders: Policy and Practice*, 92 NW. U. L. REV. 1203, 1209–10 (1998) (reporting two randomized, controlled studies that found higher recidivism rates for untreated sex offenders; in one, nearly three-quarters of untreated sex offenders reoffended, compared to one-eighth of treated offenders).

17. On the effectiveness of firm challenges, see W.L. Marshall, *Treatment Effects on Denial and Minimization in Incarcerated Sex Offenders*, 32 BEHAV. RES. & THERAPY 559, 562 (1994); *see* SALTER, *supra* note 2, at 88–95.

On the need for active challenges and the failure of passive approaches, see WILLIAM E. PRENDERGAST, TREATING SEX OFFENDERS IN CORRECTIONAL INSTI- TUTIONS AND OUTPATIENT CLINICS: A GUIDE TO CLINICAL PRACTICE 105–08, 111–12 (1991).

On the varieties of possible challenges, see *id.* at 107 (asking for explanations and details and suggesting flat rejection of the sex offender's story); MALETZKY & MCGOVERN, *supra* note 2, at 156–58, 160–61 (discussing group confrontation and role-playing); SALTER, *supra* note 2, at 112–17 (discussing confrontational group therapy); *id.* at 124–26 (discussing cognitive restructuring); Barbaree, *supra* note 2, at 32 (advocating the use of group therapy to challenge discrepancies); Gad Czudner & Ruth Mueller, *The Role of Guilt and Its Implication in the Treat- ment of Criminals*, 31 INT'L J. OFFENDER THERAPY & COMP. CRIMINOLOGY 71, 74 (1987) (suggesting group therapy involving repetition, control, and peer pressure to break down excuses); Michael J. Dougher, *Clinical Assessment of Sex Offenders*, *in* NAT'L INST. OF CORR., U.S. DEP'T OF JUSTICE, *supra* note 16, at 77, 79 (sug- gesting that "sex education, group therapy, and cognitive-behavior techniques may be useful" for dealing with cognitive distortions); Marshall, *supra* at 561–62 (recommending group therapy using "supportive but firm challenges" to test veracity and inconsistencies); Winn, *supra* chapter II note 2, at 28–33 (endors- ing indirect confrontation, challenging wrongdoers to challenge themselves, and eliciting the wrongdoer's permission to confront); Ulrich, *supra* note 3, at 298, 309–10 (suggesting that group therapy pushes, pulls, and encourages wrongdoers to confess as they see others doing so).

On the usefulness of external pressures, see Czudner & Mueller, *supra* at 73–74; *see also* O'Donohue & Letourneau, *supra* note 16, at 303.

18. On the efficacy of confessions in court, see DONALD J. NEWMAN, CONVICTION: THE DETERMINATION OF GUILT OR INNOCENCE WITHOUT TRIAL 221–23 (Frank J. Remington ed., 1966); *see also* Elizabeth Mertz & Kimberly A. Lonsway, *The*

Power of Denial: Individual and Cultural Constructions of Child Sexual Abuse, 92 Nw.
U. L. Rev. 1415, 1419, 1457–58 (1998) (noting that the legal system, by challenging denials in the adversary system, "can help to puncture false denials and reveal
unpleasant truths"); William Schma, *Judging for the New Millennium*, Ct. Rev.,
Spring 2000, at 4, 5 (noting that, once a defendant has allocuted to his guilt at a
plea hearing, the judge can use the details of that plea to confront the defendant
more effectively at sentencing with the wrongfulness of the behavior).

For evidence that unchallenged denials harden wrongdoers and make them
harder to treat, see Marshall, *supra* note 17, at 562 (noting that when defense
lawyers and therapists fail to challenge sex offenders in denial, or even encourage them to exculpate themselves, wrongdoers see these reactions as confirmation and become even more difficult to treat); Minnesota Dep't of Corrections,
Sex Offender Supervision Training, in Probation Officer Manual ch. 3, at 4,
cited in Stephanos Bibas, *Harmonizing Substantive-Criminal-Law Values and Criminal Procedure: The Case of* Alford *and Nolo Contendere Pleas*, 88 Cornell L. Rev.
1361, 1397 & nn. 180–181 (2003) (discussing *Norgaard* pleas, the Minnesota equivalent of no-contest pleas for defendants who have amnesia or were
intoxicated); *see also* Eric S. Janus & Paul E. Meehl, *Assessing the Legal Standard
for Predictions of Dangerousness in Sex Offender Commitment Proceedings*, 3 Psychol. Pub. Pol'y & L. 33, 51–59 (1997) (collecting statistics and settling on
recidivism figures of between 20% and 45% for sexual offenders); Hollida Wakefield & Ralph Underwager, *Assessing Violent Recidivism in Sexual Offenders*, 10
Issues in Child Abuse Accusations 92, 93 (1998) (listing findings of recidivism
rates of 13% within four to five years and 39% to 52% within 25 years for sexual
offenders).

19. *Cf.* Schma, *supra* note 18, at 5 (describing similar experiences).

20. Robert A. Fein, *How the Insanity Acquittal Retards Treatment, in* Therapeutic
Jurisprudence: The Law as a Therapeutic Agent 49, 52–59 (David B. Wexler
ed., 1990). On this logic, one might want to label defendants as guilty but mentally ill, rather than not guilty by reason of insanity, even if the sanction remained
mental-health treatment instead of traditional prison.

21. For a discussion of how denial affects wrongdoers more generally, see, for
example, Czudner & Miller, *supra* note 17, at 72–76 (discussing wrongdoers generally, the need for confessions as prerequisites for treatment, and the constructive
role of guilt as an inducement to reform, and giving clinical examples of wrongdoers whose crimes ranged from assault to breaking and entering to armed robbery
and attempted murder).

For a discussion of the kinds of defendants who feel the need to use *Alford*
pleas, see Alschuler, *The Defense Attorney's Role, supra* chapter II note 53, at
1304 (describing the *Alford* plea as a "crutch" that is needed for "a small group
of obviously guilty defendants who are psychologically incapable of admitting
their guilt").

22. Albert W. Alschuler, *The Changing Plea Bargaining Debate*, 69 Cal. L. Rev. 652,
661–63 (1981); Garvey, *Punishment as Atonement, supra* note 14, at 1850 & n.215
("A man should always occupy himself with Torah and good deeds, though it is not
for their own sake, for out of [doing good] with an ulterior motive there comes
[doing good] for its own sake" (alterations in original) (quoting Pesahim 50b (H.
Freedman trans.), *in* 4 The Soncino Talmud pt. 2, at 245 (I. Epstein ed., 1938)).

23. KENNETH S. BORDENS & IRWIN A. HOROWITZ, SOCIAL PSYCHOLOGY 248 (2d ed. 2002).

24. *See* Gerard V. Bradley, *Plea Bargaining and the Criminal Defendant's Obligation to Plead Guilty*, 40 S. TEX. L. REV. 65, 71 (1999) ("The pleading defendant sets himself on the path to moral reform. By accepting responsibility for his actions, he cements his status as one who recognizes the basic ends of the law of crime and punishment"); *supra* text accompanying note 19 (discussing the changes that a judge noticed in defendants and their families once the judge began refusing to allow no-contest pleas); *see also* FOUCAULT, *supra* chapter I note 70, at 37–38 (noting a community's satisfaction at a criminal's own acceptance of responsibility); William Burnham, *The Legal Context and Contributions of Dostoevsky's* Crime and Punishment, 100 MICH. L. REV. 1227, 1236 (2002) (describing Dostoevsky's "idea that confession is good for the soul and essential to gaining redemption").

25. The quotation about venting community pressures is from United States v. Lewis, 638 F. Supp. 573, 580 (W.D. Mich. 1986). As the Supreme Court put it, "public trials ha[ve] significant community therapeutic value" and bring "community catharsis." Richmond Newspapers, Inc. v. Virginia, 448 U.S. 555, 570–71 (1980).

For a discussion of the Zenger case, see FRIEDMAN, CRIME AND PUNISHMENT IN AMERICAN HISTORY, *supra* chapter I note 3, at 54–55.

This argument would support, more generally, replacing guilty pleas with jury trials. I take it for granted, however, that the United States is not about to abolish plea bargaining any time soon. Even if high-volume plea bargaining is here to stay for the foreseeable future, we can at least cut back on its most objectionable and least forthright features, including equivocal guilty pleas and charge bargaining.

26. On wrongdoers' abuse of their autonomy, see Herbert Morris, *Persons and Punishment*, 52 MONIST 475, 477–79 (1968). On humbling defendants, see Jeffrie Murphy, *Hatred: A Qualified Defense, in* MURPHY & HAMPTON, *supra* chapter II note 44, at 88, 89; Herbert Fingarette, *Punishment and Suffering*, 50 PROC. & ADDRESSES AM. PHIL. ASS'N 499, 510 (1977).

27. Alschuler, *The Defense Attorney's Role*, *supra* chapter II note 53, at 1287–90; Walburn, *supra* note 9, at 143.

28. On the role of clients' short-term desires, see David Luban, *Paternalism and the Legal Profession*, 1981 WIS. L. REV. 454, 472–74 (arguing that lawyers should disregard their clients' immediate wants when these wants conflict with the clients' values or interests); *cf.* WILLIAM H. SIMON, THE PRACTICE OF JUSTICE: A THEORY OF LAWYERS' ETHICS 8–10, 138–69 (1998) (opposing the dominant view that calls for lawyers to serve only their clients' interests, and instead proposing that lawyers take such actions "that, considering the relevant circumstances of the particular case, seem likely to promote justice").

In contrast to defense counsel, guardians are often authorized to put their wards' long-term interests above their short-term desires. *See* Frances Gall Hill, *Clinical Education and the "Best Interest" Representation of Children in Custody Disputes: Challenges and Opportunities in Lawyering and Pedagogy*, 73 IND. L.J. 605, 617–24 (1998) (defending the need for guardians *ad litem* to place minors' interests above the minors' expressed desires, because minors may lack cognitive skills, maturity, and judgment, or may harm themselves). The Model Rules of Professional Conduct distinguish between the roles of guardians and lawyers by providing that, to the extent possible, lawyers should treat disabled clients just like any other clients. MODEL RULES OF PROF'L CONDUCT R. 1.14(a) (2002). The Rules recognize, however, that in some situations, wards need guardians to make decisions for them or at least guide them in making these decisions. *Id.* at R. 1.14(b).

On how defense counsel can help their clients to confront their problems, see Friedman v. Comm'r of Pub. Safety, 473 N.W.2d 828, 834–35 (Minn. 1991) (noting the important role that defense counsel play in drunk-driving cases in encouraging problem drinkers to seek treatment); Astrid Birgden, *Dealing with the Resistant Criminal Client: A Psychologically-Minded Strategy for More Effective Legal Counseling,* 38 CRIM. L. BULL. 225, 227–29; 238–42 (2002); David B. Wexler, *Some Reflections on Therapeutic Jurisprudence and the Practice of Criminal Law,* 38 CRIM. L. BULL. 205, 206–08 (2002) (noting the example of one defense lawyer who presses clients who are habitual drunk drivers to accept responsibility and get treatment for their underlying alcoholism, which can mitigate punishment and serve clients' long-term interests, and contrasting this with the prevalent deny-guilt-at-all-costs approach of other criminal defense lawyers); Bruce J. Winick, *Redefining the Role of the Criminal Defense Lawyer at Plea Bargaining and Sentencing: A Therapeutic Jurisprudence/Preventive Law Model,* 5 PSYCHOL. PUB. POL'Y & L. 1034, 1041, 1066–76 (1999).

On defense lawyers' offering of moral advice, see MODEL RULES OF PROF'L CONDUCT R. 2.1 (2002) ("In rendering advice, a lawyer may refer not only to law but to other considerations such as moral, economic, social and political factors, that may be relevant to the client's situation.").

29. Here is one psychologist's account of how failure to challenge denials hardens defendants' denial:

> This tendency to resist challenges is all too frequently exacerbated by the fact that their [*sic*] defense lawyer has, perhaps unintentionally, encouraged them [*sic*] to present an exculpatory view of the offense. . . . This encouragement by lawyers[,] and a failure to challenge by professionals, are seen by the offender as confirmation of his claims and this, of course, makes him all the more resistant to challenges. Repeated disclosures followed by supportive challenges are, therefore, necessary.

Marshall, *supra* note 15, at 562. For criticism of client-centered counseling on this ground, see Robert F. Cochran, Jr., *Crime, Confession, and the Counselor-at-Law: Lessons from Dostoyevsky,* 35 HOUS. L. REV. 327, 381–83 (1998) (opposing client-centered counseling's emphasis on avoiding the painful consequences of confession, and proposing instead that lawyers serve as clients' friends, offering moral counsel and perhaps encouraging clients to confess in order to reap forgiveness and reconciliation). For evidence of defense lawyers' see-no-evil approach, see KENNETH MANN, DEFENDING WHITE-COLLAR CRIME: A PORTRAIT OF ATTORNEYS AT WORK 103–04 (1985).

30. *See* Carrie J. Petrucci, *Apology in the Criminal Justice Setting: Evidence for Including Apology as an Additional Component in the Legal System,* 20 BEHAV. SCI. & L. 337, 351–52 (2002) (noting that apologies correct victims' self-blame, reduce feelings of aggression and anger, promote healing, and empower victims). This lack of vindication explains why victims sometimes try to dissuade prosecutors from accepting *Alford* and no-contest pleas. *See* John M. Broder, *In a Quiet End*

to a Case, 4 Ex-Symbionese Liberation Army Members Plead Guilty to Murder, N.Y. TIMES, Nov. 8, 2002, at A18 (noting that the family of a murder victim agreed to plea bargains for four defendants on condition that each one publicly admit to his or her role in causing the victim's death); Robert Airoldi, *Ex-Priest Pleads Guilty to Sex Crime*, OAKLAND TRIBUNE, Dec. 7, 2002 (reporting that a victim insisted that a child molester plead guilty rather than no contest, stating: "It wasn't about the time he served[;] it was about admitting guilt").

In states with victims' bills of rights, victims may be able to submit written statements to courts at sentencing or make oral statements in open court. *See, e.g.*, ME. REV. STAT. ANN. tit. 17A, § 1174 (2009). Merely submitting a written statement, however, vindicates victims less than being heard at trial or receiving an admission of guilt at a guilty plea hearing.

For evidence relating specifically to victims of molestation, see O'Donohue & Letourneau, *supra* note 16, at 299–300 ("[C]ontinued denial can cause further harm to the abused child in that implicitly or explicitly, the child is being characterized as a liar and perhaps not believed by some.").

31. *See* Strang & Sherman, *supra* chapter II note 9, at 23 (noting that "discussion of apology is redundant" in light of "the dominant adversarial paradigm of the court system," which provides "no opportunity . . . for a direct exchange between [victims] and their offenders").

32. *See supra* note 23 and accompanying text (discussing the psychology of cognitive dissonance).

33. *See* Strang & Sherman, *supra* chapter II note 9, at 29 ("[A] sincere expression of remorse is . . . something victims almost never have the chance to hear in the courtroom."); *see also, e.g.*, United States v. Purchess, 107 F.3d 1261, 1269 (7th Cir. 1997) (affirming the district court's denial of a sentence reduction on the ground that the defendant's "one-sentence apology" was insufficient evidence of genuine remorse or contrition); Gregory D. Kesich, *Suspect Sentenced for Murder of Friend*, PORTLAND PRESS HERALD, Nov. 6, 2003, at 1B (noting that the victim disregarded the defendant's apology as insufficient); John P. Martin, *Barber Told To Repay $57,000*, STAR-LEDGER (Newark, N.J.), Oct. 23, 2003, at 13 (describing the defendant's reading of his apology from a single piece of paper at his sentencing for embezzlement); Monte Morin, *Fund Raiser Receives Maximum Penalty: 8 Years, Plus Restitution*, L.A. TIMES, July 25, 2002, at B5 (reporting that prosecutors rejected the defendant's open-court apology as insincere).

34. On the impact of apologies on judges' sentences, see Scott v. United States, 419 F.2d 264, 282 (D.C. Cir. 1969) (Leventhal, J., concurring in the judgment); *see* STANTON WHEELER ET AL., SITTING IN JUDGMENT: THE SENTENCING OF WHITE-COLLAR CRIMINALS 115 (1988) (interviewing judges in a pre-Guidelines study of sentencing of white-collar wrongdoers and finding that "it is important for many judges that defendants recognize the gravity of their offense, accept the blame for their misdeeds, and express remorse or contrition for them"); United States v. Beserra, 967 F.2d 254, 256 (7th Cir. 1992) (Posner, J.); *see, e.g.*, United States v. Blake, 89 F. Supp. 2d 328, 352 (E.D.N.Y. 2000) ("[The defendant] has repented by recognizing her guilt. She is remorseful over what she has done. She has also sought to apologize for her crime both to society at large and to [the victim] in particular. . . . This reflection and introspection is an aspect of her rehabilitation.");

Cloum v. State, 779 N.E.2d 84, 90 & n.3 (Ind. Ct. App. 2002) (holding that the trial judge erred in failing to consider the defendant's "tru[e] remorse" and other evidence of "his general good character," coupled with his decision to plead guilty, as a mitigating circumstance at sentencing); State v. Brown, 1986 WL 13263, at *2 (Tenn. Crim. App. Nov. 26, 1986) (reducing the defendant's sentence from two ten-year terms to two three-year terms to ensure that it was "no greater than that deserved for the offense" in light of, among other things, "the fact that the defendant expressed remorse over the incident") (internal quotation marks omitted); *Three Get Youth Detention in Rape of Retarded Teen*, CHI. TRIB., Apr. 24, 1993, § 1, at 10 (quoting the sentencing judge's observation, upon defendants' apologies, that "they are not hardened criminals" and "not without redeeming value").

Under the advisory Federal Sentencing Guidelines, for example, the two- or three-level reduction for acceptance of responsibility, plus the imposition of a sentence at the low end of the range, reduces a defendant's sentencing range by about 35%. U.S. SENTENCING GUIDELINES MANUAL § 3E1.1 (2010); Julie R. O'Sullivan, *In Defense of the U.S. Sentencing Guidelines' Modified Real-Offense System*, 91 NW. U. L. REV. 1342, 1415 & n.274 (1997) (collecting sources).

On the weight that remorse carries in capital sentencing, see Theodore Eisenberg et al., *But Was He Sorry? The Role of Remorse in Capital Sentencing*, 83 COR-NELL L. REV. 1599, 1633–35 (1998) (measuring capital jurors' beliefs and their correlations with sentencing outcomes in a multivariate empirical study); see also Riggins v. Nevada, 504 U.S. 127, 144 (1992) (Kennedy, J., concurring in the judgment) ("In a capital sentencing proceeding, assessments of character and remorse may carry great weight and, perhaps, be determinative of whether the offender lives or dies."); Eisenberg et al., *supra*, at 1632–33 (finding that "the difference . . . between jurors' beliefs about the defendant's remorse in life cases and in death cases is highly significant," and concluding that, "[i]n short, if jurors believed that the defendant was sorry for what he had done, they tended to sentence him to life imprisonment, not death"); Stephen P. Garvey, *Aggravation and Mitigation in Capital Cases: What Do Jurors Think?*, 98 COLUM. L. REV. 1538, 1559–61 (1998) (reaching same conclusion); Scott E. Sundby, *The Capital Jury and Absolution: The Intersection of Trial Strategy, Remorse, and the Death Penalty*, 83 CORNELL L. REV. 1557, 1560 (1998). As Eisenberg and his co-authors note, the presence or absence of remorse does not always exert a significant influence on capital sentencing juries. *See* Eisenberg et al., *supra*, at 1600. "[I]n highly vicious cases," they found, "a defendant's remorse may not be able to save him. But in lower viciousness cases . . . , remorse may make all the difference." *Id*. at 1636. For a good summary of how remorse can fit into a state's statutory scheme in capital cases, see *id*. at 1604–07.

35. Indeed, to apologize to his victim directly, a defendant in most cases would have to turn his back on the sentencing judge. Darrell L. Brooks did just that at his high-profile sentencing for the arson of a Baltimore rowhouse resulting in the death of two parents and their five children. *See* Gail Gibson & Laurie Willis, *Tears and Remorse Precede Life Term in Dawson Deaths: Arsonist, Victims' Family Tell Judge of Their Pain*, BALT. SUN, Aug. 28, 2003, at 1A (describing how Brooks "apologized to [Judge Marvin J.] Garbis for turning his back on the judge but said his comments were intended for the [victims'] relatives" and how he then, "[f]acing a packed courtroom, . . . went on to speak for minutes about his remorse"). In a few courtrooms, however, the victim might sit in visitors' seats that face both the judge and the defendant.

36. On the exclusion of juries from noncapital sentencing, see, for example Morris B. Hoffman, *The Case for Jury Sentencing*, 52 DUKE L.J. 951, 953 (2003); Jenia Iontcheva, *Jury Sentencing as Democratic Practice*, 89 VA. L. REV. 311, 314 (2003); Adriaan Lanni, Note, *Jury Sentencing in Noncapital Cases: An Idea Whose Time Has Come (Again)?*, 108 YALE L.J. 1775, 1790 (1999). Six states, however, retain jury sentencing in noncapital cases. King & Noble, *supra* chapter I note 81, at 886.

    Even though the Supreme Court has begun to endorse a role for jurors at sentencing, they are unlikely to dominate the process any time soon. True, *Ring v. Arizona* required that juries, not judges, find beyond a reasonable doubt all facts needed to trigger eligibility for the death penalty. 536 U.S. 584, 609 (2002). And *Blakely v. Washington* did mandate jury findings of all facts that raise maximum sentences. 542 U.S. 296, 303–05 (2004). But *United States v. Booker* solved the *Blakely* problem of judicial fact-finding under the federal sentencing guidelines not by injecting juries into the system, but by making the whole system advisory so that judges could continue to find facts and set sentences on their own. 543 U.S. 220, 258–65 (2005) (remedial majority opinion). Jurisdictions can easily follow suit. They can loosen their guidelines and raise their maximum sentences so that judges need not find specified facts before they can impose particular sentences.

    On the jury as the conscience of the community, see Witherspoon v. Illinois, 391 U.S. 510, 519 & n.15 (1968); *supra* chapter I.A.2.

    On the passivity of the jury's role, see GEORGE P. FLETCHER, WITH JUSTICE FOR SOME: VICTIMS' RIGHTS IN CRIMINAL TRIALS 228, 236 (1995); LANGBEIN, *supra* chapter I note 10, at 319–21 (tracing the "muting [of] the jury" that occurred in the eighteenth century).

37. *See* TOBOLOWSKY, *supra* chapter II note 9, at 81–86, 92–98.

38. Kahan, *What Do Alternative Sanctions Mean?*, *supra* chapter II note 44, at 597–98; *see also id.* at 598 ("In effect, the thief's behavior says to the victim, 'you matter so little, relative to me, that I can take your property without your consent.'"); Hampton, *An Expressive Theory of Retribution*, *supra* chapter II note 44, at 1, 8, 12; Jean Hampton, *Correcting Harms Versus Righting Wrongs: The Goal of Retribution*, 39 UCLA L. REV. 1659, 1677–78 (1992); *see* Jean Hampton, *Forgiveness, Resentment and Hatred*, in MURPHY & HAMPTON, *supra* chapter II note 44, at 35, 44 ("When someone wrongs another, she does not regard her victim as the sort of person who is valuable enough to require better treatment."). Jeffrie Murphy shares this view. *See* Jeffrie Murphy, *Forgiveness and Resentment*, *in id.* at 14, 25.

39. On equity theory, see Jennifer K. Robbennolt et al., *Symbolism and Incommensurability in Civil Sanctioning: Decision Makers as Goal Managers*, 68 BROOK. L. REV. 1121, 1139–44 (2003) (discussing how criminal and civil punishment restore moral balance by reaffirming victims' value and social norms and "mending the breach caused by the defendant's reprehensible actions"); *see* Alan Page Fiske & Philip E. Tetlock, *Taboo Trade-Offs: Reactions to Transactions That Transgress the Spheres of Justice*, 18 POL. PSYCHOL. 255, 286 (1997) (explaining how transgressions "throw[] into doubt the taken-for-granted assumptions that are constitutive of [social] order" and that punishment is needed "to restore the moral *status quo ante* and to reduce whatever cognitive and emotional unease was produced in individual[s] . . . by the . . . transgression"); Hampton, *Correcting Harms Versus*

Righting Wrongs, supra note 38, at 1677–82; *see also* Morris, *Persons and Punishment*, *supra* note 26, at 477–78 (arguing that crime involves seizing an unfair advantage over law-abiding citizens, so punishment is needed to "restore[] the equilibrium of benefits and burdens by taking from the [wrongdoer] what he owes").

On the importance of the relational aspect of wrongdoing, see Michelle Chernikoff Anderson & Robert J. MacCoun, *Goal Conflict in Juror Assessments of Compensatory and Punitive Damages*, 23 LAW & HUM. BEHAV. 313, 326–27 (1999); Jonathan Baron & Ilana Ritov, *Intuitions About Penalties and Compensation in the Context of Tort Law*, 7 J. RISK & UNCERTAINTY 17, 25–26 (1993); Gordon Bazemore & Mark Umbreit, *Rethinking the Sanctioning Function in Juvenile Court: Retributive or Restorative Responses to Youth Crime*, 41 CRIME & DELINQ. 296 (1995); E. Allan Lind et al., *In the Eye of the Beholder: Tort Litigants' Evaluations of Their Experiences in the Civil Justice System*, 24 LAW & SOC'Y REV. 953 (1990).

40. On apology as a relational gesture, see NICHOLAS TAVUCHIS, MEA CULPA: A SOCIOLOGY OF APOLOGY AND RECONCILIATION 13–14 (1991) (also noting that "[g]enuine apologies . . . may be taken as the symbolic foci of secular remedial rituals that serve to recall and reaffirm allegiance to codes of behavior and belief whose integrity has been tested and challenged by transgression"). On apology as affirmation of society's values, see, for example, Erik Luna, *Punishment Theory, Holism, and the Procedural Conception of Restorative Justice*, 2003 UTAH L. REV. 205, 294 ("Genuine remorse . . . signals the offender's affirmation of the legal norms of a community and his desire to be part of legitimate society."); Donna L. Pavlick, *Apology and Mediation: The Horse and Carriage of the Twenty-First Century*, 18 OHIO ST. J. ON DISP. RESOL. 829, 842–45 (2003) (discussing how remorse and apologies not only take victims seriously and validate them, but also reinforce the values underpinning membership in a moral community).

On apology as dissociation from a wrong and a plea for reconciliation, see, for example, Lee Taft, *Apology Subverted: The Commodification of Apology*, 109 YALE L.J. 1135, 1140 (2000) (explaining how an apologetic wrongdoer, while accepting responsibility for his actions, also commits himself to repent for his wrongful ways); Hiroshi Wagatsuma & Arthur Rosett, *The Implications of Apology: Law and Culture in Japan and the United States*, 20 LAW & SOC'Y REV. 461, 475 (1986) ("An apology suggests change in attitude when the apologizer expresses remorse for past hurt and the commitment that future behavior will not be hostile and will make up for the rupture in relationship created by the hurtful act. . . . [A]n apologizing individual splits herself into two parts, the part that is guilty of an offense and the part that disassociates itself from the delict and affirms a belief in the offended rule.").

Many leading criminal-law scholars are simply silent about these broader values, focusing narrowly on the wrongfulness of the wrongdoer and his crime. *See, e.g.*, MICHAEL MOORE, PLACING BLAME: A GENERAL THEORY OF THE CRIMINAL LAW (1997) (index reflects only two passing references to victims and none to remorse or apology); ANDREW VON HIRSCH, DOING JUSTICE: THE CHOICE OF PUNISHMENTS (1976) (table of contents reflects no discussion of remorse, apologies, or victims); ANDREW VON HIRSCH, PAST OR FUTURE CRIMES: DESERVEDNESS AND DANGEROUSNESS IN THE SENTENCING OF CRIMINALS (1985) (index does not mention remorse or apology and has no entry for victims apart from "[v]ictimizing acts").

Some more recent scholarship, by for example Darryl Brown, Dan Kahan, and Neal Katyal, grapples with the relational nature of crime and its interplay with social norms and social influence. *See, e.g.,* Darryl K. Brown, *Street Crime, Corporate Crime, and the Contingency of Criminal Liability*, 149 U. PA. L. REV. 1295, 1299–1301 (2001); Darryl K. Brown, *Third-Party Interests in Criminal Law*, 80 TEX. L. REV. 1383, 1395–96, 1400 (2002); Kahan, *What Do Alternative Sanctions Mean?*, *supra* chapter II note 44; Dan M. Kahan, *Social Influence, Social Meaning, and Deterrence*, 83 VA. L. REV. 349, 352–61 (1997); Neal Kumar Katyal, *Conspiracy Theory*, 112 YALE. L.J. 1307, 1316 (2003) (predicating a project on "influential [psychological] research [that] focuses on how group membership changes an individual's personal identity to produce a new social identity") (emphasis omitted).

41. On apologies' being directed to others, see TAVUCHIS, *supra* note 40, at 46–47 (emphasis omitted) (noting also that "apology is a relational concept and practice that necessarily requires an individual or collective Other to realize itself); Taft, *supra* note 40, at 1139, 1142–43 ('[A]pology does not exist in isolation; it is, rather, an intensely relational process that cannot be understood alone any more than a promise could be understood without reference to promisor and promisee.').

On apology as reaffirming community values and renewing community membership, see R.A. DUFF, PUNISHMENT, COMMUNICATION, AND COMMUNITY 114 (2001); Pavlick, *supra* note 40, at 836.

42. On the impact of face-to-face apologies, see Erin Ann O'Hara & Douglas Yarn, *On Apology and Consilience*, 77 WASH. L. REV. 1121, 1134–35 (2002); Petrucci, *supra* note 30, at 343; Strang & Sherman, *supra* chapter II note 9, at 28; *see* Kathy Elton & Michelle M. Roybal, *Restoration, A Component of Justice*, 2003 UTAH L. REV. 43, 54; Mark William Bakker, Comment, *Repairing the Breach and Reconciling the Discordant: Mediation in the Criminal Justice System*, 72 N.C. L. REV. 1479, 1483–90 (1994). The quotation in the text is from Luna, *Punishment Theory, supra* note 40, at 300; *see* Stephen P. Garvey, *Restorative Justice, Punishment, and Atonement*, 2003 UTAH L. REV. 303, 314–15 (explaining that apologetic discourse between a wrongdoer and his victim can "bring an offender to understand and appreciate the full measure of the damage he has caused, both material and moral; enable him to overcome mechanisms of defense and denial; and teach him what he must do to make amends and gain readmission into the community as a member in good standing" and that "[t]he moral education and awakening of the offender that ideally takes place . . . is thus the offender's first step on the road to atonement"); Taft, *supra* note 40, at 1142.

On the role of apologies in paving the way for forgiveness, see, for example Garvey, *Punishment as Atonement, supra* note 14, at 1840 ("[O]nce an offender has done everything possible to atone for his wrong, the burden shifts to the victim to forgive"); Luna, *Punishment Theory, supra* note 40, at 300 (noting that a wrongdoer's communication of genuine remorse to the victim in a face-to-face conference allows the victim to develop "respect for the offender as an individual capable of feeling positive emotions and taking responsibility for his actions"); Pavlick, *supra* note 195, at 845 ("Apology dispels the perception that the victim is being ignored [and] validates the victim" (citation omitted)); Petrucci, *supra* note 30, at 343 (noting that a face-to-face interaction "allows the victim to no longer feel shame because the victim sees . . . that it is the offender who is responsible for the harmful act, and not the victim"); Peter H. Rehm & Denise R. Beatty, *Legal Consequences of Apologizing*, 1996 J. DISP. RESOL. 115, 116 ("A sincere apology . . . can heal humiliation and generate forgiveness."); Taft, *supra* note 195, at 1142 ("[A]n apology sets in motion a call to the offended, a call for forgiveness.").

43. On the impact of expressions of remorse, see, for example, Jonathan R. Cohen, *Advising Clients to Apologize*, 72 S. Cal. L. Rev. 1009, 1044 (1999) (noting that "[m]any practitioners report that apologies often work 'magic' or 'miracles,'" that "often an apology triggers like conduct from the recipient," and that "even when one is highly skeptical that an apology will 'do any good,' it often does"); Stephen P. Garvey, *Can Shaming Punishments Educate?*, 65 U. Chi. . L. Rev. 733, 792 (1998) (discussing the "almost magical character" of genuine apologies); Pavlick, *supra* note 40, at 846 (observing that the effect of an apology "on the human condition often can be magical").

   For empirical studies, see Barton Poulson, *A Third Voice: A Review of Empirical Research on the Psychological Outcomes of Restorative Justice*, 2003 Utah L. Rev. 167, 189–91 & tbl. 7 (describing the empirical differences between restorative-justice and court participants as "consistently large" and statistically significant across all four studies). While three of the four studies did not involve random assignment, the fourth and largest one did. *Id.* at 169–76, 190–91. That study, the Canberra RISE study, found that 67% of the 142 wrongdoers in restorative justice apologized, while only 39% of the 132 in the court system did, a large and statistically significant difference. *Id.* at 190 tbl.7. That same randomized study found that 43% of the 296 victims in restorative justice but only 22% of the 186 victims in the court system expressed forgiveness, a large and statistically significant difference. *Id.*

44. On the reciprocal impacts of apologies, see Diane Whiteley, *The Victim and the Justification of Punishment*, Crim. Just. Ethics, Summer/Fall 1998, at 42, 51. On the high value victims put on emotional healing, see Strang & Sherman, *supra* chapter II note 9, at 17–23.

   On victims' desires to meet with wrongdoers, see Joanna Mattinson & Catriona Mirrlees-Black, Home Office, Research Study No. 200, Attitudes to Crime and Criminal Justice: Findings from the 1998 British Crime Survey 43 (2000), *available at* http://www.homeoffice.gov.uk/rds/pdfs/hors200.pdf; *see also* Deborah L. Levi, Note, *The Role of Apology in Mediation*, 72 N.Y.U. L. Rev. 1165, 1199 (1997) ("[A]pology has proven much more effective in major criminal mediations, where the injury was horribly severe, than in commercial contract cases, where the injury may be regarded as less serious." (footnotes omitted)).

45. Jeffrie Murphy, *Hatred: A Qualified Defense, in* Murphy & Hampton, *supra* chapter II note 44, at 105–06.

46. On the effect of victims' attitudes on sentences, see, for example, Susan W. Hillenbrand & Barbara E. Smith, Victims Rights Legislation: An Assessment of Its Impact on Criminal Justice Practitioners and Victims 71 tbl. 5–9 (ABA Crim. Just. Sec. Victim Witness Project 1989) (reporting that 47% of sentencing judges found victims' sentencing opinions "very useful" or "useful" in reaching their decisions, and 89% found information about the psychological impact of the crime on the victim "very useful" or "useful"); Murder Victims' Families for Reconciliation, Not in Our Name: Murder Victims' Families Speak Out Against the Death Penalty 6, 8, 11, 56, 65 (4th ed. 2003), *available at* http://www.mvfr.org/PDF/NIONbook.pdf (relating the stories of murder victims' families who successfully opposed the death penalty for their loved ones' killers). *But see* Julian V. Roberts, *Victim Impact Statements and the Sentencing Process: Recent*

Developments and Research Findings, 47 CRIM. L.Q. 365, 381–85 (2003) (reporting empirical evidence that victim-impact statements in Australia and Canada do not lead judges to impose stiffer sentences but occasionally lead to lighter ones).

Hannah Arendt memorably captured the importance of forgiveness to the forgiver: "Without being forgiven, released from the consequences of what we have done, our capacity to act would, as it were, be confined to one single deed from which we could never recover; we would remain the victims of its consequences forever, not unlike the sorcerer's apprentice who lacked the magic formula to break the spell." HANNAH ARENDT, THE HUMAN CONDITION 237 (2d ed. 1998); *see also* NORVAL MORRIS, THE FUTURE OF IMPRISONMENT 55–57 (1974) (suggesting that prosecutors include victims in plea bargaining because defendants would benefit from receiving forgiveness personally).

While expressions of forgiveness may alleviate guilt, they may be insufficient without punishment, so that the wrongdoer feels he has paid his debt. Thus, wrongdoers may benefit from forgiveness coupled with some punishment. *See* Garvey, *Punishment as Atonement*, *supra* note 14, at 1842–44 (explaining that restorative justice cannot restore wrongdoers because it does not punish them and so does not provide for atonement).

47. The quotations are from MARK S. UMBREIT ET AL., VICTIM MEETS OFFENDER: THE IMPACT OF RESTORATIVE JUSTICE AND MEDIATION 95, 101, 104 (1994) (internal quotation marks omitted). On wrongdoers' desire to explain and apologize, see Caren L. Flaten, *Victim-Offender Mediation: Application with Serious Offenses Committed by Juveniles*, *in* RESTORATIVE JUSTICE: INTERNATIONAL PERSPECTIVES 387, 396 (Burt Galaway & Joe Hudson eds., 1996); Lutz Netzig & Thomas Trenczek, *Restorative Justice as Participation: Theory, Law, Experience and Research*, *in id.* at 241, 256.

48. Strang and Sherman, for example, survey much of the existing evidence and conclude that restorative justice has always worked either as well as or in some cases better than more traditional prosecution in controlling repeat offending. They further note that all the evidence so far refutes the fear that an emphasis on restorative processes will lead to more crime. Strang & Sherman, *supra* chapter II note 9, at 38, 41.

49. On how apologies can be difficult or misfire, see TAVUCHIS, *supra* note 40, at 35; Pavlick, *supra* note 40, at 851–53; Taft, *supra* note 40, at 1142. On some participants' dissatisfaction, see, for example, Daniel W. Shuman, *The Role of Apology in Tort Law*, 83 JUDICATURE 180, 184–85 (2000); Taft, *supra*, at 1141.

50. For civil mediation scholars' recognition of the value of remorse and apology, see, for example, STEPHEN B. GOLDBERG ET AL., DISPUTE RESOLUTION: NEGOTIATION, MEDIATION AND OTHER PROCESSES 159–60 (3d ed. 1999) (stating that "[t]he first lesson of dispute resolution that many of us learn as children is the importance of apologizing" and going on to explain that an "apology is valuable in repairing whatever harm to the relationship has resulted from the dispute" and that "[m]any mediators have had one or more experiences . . . in which an apology was the key to a settlement that might otherwise not have been attainable"); Pavlick, *supra* note 40; Levi, *supra* note 44.

For mediation scholars' suggestions for reform, see, for example, KATHLEEN M. SCANLON, MEDIATOR'S DESKBOOK 68 (1999) (including "[r]ais[ing] the possibility of an apology as a component of resolving the dispute" in the checklist of mediator's techniques); O'Hara & Yarn, *supra* note 42, at 1169–83 (arguing for evidentiary reforms to better realize the value of apology in litigation); Marshall H. Tanick & Teresa J. Ayling, *Alternative Dispute Resolution by Apology: Settlement by Saying "I'm Sorry,"* HENNEPIN LAW., July–Aug. 1996, at 22, 22 (arguing for proactive use of apology in mediation); *see also* Cohen, *supra* note 43, at 1032–36, 1061–64. In light of these developments, several states have amended their evidentiary rules to provide safe harbors for apology. *See* Jonathan R. Cohen, *Toward Candor After Medical Error: The First Apology Law*, HARV. HEALTH POL'Y REV., Spring 2004, at 21, 21–22; Aviva Orenstein, *Apology Excepted: Incorporating a Feminist Analysis into Evidence Policy Where You Would Least Expect It*, 28 SW. U. L. REV. 221, 247–48 (1999); Elizabeth Latif, Note, *Apologetic Justice: Evaluating Apologies Tailored Toward Legal Solutions*, 81 B.U. L. REV. 289, 301 (2001).

51. Gerald B. Hickson et al., *Factors That Prompted Families to File Medical Malpractice Claims Following Prenatal Injuries*, 267 J. AM. MED. ASS'N 1359, 1361 (1992); Nathalie Des Rosiers et al., *Legal Compensation for Sexual Violence: Therapeutic Consequences and Consequences for the Judicial System*, 4 PSYCHOL. PUB. POL'Y & L. 433, 437, 442–43 (1998); RANDALL P. BEZANSON ET AL., LIBEL LAW AND THE PRESS: MYTH AND REALITY 79–93, 159–68, 172, 228–33 (1987) (finding also that many defamation plaintiffs would initially be content with apologies but that, after defendants rebuff their requests, many shift to litigation to vindicate and punish); *see also id.* at 159–68, 172, 228–33 (finding that plaintiffs would consider forgoing litigation if a mediation alternative were open to them, but that they sue because they lack alternative avenues of redress); *id.* at 232 (suggesting that defense lawyers might not naturally support mediation because it cuts against their financial interest).

52. *See, e.g.*, Craig A. McEwan & Richard J. Maiman, *Mediation in Small Claims Court: Consensual Processes and Outcomes, in* MEDIATION RESEARCH: THE PROCESS AND EFFECTIVENESS OF THIRD-PARTY INTERVENTION 53, 59–60 (Kenneth Kressel et al. eds., 1989); O'Hara & Yarn, *supra* note 42, at 1126; Pavlick, *supra* note 40, at 857–58; DWIGHT GOLANN, MEDIATING LEGAL DISPUTES: EFFECTIVE STRATEGIES FOR LAWYERS AND MEDIATORS § 7.1, at 188 (1996); GOLDBERG ET AL., *supra* note 50, at 159–62; Levi, *supra* note 44, at 1171.

CHAPTER IV

1. MARKUS DIRK DUBBER, VICTIMS IN THE WAR ON CRIME: THE USE AND ABUSES OF VICTIMS' RIGHTS 26 (2002).

2. This lawyer-driven state monopoly minimizes the roles of victims, wrongdoers themselves, and communities, whom it presumes are naïve, biased, or irrelevant. Thus, for example, many courts exclude testimony by victims or their surviving relatives about the proper punishment. *See* Lynn v. Reinstein, 68 P.3d 412, 414–17 (Ariz. 2003) (refusing to admit the survivor's opinion that the defendant deserved life imprisonment, not the death penalty); Wayne A. Logan, *Opining on Death: Witness Sentence Recommendations in Capital Trials*, 41 B.C. L. REV. 517, 519, 528–33 (2000) (noting that most courts are reluctant to admit capital-punishment opinions of surviving relatives, though lower courts are not unanimous and in some cases have admitted those opinions); Brian L. Vander Pol, Note, *Relevance and Reconciliation: A Proposal Regarding the Admissibility of Mercy Opinions in Capital Sentencing*, 88 IOWA L. REV. 707, 722 & nn.77–79 (2003) (noting that courts usually exclude survivors' recommendations of mercy from capital sentencing).

3. *See* Petrucci, *supra* chapter III note 30, at 359–60.

4. On the irrelevance of repentance to blameworthiness, see Murphy, *Repentance, Punishment, and Mercy, supra* chapter III note 14, at 149 ("In general, the wrongfulness of conduct at one time will not be affected by repentance at a later time. I typically do not cease to have a grievance against you simply because you are now sorry that you wronged me; nor do your debts to me disappear merely because you now lament those acts that put you into debt to me.").

On retributivists' equality objection to mercy, see, for example, Markel, *Against Mercy, supra* chapter II note 7.

On lack of remorse as a symptom of mental disorder, see AM. PSYCHIATRIC ASS'N, DIAGNOSTIC AND STATISTICAL MANUAL OF MENTAL DISORDERS § 301.7, at 650 (4th ed. 1994) (listing as one of the seven diagnostic criteria for Antisocial Personality Disorder "lack of remorse, as indicated by being indifferent to or rationalizing having hurt, mistreated, or stolen from another").

On the import of insanity and diminished-capacity defenses, see, for example, MODEL PENAL CODE § 210.3 cmt., at 71 (1980) (noting that "diminished responsibility . . . achieves a closer relation between criminal liability and moral guilt" because "[m]oral condemnation must be founded, at least in part, on some perception of the capacities and limitations of the individual actor"); Herbert Morris, *Sex, Shame, and Assorted Other Topics*, 22 QUINNIPIAC L. REV. 123, 131 (2003) (noting that individuals who suffer from a mental illness that diminishes culpability for their wrongful conduct are appropriately viewed as subjects for treatment instead of punishment); Christopher Slobogin, *An End to Insanity: Recasting the Role of Mental Disability in Criminal Cases*, 86 VA. L. REV. 1199, 1202 (2000) (explaining that the purpose of the insanity defense is to help distinguish between those wrongdoers who are blameworthy and culpable and those who are not). The same intuition underlies the criminal law's general ranking of recklessness as a more blameworthy state of mind than simple negligence. *See* MODEL PENAL CODE § 2.02(2)(c)-(d) (1980).

5. On the victim's right to inflict retribution, see William Ian Miller, *Clint Eastwood and Equity: Popular Culture's Theory of Revenge, in* LAW IN THE DOMAINS OF CULTURE 161, 167 (Austin Sarat & Thomas R. Kearns eds., 1998).

The quotation about the oddity to victims of treating society as the real victim is from WENDY KAMINER, IT'S ALL THE RAGE: CRIME AND CULTURE 75 (1995).

In a recent empirical study, Paul Robinson and his coauthors found that victims' forgiveness and views about punishment greatly influenced a large minority of respondents, particularly for crimes involving property or personal injury. Significantly more respondents were willing to heed a victim's desire for a lower punishment than would heed a victim's desire for a heavier sentence. Respondents attached even more weight to wrongdoers' remorse, acknowledgment of guilt, and apologies. Robinson et al., *Extralegal Punishment Factors, supra* chapter II note 19. Robinson's scenarios did not include restorative justice simulations, in which wrongdoers might be thought to earn mercy. The effect sizes might be even larger where the forgiveness seemed earned rather than granted fortuitously.

6. Jean Hampton, *The Retributive Idea, in* MURPHY & HAMPTON, *supra* chapter II note 44, at 111, 124–43.

7. Nils Christie, *Conflicts as Property*, 17 BRIT. J. CRIMINOLOGY 1, 2, 7–9 (1977). Even when colonists prosecuted in the state's name, they were the real parties

in interest and ran cases themselves, prosecuting *pro se*, as defendants defended themselves *pro se*. William E. Nelson, *Emerging Notions of Modern Criminal Law in the Revolutionary Era: An Historical Perspective*, 42 N.Y.U. L. REV. 450, 468 (1967). Well into the colonial era, Blackstone noted that every crime comprises both a public offense to the community and a private wrong to the victim. 4 WILLIAM BLACKSTONE, COMMENTARIES *5. Thus, until about 1900, most courts viewed victims as parties and so exempt from the general rule sequestering witnesses. Beloof & Cassell, *supra* chapter I note 51, at 491–93.

On private victims' historic control of criminal law, see, for example, J.H. BAKER, AN INTRODUCTION TO ENGLISH LEGAL HISTORY 500–01 (4th ed. 2002); 2 SIR FREDERICK POLLOCK & FREDERIC WILLIAM MAITLAND, THE HISTORY OF ENGLISH LAW BEFORE THE TIME OF EDWARD I, at 448–51 (2d ed. 1959) (describing *bot* and *wergilt* systems of pecuniary payments to victims up through the twelfth century, when criminal and tort law were one).

8. Christie, *supra* note 7, at 3–5; DURKHEIM, *supra* chapter I note 33, at 62–64.

9. This is Martha Nussbaum's reading of Adam Smith's *The Theory of Moral Sentiments*, though Smith is not nearly as explicit as Nussbaum on the need for critical distance in general. *Compare* Martha C. Nussbaum, *Emotion in the Language of Judging*, 70 ST. JOHN'S L. REV. 23, 26–28 (1996) *with* ADAM SMITH, THE THEORY OF MORAL SENTIMENTS 14–25 (Dublin: J. Beatty & C. Jackson, 6th ed. 1777).

10. *See* Jean Hampton, *The Retributive Idea, in* MURPHY & HAMPTON, *supra* chapter II note 44, at 124–32; Edna Erez, *Who's Afraid of the Big Bad Victim? Victim Impact Statements as Victim Empowerment and Enhancement of Justice*, 1999 CRIM. L. REV. 545, 550–53 ("With proper safeguards, the overall experience of providing input can be positive and empowering"; noting that giving victims a voice and some process control may matter more to their satisfaction than the outcome, as input empowers victims, communicates their stories to wrongdoers, shows that the system cares enough to listen, and helps victims to cleanse and heal).

The available empirical evidence confirms that allowing victims to testify can help them by validating their experiences and empowering them, though it also warns that forcing them to testify may cause psychological distress to some. Jamie O'Connell, *Gambling with the Psyche: Does Prosecuting Human Rights Violators Console Their Victims?*, 46 HARV. INT'L L.J. 295, 328–39 (2005).

Note that mercy is a word with multiple meanings. Sometimes, people use it loosely to specify the use of equitable discretion to tailor a rule of liability or punishment to a particular defendant's just deserts based on the wrongfulness of his crime, his criminal record, and the like. That understanding of mercy is completely consistent with retribution. Here, as elsewhere in this book, I use mercy more broadly to include leniency based on compassion, though not leniency based on bias, caprice, or corruption. For a typology of the varieties of mercy, see Markel, *Against Mercy, supra* chapter II note 7, at 1436.

11. *Cf.* Murphy, *Mercy and Legal Justice, in* MURPHY & HAMPTON, *supra* chapter II note 44, at 175–76 (explaining that mercy is easier to justify within a "private law paradigm," such as *The Merchant of Venice*, as a right-holder can always waive his claim to satisfaction of a debt).

12. *See, e.g.*, Dan M. Kahan & Martha C. Nussbaum, *Two Conceptions of Emotion in Criminal Law*, 96 COLUM. L. REV. 269, 278–301, 350–72 (1996); THE PASSIONS

OF LAW 63–214 (Susan A. Bandes ed., 1999); Samuel H. Pillsbury, *Emotional Justice: Moralizing the Passions of Criminal Punishment*, 74 CORNELL L. REV. 655 (1989).

13. Beccaria, for example, stressed that crime was not a private wrong against a person but a public wrong against the state, and that criminal justice was solely a matter of enforcing and preserving the social contract. Thus, "crimes are only to be measured by the injury done to society." BECCARIA, *supra* chapter I note 43, at 33; *see id.* at 15–21, 33–38.

On the exclusion of victims from trial, see Beloof & Cassell, *supra* chapter I note 51, at 498–503 (describing 1975 to 1982 as the nadir of victims' attendance at trial, as Federal Rule of Evidence 615 and state rules modeled on it required sequestering victims unless they could prove their presence was essential to the prosecution).

14. On twentieth-century criminal justice's insensitivity to victims, see Michael Ash, *On Witnesses: A Radical Critique of Criminal Court Procedures*, 48 NOTRE DAME LAW. 386, 399–407 (1972) (describing "a pattern of blindness and neglect" towards witnesses, exacerbated by the Warren Court's creation of new defendants' rights, and offering as one explanation that "[w]herever minor inconvenience to 'insiders' (judges, lawyers, court clerks, etc.) is to be balanced against major inconvenience to outsiders (witnesses, jurors, etc.), and the balancing is to be performed by insiders, insider interests will invariably prevail"); William F. McDonald, *Towards a Bicentennial Revolution in Criminal Justice: The Return of the Victim*, 13 AM. CRIM. L. REV. 649, 662 (1976); Stephen J. Schulhofer, *The Trouble with Trials; the Trouble with Us*, 105 YALE L.J. 825, 825 (1995) (book review).

For a survey of various victims' rights measures, see generally BELOOF ET AL., *supra* chapter II note 18, at 127–691. *E.g.*, CAL. CONST. art. 1, § 28(f)(2) (West 2008) (providing, as part of a victims' bill of rights, that victims and all other Californians have a "Right to Truth in Evidence," which purports to repeal or forbid exclusionary rules of evidence apart from privileges and hearsay rules); PRESIDENT'S TASK FORCE ON VICTIMS OF CRIME, FINAL REPORT 24–31 (1982) (proposing legislation to abolish the Fourth Amendment exclusionary rule, parole, and judicial discretion at sentencing); McCoY, *supra* chapter II note 37 (discussing California's enactment of its supposed ban on plea bargaining); JENNIFER E. WALSH, THREE STRIKES LAWS 35–44, 50 (2007) (noting the roles of victims' rights advocates and stories of victimization in passing California's and Washington's three-strikes laws).

15. Kilpatrick et al., *supra* chapter II note 17, at 4 ex. 1, 6 ex. 3.

16. For scholars fearful of emotions and biases, see, for example, Susan Bandes, *Empathy, Narrative, and Victim Impact Statements*, 63 U. CHI. L. REV. 361, 395–410 (1996); Donald J. Hall, *Victims' Voices in Criminal Court: The Need for Restraint*, 28 AM. CRIM. L. REV. 233, 255–60 (1991); Lynne N. Henderson, *The Wrongs of Victims' Rights*, 37 STAN. L. REV. 937, 994–99 (1985).

For fears that victims threaten prosecutors' neutrality, see, for example, Paul H. Robinson, *Should the Victims' Rights Movement Have Influence over Criminal Law Formulation and Adjudication?*, 33 McGEORGE L. REV. 749, 755–57 (2002).

For fears that victims inject emotion into criminal trials, see Robert P. Mosteller, Essay, *Victims' Rights and the United States Constitution: An Effort to Recast the Battle in Criminal Litigation*, 85 GEO. L.J. 1691, 1702–04 (1997).

For the centrality of harm to victims to popular intuitions of justice, see PAUL H. ROBINSON & JOHN M. DARLEY, JUSTICE, LIABILITY, AND BLAME: COMMUNITY VIEWS AND THE CRIMINAL LAW 14–27 (1995).

On the issue of moral luck: A defendant may be guilty of assault, battery, aggravated battery causing serious bodily injury, or murder depending on how well his victim dodged the blow, how quickly an ambulance responded to a 911 call, and how sturdy his victim's constitution was in bearing and recovering from it. As in tort law, a defendant takes his victim as he finds him and is responsible if his victim has an eggshell skull and suffers more extensive injury than another victim would have. Defendants can foresee that their actions may cause a range of possible harms and are accountable for the reasonably foreseeable harms that result. Similarly, the ordinary range of victims' psychological reactions should be relevant to punishment. A judge or jury can temper a victim's extreme or abnormal reaction, such as obsessive bloodthirstiness or paranoia, when setting the appropriate punishment.

On victims' right to attend trial and testify, see Beloof & Cassell, *supra* chapter I note 51, at 534–46.

17. LESLIE SEBBA, THIRD PARTIES: VICTIMS AND THE CRIMINAL JUSTICE SYSTEM 218 (1996); Sarah N. Welling, *Victim Participation in Plea Bargains*, 65 WASH. U. L.Q. 301, 311 (1987).

18. *See, e.g.*, DAVID C. BALDUS ET AL., EQUAL JUSTICE AND THE DEATH PENALTY: A LEGAL AND EMPIRICAL ANALYSIS 149–58 (1990) (reporting that a victim's race, sex, and socioeconomic status all significantly affect the likelihood that the defendant will be sentenced to death); David C. Baldus & George Woodworth, *Race Discrimination in the Administration of the Death Penalty: An Overview of the Empirical Evidence with Special Emphasis on the Post-1990 Research*, 39 CRIM. L. BULL. 194 (2003) (summarizing decades' worth of strong evidence of race-of-victim effects in capital punishment); Edward Glaeser & Bruce Sacerdote, *Sentencing in Homicide Cases and the Roles of Vengeance*, 32 J. LEGAL STUD. 363, 372 tbl.2, 373 (2003) (finding that killers of white and female victims received substantially longer prison sentences).

19. William J. Stuntz, *Unequal Justice*, 121 HARV. L. REV. 1969, 1974 (2008); *see, e.g.*, Francis X. Clines, *Death Penalty Is Suspended in Maryland*, N.Y. TIMES, May 10, 2002, at A20 (reporting the Maryland governor's decision to impose a moratorium on executions because of concerns about unfairness and racial inequality); Carrie Johnson, *Bill Targets Sentencing Rules for Crack and Powder Cocaine*, WASH. POST, Oct. 16, 2009, at A6; Carrie Johnson, *Parity in Cocaine Sentences Gains Momentum*, WASH. POST, July 25, 2009, at A2 (noting that while campaigning for office, President Obama and Vice-President Biden had supported equalizing sentences for crack and powder cocaine, and that Attorney General Holder and congressional committees were moving forward with bills to equalize the penalties); David Kocieniewski, *Amid Pomp, McGreevey Signs Racial-Profiling Bill*, N.Y. TIMES, Mar. 15, 2003, at B5; New Jersey Black and Latino Caucus, *A Report on Discriminatory Practices Within the New Jersey State Police*, 26 SETON HALL LEGIS. J. 273 (2002).

20. *See, e.g.*, 31 U.S.C. § 3730(b)(1), (c) (2006) (requiring court and government approval to dismiss (and thus settle) a *qui tam* suit, and giving the government the right to intervene and take over a *qui tam* action or to dismiss a *qui tam* action after giving the relator notice and an opportunity to be heard in court); 33 U.S.C. § 1365(b), (c)(2) (2006) (authorizing citizen suits under the Clean Water Act but requiring notice to the federal government and giving the federal government the right to intervene or preempt citizen suits by filing a civil or criminal action of its own).

21. On European victims' rights movements, see Heather Strang, *The Crime Victim Movement as a Force in Civil Society, in* RESTORATIVE JUSTICE AND CIVIL SOCIETY 69, 70–76 (Heather Strang & John Braithwaite eds., 2001).

    On American academic support for giving victims procedural rights, see generally BELOOF ET AL., *supra* chapter II note 18 (addressing victims' rights in criminal procedure as procedural rights to receive information and take part but not including exclusionary rules, sentence enhancements, or parole restrictions).

    On American victims' rights rhetoric as a cloak for tough-on-crime measures, see, for example, DAVID GARLAND, THE CULTURE OF CONTROL: CRIME AND SOCIAL ORDER IN CONTEMPORARY SOCIETY 143–44 (2001); Andrew Ashworth, *Victims' Rights, Defendants' Rights and Criminal Procedure, in* INTEGRATING A VICTIM PERSPECTIVE WITHIN CRIMINAL JUSTICE: INTERNATIONAL DEBATES 185, 186 (Adam Crawford & Jo Goodey eds., 2000) (dubbing this phenomenon "victims in the service of severity"); *see also* JONATHAN SIMON, GOVERNING THROUGH CRIME: HOW THE WAR ON CRIME TRANSFORMED AMERICAN DEMOCRACY AND CREATED A CULTURE OF FEAR (2007).

    On the Doris Tate Crime Victims' Bureau, see KATHERINE BECKETT & THEODORE SASSON, THE POLITICS OF INJUSTICE: CRIME AND PUNISHMENT IN AMERICA 148 (2d ed. 2003).

22. PROTECT Act, Pub. L. No. 108–21, 117 Stat. 650 (2003); Bibas, *The Feeney Amendment, supra* chapter II note 35, at 296–301; Daniel Richman, *Federal Sentencing in 2007: The Supreme Court Holds—The Center Doesn't*, 117 YALE L.J. 1374, 1388–90 (2008).

23. McCOY, *supra* chapter II note 37, at xvii, 23–31, 37–40, 156–61.

24. On the zero-sum mentality, see, for example, Thomas Weigend, *Problems of Victim/Witness Assistance Programs*, 8 VICTIMOLOGY: INT'L J. 91, 98 (1983) (acknowledging as a "fact that in the zero sum game of criminal justice no one can gain except by someone else's loss").

    Indeed, victims often care more about fair, respectful treatment and apologies than they do about maximizing punishment. Giving them a voice and listening to them has the expressive benefit of taking them seriously and respecting their stake. *See, e.g.*, BHARAT B. DAS, VICTIMS IN THE CRIMINAL JUSTICE SYSTEM 126–27, 131 (1997); SEBBA, *supra* note 17, at 116–19; WEMMERS, *supra* chapter II note 9, at 71–77, 207–08; Carolyn Hoyle & Lucia Zedner, *Victims, Victimization, and Criminal Justice, in* THE OXFORD HANDBOOK OF CRIMINOLOGY 461, 481–82 (Mike Maguire et al. eds., 4th ed. 2007) ("Victim surveys have consistently revealed that victims are no more punitive than the general public, and many are willing to engage in direct mediation, or to receive compensation from their offender. . . . There is clearly an appetite for restorative justice"); Joanna Shapland, *Victims and the Criminal Justice System, in* FROM CRIME POLICY TO VICTIM POLICY: REORIENT-ING THE JUSTICE SYSTEM 210, 213–14 (Ezzat A. Fattah ed., 1986). As discussed earlier, sometimes victims want to show mercy and forgive, but the system stifles them. *See supra* note 2.

25. Paul Gewirtz, *Victims and Voyeurs: Two Narrative Problems at the Criminal Trial, in* LAW'S STORIES: NARRATIVE AND RHETORIC IN THE LAW 135, 142–43 (Peter Brooks & Paul Gewirtz eds., 1996); Bandes, *supra* note 16, at 409; *see also* Mosteller, *supra* note 16, at 1712–13 (equating victims' rights with harsh sentences and advocating instead mercy toward defendants).

26. John Braithwaite, *Restorative Justice: Assessing Optimistic and Pessimistic Accounts, in* 25 CRIME & JUST.: REV. RES. 1, 7 (Michael Tonry ed., 1999) (source of the first quotation); JOHN BRAITHWAITE, RESTORATIVE JUSTICE AND RESPONSIVE REGU-LATION 129 (2002); Susan M. Olson & Albert W. Dzur, *Reconstructing Professional Roles in Restorative Justice Programs*, 2003 UTAH L. REV. 57, 77; John Braithwaite, *A Future Where Punishment Is Marginalized: Realistic or Utopian?*, 46 UCLA L. REV. 1727, 1727 (1999) (title is the source of the second quotation); John Braithwaite & Heather Strang, *Connecting Philosophy and Practice, in* RESTORATIVE JUSTICE: PHILOSOPHY TO PRACTICE 203, 210–11 fig.12.1 (Heather Strang & John Braith-waite eds., 2000) (depicting a pyramid in which restorative justice is the broad base and presumptive response to crime, deterrence is needed when restor-ative justice repeatedly fails, and incapacitation is the apex needed only when deterrence fails). Even when Braithwaite leaves the door open to punishment, he still veers away from conceding the need for it. In more recent writings, he admits that "when criminals eschew atonement, punishment—or at least some solemn public condemnation of the crime—is needed to affirm that moral order and to vindicate victims." John Braithwaite, *Holism, Justice, and Atonement*, 2003 UTAH L. REV. 389, 404. Note carefully his choice of words. Even this concession suggests that the state could simply condemn an unrepentant wrongdoer's crime in words and symbols without backing up those words with punishment.

27. *See* JOHN BRAITHWAITE, CRIME, SHAME, AND REINTEGRATION 54–61 (1989). Crimes that are not inherently wrong (*mala prohibita*) and truly victimless crimes do not fit within this account, but they are not the focus of restorative justice nor of this book. But many seemingly victimless crimes, such as drug deal-ing, often have spillover effects that harm a neighborhood and so would fit within restorative justice and my focus here.

28. On the various models of restorative justice procedures, see Gordon Bazemore & Mark Umbreit, *A Comparison of Four Restorative Justice Conferencing Models*, JUV. JUST. BULL., Feb. 2001, at 2–6. On the roles of the various parties and their friends and relatives, see Braithwaite, *Restorative Justice, supra* note 26, at 47–49.

29. *See* Poulson, *supra* chapter III note 43, at 177–98 (also reporting that all of these measured advantages of restorative justice were statistically significant except for consideration of victims' opinions and wrongdoers' satisfaction with outcomes). One must be cautious, however, in extrapolating from these seven studies. Five of them focused on juvenile wrongdoers, and six focused on misdemeanors or at most lesser felonies, not violent crimes beyond minor assaults. They did not emphasize serious crimes by adults.

30. Paul H. Robinson, *The Virtues of Restorative Processes, The Vices of "Restorative Justice,"* 2003 UTAH L. REV. 375, 384–85.

31. On the messages sent by restoration and fines, see Kahan, *What Do Alternative Sanctions Mean?, supra* chapter II note 44, at 619–24; Garvey, *Punishment as Atonement, supra* chapter III note 14, at 1844 (source of the quotation in the text); *accord* Antony Duff, *Restoration and Retribution, in* RESTORATIVE JUSTICE AND CRIMINAL JUSTICE: COMPETING OR RECONCILABLE PARADIGMS? 43, 44 (Andrew von Hirsch et al. eds., 2003) (insisting that restoration is impossible without retributive punishment).

    Admittedly, the preliminary findings that restoration is no substitute for punishing moderately serious offenses but can warrant lower sentences come from psychology studies done in laboratories rather than from real-world interviews with victims, defendants, and citizens affected by crimes. Dena M. Gromet & John M. Darley, *Restoration and Retribution: How Including Retributive Components Affects the Acceptability of Restorative Justice Procedures,* 19 SOC. JUST. RES. 395, 406 tbl.1, 409–11, 418 fig.5, 420–23 (2006); *see also* Dena M. Gromet & John M. Darley, *Punishment and Beyond: Achieving Justice Through Satisfaction of Multiple Goals,* 43 LAW & SOC'Y REV. 1, 23–25 (2009) (finding that when study subjects read serious-crime scenarios and were told to focus on offenders, they were more punitive, but when they focused on victims or communities' interests they chose sanctions that were somewhat less punitive and more directed toward restoring victims or communities, respectively).

32. R.A. DUFF, ANSWERING FOR CRIME: RESPONSIBILITY AND LIABILITY IN THE CRIMINAL LAW 88 (2007) (internal citations omitted). *Cf. Ecclesiastes* 3:1, 3, 5 (King James Version) ("To everything there is a season, and a time to every purpose under the heaven . . . A time to kill, and a time to heal . . . a time to embrace, and a time to refrain from embracing. . . .").

33. The quotation in the text is from ANNALISE ACORN, COMPULSORY COMPASSION: A CRITIQUE OF RESTORATIVE JUSTICE 19 (2004). On the classic traits of criminals, see MICHAEL R. GOTTFREDSON & TRAVIS HIRSCHI, A GENERAL THEORY OF CRIME 85–111 (1990) (identifying poor self-control, which includes impulsive gratification of desires, as the hallmark of criminality); JAMES Q. WILSON & RICHARD J. HERRNSTEIN, CRIME AND HUMAN NATURE: THE DEFINITIVE STUDY OF THE CAUSES OF CRIME 204–05 (1985) (noting the link between impulsiveness and criminality).Psychopaths exhibit no empathy nor remorse for anything except being caught. *See* HERVEY CLECKLEY, THE MASK OF SANITY: AN ATTEMPT TO REINTERPRET THE SO-CALLED PSYCHOPATHIC PERSONALITY 241–43, 258 (1941); ROBERT D. HARE, WITHOUT CONSCIENCE: THE DISTURBING WORLD OF THE PSYCHOPATHS AMONG US 40–45, 58–60 (1999).

    Even repentant wrongdoers are at great risk of relapsing. For example, a sober wife-beater may be genuinely remorseful, but the next time he is tempted to drink he is likely to fly into a violent rage again. Indeed, this cycling of violence and contrition is characteristic of batterers in general, not just alcoholics. *See, e.g.,* LENORE E. WALKER, THE BATTERED WOMAN 55–70 (1979) (documenting the cycle of abuse, apology, and reconciliation); LENORE E.A. WALKER, THE BATTERED WOMAN SYNDROME 91–96, 98–105 (3d ed. 2009) (reporting clinical evidence confirming the Walker Cycle Theory of Violence).

34. The anecdote and quotations in the text are from MARK S. UMBREIT, THE HANDBOOK OF VICTIM-OFFENDER MEDIATION: AN ESSENTIAL GUIDE TO PRACTICE

AND RESEARCH 88–89 (2001). Umbreit, a major scholar of restorative justice, endorsed the mediator's deflection of the victim's complaints: "The co-mediator's comment appeared to have validated some of [the burglar]'s concern that he was being 'dumped on.' The interaction between the mediator and [the burglar] also evidently had a positive impact on [the victim]. From this point on, [the victim]'s communication to [the burglar] was far less emotional, and his body language slowly began to loosen up." *Id.* at 89.

On mediators' responsibility to interrupt and deflect victims' outrage, see Thomas J. Scheff, *Working with Shame and Anger in Community Conferencing, in* JUDGING IN A THERAPEUTIC KEY: THERAPEUTIC JURISPRUDENCE AND THE COURTS 231, 231, 240–45 (Bruce J. Winick & David B. Wexler eds., 2003) (treating restorative justice and therapeutic jurisprudence as two vectors of a single movement, and discussing the restorative justice procedure of community conferencing, based on first-hand observations of conferences in three Australian cities).

On the conflict between restorative justice's hostility to punishment and its efficacy, see Kahan, *What's* Really *Wrong with Shaming Sanctions, supra* chapter II note 45, at 2094 (noting the danger that anti-punishment restorative justice zealots may suppress victims' anger and thus hobble restorative justice's expressiveness and public support).

35. On how the agenda of restorative justice professionals differs from that of laymen, see, for example, Olson & Dzur, *supra* note 26, at 77 ("'Retributive,' 'punitive,' and 'offender-based' perspectives are seen as in tension with the value of restoration, and it is the job of the restorative justice professional to correct or modify these perspectives"). The Braithwaite example in the text is from BRAITHWAITE, RESTORATIVE JUSTICE AND RESPONSIVE REGULATION, *supra* note 26, at 160 box 5.3.

36. Howard Zehr, Book Review, 43 BRIT. J. CRIMINOLOGY 653, 654 (2003) (reviewing THE SPIRITUAL ROOTS OF RESTORATIVE JUSTICE (Michael L. Hadley ed., 2001)). For examples of retributive elements found in some restorative processes, see Kathleen Daly, *Revisiting the Relationship Between Retributive and Restorative Justice, in* RESTORATIVE JUSTICE: PHILOSOPHY TO PRACTICE, *supra* note 26, at 33, 45. On restorativist blindness to retributive elements, see Charles Barton, *Empowerment and Retribution in Criminal Justice, in id.* at 55, 61–64 (citing multiple authors who deny that the Australian aboriginal practice of ritual spearing was retributive, even though it often causes wrongdoers' deaths or serious injuries).

37. The Wisconsin project is described at Frank J. Remington Ctr., Restorative Justice Project, http://www.law.wisc.edu/fjr/clinicals/rjp.html (last visited May 5, 2011). The example in the text is from Tag Evers, *Blessed Are the Peace Makers*, ISTHMUS (Madison, Wis.), Apr. 10–16, 1998, at 9.

The descriptions of practice in Iowa and Minnesota are from my telephone interview with Bruce Kittle, member of the board of directors of the Victim-Offender Mediation Ass'n and chaplain, Iowa Dep't of Corr. Servs. (Feb. 27, 2004); Iowa Dep't of Corr., *History of Victim and Restorative Justice Programs*, http://www.doc.state.ia.us/VictimHistory.asp (last visited May 5, 2011); Minn. Dep't of Corr., *Restorative Justice: Victims & Offenders in Communication Experiences*, http://www.doc.state.mn.us/rj/Options.htm (last visited May 5, 2011).

In authoritative models of mediation, for example, mediators can make suggestions, place a thumb on the scale, or even decide cases if mediation breaks down.

See CHRISTOPHER W. MOORE, THE MEDIATION PROCESS: PRACTICAL STRATEGIES FOR RESOLVING CONFLICT 44–52 (3d ed. Rev. 2003). Though most examples of authoritative mediation come from civil contexts, they could also be adapted to criminal restorative processes.

Rwanda and South Africa exemplify two quite different ways of using restorative justice in the wake of mass atrocities. In 1994, members of the Hutu tribe in Rwanda massacred close to a million Tutsis and moderate Hutus. Because the International Criminal Tribunal for Rwanda could prosecute only a handful of the worst defendants, lay-run gacaca courts handled the rest. Gacaca tribunals held public trials, in which victims and villagers could confront defendants. Defendants could contest their guilt or confess and name other participants in exchange for lighter sentences. Importantly, gacaca courts did not treat victim confrontation, confession, or apology as a substitute for deserved punishment, but rather as a complement to it. Punishment was part of a broader reconciliation process, not an alternative to it. True, gacaca courts have been overwhelmed with thousands of cases, and some criticize them for lacking adequate safeguards. Nevertheless, their effort to blend retribution and restoration is promising. And unlike domestic restorative processes, which mostly substitute for or follow sentencing, gacaca courts also involve victims and villagers in determining guilt. Thus, they are closer to the colonial model of a morality play. *See* MARK A. DRUMBL, ATROCITY, PUNISHMENT, AND INTERNATIONAL LAW 85–99 (2007); Nat'l Serv. of Gacaca Jurisdictions, *Sentences Applicable in the GACACA Courts*, http://www.inkiko-gacaca.gov.rw/En/EnSentence.htm (last visited May 5, 2011); Davan Maharaj, *People's Court for Genocide: Eight Years After the Rwandan Slaughter, the Overwhelmed Justice System Turns to Villagers, Including Survivors, to Pass Judgment*, L.A. TIMES, May 29, 2002, at A1; Andrew Meldrum, *One Million Rwandans to Face Killing Charges in Village Courts*, THE GUARDIAN (London), Jan. 15, 2005, at 16.

In contrast, South Africa's example cautions against simply substituting storytelling for justice. After it dismantled the racist system of apartheid, South Africa could not air, prosecute, and prove the countless human rights abuses committed under that system. In order to bring the abuses of apartheid to light, the South African Truth and Reconciliation Commission offered the possibility of amnesty for politically motivated crimes in exchange for full disclosure. The hope was that bringing these crimes to light, out in the open, would provide a measure of healing and closure. *See generally* 1 TRUTH AND RECONCILIATION COMM'N, TRUTH AND RECONCILIATION COMMISSION OF SOUTH AFRICA REPORT 49–134 (1998). In response, thousands of wrongdoers testified, though only a small minority of them received amnesty. Truth and Reconciliation Comm'n, *Amnesty Hearings and Decisions: Summary of Amnesty Decisions, 1.11.2000*, www.doj.gov.za/trc/amntrans/index.htm (last visited May 5, 2011). Many victims of apartheid, unfortunately, questioned whether the commission had not reconciled blacks and whites because it had not done justice. Reconciliation was no substitute for justice; on the contrary, many victims saw justice as a precondition for reconciliation. Jay A. Vora & Erika Vora, *The Effectiveness of South Africa's Truth and Reconciliation Commission: Perceptions of Xhosa, Afrikaner, and English South Africans*, 34 J. BLACK STUD. 301, 309–10 & tbl.1, 314–19 (2004); Center for the Study of Violence and Reconciliation & the Khulumani Support Group, *Survivors' Perceptions of the Truth and Reconciliation Commission and Suggestions for the Final Report*, *available at* www.csvr.org.za/wits/papers/papakhul.htm.. Given the difficulties of prosecuting countless thousands of crimes years after the fact, perhaps the best one could hope for was simply to air the truth. But without justice, victims understandably found it much harder to find closure and forgive.

38. Christopher Slobogin, *Therapeutic Jurisprudence: Five Dilemmas to Ponder*, 1 PSYCHOL. PUB. POL'Y & L. 193, 196 (1995); Bruce J. Winick, *The Jurisprudence of Therapeutic Jurisprudence*, *in* LAW IN A THERAPEUTIC KEY: DEVELOPMENTS IN THERAPEUTIC JURISPRUDENCE 645, 647–52 (David B. Wexler & Bruce J. Winick eds., 1996). *Cf.* John Braithwaite, *Restorative Justice and Therapeutic Jurisprudence*, 38 CRIM. L. BULL. 244 (2002) (outlining the empathy and holism that both approaches share, while contrasting aspects such as therapeutic jurisprudence's somewhat greater tolerance for paternalism). *See generally* JUDGING IN A THERAPEUTIC KEY, *supra* note 34; PRACTICING THERAPEUTIC JURISPRUDENCE: LAW AS A HELPING PROFESSION (Dennis P. Stolle et al. eds., 2000); LAW IN A THERAPEUTIC KEY, *supra*; ESSAYS IN THERAPEUTIC JURISPRUDENCE (David B. Wexler & Bruce J. Winick eds., 1991).

39. On insanity verdicts, see Fein, *supra* chapter III note 20, at 52–57 (basing this claim on several reported clinical cases from the author's experience at a state mental hospital with patients who had been acquitted by reason of insanity). This claim is controversial and may hold for only a subset of insanity acquittees. Others, especially those who are clinically depressed, may over-blame themselves and not need pressure to take responsibility.

On the Federal Sentencing Guidelines, see, for example, Keri A. Gould, *Turning Rat and Doing Time for Uncharged, Dismissed, or Acquitted Crimes: Do the Federal Sentencing Guidelines Promote Respect for the Law?*, *in* LAW IN A THERAPEUTIC KEY, *supra* note 38, at 171; *see also* Kevin R. Reitz, *Sentencing Facts: Travesties of Real-Offense Sentencing*, 45 STAN. L. REV. 523 (1993).

40. On acceptance of responsibility and apologies at sentencing, see Richard P. Wiebe, *The Mental Health Implications of Crime Victims' Rights*, *in* LAW IN A THERAPEUTIC KEY, *supra* note 38, at 213, 227 (suggesting the possibility that victim testimony and victim-impact statements may help some victims psychologically); Petrucci, *supra* chapter III note 30, at 354–58 (apology); Amy D. Ronner, *Dostoyevsky and the Therapeutic Jurisprudence Confession*, 40 J. MARSHALL L. REV. 41, 47–57, 109, 111 (2006) (describing defense counsel's role in listening to and eliciting the client's voice and confession).

On defense lawyers' counseling of their drunk-driving clients, see, for example, Wexler, *Some Reflections on Therapeutic Jurisprudence*, *supra* chapter III note 28, at 206–07 (discussing John V. McShane, The How and Why of Therapeutic Jurisprudence in Criminal Defense Work (2000) (unpublished paper distributed at the American-Psychology-Law Society Conference, New Orleans, Louisiana, Mar. 12, 2000), which described McShane's handling of these cases in private practice).

41. Amy D. Ronner & Bruce J. Winick, *The Antitherapeutic Per Curiam Affirmance*, *in* JUDGING IN A THERAPEUTIC KEY, *supra* note 34, at 316, 319.

42. On the relationship between therapeutic jurisprudence and problem-solving courts, see Bruce J. Winick & David B. Wexler, *Drug Treatment Court: Therapeutic Jurisprudence Applied*, 18 TOURO L. REV. 479, 480 (2002) ("Specialized treatment courts—including drug treatment courts—are *related* to therapeutic jurisprudence, but they are not identical with the concept. These courts can be seen as applications of therapeutic jurisprudence.") (internal citation omitted).

On drug courts specifically, see Peggy Fulton Hora et al., *Therapeutic Jurisprudence and the Drug Treatment Court Movement: Revolutionizing the Criminal Justice System's Response to Drug Abuse and Crime in America*, 74 NOTRE DAME L. REV. 439 (1999); Bruce J. Winick, *Therapeutic Jurisprudence and Problem-Solving Courts*, 30 FORDHAM URB. L.J. 1055 (2003).

On "therapeutic theater," see JAMES L. NOLAN, JR., REINVENTING JUSTICE: THE AMERICAN DRUG COURT MOVEMENT 5–11, 71–73, 75–89, 100–02 (2001); Richard C. Boldt, *The Adversary System and Attorney Role in the Drug Treatment Court Movement*, *in* DRUG COURTS IN THEORY AND PRACTICE 115, 119–20 (James L. Nolan, Jr. ed., 2002); Philip Bean, *Drug Courts, the Judge, and the Rehabilitative Ideal*, *in id.* at 235, 236–38; James J. Chriss, *The Drug Court Movement: An Analysis of Tacit Assumptions*, *in id.* at 189, 198–200; James L. Nolan, Jr., *Separated by an Uncommon Law: Drug Courts in Great Britain and America*, *in id.* at 89, 103, 105–06; Sara Steen, *West Coast Drug Courts: Getting Offenders Morally Involved in the Criminal Justice Process*, *in id.* at 51, 58–65; Elaine M. Wolf, *Systemic Constraints on the Implementation of a Northeast Drug Court*, *in id.* at 27, 40–44.

On criticisms of problem-solving courts, see Morris B. Hoffman, *Therapeutic Jurisprudence, Neo-Rehabilitationism, and Judicial Collectivism: The Least Dangerous Branch Becomes Most Dangerous*, 29 FORDHAM URB. L.J.2063 (2002); James L. Nolan, Jr., *Redefining Criminal Courts: Problem-Solving and the Meaning of Justice*, 40 AM. CRIM. L. REV. 1541, 1554–63 (2003) (criticizing problem-solving courts' use of euphemism, retreat from the language of justice, and substitution of treatment for just retribution).

43. *See, e.g.*, Tom R. Tyler, *The Psychological Consequences of Judicial Procedures: Implications for Civil Commitment Hearings*, *in* LAW IN A THERAPEUTIC KEY, *supra* note 38, at 3, 15 (noting that civil-commitment procedures can have important psychological impacts on people's trust, vulnerability, and self-worth, quite apart from whether those procedures lead to accurate outcomes).

44. David B. Wexler, *The TJ Criminal Lawyer: Therapeutic Jurisprudence and Criminal Law Practice*, *in* THE AFFECTIVE ASSISTANCE OF COUNSEL: PRACTICING LAW AS A HEALING PROFESSION 367, 379–98 (Marjorie A. Silver ed., 2007).

45. The need to individualize justice and retreat from overbroad abstract rules is one of the insights of the storytelling movement in law. *See* Toni M. Massaro, *Empathy, Legal Storytelling, and The Rule of Law: New Words, Old Wounds?*, 87 MICH. L. REV. 2099, 2101, 2106–20 (1989) (acknowledging this impulse, while going on to critique the storytelling movement as driven by an underlying progressive political agenda and so selectively emphasizing the stories of minorities and other disempowered groups).

On problem-solving courts' excessive hostility to equality, see, for example, NOLAN, REINVENTING JUSTICE, *supra* note 42, at 103–04 (relaying anecdotes belying drug court judges' open hostility to inquiries about equality and efforts to be consistent).

46. On lawyers' personalities, see Susan Daicoff, *Lawyer Personality Traits and Their Relationship to Various Approaches to Lawyering*, *in* THE AFFECTIVE ASSISTANCE OF COUNSEL, *supra* note 44, at 79, 81–94.

The text's emphasis on listening and empathy complements feminist critiques of cold, stereotypically male approaches to litigation. Linda G. Mills, *Affective Lawyering: The Emotional Dimensions of the Lawyer-Client Relation*, *in* PRACTICING

THERAPEUTIC JURISPRUDENCE, *supra* note 38, at 419, 426–32; Marjorie A. Silver, *Love, Hate, and Other Emotional Interference in the Lawyer/Client Relationship, in id.* at 357, 358; Bruce J. Winick, *Redefining the Role of the Criminal Defense Lawyer at Plea Bargaining and Sentencing: A Therapeutic Jurisprudence/Preventive Law Model, in id.* at 245, 293–98; Bruce J. Winick, *Therapeutic Jurisprudence and the Role of Counsel in Litigation, in id.* at 309, 321–22.

47. For discussions of therapeutic jurisprudence's paternalism, compare, for example, Winick & Wexler, *supra* note 42, at 483 (cautioning about the need for drug-treatment courts to guard against coercion) *with* NOLAN, REINVENTING JUSTICE, *supra* note 42, at 200 (reporting a judge's admission that "I probably pushed too hard on that one" by threatening the client with the expense of hiring a private lawyer and going to jail if he did not choose the drug-court route) *and* Winick, *Therapeutic Justice and Problem-Solving Courts, supra* note 42, at 1071–78 (suggesting that judges respect autonomy and avoid paternalism, but reporting advocates' praise of "benevolent coercion" and suggesting that use of legal levers to pressure change is no more problematic than it is in plea bargaining).

   For the threat therapeutic jurisprudence poses to proportionality, see Hoffman, *Therapeutic Jurisprudence, Neo-Rehabilitationism, and Judicial Collectivism, supra* note 42, at 2078–83. As James Nolan perceptively notes, the new therapeutic ideology differs in its emphasis from classic rehabilitation. Rehabilitationism strove to adapt wrongdoers to live in society by inculcating an ethic of self-denial. It diagnosed the problem as a disease of the individual. The modern therapeutic ethos, in contrast, emphasizes "self-actualization," liberating the authentic self from oppressive societal causes of crime. Thus, drug courts stress building up clients' self-esteem and eschew ascribing guilt. NOLAN, REINVENTING JUSTICE, *supra* note 42, at 138–43, 179–80. In short, therapeutic ideology has moved even further away from the popular morality of guilt and blame.

   For therapists' redefinition of justice to include whatever treatment demands, see *id.* at 191–201. For the divergence of professionals' views from those of their clients, see John Petrila, *Paternalism and the Unrealized Promise of* Essays in Therapeutic Jurisprudence, *in* LAW IN A THERAPEUTIC KEY, *supra* note 38, at 685, 701.

48. NOLAN, REINVENTING JUSTICE, *supra* note 42, at 75.

49. For some problem-solving courts' rejection of retribution and blame, see Hora et al., *supra* note 42, at 520; *see also* NOLAN, REINVENTING JUSTICE, *supra* note 42, at 144–50; Nolan, *Redefining Criminal Courts, supra* note 42, at 1548 (quoting remarks of Bruce Winick, cofounder of therapeutic jurisprudence, criticizing restorative justice for using the language of "reintegrative shaming" and not focusing enough on rehabilitation). In fairness, I should note that in other places, some therapeutic jurisprudence advocates contend that blame can sometimes be therapeutic. *See, e.g.,* chapter III note 20 and accompanying text (discussing possibly antitherapeutic consequences of labeling some mentally ill defendants as not guilty). Even so, treating ascriptions of blame as mere therapeutic means to an end is at best incomplete; it lacks the moral force of true blame.

   On the diversion of cases to problem-solving courts before any adjudication, see NOLAN, REINVENTING JUSTICE, *supra* note 42, at 141.

50. For this very reason, British observers of American drug courts are often shocked to see drug-court judges emoting, hugging, and acting like talk-show hosts instead of dignified authorities. Nolan, *Separated by an Uncommon Law, supra* note 42, at 89, 102–08.

CHAPTER V

1. For judicial and scholarly emphases on efficiency, see Santobello v. New York, 404 U.S. 257, 260–61 (1971) (plea bargaining "is to be encouraged" because it is fast and final, and "[i]f every criminal charge were subjected to a full-scale trial, the States and the Federal Government would need to multiply by many times the number of judges and court facilities"); Chief Justice Warren E. Burger, *The State of the Judiciary*, 56 A.B.A. J. 929, 929, 931 (1970) (criticizing "antiquated, rigid procedures which not only permit delay but often encourage it" and instead endorsing plea bargaining as a modern, efficient, businesslike technique); HEUMANN, *supra* chapter I note 61, at 148 (noting, based on interviews of judges, that judicial culture and training value "disposing of cases" and "efficiently moving the business" even when case pressures do not force them to do so); *infra* note 12 and accompanying text (citing law and economics scholars who evaluate criminal justice in terms of efficiency); *see also* Apprendi v. New Jersey, 550 U.S. 466, 555 (2000) (Breyer, J., dissenting) ("[T]he real world . . . cannot hope to meet any [jury-trial] ideal. It can function only with the help of procedural compromises").

   The speedy-trial provisions are found at U.S. CONST. amend. VI; 18 U.S.C. § 3161(c) (2006) (Speedy Trial Act).

2. PACKER, *supra* Introduction note 9, at 159.

3. *Id.* at 163–71.

4. The first quotation in the textual paragraph is from Chesterton, *supra* chapter II note 21, at 86. For a discussion of jurors' checking function, see Rachel E. Barkow, *Recharging the Jury: The Criminal Jury's Constitutional Role in an Era of Mandatory Sentencing*, 152 U. PA. L. REV. 33, 48–54 (2003). The Tocqueville quotations are from 1 TOCQUEVILLE, *supra* chapter II note 48, at 284–85.

5. *See generally* Stephanos Bibas, *The Real-World Shift in Criminal Procedure*, 93 J. CRIM. L. & CRIMINOLOGY 789, 795–804 (2003) (reviewing RONALD JAY ALLEN ET AL., COMPREHENSIVE CRIMINAL PROCEDURE (2001) and MARC L. MILLER & RONALD F. WRIGHT, CRIMINAL PROCEDURES: CASES, STATUTES, AND EXECUTIVE MATERIALS (1998)).

6. Amar's discussion of the Bill of Rights' populist, majoritarian character is in Akhil Reed Amar, *The Bill of Rights as a Constitution*, 100 YALE L.J. 1131, 1132–33 (1991). For discussion of the jury as the conscience of the community, see Witherspoon v. Illinois, 391 U.S. 510, 519 & n.15 (1968) (the source of the quotation in the text); *see also* AMAR, THE CONSTITUTION AND CRIMINAL PROCEDURE, *supra* Introduction note 1, at 122–24.

7. For discussion of how workloads encourage plea bargaining, see FISHER, *supra* Introduction note 4, at 13; *accord id.* at 15–16; Bibas, *Plea Bargaining Outside the Shadow of Trial*, *supra* chapter I note 83, at 2479–80.

   For a study of prosecutorial elections, see Ronald F. Wright, *How Prosecutor Elections Fail Us*, 6 OHIO ST. J. CRIM. L. 581, 600–01 tbl.3 (2009) (reporting, in an empirical study of print news coverage of 67 prosecutor election campaigns, that 39 campaigns mentioned case backlogs or processing time, 27 mentioned conviction rates, and 23 mentioned aggregate sentence severity).

   For metrics of police officers' efficacy, see JEROME H. SKOLNICK & JAMES J. FYFE, ABOVE THE LAW: POLICE AND THE EXCESSIVE USE OF FORCE 125 (1993);

Barbara E. Armacost, *Organizational Culture and Police Misconduct*, 72 GEO. WASH. L. REV. 453, 519 (2004).

For bureaucratic rewards for quantifiable successes, see Geoffrey P. Alpert & Mark H. Moore, *Measuring Police Performance in the New Paradigm of Policing, in* PERFORMANCE MEASURES FOR THE CRIMINAL JUSTICE SYSTEM, NCJ 143505, at 109, 129 (1993); Erik Luna, *The Overcriminalization Phenomenon*, 54 AM. U. L. REV. 703, 723 (2005).

8. HEUMANN, *supra* chapter I note 61, at 144–48. As one thoughtful judge observed:

> You know, we're all trying to rush the things through the court, and if you think about it, it has become kind of a phobia. We certainly don't have much to gain by it; the only one who might benefit is a part-time prosecutor because he has a private practice also. I don't have any reason to rush. I get paid no matter if I'm here or there, and I've got the time to handle all of the business. I'm perfectly willing to sit here till five o'clock every day, so it's kind of a fantasy, this idea of rushing things through. But I still do it. I guess it's that you get tired of these things after a while. Maybe it's human nature. You know you can do it quicker, so that's how you do it. I'm not sure.

> *Id.* at 148 (quoting an anonymous state judge).

9. Barkow, *supra* chapter I note 77, at 1336–55.

10. For the shakiness of morality as a foundation for consensus, see Richard A. Posner, *The Problematics of Moral and Legal Theory*, 111 HARV. L. REV. 1637, 1638–42 (1998); Richard A. Posner, *Conceptions of Legal "Theory": A Response to Ronald Dworkin*, 29 ARIZ. ST. L.J. 377, 382–84 (1997); Peter Cane, *Taking Law Seriously: Starting Points of the Hart/Devlin Debate*, 10 J. ETHICS 21, 49–50 (2006).

For discussions of efforts to raise cultural defenses to crimes, see generally MULTICULTURAL JURISPRUDENCE: COMPARATIVE PERSPECTIVES ON THE CULTURAL DEFENSE (Marie-Claire Foblets & Alison Dundes Renteln eds., 2009); ALISON DUNDES RENTELN, THE CULTURAL DEFENSE (2004).

11. Neil MacCormick & David Garland, *Sovereign States and Vengeful Victims: The Problem of the Right to Punish, in* FUNDAMENTALS OF SENTENCING THEORY 11, 14–15 (Andrew Ashworth & Martin Wasik eds., 1998) (source of the quotation in the text); *accord* GARLAND, *supra* chapter IV note 21, at 9 (lamenting the return "of an explicitly retributive discourse," which uses "[t]he language of condemnation and punishment" to serve "symbolic, expressive, and communicative" functions instead of "professional judgment"). For Rawls's idea of neutrality, see generally JOHN RAWLS, POLITICAL LIBERALISM (1996).

12. On nonjudgmentalism in criminal justice policy, see Dan M. Kahan, *The Secret Ambition of Deterrence*, 113 HARV. L. REV. 413, 445–46 (1999). For examples of scholarship that treats quantifiable metrics as the dominant if not the only criteria for criminal justice, see Gary S. Becker, *Crime and Punishment: An Economic Approach*, 76 J. POL. ECON. 169, 207–09 (1968); Frank H. Easterbrook, *Criminal Procedure as a Market System*, 12 J. LEGAL STUD. 289, 290 (1983) (criticizing wrongful convictions for undermining marginal deterrence); Frank H. Easterbrook, *Plea Bargaining as Compromise*, 101 YALE L.J. 1969, 1970, 1975 (1992) (praising plea bargaining as a system for efficiently selling rights in exchange for lower

sentences); Richard A. Posner, *An Economic Theory of the Criminal Law*, 85 COLUM. L. REV. 1193, 1193–95 (1985).

13. ALAN WOLFE, ONE NATION, AFTER ALL 54 (1998).

14. Kahan, *The Secret Ambition, supra* note 12, at 425–35, 477–85.

15. *Id.* at 437–45, 451–59; Phoebe C. Ellsworth & Lee Ross, *Public Opinion and Capital Punishment: A Close Examination of the Views of Abolitionists and Retentionists*, 29 CRIME & DELINQ. 116, 146–49 (1983) (using empirical data to show that deterrence is not the basis of people's beliefs about the death penalty).

16. For evidence of popular consensus on criminal justice, see PETER H. ROSSI & RICHARD A. BERK, U.S. SENTENCING COMM'N, A NATIONAL SAMPLE SURVEY: PUBLIC OPINION ON SENTENCING FEDERAL CRIMES 11–12 (1995) ("[A] [f]airly strong consensus exists on the seriousness ordering of crimes, with those involving actual or threatened physical harm to victims generally considered to be the most serious"); *see also* THORSTEN SELLIN & MARVIN E. WOLFGANG, THE MEASUREMENT OF DELINQUENCY 268–71, 324 (1964).

Robinson's empirical study is Paul H. Robinson & Robert Kurzban, *Concordance and Conflict in Intuitions of Justice*, 91 MINN. L. REV. 1829, 1867–73, 1883–87 (2007). These agreements are on relative rankings rather than absolute punishment amounts, which vary more. Chapter VI will suggest ways to produce consensus on absolute punishments. For example, sentencing judges or juries could consider recommended punishment guidelines and frequency distributions of punishments imposed in similar crimes. These would serve as mental anchors or benchmarks, leading sentencers to sentence based on how wrongful a particular crime was relative to the average one in that category. Note that many of the more controversial crimes studied, such as late-term abortions and bestiality, are rarely prosecuted in practice, so people's disagreements about them have limited practical importance.

Some authors emphasize the remaining areas of disagreement rather than consensus, but that emphasis does not contradict the existence of large areas of consensus. *See* Donald Braman et al., *Some Realism About Punishment Naturalism*, 77 U. CHI. L. REV. 1531, 1545 (2010).

For Durkheim's emphasis on criminal law's function of reinforcing social solidarity, see DURKHEIM, *supra* chapter I note 33, at 62–64.

17. Kevin M. Carlsmith et al., *Why Do We Punish? Deterrence and Just Deserts as Motives for Punishment*, 83 J. PERSONALITY & SOC. PSYCHOL. 284, 288–97 (2002); John M. Darley et al., *Incapacitation and Just Deserts as Motives for Punishment*, 24 LAW & HUM. BEHAV. 659, 661–71, 676 (2000). The only partial exception to respondents' focus on retribution was that they were also willing to incapacitate those who committed crimes because of brain tumors. *Id.* at 671–76.

18. *See supra* text accompanying chapter II note 13.

19. TYLER, *supra* Introduction note 8, at 125–30, 135–40, 163–65. Procedural justice and process control are consistently important across an array of cultures. In studies from Europe to East Asia to America, "[s]ome procedural justice *effects* are clearly variable [such as the American preference for the adversarial process], but basic procedural justice *processes* are remarkably invariant across the contexts and cultures studied thus far." LIND & TYLER, *supra* chapter II note 17, at 141–45.

20. TYLER, *supra* Introduction note 8, at 137–40.

21. JOHN LOCKE, A LETTER CONCERNING TOLERATION 6 (Huddersfield: J. Brook 1796) (1689) ("appeal[ing] to the consciences of those that persecute, torment, destroy, and kill other men upon pretence of religion"). There is certainly room to debate whether the criminal law ought to reach beyond crimes that involve harm to others. That argument, however, is a debate around the edges rather than at the heart of the criminal law. A substantial majority of crimes in America involve clear harm to others. *See* WILLIAM J. SABOL ET AL., U.S. DEP'T OF JUSTICE, NCJ 228417, PRISONERS IN 2008, at 37 appx. tbl. 16 (2009) (reporting that in 2006, 50.2% of state inmates were incarcerated for violent crimes, 20.9% for property offenses, 20% for drug offenses, and only 8.4% for public-order offenses). Even many so-called victimless crimes, such as neighborhood drug dealing, are committed in ways that produce substantial violence and harm to others. *See generally* Bernard E. Harcourt, *The Collapse of the Harm Principle*, 90 J. CRIM. L. & CRIMINOLOGY 109 (1999). The next chapter discusses how making criminal justice more responsive to local community needs would further steer enforcement towards crimes that harm others and away from truly victimless crimes.

22. 2 TOCQUEVILLE, *supra* chapter II note 48, at 121–27 (discussing how American religious beliefs and moral habits inculcate selflessness, self-sacrifice, and self-restraint); *see* BARRY SCHWARTZ, THE BATTLE FOR HUMAN NATURE: SCIENCE, MORALITY AND MODERN LIFE 19–20 (1987) (expounding Tocqueville's vision of the productive tension between individualism and shared virtues).

23. *See* David Luban, *A Theory of Crimes Against Humanity*, 29 YALE J. INT'L L. 85, 126 n.145 (2004).

24. *See* Michael Tonry, *Punishment Policies and Patterns in Western Countries*, *in* SENTENCING AND SANCTIONS IN WESTERN COUNTRIES 3, 15, 18 (Michael Tonry & Richard S. Frase eds., 2001) (decrying America's "punitive populism" and "moralism" as setting it apart from other Western countries); Michael Tonry, *Determinants of Penal Policies*, *in* CRIME, PUNISHMENT, AND POLITICS IN COMPARATIVE PERSPECTIVE 1, 26, 33 (Michael Tonry ed., 2007) (blaming America for not insulating criminal-justice policy from "ill-informed, mercurial, [] mean-spirited," and "emotional" mob rule the way that other Western countries do); Michael Tonry, *Rethinking Unthinkable Punishment Policies in America*, 46 UCLA L. REV. 1751, 1752–53, 1771, 1788–89 (1998) (blaming American criminal justice policy on moral panics driven by "ideology, exaggerated fears, and political opportunism" and decrying the importance that punishment policies accord to "public edification"); WHITMAN, HARSH JUSTICE, *supra* chapter II note 23, at 14–15, 55; GARLAND, *supra* chapter IV note 21, at 9–10, 13, 35, 142, 145, 151, 184; Ian Loader, *Fall of the "Platonic Guardians": Liberalism, Criminology and Political Responses to Crime in England and Wales*, 46 BRIT. J. CRIMINOLOGY 561, 568, 582 (2006) (noting that liberal elites valued criminal-justice policymakers as Platonic guardians and lamented their failure to fulfill that role).

25. For scholarly condemnations of shaming punishments, see MARTHA NUSSBAUM, HIDING FROM HUMANITY: DISGUST, SHAME, AND THE LAW 71–171, 227–50, 335–40 (2004) (rejecting shaming penalties because they are "connected to hierarchy and degradation," particularly of homosexuals and other minorities, but leaving the door open to shaming "powerful organizations—corporations, law

firms—[for their] hubris and narcissism"); Markel, *Are Shaming Punishments Beautifully Retributive?*, *supra* chapter II note 45, at 2216–28 (opposing shaming punishments because they are too degrading and illiberal, create spillover effects, and depend on unpredictable mob reactions); Massaro, *Shame, Culture, and American Criminal Law*, *supra* chapter II note 45, at 1942–43 (opposing shaming penalties in part because they degrade offenders' dignity); Whitman, *What Is Wrong with Inflicting Shame Sanctions?*, *supra* chapter II note 45, at 1088–92.

Note that I am not taking a position in favor of shaming sanctions specifically. Rather, I am criticizing opponents' rhetoric and reasoning for its aversion to popular input and popular moral language.

26. *See* Stuntz, *Unequal Justice*, *supra* chapter IV note 19, at 1970–71 (collecting statistics showing that blacks make up about one-eighth of the general population but almost half of the prison population; black men are locked up at nearly seven times the rate of their white counterparts, while Latino men are imprisoned at almost three times the rate for white men; on drug charges, black men are imprisoned at nearly thirteen times the rate for whites, even though they are only slightly more likely to use illegal drugs).

27. *See generally* Prison Fellowship, *What Is Prison Fellowship?*, http://www.prisonfellowship.org/why-pf (last visited June 10, 2011).

28. Bandes, *supra* chapter IV note 16, at 409; Robert C. Solomon, *Justice v. Vengeance: On Law and the Satisfaction of Emotion*, *in* THE PASSIONS OF LAW, *supra* chapter IV note 12, at 123, 125.

29. As C.S. Lewis put it:

Mercy, detached from Justice, grows unmerciful. That is the important paradox. As there are plants which will flourish only in mountain soil, so it appears that Mercy will flower only when it grows in the crannies of the rock of Justice: trans-planted to the marshlands of mere Humanitarianism, it becomes a man-eating weed, all the more dangerous because it is still called by the same name as the mountain variety.

C.S. Lewis, *The Humanitarian Theory of Punishment*, *in* GOD IN THE DOCK: ESSAYS ON THEOLOGY AND ETHICS 287, 294 (Walter Hooper ed., 1970).

30. Solomon, *supra* note 28, at 140–41; *see also supra* text accompanying chapter III note 15 (discussing Hampton's idea of punishment as vindication of victims).

31. *See, e.g.*, MICHAEL R. RAND, U.S. DEP'T OF JUSTICE, NCJ 227777, CRIMINAL VICTIMIZATION 2008, at 5 (2009) (reporting that in 2008, family, friends, and acquaintances were responsible for committing almost three-fifths of violent crimes).

32. *See, e.g.*, Thomas F. Pettigrew & Linda R. Tropp, *A Meta-Analytic Test of Intergroup Contact Theory*, 90 J. PERSONALITY & SOC. PSYCHOL. 751, 752, 766 (2006) (citing multiple studies, and reporting results of a meta-analysis, finding that "intergroup contact typically reduces intergroup prejudice"); Jeffrey J. Rachlinski et al., *Does Unconscious Racial Bias Affect Trial Judges?*, 84 NOTRE DAME L. REV. 1195, 1221–25 (2009) (noting that explicitly confronting the racial issue may help to reduce the impact of bias). *Cf.* Cass R. Sunstein, *Moral Heuristics*, 28 BEHAV.

& BRAIN SCI. 531, 541–42 (2005) (noting the dangers of moral reasoning from exotic, unrepresentative hypothetical cases).

33. Tracey L. Meares & Dan M. Kahan, *The Wages of Antiquated Procedural Thinking: A Critique of* Chicago v Morales, 1998 U. CHI. LEGAL F. 197; *see supra* text accompanying chapter II note 51, chapter IV note 19 (discussing Stuntz's work and democratic responses to inequality).

CHAPTER VI

1. On inmates' employment before their incarceration, see LAUREN E. GLAZE & LAURA M. MARUSCHAK, U.S. DEP'T OF JUSTICE, NCJ 222984, PARENTS IN PRISON AND THEIR MINOR CHILDREN 18 (2010).

   On the contributions inmates were making to their families before being incarcerated, see, for example, DONALD BRAMAN, DOING TIME ON THE OUTSIDE: INCARCERATION AND FAMILY LIFE IN URBAN AMERICA 98, 109, 155–56 (2004).

   On the choking off of the market for prison-made goods, see *supra* text accompanying chapter I note 71; JEREMY TRAVIS ET AL., FROM PRISON TO HOME: THE DIMENSIONS AND CONSEQUENCES OF PRISONER REENTRY 18 (2001) (reporting that only 7% of prisoners take part in prison industries, while 24% are completely idle); THE 2002 CORRECTIONS YEARBOOK, *supra* chapter I note 71, at 118 (reporting that at the start of 2002, only 7.8% of federal and state inmates combined worked in prison industries and only 3.6% worked on prison farms); Garvey, *Freeing Prisoners' Labor*, *supra* chapter I note 71, at 358–67 (discussing history).

   On how few prisoners cultivate marketable skills, see AMY SOLOMON ET AL., URBAN INSTITUTE, FROM PRISON TO WORK: THE EMPLOYMENT DIMENSIONS OF PRISONER REENTRY 16–17 fig. 5 (2004). At the start of 2002, only 47% of federal and state inmates combined had some work detail in prison. THE 2002 CORRECTIONS YEARBOOK, *supra* chapter I note 71, at 118.

   On the pittance prisoners are paid, see BRAMAN, *supra*, at 140–42; JEREMY TRAVIS ET AL., URBAN INST. JUSTICE POL'Y CTR., FAMILIES LEFT BEHIND: THE HIDDEN COSTS OF INCARCERATION AND REENTRY 5 (2005) ("Sharing income with one's family is all but eliminated as most prisoners, even those with prison jobs, earn as little as $350 per year"); THE 2002 CORRECTIONS YEARBOOK, *supra* chapter I note 71, at 120 (reporting average prisoner wages of $2.63 to $7.64 per day in prison-run industries, $21.43 to $36.50 per day in privately run industries, and $1.14 to $5.99 per day for non-industry prison jobs such as farm work; also reporting average work days as 6.7 to 6.8 hours long).

   At the start of 2002, only 12.4% of federal and state inmates combined were enrolled in full-time academic or vocational training programs, and only 14.5% were enrolled in part-time programs. THE 2002 CORRECTIONS YEARBOOK, *supra* chapter I note 71, at 118. A 1997 study of inmates who were to be released in the next year found only 27% enrolled in vocational programs and 35% in educational programs. TRAVIS ET AL., FROM PRISON TO HOME, *supra*, at 17 fig. 8.

   The law that ended Pell grants for prisoners was the Violent Crime Control and Law Enforcement Act of 1994, Pub. L. 103–322, § 20411, 108 Stat. 1796 (amending 20 U.S.C. § 1070a(b)(8)); *see also* Richard Tewksbury & Jon Marc Taylor, *The Consequences of Eliminating Pell Grant Eligibility for Students in Post-Secondary Correctional Education Programs*, 60 FED. PROBATION 60, 61 (1994) (noting that nearly a quarter of prison systems had completely eliminated post-secondary education in the wake of the elimination of Pell grants, and another 31.6% of systems recorded a significant drop in the number of students enrolled); Robert Worth, *A Model Prison*, ATLANTIC MONTHLY, Nov. 1995, at 38, 42 (noting that at least 25 states had cut their vocational and technical training for inmates in recent years).

On the inadequate supply of treatment in prison, see TRAVIS ET AL., FROM PRISON TO HOME, *supra*, at 26–27 (2001) (reporting that only 18% of soon-to-be-released inmates who had been using drugs in the month before entering prison had taken part in drug treatment while in prison); NATIONAL CENTER ON ADDICTION AND SUBSTANCE ABUSE, BEHIND BARS: SUBSTANCE ABUSE AND AMERICA'S PRISON POPULATION 10–11, 111–35 (1998) (estimating that while 70% to 85% of state inmates and 31% of federal inmates need substance-abuse treatment, only 13% of state prison inmates, 10% of federal prison inmates, and 8% of jail inmates were in any form of treatment in 1996, and few treatment slots are in intensive residential programs, the most effective type).

On the demise of orderly work and good habits in prison, see FRIEDMAN, CRIME AND PUNISHMENT IN AMERICAN HISTORY, *supra* chapter I note 3, at 155–56.

2. On the roles of marriage and fatherhood in taming crime, Kathryn Edin et al., *Fatherhood and Incarceration as Potential Turning Points in the Criminal Careers of Unskilled Men, in* IMPRISONING AMERICA: THE SOCIAL EFFECTS OF MASS INCARCERATION 46, 53 (Mary Patillo et al. eds., 2004); Robert J. Sampson et al., *Does Marriage Reduce Crime? A Counterfactual Approach to Within-Individual Causal Effects*, 44 CRIMINOLOGY 465, 498 (2006) (finding, in long longitudinal study, that marriage is associated with 35% reduction in crime and appears to causally inhibit it).

On the link between maintaining family relationships in prison and crime after release, see Bonnie F. Carlson & Neil Cervera, *Inmates and Their Families: Conjugal Visits, Family Contact, and Family Functioning*, 18 CRIM. JUST. & BEHAV. 318, 320 (1991); Creasie Finney Hairston, *Family Ties During Imprisonment: Important to Whom and for What?*, 18 J. SOCIOLOGY & SOC. WELFARE 87, 97–98 (1991); Creasie Finney Hairston, *Family Ties During Imprisonment: Do They Influence Future Criminal Activity?*, 52 FED. PROBATION 48, 48–49 (1988); Ginger L. Wilczak & Carol A. Markstrom, *The Effects of Parent Education on Parental Locus of Control and Satisfaction of Incarcerated Fathers*, 43 INT'L J. OFFENDER THERAPY & COMP. CRIMINOLOGY 90, 92 (2006) ("[T]he single best predictor of successful release from prison is whether the individual has solid family relationships to which they [*sic*] can return").

Far from removing wrongdoers from criminogenic environments, prisons distill a hyper-criminal concentration of human capital. Sending a greenhorn to prison risks confirming him in a career of crime. *See* Edwin J. Latessa & Christopher Lowenkamp, *What Works in Reducing Recidivism?*, 3 U. ST. THOMAS L.J. 521, 522 & n. 2 (2006); Christopher T. Lowenkamp & Edward J. Latessa, *Understanding the Risk Principle: How and Why Correctional Interventions Can Harm Low-Risk Offenders*, TOPICS IN COMMUNITY CORRECTIONS 3, 5 (2004).

3. *Cf.* DICKENS, *supra* chapter I note 70, at 111–13 ("[B]ecause [imprisonment's] wounds are not upon the surface, and it extorts few cries that human ears can hear; therefore I the more denounce it, as a secret punishment which slumbering humanity is not roused up to stay."); Louis D. Brandeis, *What Publicity Can Do*, HARPER'S WEEKLY, Dec. 20, 1913, at 10 ("Sunlight is said to be the best of

disinfectants; electric light the most efficient policeman."), *reprinted in* OTHER PEOPLE'S MONEY 92 (1914).

4. Braman, *supra* chapter I note 35, at 1149–53, 1188–91, 1195 tbls. A, B (summarizing data from 1995 *National Opinion Survey of Crime and Justice*), 1197 tbl. C (finding at least 85% support in each political subgroup for mandatory prison labor, work in the community, education, and job training), 1198 (describing support for judicially supervised drug treatment as exceeding a five-to-one margin).

5. *See supra* note 1.

6. ALEXANDER SOLZHENITSYN, ONE DAY IN THE LIFE OF IVAN DENISOVICH 75–88 (Ralph Parker trans. 2008).

7. We would not want to insist on full repayment before release. Doing so would re-create the old debtors' prisons, releasing the rich but holding the poor indefinitely solely because they remain too poor to pay. The state could, however, continue to garnish wages after release to fulfill the remaining restitution that convicts owe to victims.

8. *See* Mark S. Fleisher & Richard H. Rison, *United States of America: Inmate Work and Consensual Management in the Federal Bureau of Prisons, in* PRISON LABOR: SALVATION OR SLAVERY? INTERNATIONAL PERSPECTIVES 281, 289 tbls. 16.4, 16.5 (Dirk van Zyl Smit & Frieder Dünkel eds. 1999) (noting that inmates who work in federal prison industries commit fewer infractions); Marilyn C. Moses & Cindy J. Smith, *Factories Behind Fences: Do Prison "Real Work" Programs Work?*, NAT'L INST. JUST. J., June 2007, at 32 (finding that prisoners who take part in prison industries recidivate less, find work more quickly after release, and contribute toward the expenses of their room and board while in prison); THOMAS W. PETERSIK ET AL., NAT'L CORRECTIONAL INDUS. ASS'N, IDENTIFYING BENEFICIARIES OF PIE INMATE INCOMES: WHO BENEFITS FROM WAGE EARNINGS OF INMATES WORKING IN THE PRISON INDUSTRY ENHANCEMENT (PIE) PROGRAM? (2003), *available at* www.nationalcia.org/wp-content/uploads/2008/09/researchfullrpt1.pdf.

9. For examples from history, see, for example, HUGH F. RANKIN, CRIMINAL TRIAL PROCEEDINGS IN THE GENERAL COURT OF COLONIAL VIRGINIA 110, 171 (1965) (noting two examples of sentences to military service in colonial Virginia); Peter King, *War as a Judicial Resource: Press Gangs and Prosecution Rates, 1740–1830, in* LAW, CRIME AND ENGLISH SOCIETY, 1660–1830, at 97, 106 (2002) (discussing English wartime impressment of young male property offenders as an alternative to prosecution, and concluding that "[p]ress gangs made better magistrates than Middlesex justices"); Edith Abbott, *Crime and the War*, 9 J. AM. INST. CRIM. L. & CRIMINOLOGY 32, 42 (1918) (noting one view that crime rose after the Civil War because convicts had been sentenced to military service); Hans W. Mattick, *Parolees in the Army During World War II*, 24 FED. PROBATION 49 (1960) (noting World War I parolees who worked in wartime industries and discussing Illinois program during World War II of paroling inmates directly or indirectly to the Army, which succeeded in reducing recidivism and improving behavior).

On the American military's current ban on enlisting convicts, see John F. Frana & Ryan D. Schroeder, *Alternatives to Incarceration*, JUST. POL'Y, Fall 2008, at 8 (noting that every military branch except for the Navy explicitly forbids enlistment in lieu of prosecution or punishment).

10. CHARLES C. MOSKOS & JOHN SIBLEY BUTLER, ALL THAT WE CAN BE: BLACK LEADERSHIP AND RACIAL INTEGRATION THE ARMY WAY 1–3 (1997); Jennifer Hickes Lundquist, *Ethnic and Gender Satisfaction in the Military: The Effect of a Meritocratic Institution*, 73 AM. SOC. REV. 477, 480 (2008); Aline O. Questor & Curtis L. Gilroy, *Women and Minorities in America's Volunteer Army*, 20 CONTEMP. ECON. POL'Y 111 (2002); Steven A. Holmes, *Time and Money Producing Racial Harmony in the Military*, N.Y. TIMES, Apr. 5, 1995, at A1.

11. *See* Mattick, *supra* note 9.

12. There would need to be some sanctions for drug use and failure to engage in education or training. At the same time, one would not want to lengthen sentences indefinitely for these violations, for that would amount to net-widening, punishing inmates' uncooperativeness more than the underlying crime itself. Uncooperativeness could prevent inmates from claiming good-time sentence credits that ordinarily reduce their total sentences by 15% or so. Serious infractions, such as violence or drug dealing, would merit additional convictions and sentences. Other carrots and sticks would involve prison privileges such as exercise and outdoors time, showers, haircuts, desserts, visitor privileges, and television and telephone access.

13. On the so-called collateral consequences of criminal convictions, see generally Nora V. Demleitner, *Preventing Internal Exile: The Need for Restrictions on Collateral Sentencing Consequences*, 11 STAN. L. & POL'Y REV. 153, 154 (1999); Brian C. Kalt, *The Exclusion of Felons from Jury Service*, 53 AM. U. L. REV. 65, 67 nn. 4–5 (2003).

On restrictions on felons' employment, see Bruce E. May, *The Character Component of Occupational Licensing Laws: A Continuing Barrier to the Ex-Felon's Employment Opportunities*, 71 N.D. L. REV. 187, 190–91 (1995) (noting that occupational licensing laws typically govern accountants, alcohol sellers, ambulance drivers, attorneys, barbers, billiard room employees, contractors, embalmers, nurses, pharmacists, physicians, real estate professionals, and septic tank cleaners, among others).

On the breadth of crimes lumped together as sex offenses, see, for example, HUMAN RIGHTS WATCH, vol. 19, no. 4(G), NO EASY ANSWERS: SEX OFFENDER LAWS IN THE US 39–40 (Sept. 2007), *available at* http://www.hrw.org/en/reports/2007/09/11/no-easy-answers (cataloguing five states that require registration for adult prostitution-related crimes, 13 states that require it for public urination, 29 states that require it for consensual sex between teenagers, and 32 that require it for exposing genitals in public); Corey Rayburn Yung, *The Emerging Criminal War on Sex Offenders*, 45 HARV. C.R.-C.L. L. REV. 435, 455–56 (2010).

14. Colorado Sex Offender Mgmt. Bd., Colo. Dep't of Pub. Safety, White Paper on the Use of Residence Restrictions as a Sex Offender Management Strategy 2–4 (June 2009), *available at* http://dcj.state.co.us/odvsom/sex_offender/SO_Pdfs/Residence%20Restrictions.PP.pdf; Minnesota Dep't of Corrections, Residential Proximity and Sex Offense Recidivism in Minnesota 2 (Apr. 2007), *available at* http://www.nacdl.org/sl_docs.nsf/issues/SexOffender_attachments/$FILE/MN_Residence.pdf; Minnesota Dep't of Corrections, Level Three Sex Offenders Residential Placement Issues, 2003 Report to the Legislature 9–11, 19–21 App. C-1 to C-3 (Jan. 2003) (finding no evidence that residential proximity to schools or parks affected reoffending, and also noting that a 1500-foot exclusion zone would exclude offenders from all but slivers of every residential area of

Minneapolis and St. Paul); Iowa Cnty. Attorneys Ass'n, Statement on Sex Offender Residency Restrictions in Iowa (Dec. 11, 2006) (concluding that a 2000-foot residency restriction does not reduce sex offenses or protect children, is too costly to enforce, and harms convicts' families), *available at* http://www.iowa-icaa.com/ICAA%20STATEMENTS/Sex%20Offender%20Residency%20Statement%20Dec%2011%2006.pdf.

15. *Cf. Ecclesiastes* 3:1, 5 (King James Version) ("To everything there is a season, and a time to every purpose under the heaven; . . . A time to cast away stones, and a time to gather stones together; a time to embrace, and a time to refrain from embracing.").

16. Braithwaite, Crime, Shame, and Reintegration *supra* chapter IV note 27, at 54–107.

17. Winston Churchill, Home Secretary, Speech Delivered to House of Commons (July 20, 1910), *in* Winston S. Churchill, His Complete Speeches: 1897–1963, Volume II: 1908–1913, at 1589, 1598 (Robert Rhodes James ed., 1974). *Cf. Luke* 15:11–32 (parable of the prodigal son).

18. On the right's recent interest in prison reform and re-entry, see Chris Suellentrop, *The Right Has a Jailhouse Conversion: How Conservatives Came to Embrace Prison Reform*, N.Y. Times, Dec. 24, 2006, § E (Magazine), at 46; Erik Eckholm, *U.S. Shifting Prison Focus to Re-Entry into Society*, N.Y. Times, Apr. 8, 2008, at A23 (noting that Congress passed the Second Chance Act with overwhelming bipartisan support and President George W. Bush would sign it); Justice Fellowship, Prison Fellowship, *Clemency and Overcoming Barriers to Reentry*, http://www.justicefellowship.org/key-issues/issues-in-criminal-justice-reform/clemency (last visited June 15, 2011).

19. Abraham Lincoln, *First Inaugural Address, Monday, March 4, 1861*, in Inaugural Addresses of the Presidents of the United States 133, 141 (1989). *Cf.* 1 *Corinthians* 13:13 (New King James Version) (listing faith, hope, and love as the three great virtues, of which the greatest is love).

20. On the woeful inadequacy of public reentry support, see Travis et al., From Prison to Home, *supra* note 1, at 19. On the InnerChange Freedom Initiative, see Byron R. Johnson with David B. Larson, Ctr. for Res. on Religion & Civil Soc'y, The InnerChange Freedom Initiative: A Preliminary Evaluation of a Faith-Based Prison Program 16–22, 47–50 (June 2003), *available at* http://www.prisonfellowship.org/images/pdfs/ifi_study.pdf; Brittani Trusti & Michael Eisenberg, Crim. Just. Pol'y Council, Initial Process and Outcome Evaluation of the InnerChange Freedom Initiative: The Faith-Based Prison Program in TDCJ 25 (Feb. 2003). Needless to say, such studies are always open to criticisms about selection biases and control groups, which tempers the strength of the conclusions one can draw.

On possible Establishment Clause problems, see Ams. United for Separation of Church and State v. Prison Fellowship Ministries, Inc., 509 F.3d 406, 418–19, 423–25 (8th Cir. 2007) (holding that InnerChange Freedom Initiative program in Iowa violated the Establishment Clause because 1) accounting was inadequate to ensure that direct government aid was not spent on religious activities; 2) the state gave inmates in the program better cells with more privacy, more family visits, and more computer access than other inmates received; 3) InnerChange staffers were inappropriately empowered to discipline inmates; and 4) inmates were given no choice of a secular alternative program).

21. *See* Wright & Miller, *The Screening/Bargaining Tradeoff, supra* chapter II note 10, at 60–61, 113–16.

22. *Id.* at 111–13.

23. For examples of published prosecutorial policies, see, for example, Richard H. Kuh, *Plea Bargaining: Guidelines for the Manhattan District Attorney's Office,* 11 CRIM. L. BULL. 48 (1975) (publishing internal memorandum from New York County District Attorney's Office on plea-bargaining guidelines); Richard H. Kuh, *Sentencing: Guidelines for the Manhattan District Attorney's Office,* 11 CRIM. L. BULL. 62 (1975) (same, for sentencing); Mario Merola, *Modern Prosecutorial Techniques,* 16 CRIM. L. BULL. 232, 237–40, 251–58 (1980) (publishing some details of Bronx County District Attorney's Office's internal screening and plea-bargaining procedures).

On repeat defense counsel's knowledge, see JONATHAN D. CASPER, AMERICAN CRIMINAL JUSTICE: THE DEFENDANT'S PERSPECTIVE 108 (1972); HEUMANN, *supra* chapter I note 61, at 76–78, 90. Because the point of publishing prosecutorial policies is to provide information rather than legal rights, the policies would not need to be enforceable, thus avoiding collateral litigation.

On the relative importance of certainty and severity for deterrence, see Jeffrey Grogger, *Certainty vs. Severity of Punishment,* 29 ECON. INQUIRY 297, 307–08 (1991); Ann Dryden Witte, *Estimating the Economic Model of Crime with Individual Data,* 94 Q.J. ECON. 57, 79 (1980).

24. On the limited data collected by police, the role of citizen review boards, and the efficacy of regulation by disclosure, see William J. Stuntz, *The Political Constitution of Criminal Justice,* 119 HARV. L. REV. 780, 826–28 (2006). On the roles of community review boards, videotaping, mandatory record-keeping, and sharing of crime maps, see Erik Luna, *Transparent Policing,* 85 IOWA L. REV. 1107, 1167–70, 1177–78, 1192–93 (2000). For a thoughtful assessment of this participatory trend in the policing literature, see generally Sklansky, *Police and Democracy, supra* chapter I note 48.

25. On the subject of police collaboration with neighborhood residents, see Erik Luna, *Race, Crime, and Institutional Design,* 66 LAW & CONTEMP. PROBS. 183, 207–11 (Summer 2003). In addition, better police recruitment, training, performance standards, oversight, and discipline can likewise help check police actions that might breed antagonism and mistrust. *Id.* at 211–17.

For an overview of community policing and its two core principles of community partnership and joint problem-solving, see BUREAU OF JUSTICE ASSISTANCE, U.S. DEP'T OF JUSTICE, NCJ 148457, UNDERSTANDING COMMUNITY POLICING: A FRAMEWORK FOR ACTION (Aug. 1994).

On possible changes to pay and promotion criteria, see Stephanos Bibas, *Rewarding Prosecutors for Performance,* 6 OHIO ST. J. CRIM. L. 441 (2009) (suggesting combination of incentive pay, promotions, and awards to motivate prosecutors to pursue improved metrics of success that reflect public and peer evaluations of performance, not just conviction rates).

For Luna's proposal for public rulemaking, see Erik Luna, *Principled Enforcement of Penal Codes,* 4 BUFF. CRIM. L. REV. 515, 598–622 (2000).

26. *See* Dan M. Kahan & Tracey L. Meares, *Foreword: The Coming Crisis in Criminal Procedure*, 86 GEO. L.J. 1153, 1153–54 (1998); RANDALL KENNEDY, RACE, CRIME, AND THE LAW 19 (1997) (developing the theme "that the principal injury suffered by African-Americans in relation to criminal matters is not overenforcement but underenforcement").

27. *See* Tracey L. Meares, *Praying for Community Policing*, 90 CAL. L. REV. 1593 (2002) (offering this explanation for the crime-fighting potency of the prayer vigils organized by Chicago police, which brought together ministers and congregations which previously had had no contact).

28. *See, e.g.*, James Vorenberg, *Decent Restraint of Prosecutorial Power*, 94 HARV. L. REV. 1521, 1567 (1981) (favoring legislation to restrict prosecutorial discretion ex ante).

29. *Cf.* Lior Jacob Strahilevitz, *"How's My Driving?" for Everyone (and Everything?)*, 81 N.Y.U. L. REV. 1699, 1760, 1764 (2006) (proposing distributed-feedback approaches to "replace state policing with citizen policing, laws with norms, and, to some extent, rules with standards," including a "How's My Policing?" feedback program to generate data about bad or rude police).

30. Kevin K. Washburn, *Restoring the Grand Jury*, 76 FORDHAM L. REV. 2333, 2378–88 (2008); Jason Mazzone, *The Waiver Paradox*, 97 NW. U. L. REV. 801, 872–78 (2003); Josh Bowers, Outsourcing Equitable Discretion (Aug. 24, 2010) (unpublished manuscript, on file with the Columbia Law Review); Laura I. Appleman, *The Plea Jury*, 85 IND. L.J. 731, 750–68 (2010); Bibas & Bierschbach, *supra* chapter II note 6, at 141, 144.

31. Lay judges in Germany, for example, routinely defer to the professional judges with whom they sit, so they have little influence. Gerhard Casper & Hans Zeisel, *Lay Judges in the German Criminal Courts*, 1 J. LEGAL STUD. 135, 186–91 (1972) (noting that, in cases where there is disagreement, lay judges influence only 21% of guilty verdicts and 32% of sentencing decisions; in 70% of guilty verdicts they simply surrender their positions). Giving laymen equal information and involvement in the process, however, might ameliorate the problem. *See* Jenia Iontcheva Turner, *Judicial Participation in Plea Negotiations: A Comparative View*, 54 AM. J. COMP. L. 199, 221 (2006) (explaining German lay judges' deference in terms of lay judges' uninvolvement in negotiations and lack of direct access to the case file).

32. One might expect victims and affected locals to be imperfect proxies for the public if one fears that they are too vengeful. But if one believes the evidence that victims are not on average more punitive than anyone else, then they can serve as reasonable agents of the public's sense of justice. And that is doubly so of affected local residents.

33. TOBOLOWSKY, *supra* chapter II note 9, at 36–39; Bibas & Bierschbach, *supra* chapter II note 6, at 137. For a discussion of the gap between victims' statutory rights and their implementation in procedural rules, see generally Paul G. Cassell, *Recognizing Victims in the Federal Rules of Criminal Procedure: Proposed Amendments in Light of the Crime Victims' Rights Act*, 2005 BYU L. REV. 835.

34. WEMMERS, *supra* chapter II note 9, at 208 (the source of the quotation in the text); Strang & Sherman, *supra* chapter II note 9, at 18, 21. On the importance of participation and process control, LIND & TYLER, *supra* chapter II note 19, at 106, 206–11, 215; TYLER, *supra* Introduction note 8, at 125–34; Tom R. Tyler

et al., *Influence of Voice on Satisfaction with Leaders: Exploring the Meaning of Process Control*, 48 J. PERSONALITY & SOC. PSYCHOL. 72, 75–80 (1985); Paul H. Robinson & Josh Bowers, *Perceptions of Injustice: The Shared Aims and Occasional Conflicts of Legitimacy and Moral Credibility* 4–6, http://lsr.nellco.org/upenn_wps/365 (Apr. 22, 2011) (last visited June 24, 2011).

35. Poulson, *supra* chapter III note 43, at 178–98.

36. *See, e.g.*, State v. Casey, 44 P. 3d 756, 766–67 (Utah 2002) (Wilkins, J., concurring) (victim was not timely heard at plea hearing, so trial judge informally reopened the plea hearing, purported to consider the victim's concerns, and summarily reaffirmed the previously accepted plea; the concurrence lamented the inadequacy of belated input once the plea was a fait accompli).

37. *See* BUREAU OF JUSTICE STATISTICS, SOURCEBOOK OF CRIMINAL JUSTICE STATISTICS ONLINE, *supra* chapter I note 62, tbl. 5.51.2006, *available at* http://www.albany.edu/sourcebook/pdf/t5512006.pdf (last visited June 24, 2011) (reporting that, in the 75 most populous counties in the United States in 2006, roughly 23% of arrests were for violent offenses, 29% were for property offenses, 37% were for drug offenses, and 11% were for public-order offenses).

38. *See* Dan Christensen, *No More Instant Plea Deals, Says Public Defender*, DAILY BUS. REV. (Miami), June 6, 2005, at 1, *available at* http://www.nlada.org/DMS/Documents/1118065097.48/article.jsp%3Fid%3D1117789520360 (describing the policy as "end[ing] the practice at arraignment of 'meet, greet and plead'"); *see also* NEW YORK CRIMINAL JUSTICE AGENCY, INC., CJA ANNUAL REPORT 2008, at 18 exh. 10, 36 exh. 26 (reporting that in the Bronx, a majority of criminal cases at every level of severity are disposed of at arraignment in Criminal Court, and that across New York City a substantial minority of defendants plead guilty at arraignment in the Supreme Court).

39. *See, e.g.*, FED. R. EVID. 404, 609.

40. Josh Bowers makes this point brilliantly. Josh Bowers, *Legal Guilt, Normative Innocence, and the Equitable Decision Not to Prosecute*, 110 COLUM. L. REV. 1655, 1689 (2010).

41. On the need for large, heterogeneous groups to prevent polarization, see Cass R. Sunstein, *Deliberative Trouble? Why Groups Go to Extremes*, 110 YALE L.J. 71, 85–90 (2000). Capital juries generally require unanimity before they may return death sentences. 18 U.S.C. § 3593(e) (2006) (requiring a unanimous jury recommendation in favor of the death penalty in federal capital cases); Raoul G. Cantero & Robert M. Kline, *Death Is Different: The Need for Jury Unanimity in Death Penalty Cases*, 22 ST. THOMAS L. REV. 4, 10–11 (2009) (collecting citations to show that, of 35 states that retain capital punishment, 34 require jury unanimity on the existence of an aggravating circumstance and 27 require a unanimous jury recommendation in favor of the death penalty). Presumably capital sentencing ought to remain very formal and trial-like, given the extreme stakes, but even in capital cases there could be more room for defendants to apologize and victims' families to forgive.

42. *See, e.g.*, Rummel v. Estelle, 445 U.S. 263, 265–66, 285 (1980) (affirming life sentence with the possibility of parole for a defendant who had previously committed six minor frauds and was then convicted of a felony theft by fraud of $120.75); Almond v. United States, 854 F. Supp. 439, 445 (W.D. Va. 1994) (affirming

fifteen-year prison sentence for a defendant who had a thirty-year-old conviction for burglary of an unoccupied building and a twenty-five-year-old conviction for throwing a rock at his father-in-law's car and for breaking and entering an office, who decades later picked up his son's gun and shot his own television, thereby becoming a felon in possession of a firearm); Paul H. Robinson et al., *The Disutility of Injustice*, 85 NYU L. Rev. 1940, 1950 (2010).

43. Rich Schragger calls these accounts of community deep and dualist, respectively. *See* Richard C. Schragger, *The Limits of Localism*, 100 Mich. L. Rev. 371, 393–403 (2001).

44. For a cogent articulation of both the equality and certainty objections to restorative justice, see Dan Markel, *Wrong Turns on the Road to Alternative Sanctions: Reflections on the Future of Shaming Punishments and Restorative Justice*, 85 Tex. L. Rev. 1385, 1407–09 (2007).

    Michael O'Hear has admirably explored the different kinds of sentencing uniformity one might wish to pursue and how compatible restorative justice is with each. He concludes that restorative justice can conflict with two static approaches to uniformity: (1) the desire to make sentences predictable to prospective wrongdoers, and to some extent (2) classical retributive judgments based solely on the amount of harm and the wrongdoer's mental state. But he argues persuasively that restorative justice complements approaches to uniformity that emphasize (3) making consequences predictable to defendants once they are in the system, (4) linking punishments to the purposes or justifications of punishment, and (5) preventing subjugation of defendants and giving them genuine opportunities to be heard. Michael M. O'Hear, *Is Restorative Justice Compatible with Sentencing Uniformity?*, 89 Marq. L. Rev. 305 (2005).

    On the lack of evidence about noncapital jury sentencing, see King & Noble, *supra* chapter I note 81, at 887; Nancy J. King & Rosevelt L. Noble, *Jury Sentencing in Noncapital Cases: Comparing Severity and Variance with Judicial Sentencing in Two States*, 2 J. Empirical Legal Stud. 331, 332, 361–62 (2005); Lanni, *supra* chapter III note 36, at 1798–1801.

45. Rachlinski et al., *supra* chapter V note 32, at 1210–22 (noting that white judges have, if anything, slightly stronger implicit racial associations than white respondents in online surveys, while some black judges and jurors have less implicit bias, and thus concluding that "[p]erhaps the only entity in the system that might avoid the influence of the bigot in the brain is a diversely composed jury"); Baldus & Woodworth, *supra* chapter IV note 18, at 214 (source of the quotation in the text, based on a review of the literature and empirical studies).

BIBLIOGRAPHY

CASES

Allison v. State, 495 So. 2d 739, 741 (Ala. Crim. App. 1986) 200-201n8

In re *Alvernaz*, 830 P.2d 747 (Cal. 1992) 200-201n8

Ams. United for Separation of Church and State v. *Prison Fellowship*
      Ministries, Inc., 509 F.3d 406 (8th Cir. 2007) 237n20

Apprendi v. New Jersey, 530 U.S. 466 (2000). 182n81, 229n1

Argersinger v. Hamlin, 407 U.S. 25 (1972) 176n50

Banegura v. Taylor, 541 A.2d 969 (Md. 1988) 201n8

Blakely v. Washington, 542 U.S. 296 (2004). 211n36

Boykin v. Garrison, 658 So. 2d 1090 (Fla. Dist. Ct. App. 1995) 201n8

Brown v. State, 45 S.W.3d 506 (Mo. Ct. App. 2001). 201n8

Carroll v. State, 474 S.E.2d 737 (Ga. Ct. App. 1996) 202-203n13

Cloum v. State, 779 N.E.2d 84 (Ind. Ct. App. 2002) 210n34

Coker v. Georgia, 433 U.S. 584 (1977) 180n72

Commonwealth v. Cabrera, 2 N. Mar. I. 311 (1991) 200-201n8

Commonwealth v. Corey, 826 S.W.2d 319 (Ky. 1992) 200-201n8

Commonwealth v. Fluharty, 632 A.2d 312 (Pa. Super. Ct. 1993). 200-202n8

Commonwealth v. Lewis, 506 N.E.2d 891 (Mass. 1987). 200-201n8

Deal v. State, 527 S.E.2d 112 (S.C. 2000) 200-201n8

Duren v. Missouri, 439 U.S. 357 (1979) 171-172n18

In re *Fogel*, 728 A.2d 668 (D.C. 1999) 200-201n8

Friedman v. Comm'r of Pub. Safety, 473 N.W.2d 828 (Minn. 1991) 207-208n28

Furman v. Georgia, 408 U.S. 232 (1972). 180n72

Gaines v. State, 517 S.E. 2d 439 (S.C. 1999) 200-202n8

Gideon v. Wainwright, 372 U.S. 335 (1963) 170n11, 176n50

Gollaher v. United States, 419 F.2d 520 (9th Cir. 1969) .204n16

Goodman v. Davis, 287 S.E.2d 26 (Ga. 1982) 200-201n8

Gregg v. Georgia, 428 U.S. 153 (1976) 180n72

Harris v. State, 620 S.W.2d 289 (Ark. 1981) 200-201n8

Harris v. United States, 536 U.S. 545 (2004) 181-182n81

Johnson v. State, 478 S.W.2d 954 (Tex. Crim. App. 1972). 200-202n8

Johnston v. State, 829 P.2d 1179 (Wyo. 1992) 200-202n8

Jones v. Barnes, 463 U.S. 745 (1983) 197n53

Kennedy v. Frazier, 357 S.E.2d 43 (W. Va. 1987) 200-202n8

Kennedy v. Louisiana, 554 U.S. 407 (2008) 180n72

Kibler v. State, 227 S.E.2d 199 (S.C. 1976) 200-201n8

Lynn v. Reinstein, 68 P.3d 412 (Ariz. 2003) 216n2

McKune v. Lile, 536 U.S. 24 (2002) 204n16

North Carolina v. Alford, 400 U.S. 25 (1970) 200*n*6

Ocampo v. State, 778 P.2d 920 (Okla. Crim. App. 1989) 201–202*n*8

People v. Barker, 415 N.E.2d 404 (Ill. 1980) 200–201*n*8

People v. Booth, 324 N.W.2d 741, 748 (Mich. 1982)..................... 200–202*n*8

People v. Canino, 508 P.2d 1273 (Colo. 1973) 200–201*n*8

People v. Hicks, 608 N.Y.S.2d 543 (N.Y. App. Div. 1994) 200–201*n*8

Perry v. Commonwealth, 533 S.E. 2d 651 (Va. Ct. App. 2000)............. 200–202*n*8

Powell v. Alabama, 287 U.S. 45 (1932) 170*n*11

Recorder's Court Bar Ass'n v. Wayne Cir. Ct.,
     503 N.W.2d 885 (Mich. 1993).....................................197*n*53

Reynolds v. State, 521 So. 2d 914 (Miss. 1988)......................... 200–201*n*8

Richmond Newspapers, Inc. v. Virginia, 448 U.S. 555 (1980)................207*n*25

Riggins v. Nevada, 504 U.S. 127 (1992) 209–210*n*34

Ring v. Arizona, 536 U.S. 584 (2002) 182*n*82, 211*n*36

Robinson v. State, 291 A.2d 279 (Del. 1972)..........................200-201*n*8

Rummel v. Estelle, 445 U.S. 263 (1980) 241*n*42

Santobello v. New York, 404 U.S. 257 (1971) 229*n*1

Scott v. United States, 419 F.2d 264 (D.C. Cir. 1969) 209*n*34

Shannon v. United States, 512 U.S. 573 (1994) 182*n*82

Sparf v. United States, 156 U.S. 51 (1895)...............................177*n*55

Sparrow v. State, 625 P.2d 414 (Idaho 1981)......................... 200–201*n*8

State ex rel. Juvenile Dep't v. Welch, 501 P.2d 991 (Or. Ct. App. 1972) 200–202*n*8

State ex rel. McDougall v. Nastro, 800 P.2d 974 (Ariz. 1990)............. 200–201*n*8

State v. Amarillo, 503 A.2d 146 (Conn. 1986)......................... 200–201*n*8

State v. Bates, 726 N.W.2d 595 (N.D. 2007) 200–202*n*8

State v. Blanchard, 786 So. 2d 701 (La. 2001)........................ 200–201*n*8

State v. Brown, 1986 WL 13263 (Tenn. Crim. App. Nov. 26, 1986)....... 209–210*n*34

State v. Cameron, 830 P.2d 1284 (Mont. 1992), overruled on
    other grounds by *Montana v. Deserly*, 188 P.3d 1057
    (Mont. 2008) 200–201*n*8

State v. Casey, 44 P.3d 756 (Utah 2002)..................................241*n*36

State v. Dillon, 748 P.2d 856 (Kan. 1988) 200–201*n*8

State v. Engelmann, 541 N.W. 2d 96 (S.D. 1995)...................... 200–202*n*8

State v. Fisk, 682 A.2d 937 (Vt. 1996).............................. 200–202*n*8

State v. Fontaine, 559 A.2d 622 (R.I. 1989).......................... 200–202*n*8

State v. Garcia, 532 N.W.2d 111 (Wis. 1995) 200–202*n*8

State v. Gardner, 885 P.2d 1144 (Idaho Ct. App. 1994)................ 202–203*n*13

State v. Gomes, 930 P.2d 701 (Nev. 1996) 200–201*n*8

State v. Goulette, 258 N.W.2d 758 (Minn. 1977) 200–201*n*8

State v. Hansen, 344 N.W.2d 725 (Iowa App.1983) 200–201*n*8

State v. Hodge, 882 P.2d 1 (N.M. 1994) 200–201*n*8

State v. LaForest, 665 A.2d 1083 (N.H. 1995)....................... 189–190*n*27

State v. Malo, 577 A.2d 332 (Me. 1990)............................. 200–201*n*8

State v. McClure, 185 S.E.2d 693 (N.C. 1972)....................... 200–201*n*8

State v. Munsch, 338 S.E.2d 329 (S.C. 1985)........................ 200–201*n*8

State v. Osborne, 684 N.E.2d 683 (Wash. 1984) 200–202*n*8

State v. Padgett, 586 N.E.2d 1194 (Ohio Ct. App. 1990)................ 200–201*n*8

State v. Peart, 621 So. 2d 780 (La. 1993)........................183n4, 197*n*54

State v. Rhodes, 445 N.W.2d 622 (Neb. 1989)........................ 200–201*n*8

State v. Smith, 606 P.2d 86 (Haw. 1980) 200–201*n*8

State v. Stilling, 856 P.2d 666 (Utah Ct. App. 1993)................... 200–202*n*8

CONSTITUTIONS, STATUTES, AND RULES

MD. CODE ANN., MD. R. § 4–242 (WEST 2010) 200–201n8
ME. R. CRIM. P. 11 . . . . 200–201n8
ME. REV. STAT. ANN. tit. 17A, § 1174 (2009) 208–209n30
MICH. CT. R. 6.301 . . . . 200–201n8
MISS. UNIF. CIR. & CTY. CT. R. 8.04 . . . . 200–201n8
MODEL PENAL CODE § 2.02 (1980) 217n4
MODEL PENAL CODE § 210.3 cmt. (1980) 217n4
MODEL RULES OF PROF'L CONDUCT R. 1.14 (2002) 207–208n28
MODEL RULES OF PROF'L CONDUCT R. 2.1 (2002). 207–208n28
MONT. CODE ANN. § 46–12–204 (2009) 200–201n8
N.C. GEN. STAT. ANN. § 7A-272 (West 2009) 200–201n8
N.C. GEN. STAT. ANN. § 90–95 (West 2010) 194n42
N.H. REV. STAT. ANN. § 605:6 (2010) 200–201n8
N.M. DIST. CT. R. CRIM. P. 5–304.A 200–201n8
N.M. MAGISTRATE CT. R. CRIM. P. 6–302.A 200–201n8
N.M. METRO. CT. R. CRIM. P. 7–302.A. 200–201n8
N.Y. CRIM. PROC. LAW § 220.10 (McKinney 2005) 192n36
NEB. REV. STAT. § 29–1819.01 (2010) 200–201n8
NEV. REV. STAT. ANN. § 174.035 (2009) 200–201n8
OKLA. STAT. ANN. tit. 22, § 513 (2010) 200–201n8
OR. REV. STAT. ANN. § 135.335 (West 2010) 200–201n8
PA. R. CRIM. P. 590 . . . . 200–201n8
PROTECT Act, Pub. L. No. 108–21, § 401, 117 Stat. 650,
   667–76 (2003) (codified as amended at scattered
   sections of 18 U.S.C. & 28 U.S.C.). 45, 47, 93, 191n35, 221n22
R.I. SUPER. CT. R. CRIM. P. 11 . . . . 200–201n8
S.C. CODE ANN. § 17–23–40 (2010). 200–201n8
S.D. CODIFIED LAWS § 23A-7–2 (2010) 200–201n8
TENN. R. CRIM. P. 11. . . . . 200–201n8
TEX. CODE CRIM. PROC. ANN. § 27.02 (West 2009). 200–201n8
18 U.S.C. § 924 (2006) 181–182n81, 191–182n35
18 U.S.C. § 1761 (2006). 180n71
18 U.S.C. § 3161 (2006). 229n1
18 U.S.C. § 3593(e) (2006) 241n41
18 U.S.C. § 3624(b) (2006) 181n80
18 U.S.C. § 3553(e) (2006) 194n42
21 U.S.C. § 841 (2006) 181–182n81,
                                                                   191–192n35, 194n41
21 U.S.C. § 843 (2006) 194n41
21 U.S.C. § 846 (2006) 181–182n81
21 U.S.C. § 848 (2006) 181–182n81
21 U.S.C. § 960 (2006) 181–182n81
31 U.S.C. § 3730 (2006). 221n20
33 U.S.C. § 1365 (2006). 221n20
UTAH CODE ANN. § 77–13–1 (LexisNexis 2010) 200–201n8
VA. CODE ANN. § 18.2–248.H2.5 (2005). 194n42
VA. CODE ANN. § 19.2–254 (West 2010) 200–201n8
Violent Crime Control and Law Enforcement Act of 1994,
   Pub. L. 103–322, § 20411, 108 Stat. 1796 . . . . 234n1
VT. R. CRIM. P. 11 . . . . 200–201n8

W. VA. MAGISTRATE CTS. CRIM. P. R. 10 . . . . 200–201n8
W. VA. R. CRIM. P. 11 . . . . 200–201n8
WIS. STAT. § 968.075 (2003–2004) 192n36
WIS. STAT. ANN. § 971.06 (West 2009) 200–201n8
WYO. R. Crim. P. 11 . . . . 200–201n8

SECONDARY SOURCES

Abbott, Edith, *Crime and the War*, 9 J.AM. INST. CRIM. L. & CRIMINOLOGY 32 (1918).

Abel, Gene G. et al., *Sexual Offenders: Results of Assessment and Recommendations for Treatment*, in CLINICAL CRIMINOLOGY: THE ASSESSMENT AND TREATMENT OF CRIMINAL BEHAVIOR 191 (Mark H. Ben-Aron et al., eds., 1985).

Abel, Gene G. et al., *Complications, Consent, and Cognitions in Sex Between Children and Adults*, 7 INT'L J. L. & PSYCHIATRY 89 (1984).

An ACCOUNT OF THE ROBBERIES COMMITTED BY JOHN MORRISON. (Philadelphia: s.n., 1750).

Acorn, Annalise, COMPULSORY COMPASSION: A CRITIQUE OF RESTORATIVE JUSTICE (2004).

THE AFFECTIVE ASSISTANCE OF COUNSEL: PRACTICING LAW AS A HEALING PROFESSION (Marjorie A. Silver ed., 2007).

Airoldi, Robert, *Ex-Priest Pleads Guilty to Sex Crime*, OAKLAND TRIBUNE, Dec. 7, 2002.

ALCOHOLICS ANONYMOUS, TWELVE STEPS AND TWELVE TRADITIONS (1981).

ALLEN, RONALD JAY ET AL., COMPREHENSIVE CRIMINAL PROCEDURE (2001).

Alpert, Geoffrey P. & Mark H. Moore, *Measuring Police Performance in the New Paradigm of Policing*, in PERFORMANCE MEASURES FOR THE CRIMINAL JUSTICE SYSTEM, NJC 143505 (1993).

Alschuler, Albert W., *Straining at Gnats and Swallowing Camels: The Selective Morality of Professor Bibas*, 88 CORNELL L. REV. 1412 (2003).

———, *The Changing Plea Bargaining Debate*, 69 CAL. L. REV. 652 (1981).

———, *Plea Bargaining and Its History*, 13 LAW & SOC'Y REV. 211 (1979).

———, *The Defense Attorney's Role in Plea Bargaining*, 84 YALE L.J. 1179 (1975).

———, *The Prosecutor's Role in Plea Bargaining*, 36 U. CHI. L. REV. 50 (1968).

AMAR, AKHIL REED, THE BILL OF RIGHTS: CREATION AND RECONSTRUCTION (2000).

———, THE CONSTITUTION AND CRIMINAL PROCEDURE: FIRST PRINCIPLES (1998).

———, *The Bill of Rights as a Constitution*, 100 YALE L.J. 1131 (1991).

AM. BAR ASS'N, GIDEON BROKEN PROMISE: AMERICA'S CONTINUING QUEST FOR EQUAL JUSTICE: A REPORT ON THE AMERICAN BAR ASSOCIATION'S HEARINGS ON THE RIGHT TO COUNSEL IN CRIMINAL PROCEEDINGS (2004).

AM. PSYCHIATRIC ASS'N, DIAGNOSTIC AND STATISTICAL MANUAL OF MENTAL DISORDERS (4th ed. 1994) (DSM-IV).

Anderson, Michelle Chernikoff & Robert J. MacCoun, *Goal Conflict in Juror Assessments of Compensatory and Punitive Damages*, 23 LAW & HUM. BEHAV. 313 (1999).

Applegate, Brandon K. et al., *Assessing Public Support for Three-Strikes-and-You're-Out Laws: Global versus Specific Attitudes*, 42 CRIME & DELINQ. 517 (1996).

Appleman, Laura I., *The Plea Jury*, 85 IND. L. J. 731 (2010).

53 ARCHIVES OF MARYLAND (1936).

ARENDT, HANNAH, THE HUMAN CONDITION (2d ed. 1998).

Arenella, Peter, *Rethinking the Functions of Criminal Procedure: The Warren and Burger Courts' Competing Ideologies*, 72 GEO. L. J. 185 (1983).

Armacost, Barbara E., *Organizational Culture and Police Misconduct*, 72 GEO. WASH. L. REV. 453 (2004).

Armstrong, Ken & Justin Mayo, *Frustrated Attorney: "You Just Can't Help People,"* SEATTLE TIMES, Apr. 6, 2004, at A1.

Armstrong, Ken et al., *Attorney Profited, But His Clients Lost*, SEATTLE TIMES, Apr. 5, 2004, at A1.

———, *For Some, Free Counsel Comes at a High Cost*, SEATTLE TIMES, Apr. 4, 2004, at A1.

Arnold, Thurman, *The Criminal Trial as a Symbol of Public Morality, in* CRIMINAL JUSTICE IN OUR TIME 137 (A.E. Dick Howard ed., 1965).

Ash, Michael, *On Witnesses: A Radical Critique of Criminal Court Procedures*, 48 NOTRE DAME LAW. 386 (1972).

Ashworth, Andrew, *Victims' Rights, Defendants' Rights and Criminal Procedure, in* INTEGRATING A VICTIM PERSPECTIVE WITHIN CRIMINAL JUSTICE: INTERNATIONAL DEBATES 185 (Adam Crawford & Jo Goodey eds., 2000).

4 THE BABYLONIAN TALMUD (I. Epstein ed., 1938).

BAKER, J. H., AN INTRODUCTION TO ENGLISH LEGAL HISTORY (4th ed. 2002).

Baker, Katharine K., *Sex, Rape, and Shame*, 79 B.U. L. REV. 663 (1999).

Bakker, Mark William, *Repairing the Breach and Reconciling the Discordant: Mediation in the Criminal Justice System*, 72 N.C. L. REV. 1479 (1994).

Baldus, David C. & George Woodworth, *Race Discrimination in the Administration of the Death Penalty: An Overview of the Empirical Evidence with Special Emphasis on the Post-1990 Research*, 39 CRIM. L. BULL. 194 (2003).

BALDUS, DAVID C. ET AL., EQUAL JUSTICE AND THE DEATH PENALTY: A LEGAL AND EMPIRICAL ANALYSIS (1990).

Bandes, Susan, *Empathy, Narrative, and Victim Impact Statements*, 63 U. CHI. L. REV. 361 (1996).

BANNER, STUART, THE DEATH PENALTY: AN AMERICAN HISTORY (2002).

Barbaree, Howard E., *Denial and Minimization among Sex Offenders: Assessment and Treatment Outcome*, 3 F. ON CORRECTIONS RES., no. 4 (1991).

Barkow, Rachel E., *The Ascent of the Administrative State and the Demise of Mercy*, 121 HARV. L. REV. 1332 (2008).

———, *Administering Crime*, 52 UCLA L. REV. 715 (2005).

———, *Federalism and the Politics of Sentencing*, 105 COLUM. L. REV. 1276 (2005).

———, *Recharging the Jury: The Criminal Jury's Constitutional Role in an Era of Mandatory Sentencing*, 152 U. PA. L. REV. 33 (2003).

Barnard, Jayne W., *Reintegrative Shaming in Corporate Sentencing*, 72 S. CAL. L. REV. 959 (1999).

Baron, Jonathan & Ilana Ritov, *Intuitions about Penalties and Compensation in the Context of Tort Law*, 7 J. RISK & UNCERTAINTY 17 (1993).

Barton, Charles, *Empowerment and Retribution in Criminal Justice, in* RESTORATIVE JUSTICE: PHILOSOPHY TO PRACTICE 55 (Heather Strang & John Braithwaite eds., 2000).

Bazemore, Gordon & Mark Umbreit, *A Comparison of Four Restorative Justice Conferencing Models*, JUV. JUST. BULL., Feb. 2001.

———, *Rethinking the Sanctioning Function in Juvenile Court: Retributive or Restorative Responses to Youth Crime*, 41 CRIME & DELINQUENCY 296 (1995).

Beale, Sara Sun, *Still Tough on Crime? Prospects for Restorative Justice in the United States*, 2003 UTAH L. REV. 413.

———, *What's Law Got to Do with It? The Political, Social, Psychological and Other Non-Legal Factors Influencing the Development of (Federal) Criminal Law*, 1 BUFF. CRIM. L. REV. 23 (1997).

Bean, Philip, *Drug Courts, the Judge, and the Rehabilitative Ideal, in* DRUG COURTS IN THEORY AND PRACTICE 235 (James L. Nolan, Jr. ed., 2002).

BEATTIE, J.M., CRIME AND THE COURTS IN ENGLAND, 1660–1800 (1986).

BECCARIA, CESARE, AN ESSAY ON CRIMES AND PUNISHMENTS (Philadelphia: Edward D. Ingraham trans., Philip H. Nicklin 2d Am. ed., 1819).

Becker, Gary S., *Crime and Punishment: An Economic Approach*, 76 J. POL. ECON. 169 (1968).

BECKETT, KATHERINE & THEODORE SASSON, THE POLITICS OF INJUSTICE: CRIME AND PUNISHMENT IN AMERICA (2d ed. 2003).

Bedau, Hugo Adam & Michael L. Radelet, *Miscarriages of Justice in Potentially Capital Cases*, 40 STAN. L. REV. 21 (1987).

Beha, James J., II, Note, *Redemption to Reform: The Intellectual Origins of the Prison Reform Movement*, 63 N.Y.U. ANN. SURV. AM. L. 773 (2008).

Beloof, Douglas E. & Paul G. Cassell, *The Crime Victim's Right to Attend the Trial: The Reascendent National Consensus*, 9 LEWIS & CLARK L. REV. 481 (2005).

BELOOF, DOUGLAS E., PAUL G. CASSELL & STEVEN J. TWIST, VICTIMS IN CRIMINAL PROCEDURE (2d ed. 2006).

BENTHAM, JEREMY, AN INTRODUCTION TO THE PRINCIPLES OF MORALS AND LEGISLATION (Oxford: Clarendon Press 1907) (new corrected ed. 1823).

Berliner, Lucy, *Sex Offenders: Policy and Practice*, 92 NW. U. L. REV. 1203 (1998).

Best, Joel, *Monster Hype*, EDUC. NEXT, Summer 2002, at 50, *available at* http://www.educationnext.org/monster-hype/.

BEZANSON, RANDALL P. ET AL., LIBEL LAW AND THE PRESS: MYTH AND REALITY (1987).

Bibas, Stephanos, *Rewarding Prosecutors for Performance*, 6 OHIO ST. J. CRIM. L. 441 (2009).

———, *Regulating Local Variations in Federal Sentencing*, 58 STAN. L. REV. 137 (2005).

———, *The Feeney Amendment and the Continuing Rise of Prosecutorial Power to Plea Bargain*, 94 J. CRIM. L. & CRIMINOLOGY 295 (2004).

———, *Plea Bargaining Outside the Shadow of Trial*, 117 HARV. L. REV. 2464 (2004).

———, *Harmonizing Substantive-Criminal-Law Values and Criminal Procedure: The Case of Alford and Nolo Contendere Pleas*, 88 CORNELL L. REV. 1361 (2003).

———, *The Real-World Shift in Criminal Procedure*, 93 NW. U. L. REV. 789 (2003) (reviewing RONALD JAY ALLEN ET AL., COMPREHENSIVE CRIMINAL PROCEDURE (2001) and MARC L. MILLER & RONALD F. WRIGHT, CRIMINAL PROCEDURES: CASES, STATUTES, AND EXECUTIVE MATERIALS (1998)).

Bibas, Stephanos & Richard A. Bierschbach, *Integrating Remorse and Apology into Criminal Procedure*, 114 YALE L.J. 85 (2004).

THE BIBLE (King James Version).

THE BIBLE (New King James Version).

Birgden, Astrid, *Dealing with the Resistant Criminal Client: A Psychologically-Minded Strategy for More Effective Legal Counseling*, 38 CRIM. L. BULL. 225 (2002).

Bjerk, David, *Making the Crime Fit the Penalty: The Role of Prosecutorial Discretion under Mandatory Minimum Sentencing*, 48 J.L. & ECON. 591 (2005).

BLACKSTONE, WILLIAM COMMENTARIES ON THE LAWS OF ENGLAND (1765).

Blumberg, Abraham S., *The Practice of Law as Confidence Game: Organizational Cooptation of a Profession*, 1 LAW & SOC'Y REV. 15 (1967).

Boldt, Richard C., *The Adversary System and Attorney Role in the Drug Treatment Court Movement, in* DRUG COURTS IN THEORY AND PRACTICE 115 (James L. Nolan, Jr. ed., 2002).

BORDENS, KENNETH S. & IRWIN A. HOROWITZ, SOCIAL PSYCHOLOGY (2002).

Bowers, Josh, *Legal Guilt, Normative Innocence, and the Equitable Decision Not to Prosecute*, 110 COLUM. L. REV. 1655 (2010).

———, Outsourcing Equitable Discretion (Aug. 24, 2010) (unpublished manuscript) (on file with the *Columbia Law Review*).

———, *Punishing the Innocent*, 156 U. PA. L. REV. 1117 (2008).

———, Note, *"The Integrity of the Game Is Everything": The Problem of Geographic Disparity in Three Strikes*, 76 N.Y.U. L. REV. 1164 (2001).

Bowman, Frank O., III & Michael Heise, *Quiet Rebellion II: An Empirical Analysis of Declining Federal Drug Sentences Including Data from the District Level*, 87 IOWA L. REV. 477 (2002).

———, *Quiet Rebellion? Explaining Nearly a Decade of Declining Federal Drug Sentences*, 86 IOWA L. REV. 1043 (2001).

Bradley, Gerard V., *Plea Bargaining and the Criminal Defendant's Obligation to Plead Guilty*, 40 S. TEX. L. REV. 65 (1999).

Braithwaite, John, *Holism, Justice, and Atonement*, 2003 UTAH L. REV. 389.

———, RESTORATIVE JUSTICE AND RESPONSIVE REGULATION (2002).

———, *Restorative Justice and Therapeutic Jurisprudence*, 38 CRIM. L. BULL. 244 (2002).

———, *A Future Where Punishment Is Marginalized: Realistic or Utopian?*, 46 UCLA L. REV. 1727 (1999).

———, *Restorative Justice: Assessing Optimistic and Pessimistic Accounts*, 25 CRIME & JUST.: REV. RES. 1 (Michael Tonry ed., 1999).

———, CRIME, SHAME AND REINTEGRATION (1989).

Braithwaite, John & Heather Strang, *Connecting Philosophy and Practice*, in RESTORATIVE JUSTICE: PHILOSOPHY TO PRACTICE 203 (Heather Strang & John Braithwaite eds., 2000).

BRAMAN, DONALD, DOING TIME ON THE OUTSIDE: INCARCERATION AND FAMILY LIFE IN URBAN AMERICA (2004).

———, *Punishment and Accountability: Understanding and Reforming Criminal Sanctions in America*, 53 UCLA L. REV. 1143 (2006).

Braman, Donald et al., *Some Realism about Punishment Naturalism*, 77 U. CHI. L. REV. 1531 (2010).

Brandeis, Louis D., *What Publicity Can Do*, HARPER'S WEEKLY, Dec. 20, 1913, *reprinted in* OTHER PEOPLE'S MONEY 92 (1914).

Broder, John M., *In a Quiet End to a Case, 4 Ex-Symbionese Liberation Army Members Plead Guilty to Murder*, N.Y. TIMES, Nov. 8, 2002, at A14.

Brown, Darryl K., *Democracy and Decriminalization*, 86 TEX. L. REV. 223 (2007).

———, *Rationing Criminal Defense Entitlements: An Argument from Institutional Design*, 104 COLUM. L. REV. 801 (2004).

———, *Third-Party Interests in Criminal Law*, 80 TEX. L. REV. 1383 (2002).

———, *Street Crime, Corporate Crime, and the Contingency of Criminal Liability*, 149 U. PA. L. REV. 1295 (2001).

BUREAU OF JUSTICE ASSISTANCE, U.S. DEP'T OF JUSTICE, NCJ 148457, UNDERSTANDING COMMUNITY POLICING: A FRAMEWORK FOR ACTION (Aug. 1994).

BUREAU OF JUSTICE STATISTICS, U.S. DEP'T OF JUSTICE, NCJ 143505, PERFORMANCE MEASURES FOR THE CRIMINAL JUSTICE SYSTEM (1993).

———, SOURCEBOOK OF CRIMINAL JUSTICE STATISTICS ONLINE, *available at* http://www.albany.edu/sourcebook/tost_5.html.

Burger, Warren E., *The State of the Judiciary*, 56 A.B.A. J. 929 (1970).

BURKE, ROBERT ET AL., NAT'L LEGAL AID & DEFENDER ASS'N, INDIGENT CASELOADS AND COMMON SENSE: AN UPDATE (1992).

Burnham, William, *The Legal Context and Contributions of Dostoevsky's* Crime and Punishment, 100 MICH. L. REV. 1227 (2002).

Butterfield, Fox, *As Crime Falls, Pressure Rises to Alter Data*, N.Y. TIMES, Aug. 3, 1998, at A1.

Cane, Peter, *Taking Law Seriously: Starting Points of the Hart/Devlin Debate*, 10 J. ETHICS 21 (2006).

Cantero, Raoul G. & Robert M. Kline, *Death Is Different: The Need for Jury Unanimity in Death Penalty Cases*, 22 ST. THOMAS L. REV. 4 (2009).

Cardenas, Juan, *The Crime Victim in the Prosecutorial Process*, 9 HARV. J.L. & PUB. POL'Y 357 (1986).

Carlson, Bonnie F. & Neil Cervera, *Inmates and Their Families: Conjugal Visits, Family Contact, and Family Functioning*, 18 CRIM. JUST. & BEHAV. 318, 320 (1991).

Carlsmith, Kevin M. et al., *Why Do We Punish? Deterrence and Just Deserts as Motives for Punishment*, 83 J. PERSONALITY & SOC. PSYCHOL. 284 (2002).

Casper, Gerhard & Hans Zeisel, *Lay Judges in the German Criminal Courts*, 1 J. LEGAL STUD. 135 (1972).

CASPER, JONATHAN D., AMERICAN CRIMINAL JUSTICE: THE DEFENDANT'S PERSPECTIVE (1972).

Cassell, Paul G., *Treating Crime Victims Fairly: Integrating Victims into the Federal Rules of Criminal Procedure*, 2007 UTAH L. REV. 861.

———, *Recognizing Victims in the Federal Rules of Criminal Procedure: Proposed Amendments in Light of the Crime Victims' Rights Act*, 2005 BYU L. REV. 835.

CENTRE FOR THE STUDY OF VIOLENCE AND RECONCILIATION & THE KHULUMANI SUPPORT GROUP, SUBMISSION TO THE TRUTH AND RECONCILIATION COMMISSION: SURVIVORS' PERCEPTIONS OF THE TRUTH AND RECONCILIATION COMMISSION AND SUGGESTIONS FOR THE FINAL REPORT, *available at* "http://www.csvr.org.za/wits/papers/papakhul.htm.

CHANGING ATTITUDES TO PUNISHMENT: PUBLIC OPINION, CRIME, AND JUSTICE (Julian V. Roberts & Mike Hough eds., 2002).

Chesterton, G.K., *The Twelve Men, in* TREMENDOUS TRIFLES (1909).

Chriss, James J., *The Drug Court Movement: An Analysis of Tacit Assumptions, in* DRUG COURTS IN THEORY AND PRACTICE 189 (James L. Nolan, Jr. ed., 2002).

Christensen, Dan, *No More Instant Plea Deals, Says Public Defender*, DAILY BUS. REV., June 6, 2005, at 1, *available at* http://www.nlada.org/DMS/Documents/1118065097.48/article.jsp%3Fid%3D1117789520360.

Christie, Nils, *Conflicts as Property*, 17 BRIT. J. CRIMINOLOGY 1 (1977).

Churchill, Winston, Home Secretary, *Speech Delivered to House of Commons* (July 20, 1910), *in* WINSTON S. CHURCHILL, HIS COMPLETE SPEECHES: 1897–1963, VOL. II: 1908–1913, at 1589 (Robert Rhodes James ed., 1974).

CHURCHILL, WINSTON S., HIS COMPLETE SPEECHES: 1897–1963, Vol. II: 1908–1913 (Robert Rhodes James ed., 1974).

CLECKLEY, HERVEY, THE MASK OF SANITY: AN ATTEMPT TO REINTERPRET THE SO-CALLED PSYCHOPATHIC PERSONALITY (1941).

Clines, Francis X., *Death Penalty Is Suspended in Maryland*, N.Y. TIMES, May 10, 2002, at A20.

CLINICAL CRIMINOLOGY: THE ASSESSMENT AND TREATMENT OF CRIMINAL BEHAVIOR (Mark H. Ben-Aron et al. eds., 1985).

Cochran, Robert F., Jr., *Crime, Confession, and the Counselor-at-Law: Lessons from Dostoyevsky*, 35 HOUS. L. REV. 327 (1998).

COHEN, DANIEL A., PILLARS OF SALT, MONUMENTS OF GRACE: NEW ENGLAND CRIME LITERATURE AND THE ORIGINS OF AMERICAN POPULAR CULTURE, 1674–1860 (1993).

Cohen, Jonathan R., *Toward Candor after Medical Error: The First Apology Law*, HARV. HEALTH POL'Y REV., Spring 2004, at 21.

———, *Advising Clients to Apologize*, 72 S. CAL. L. REV. 1009 (1999).

COLORADO SEX OFFENDER MGMT. BD., COLO. DEP'T OF PUB. SAFETY, WHITE PAPER ON THE USE OF RESIDENCE RESTRICTIONS AS A SEX OFFENDER MANAGEMENT STRATEGY (June 2009), *available at* http://dcj.state.co.us/odvsom/sex_offender/SO_Pdfs/Residence%20Restrictions.PP.pdf.

Corsilles, Angela, Note, *No-Drop Policies in the Prosecution of Domestic Violence Cases: Guarantee to Action or Dangerous Solution?*, 63 FORDHAM L. REV. 853 (1994).

1 EDWARD COKE, THE FIRST INSTITUTES OF THE LAWES OF ENGLAND, OR A COMMENTARY ON LITTLETON (1628).

Coughlin, Anne M., *Sex and Guilt*, 84 VA. L. REV. 1 (1998).

CRIME, PUNISHMENT, AND POLITICS IN COMPARATIVE PERSPECTIVE (Michael Tonry ed., 2007).

CRIMINAL JUSTICE IN OUR TIME (A.E. Dick Howard ed., 1965).

CSI: *Crime Scene Investigation* (CBS television series).

Cutler, Brian L. & Donna M. Hughes, *Judging Jury Service: Results of the North Carolina Administrative Office of the Courts Juror Survey*, 19 BEHAV. SCI. & L. 305 (2001).

Czudner, Gad & Ruth Mueller, *The Role of Guilt and Its Implication in the Treatment of Criminals*, 31 INT'L J. OFFENDER THERAPY & COMP. CRIMINOLOGY 71 (1987).

Daicoff, Susan, *Lawyer Personality Traits and Their Relationship to Various Approaches to Lawyering, in* THE AFFECTIVE ASSISTANCE OF COUNSEL: PRACTICING LAW AS A HEALING PROFESSION 79 (Marjorie A. Silver ed., 2007).

Daly, Kathleen, *Revisiting the Relationship Between Retributive and Restorative Justice, in* RESTORATIVE JUSTICE: PHILOSOPHY TO PRACTICE 33 (Heather Strang & John Braithwaite eds., 2000).

Darley, John M. et al., *Incapacitation and Just Deserts as Motives for Punishment*, 24 LAW & HUM. BEHAV. 659 (2000).

DAS, BHARAT B., VICTIMS IN THE CRIMINAL JUSTICE SYSTEM (1997).

DE BEAUMONT, GUSTAVE & ALEXIS DE TOCQUEVILLE, ON THE PENITENTIARY SYSTEM IN THE UNITED STATES AND ITS APPLICATION IN FRANCE (S. Ill. Univ. Press 1964) (Francis Lieber trans. 1833).

THE DECLARATION OF INDEPENDENCE (U.S. 1776).

Demleitner, Nora V., *"Collateral Damage": No Re-Entry for Drug Offenders*, 47 VILL. L. REV. 1027 (2002).

———, *Preventing Internal Exile: The Need for Restrictions on Collateral Sentencing Consequences*, 11 STAN. L. & POL'Y REV. 153 (1999).

DEP'T OF JUSTICE, U.S. CORRECTIONAL POPULATION REACHES 6.3 MILLION MEN AND WOMEN: REPRESENTS 3.1 PERCENT OF THE ADULT U.S. POPULATION (2000), *available at* http://bjs.ojp.usdoj.gov/content/pub/pdf/pp99pr.pdf.

Department of Justice Authorization and Oversight, 1981: Hearings before the Senate Comm. on the Judiciary, 96th Cong. 1046 (supplemental statement of Assistant Attorney General Philip Heymann).

Des Rosiers, Nathalie et al., *Legal Compensation for Sexual Violence: Therapeutic Consequences and Consequences for the Judicial System*, 4 PSYCHOL. PUB. POL'Y & L. 433 (1998).

I ALEXIS DE TOCQUEVILLE, DEMOCRACY IN AMERICA (Philips Bradley ed., Francis Bowen rev., Henry Reeve trans., Vintage Books 1990) (1835).

Dharmapala, Dhammika et al., *Legislatures, Judges, and Parole Boards: The Allocation of Discretion under Determinate Sentencing*, 62 FLA. L. REV. 1037 (2009).

Diamond, Shari Seidman & Loretta J. Stalans, *The Myth of Judicial Leniency in Sentencing*, 7 BEHAV. SCI. & L. 73 (1989).

DICKENS, CHARLES, AMERICAN NOTES FOR GENERAL CIRCULATION (Patricia Ingram ed., Penguin Classics 2000) (1842).

DOBLE, JOHN, CRIME AND PUNISHMENT: THE PUBLIC'S VIEW (1987).

Doob, Anthony N. & Julian Roberts, *Public Punitiveness and Public Knowledge of the Facts: Some Canadian Surveys*, in PUBLIC ATTITUDES TO SENTENCING: SURVEYS FROM FIVE COUNTRIES 111 (Nigel Walker & Mike Hough eds., 1988).

DRUG COURTS IN THEORY AND PRACTICE (James L. Nolan, Jr. ed., 2002).

DRUMBL, MARK A., ATROCITY, PUNISHMENT, AND INTERNATIONAL LAW (2007).

DUBBER, MARKUS DIRK, VICTIMS IN THE WAR ON CRIME: THE USE AND ABUSES OF VICTIMS' RIGHTS (2002).

Duff, Antony, *Restoration and Retribution*, in RESTORATIVE JUSTICE AND CRIMINAL JUSTICE: COMPETING OR RECONCILABLE PARADIGMS? 43 (Andrew von Hirsch et al. eds., 2003).

DUFF, R.A., ANSWERING FOR CRIME: RESPONSIBILITY AND LIABILITY IN THE CRIMINAL LAW (2007).

———, PUNISHMENT, COMMUNICATION, AND COMMUNITY (2001).

———, TRIALS AND PUNISHMENTS (1986).

DURKHEIM, EMILE, THE DIVISION OF LABOR IN SOCIETY (The Free Press: W.D. Halls trans., 1st paperback ed. 1997) (1893).

THE DYING PENITENT; OR, THE AFFECTING SPEECH OF LEVI AMES, TAKEN FROM HIS OWN MOUTH, AS DELIVERED BY HIM AT THE GOAL [*sic*] IN BOSTON THE MORNING OF HIS EXECUTION (Boston: s.n., 1773).

Easterbrook, Frank H., *Plea Bargaining as Compromise*, 101 YALE L.J. 1969 (1992).

———, *Criminal Procedure as a Market System*, 12 J. LEGAL STUD. 289 (1983).

Eckholm, Erik, *U.S. Shifting Prison Focus to Re-Entry into Society*, N.Y. TIMES, Apr. 8, 2008, at A23.

Edin, Kathryn et al., *Fatherhood and Incarceration as Potential Turning Points in the Criminal Careers of Unskilled Men*, in IMPRISONING AMERICA: THE SOCIAL EFFECTS OF MASS INCARCERATION 46 (Mary Patillo et al. eds., 2004).

EDWARDS, LAURA F., THE PEOPLE AND THEIR PEACE: LEGAL CULTURE AND THE TRANSFORMATION OF INEQUALITY IN THE POST-REVOLUTIONARY SOUTH (2009).

Eisenberg, Theodore & Martin T. Wells, *Deadly Confusion: Juror Instructions in Capital Cases*, 79 CORNELL L. REV. 1 (1993).

Eisenberg, Theodore et al., *But Was He Sorry? The Role of Remorse in Capital Sentencing*, 83 CORNELL L. REV. 1599 (1998).

EISENSTEIN, JAMES, COUNSEL FOR THE UNITED STATES: U.S. ATTORNEYS IN THE POLITICAL AND LEGAL SYSTEMS (1978).

Ellsworth, Phoebe C. & Lee Ross, *Public Opinion and Capital Punishment: A Close Examination of the Views of Abolitionists and Retentionists*, 29 CRIME & DELINQ. 116 (1983).

Elton, Kathy & Michelle M. Roybal, *Restoration, a Component of Justice*, 2003 UTAH L. REV. 43.

Erez, Edna, *Who's Afraid of the Big Bad Victim? Victim Impact Statements as Victim Empowerment and Enhancement of Justice*, 1999 CRIM. L. REV. 545.

ERIKSON, KAI T., WAYWARD PURITANS: A STUDY IN THE SOCIOLOGY OF DEVIANCE (1966).

ESSAYS IN THERAPEUTIC JURISPRUDENCE (David B. Wexler & Bruce J. Winick eds., 1991).

Etienne, Margareth, *The Declining Utility of the Right to Counsel in Federal Criminal Courts: An Empirical Study on the Role of Defense Attorney Advocacy Under the Sentencing Guidelines*, 92 CAL. L. REV. 425 (2004).

———, *Remorse, Responsibility, and Regulating Advocacy: Making Defendants Pay for the Sins of Their Lawyers*, 78 N.Y.U. L. REV. 2103 (2003).

Evers, Tag, *Blessed Are the Peace Makers*, ISTHMUS (Madison, Wis.), Apr. 10–16, 1998, at 9.

Faber, Eli, *Puritan Criminals: The Economic, Social, and Intellectual Background to Crime in Seventeenth-Century Massachusetts*, in XI PERSPECTIVES IN AMERICAN HISTORY 83 (Donald Fleming ed., 1978).

Farnham, Alan & Tricia Walsh, *U.S. Suburbs Are under Siege*, FORTUNE, Dec. 28, 1992, at 42.

Feeley, Malcolm M., *Legal Complexity and the Transformation of the Criminal Process: The Origins of Plea Bargaining*, 31 ISRAEL L. REV. 183 (1997).

Fein, Robert A., *How the Insanity Acquittal Retards Treatment*, in THERAPEUTIC JURISPRUDENCE: THE LAW AS A THERAPEUTIC AGENT 49 (David B. Wexler ed., 1990).

FEINBERG, JOEL, *The Expressive Function of Punishment*, in DOING & DESERVING: ESSAYS IN THE THEORY OF RESPONSIBILITY 95 (1970).

FERDINAND, THEODORE, BOSTON'S LOWER CRIMINAL COURTS, 1814–50 (1992).

Fingarette, Herbert, *Punishment and Suffering*, 50 PROC. & ADDRESSES AM. PHIL. ASS'N 499 (1977).

FISHER, GEORGE, PLEA BARGAINING'S TRIUMPH: A HISTORY OF PLEA BARGAINING IN AMERICA (2003).

Fiske, Alan Page & Philip E. Tetlock, *Taboo Trade-Offs: Reactions to Transactions That Transgress the Spheres of Justice*, 18 POL. PSYCHOL. 255 (1997).

Flaten, Caren L., *Victim-Offender Mediation: Application with Serious Offenses Committed by Juveniles*, in RESTORATIVE JUSTICE: INTERNATIONAL PERSPECTIVES 387 (Burt Galaway & Joe Hudson eds., 1996).

Fleisher, Mark S. & Richard H. Rison, *United States of America: Inmate Work and Consensual Management in the Federal Bureau of Prisons*, in PRISON LABOR: SALVATION OR SLAVERY? INTERNATIONAL PERSPECTIVES 281 (Dirk van Zyl Smit & Frieder Dünkel eds., 1999).

FLETCHER, GEORGE P., WITH JUSTICE FOR SOME: VICTIMS' RIGHTS IN CRIMINAL TRIALS (1995).

Ford, Andrea, *The Simpson Verdicts; The Prosecution: Another Stumble; The D.A.'s Office Adds to Its List of High-Profile Defeats, Which Could Leave Gil Garcetti Vulnerable in Next Year's Election*, L.A. TIMES, Oct. 4, 1995, at A3.

FOUCAULT, MICHEL, DISCIPLINE AND PUNISH: THE BIRTH OF THE PRISON (Alan Sheridan trans., Vintage Books 2d ed. 1995) (1975).

Frana, John F. & Ryan D. Schroeder, *Alternatives to Incarceration*, JUST. POL'Y, Fall 2008, at 8.

Frank J. Remington Ctr. *Restorative Justice Project*, http://www.law.wisc.edu/fjr/clinicals/rjp.html (last visited May 5, 2011).

Frankel, Bruce & Dennis Cauchon, *"Young & The Restless": Crime in 1992 More Violent*, USA TODAY, Dec. 31, 1992, at 7A.

FRANKEL, MARVIN E., CRIMINAL SENTENCES: LAW WITHOUT ORDER (1972).

Frase, Richard S., *State Sentencing Guidelines: Diversity, Consensus, and Unresolved Policy Issues*, 105 COLUM. L. REV. 1190 (2005).

Friedman, Lawrence M., Crime and Punishment in American History (1993).

————, A History of American Law (1973).

Friedman, Lawrence M. & Robert V. Percival, The Roots of Justice: Crime and Punishment in Alameda County, California 1870–1910 (1981).

Friendly, Fred W., *On Judging the Judges, in* State Courts: A Blueprint for the Future 70 (Theodore J. Fetter ed., 1978).

From Crime Policy to Victim Policy: Reorienting the Justice System (Ezzat A. Fattah ed., 1986).

Fundamentals of Sentencing Theory (Andrew Ashworth & Martin Wasik eds., 1998).

Gallup Poll, June 2009, retrieved June 9, 2010 from the iPOLL Databank, The Roper Center for Public Opinion Research, University of Connecticut, http:/www. ropercenter.uconn.edu/data_access/ipoll.ipoll.htm (last visited July 14, 2010).

Garland, David, The Culture of Control: Crime and Social Order in Contemporary Society (2001).

Garvey, Stephen P., *Restorative Justice, Punishment, and Atonement,* 2003 Utah L. Rev. 303.

————, *Punishment as Atonement,* 46 UCLA L. Rev. 1801 (1999).

————, *Aggravation and Mitigation in Capital Cases: What Do Jurors Think?,* 98 Colum. L. Rev. 1538 (1998).

————, *Can Shaming Punishments Educate?,* 65 U. Chi. L. Rev. 733 (1998).

————, *Freeing Prisoners' Labor,* 50 Stan. L. Rev. 339 (1998).

Gatrell, V.A.C., The Hanging Tree: Execution and the English People 1770–1868 (1994).

Gershowitz, Adam M. & Laura R. Killinger, *The State (Never) Rests: How Excessive Prosecutor Caseloads Harm Criminal Defendants,* 105 Nw. U. L. Rev. 261 (2011).

Gewirtz, Paul, *Victims and Voyeurs: Two Narrative Problems at the Criminal Trial, in* Law's Stories: Narrative and Rhetoric in the Law 135 (Peter Brooks & Paul Gewirtz eds., 1996).

Gibson, Gail & Laurie Willis, *Tears and Remorse Precede Life Term in Dawson Deaths: Arsonist, Victims' Family Tell Judge of Their Pain,* Balt. Sun, Aug. 28, 2003, at 1A.

Glaeser, Edward & Bruce Sacerdote, *Sentencing in Homicide Cases and the Roles of Vengeance,* 32 J. Legal Stud. 363 (2003).

Glaze, Lauren E. & Thomas P. Bonczar, U.S. Dep't of Justice, NCJ 228230, Probation and Parole in the United States, 2008 (2009), *available at* http://bjs.ojp.usdoj.gov/content/pub/pdf/ppus08.pdf.

Glaze, Lauren E. & Laura M. Maruschak, U.S. Dep't of Justice, NCJ 222984, Parents in Prison and their Minor Children (2008).

Glenn, Myra C., Campaigns Against Corporal Punishment: Prisoners, Sailors, Women, and Children in Antebellum America (1984).

Goebel, Julius, Jr. & T. Raymond Naughton, Law Enforcement in Colonial New York: A Study in Criminal Procedure (1664–1776) (1944).

Golann, Dwight, Mediating Legal Disputes: Effective Strategies for Lawyers and Mediators (1996).

Goldberg, Stephen B. et al., Dispute Resolution: Negotiation, Mediation and Other Processes (3d ed. 1999).

Goldman, Mayer C., *Public Defenders for the Poor in Criminal Cases,* 26 Va. L. Rev. 275 (1940).

————, *The Need for a Public Defender,* 8 J. Crim. L. & Criminology 273 (1917).

Goldstein, Abraham S., *Converging Criminal Justice Systems: Guilty Pleas and the Public Interest*, 49 SMU L. REV. 567 (1996).

Gordon, Loren, *Where to Commit a Crime If You Can Only Spare a Few Days to Serve the Time: The Constitutionality of California's Wobbler Statutes As Applied in the State Today*, 33 SW. U. L. REV. 497 (2004).

GOTTFREDSON, MICHAEL R. & TRAVIS HIRSCHI, A GENERAL THEORY OF CRIME (1990).

Gould, Keri A., *Turning Rat and Doing Time for Uncharged, Dismissed, or Acquitted Crimes: Do the Federal Sentencing Guidelines Promote Respect for the Law?*, in LAW IN A THERAPEUTIC KEY: DEVELOPMENTS IN THERAPEUTIC JURISPRUDENCE 171 (David B. Wexler & Bruce J. Winick eds., 1996).

Green, Randy, *Comprehensive Treatment Planning for Sex Offenders*, in NAT'L INST. OF CORR., U.S. DEP'T OF JUSTICE, A PRACTITIONER'S GUIDE TO TREATING THE INCARCERATED MALE SEX OFFENDER 71 (1988), *reprinted in* 1 THE SEX OFFENDER: CORRECTIONS, TREATMENT AND LEGAL PRACTICE 10–1 (1995).

GREEN, THOMAS ANDREW, VERDICT ACCORDING TO CONSCIENCE (1985).

GREENBERG, DOUGLAS, *Crime, Law Enforcement, and Social Control in Colonial America*, 26 AM. J. LEGAL HIST. 293 (1982).

———, CRIME AND LAW ENFORCEMENT IN THE COLONY OF NEW YORK, 1691–1776 (1974).

Grogger, Jeffrey, *Certainty vs. Severity of Punishment*, 29 ECON. INQUIRY 297 (1991).

Gromet, Dena M. & John M. Darley, *Punishment and Beyond: Achieving Justice through Satisfaction of Multiple Goals*, 43 LAW & SOC'Y REV. 1 (2009).

———, *Restoration and Retribution: How Including Retributive Components Affects the Acceptability of Restorative Justice Procedures*, 19 SOC. JUST. RES. 395 (2006).

GUTMANN, AMY & DENNIS THOMPSON, DEMOCRACY AND DISAGREEMENT (1996).

Hairston, Creasie Finney, *Family Ties During Imprisonment: Important to Whom and for What?*, 18 J. SOCIOLOGY & SOC. WELFARE 87 (1991).

———, *Family Ties During Imprisonment: Do They Influence Future Criminal Activity?*, 52 FED. PROBATION 48 (1988).

Hall, Donald J., *Victims' Voices in Criminal Court: The Need for Restraint*, 28 AM. CRIM. L. REV. 233 (1991).

Hampton, Jean, *The Moral Education Theory of Punishment*, in PUNISHMENT: A PHILOSOPHY & PUBLIC AFFAIRS READER 112 (A. John Simmons et al. eds., 1995).

———, *An Expressive Theory of Retribution*, in 1 RETRIBUTIVISM AND ITS CRITICS (Wesley Cragg ed., 1992).

———, *Correcting Harms Versus Righting Wrongs: The Goal of Retribution*, 39 UCLA L. REV. 1659 (1992).

———, *The Retributive Idea*, in JEFFRIE G. MURPHY & JEAN HAMPTON, FORGIVENESS AND MERCY 111 (1988).

THE HANDBOOK OF CRIME & PUNISHMENT (Michael Tonry ed. 1998).

Hanna, Cheryl, *No Right to Choose: Mandated Victim Participation in Domestic Violence Prosecutions*, 109 HARV. L. REV. 1849 (1996).

HANS, VALERIE P. & NEIL VIDMAR, JUDGING THE JURY (1986).

Happel, Richard M. & Joseph J. Auffrey, *Sex Offender Assessment: Interrupting the Dance of Denial*, 13 AM. J. FORENSIC PSYCHOL., No. 2 1995, at 5.

Harcourt, Bernard E., *The Collapse of the Harm Principle*, 90 J. CRIM. L. & CRIMINOLOGY 109 (1999).

HARE, ROBERT D., WITHOUT CONSCIENCE: THE DISTURBING WORLD OF THE PSYCHOPATHS AMONG US (1999).

HARLOW, CAROLINE WOLF, DEFENSE COUNSEL IN CRIMINAL CASES, BUREAU JUST. STAT. SPECIAL REP., Nov. 2000, at 1, *available at* http://bjs.ojp.usdoj.gov/content/pub/pdf/dccc.pdf.

Harrington, Matthew P., *The Law-Finding Function of the American Jury*, 1999 WIS. L. REV. 377.

Hart, Henry M., Jr., *The Aims of the Criminal Law*, 23 LAW & CONTEMP. PROBS. 401 (1958).

HASKINS, GEORGE LEE, LAW AND AUTHORITY IN EARLY MASSACHUSETTS: A STUDY IN TRADITION AND DESIGN 206–11 (1960).

HAWTHORNE, NATHANIEL, THE SCARLET LETTER (Bantam Classic 2003) (1850).

Heft, Richard Kelly, *Legislating with a Vengeance: Criminals in California Now Face Life Sentences After Their Third Offence Under the "Three Strikes, You're Out" Law*, INDEP. (London), Apr. 26, 1995, at 27.

Heise, Michael, *Mercy by the Numbers: An Empirical Analysis of Clemency and Its Structure*, 89 VA. L. REV. 239 (2003).

Henderson, Lynne N., *The Wrongs of Victims' Rights*, 37 STAN. L. REV. 937 (1985).

Henry, William A., III, *Reporting the Drug Problem: Have Journalists Overdosed on Print and TV Coverage?*, TIME, Oct. 6, 1986, at 73.

HERMAN, G. NICHOLAS, PLEA BARGAINING (1997).

HERMAN, JUDITH LEWIS, FATHER-DAUGHTER INCEST (1981).

HERRUP, CYNTHIA B., THE COMMON PEACE: PARTICIPATION AND THE CRIMINAL LAW IN SEVENTEENTH-CENTURY ENGLAND (1987).

HEUMANN, MILTON, PLEA BARGAINING: THE EXPERIENCES OF PROSECUTORS, JUDGES, AND DEFENSE ATTORNEYS (1978).

HIBBING, JOHN R. & ELIZABETH THEISS-MORSE, STEALTH DEMOCRACY: AMERICANS' BELIEFS ABOUT HOW GOVERNMENT SHOULD WORK (2002).

HICKMAN, MATTHEW J., BUREAU OF JUSTICE STATISTICS, COMMUNITY POLICING IN LOCAL POLICE DEPARTMENTS, 1997 AND 1999 (2001).

Hicks, Jonathan P., *Steady Work, If You Can Get It: District Attorneys Hold Surest Elective Posts in City*, N.Y. TIMES, Apr. 17, 2005, § 1, at 33.

Hickson, Gerald B. et al., *Factors That Prompted Families to File Medical Malpractice Claims Following Prenatal Injuries*, 267 J. AM. MED. ASS'N 1359 (1992).

Hildebran, Diane D. & William D. Pithers, *Relapse Prevention: Application and Outcome*, *in* 2 THE SEXUAL ABUSE OF CHILDREN: CLINICAL ISSUES 365 (William O'Donohue & James H. Geer eds., 1992).

Hill, Frances Gall, *Clinical Education and the "Best Interest" Representation of Children in Custody Disputes: Challenges and Opportunities in Lawyering and Pedagogy*, 73 IND. L.J. 605 (1998).

HILLENBRAND, SUSAN W. & BARBARA E. SMITH, VICTIMS RIGHTS LEGISLATION: AN ASSESSMENT OF ITS IMPACT ON CRIMINAL JUSTICE PRACTITIONERS AND VICTIMS (ABA Crim. Just. Sec. Victim Witness Project 1989).

HINDUS, MICHAEL STEPHEN, PRISON AND PLANTATION: CRIME, JUSTICE, AND AUTHORITY IN MASSACHUSETTS AND SOUTH CAROLINA, 1767–1878 (1980).

HIRSCH, ADAM JAY, THE RISE OF THE PENITENTIARY: PRISONS AND PUNISHMENT IN EARLY AMERICA (1992).

HIRSCHMAN, ALBERT O., EXIT, VOICE, AND LOYALTY: RESPONSES TO DECLINE IN FIRMS, ORGANIZATIONS, AND STATES (1970).

HOBBES, THOMAS, LEVIATHAN (Michael Oakeshott ed., Basil Blackwell 1960) (1651).

Hofer, Paul J., *Federal Sentencing for Violent and Drug Trafficking Crimes Involving Firearms: Recent Changes and Prospects for Improvement*, 37 AM. CRIM. L. REV. 41 (2000).

Hoffman, Morris B., *The Case for Jury Sentencing*, 52 DUKE L.J. 951 (2003).

————, *Therapeutic Jurisprudence, Neo-Rehabilitationism, and Judicial Collectivism: The Least Dangerous Branch Becomes Most Dangerous*, 29 FORDHAM URB. L.J. 2063 (2002).

Holmes, Steven A., *Time and Money Producing Racial Harmony in the Military*, N.Y. TIMES, Apr. 5, 1995, at A1.

Hood, William W., III, Note, *The Meaning of "Life" for Virginia Jurors and Its Effect on Reliability in Capital Sentencing*, 75 VA. L. REV. 1605 (1989).

Hora, Peggy Fulton et al., *Therapeutic Jurisprudence and the Drug Treatment Court Movement: Revolutionizing the Criminal Justice System's Response to Drug Abuse and Crime in America*, 74 NOTRE DAME L. REV. 439 (1999).

Hoyle, Carolyn & Lucia Zedner, *Victims, Victimization, and Criminal Justice, in* THE OXFORD HANDBOOK OF CRIMINOLOGY 461 (Mike Maguire et al. eds., 4th ed. 2007).

Huigens, Kyron, *Virtue and Inculpation*, 108 HARV. L. REV. 1423 (1995).

HUMAN RIGHTS WATCH, vol. 19, no. 4(G), NO EASY ANSWERS: SEX OFFENDER LAWS IN THE US (Sept. 2007), *available at* http://www.hrw.org/en/reports/2007/09/11/no-easy-answers.

IMPRISONING AMERICA: THE SOCIAL EFFECTS OF MASS INCARCERATION 46 (Mary Patillo et al. eds., 2004).

INAUGURAL ADDRESSES OF THE PRESIDENTS OF THE UNITED STATES (1989).

INTEGRATING A VICTIM PERSPECTIVE WITHIN CRIMINAL JUSTICE (Adam Crawford & Jo Goodey eds., 2000).

Iontcheva, Jenia, *Jury Sentencing as Democratic Practice*, 89 VA. L. REV. 311 (2003).

IOWA Cnty. ATTORNEYS ASS'N, STATEMENT ON SEX OFFENDER RESIDENCY RESTRICTIONS IN IOWA (Dec. 11, 2006), *available at* http://www.iowa-icaa.com/ICAA%20STATEMENTS/Sex%20Offender%20Residency%20Statement%20Dec%2011%2006.pdf.

Iowa Dep't of Corr., *History of Victim and Restorative Justice Programs*, http://www.doc.state.ia.us/VictimHistory.asp (last visited May 5, 2011).

JACOBY, JOAN, THE AMERICAN PROSECUTOR: A SEARCH FOR IDENTITY (1980).

Janus, Eric S. & Paul E. Meehl, *Assessing the Legal Standard for Predictions of Dangerousness in Sex Offender Commitment Proceedings*, 3 PSYCHOL. PUB. POL'Y & L. 33 (1997).

JENSEN, CHRISTEN, THE PARDONING POWER IN THE AMERICAN STATE (1922).

JOHN DOBLE RESEARCH ASSOCIATES, INC. & JUDITH GREENE, ATTITUDES TOWARD CRIME AND PUNISHMENT IN VERMONT: PUBLIC OPINION ABOUT AN EXPERIMENT WITH RESTORATIVE JUSTICE (2000), *available at* http://www.ncjrs.gov/pdffiles1/nij/grants/182361.pdf.

JOHNSON, BYRON R. WITH DAVID B. LARSON, CTR. FOR RES. ON RELIGION & CIVIL SOC'Y, THE INNERCHANGE FREEDOM INITIATIVE: A PRELIMINARY EVALUATION OF A FAITH-BASED PRISON PROGRAM (June 2003), *available at* http://www.prisonfellowship.org/images/pdfs/ifi_study.pdf.

Johnson, Carrie, *Bill Targets Sentencing Rules for Crack and Powder Cocaine*, WASH. POST, Oct. 16, 2009, at A6.

————, *Parity in Cocaine Sentences Gains Momentum*, WASH. POST, July 25, 2009, at A2.

Johnston, David, *U.S. Is Beginning Criminal Inquiry in Pardon of Rich*, N.Y. TIMES, Feb. 15, 2001, at A1.

JOINT COMM. ON N.Y. DRUG LAW EVALUATION, THE NATION'S TOUGHEST DRUG LAW: EVALUATING THE NEW YORK EXPERIENCE (1977).

JONES, DAVID A., CRIME WITHOUT PUNISHMENT (1979).

JUDGING IN A THERAPEUTIC KEY: THERAPEUTIC JURISPRUDENCE AND THE COURTS (Bruce J. Winick & David B. Wexler eds., 2003).

Juror Evaluation Forms, U.S. Dist. Ct., S.D. Iowa (on file with the author).

Justice Fellowship, *Prison Fellowship, Clemency and Overcoming Barriers to Reentry*, http://www.justicefellowship.org/key-issues/issues-in-criminal-justice-reform/clemency (last visited June 15, 2011).

Kahan, Dan M., *What's Really Wrong with Shaming Sanctions*, 84 TEX. L. REV. 2075 (2006).

———, *The Secret Ambition of Deterrence*, 113 HARV. L. REV. 413 (1999).

———, *Social Influence, Social Meaning, and Deterrence*, 83 VA. L. REV. 349 (1997).

———, *What Do Alternative Sanctions Mean?*, 63 U. CHI. L. REV. 591 (1996).

Kahan, Dan M. & Tracey L. Meares, *Foreword: The Coming Crisis in Criminal Procedure*, 86 GEO. L.J. 1153 (1998).

Kahan, Dan M. & Martha C. Nussbaum, *Two Conceptions of Emotion in Criminal Law*, 96 COLUM. L. REV. 269 (1996).

Kalt, Brian C., *The Exclusion of Felons from Jury Service*, 53 AM. U. L. REV. 65 (2003).

KALVEN, HARRY, JR. & HANS ZEISEL, THE AMERICAN JURY (1966).

KAMINER, WENDY, IT'S ALL THE RAGE: CRIME AND CULTURE (1995).

KANT, IMMANUEL: PHILOSOPHICAL CORRESPONDENCE 1795–99 (Arnulf Zweig ed. & trans., 1967).

———, *Letter from Immanuel Kant to J.B. Erhard* (Dec. 21, 1792) *in* KANT: PHILOSOPHICAL CORRESPONDENCE 1795–99, at 199 (Arnulf Zweig ed. & trans., 1967).

Katyal, Neal Kumar, *Conspiracy Theory*, 112 YALE. L.J. 1307 (2003).

KENNEDY, RANDALL, RACE, CRIME, AND THE LAW (1997).

Kesich, Gregory D., *Suspect Sentenced for Murder of Friend*, PORTLAND PRESS HERALD, Nov. 6, 2003, at 1B.

Kilpatrick, Dean G. et al., *The Rights of Crime Victims—Does Legal Protection Make a Difference?*, NAT'L INST. JUST. : RES. IN BRIEF, Dec. 1998 (1998) (NCJ 173839), *available at* http://ncjrs.org/pdffiles/173839.pdf.

King, Nancy J., *Priceless Process: Nonnegotiable Features of Criminal Litigation*, 47 UCLA L. REV. 113 (1999).

King, Nancy J. & Rosevelt L. Noble, *Jury Sentencing in Noncapital Cases: Comparing Severity and Variance with Judicial Sentencing in Two States*, 2 J. EMPIRICAL LEGAL STUD. 331 (2005).

———, *Felony Jury Sentencing in Practice—A Three-State Study*, 57 VAND. L. REV. 885 (2004).

King, Peter, *War as a Judicial Resource: Press Gangs and Prosecution Rates, 1740–1830*, in LAW, CRIME AND ENGLISH SOCIETY, 1660–1830, at 97 (2002).

———, CRIME, JUSTICE, AND DISCRETION IN ENGLAND: 1740–1820 (2000).

Klein, Richard, *The Emperor Gideon Has No Clothes: The Empty Promise of the Constitutional Right to the Effective Assistance of Counsel*, 13 HASTINGS CONST. L.Q. 625 (1986).

KLEIN, RICHARD & ROBERT SPANGENBERG, THE INDIGENT DEFENSE CRISIS (1993).

Know the Cases: Browse the Profiles, The Innocence Project, http://www.innocenceproject.org/know/Browse-Profiles.php (last visited Mar. 17, 2009).

Kocieniewski, David, *Amid Pomp, McGreevey Signs Racial-Profiling Bill*, N.Y. TIMES, Mar. 15, 2003, at B5.

Korobkin, Russell & Chris Guthrie, *Psychological Barriers to Litigation Settlement: An Experimental Approach*, 93 MICH. L. REV. 107 (1994).

———, *Psychology, Economics, and Settlement: A New Look at the Role of the Lawyer*, 76 TEX. L. REV. 77 (1997).

Kuh, Richard H., *Plea Bargaining: Guidelines for the Manhattan District Attorney's Office*, 11 CRIM. L. BULL. 48 (1975).

———, *Sentencing: Guidelines for the Manhattan District Attorney's Office*, 11 CRIM. L. BULL. 62 (1975).

L. A. *LAW* (NBC television series).

Lamar, Jacob V., Jr. et al., *Crack: A Cheap and Deadly Cocaine Is a Spreading Menace*, TIME, June 2, 1986, at 16.

Landsberg, Mitchell, *Garcetti's Chances Were Slim, Analysts Say*, L.A. TIMES, Nov. 12, 2000, at B1.

LANGBEIN, JOHN H., THE ORIGINS OF ADVERSARY CRIMINAL TRIAL (2003).

———, *Torture and Plea Bargaining*, 46 U. CHI. L. REV. 3 (1978).

Lanni, Adriaan, Note, *Jury Sentencing in Noncapital Cases: An Idea Whose Time Has Come (Again)?*, 108 YALE L.J. 1775 (1999).

Latessa, Edwin J. & Christopher Lowenkamp, *What Works in Reducing Recidivism?*, 3 U. ST. THOMAS L.J. 521 (2006).

Latif, Elizabeth, Note, *Apologetic Justice: Evaluating Apologies Tailored Toward Legal Solutions*, 81 B.U. L. REV. 289 (2001).

LAW AND THE DOMAINS OF CULTURE (Austin Sarat & Thomas R. Kearns eds., 1998).

LAW IN A THERAPEUTIC KEY: DEVELOPMENTS IN THERAPEUTIC JURISPRUDENCE (David B. Wexler & Bruce J. Winick eds., 1996).

LAW'S STORIES (Peter Brooks & Paul Gewirtz eds., 1996).

Legislation—Indeterminate Sentencing Laws—The Adolescence of Peno-correctional Legislation, 50 HARV. L. REV. 677 (1937).

Lerman, Lisa G., *Lying to Clients*, 138 U. PA. L. REV. 659 (1990).

Lester, Charles & Malcolm M. Feeley, *Legal Complexity and the Transformation of the Criminal Process*, in SUBJEKTIVIERUNG DES JUSTIZIELLEN BEWEISVERFAHRENS 355 (André Gouron et al. eds., 1994).

Levi, Deborah L., Note, *The Role of Apology in Mediation*, 72 N.Y.U. L. REV. 1165 (1997).

LEWIS, C.S., *The Humanitarian Theory of Punishment, in* GOD IN THE DOCK: ESSAYS ON THEOLOGY AND ETHICS 287 (Walter Hooper ed., 1970).

———, THE PROBLEM OF PAIN (1962).

Lincoln, Abraham, *First Inaugural Address, Monday, March 4, 1861, in* INAUGURAL ADDRESSES OF THE PRESIDENTS OF THE UNITED STATES 133 (1989).

LIND, E. ALLAN & TOM R. TYLER, THE SOCIAL PSYCHOLOGY OF PROCEDURAL JUSTICE (1988).

Lind, E. Allan et al., *In the Eye of the Beholder: Tort Litigants' Evaluations of Their Experiences in the Civil Justice System*, 24 LAW & SOC'Y REV. 953 (1990).

LIPSKY, MICHAEL, STREET-LEVEL BUREAUCRACY: DILEMMAS OF THE INDIVIDUAL IN PUBLIC SERVICES (updated ed. 2010).

LIPTON, D., R. MARTINSON & J. WILKS, EFFECTIVENESS OF CORRECTIONAL TREATMENT—A SURVEY OF TREATMENT EVALUATION STUDIES (1975).

Loader, Ian, *Fall of the "Platonic Guardians": Liberalism, Criminology and Political Responses to Crime in England and Wales*, 46 BRIT. J. CRIMINOLOGY 561 (2006).

LOCKE, JOHN, A LETTER CONCERNING TOLERATION (Huddersfield: J. Brook 1796) (1689).

Logan, Wayne A., *Opining on Death: Witness Sentence Recommendations in Capital Trials*, 41 B.C. L. REV. 517 (2000).

LOMBROSO, CESARE, CRIMINAL MAN (Mary Gibson & Nicole Hahn Rafter trans., Duke Univ. Press 2006) (1876–97).

LOVE, MARGARET COLGATE, RELIEF FROM THE COLLATERAL CONSEQUENCES OF A CRIMINAL CONVICTION: A STATE-BY-STATE RESOURCE GUIDE (2006).

Lowenkamp, Christopher T. & Edward J. Latessa, *Understanding the Risk Principle: How and Why Correctional Interventions Can Harm Low-Risk Offenders*, in TOPICS IN COMMUNITY CORRECTIONS (2004).

Lowry, Dennis T. et al., *Setting the Public Fear Agenda: A Longitudinal Analysis of Network TV Crime Reporting, Public Perceptions of Crime, and FBI Crime Statistics*, 53 J. COMM. 61 (2003).

Luban, David, *A Theory of Crimes Against Humanity*, 29 YALE J. INT'L L. 85 (2004).

———, *Are Criminal Defenders Different?*, 91 MICH. L. REV. 1729 (1993).

———, *Paternalism and the Legal Profession*, 1981 WIS. L. REV. 454.

Luna, Erik G., *The Overcriminalization Phenomenon*, 54 AM. U. L. REV. 703 (2005).

———, *Punishment Theory, Holism, and the Procedural Conception of Restorative Justice*, 2003 UTAH L. REV. 205.

———, *Race, Crime, and Institutional Design*, 66 LAW & CONTEMP. PROBS. 183 (Summer 2003).

———, *Principled Enforcement of Penal Codes*, 4 BUFF. CRIM. L. REV. 515 (2000).

———, *Transparent Policing*, 85 IOWA L. REV. 1107 (2000).

———, *Foreword: Three Strikes in a Nutshell*, 20 T. JEFFERSON L. REV. 1 (1998).

Lundquist, Jennifer Hickes, *Ethnic and Gender Satisfaction in the Military: The Effect of a Meritocratic Institution*, 73 AM. SOC. REV. 477 (2008).

Luo, Michael, *Rapist's Parole and AIDS View from 1990s Follow Huckabee*, N.Y. TIMES, Dec. 9, 2007, § 1, at 1.

Lynch, James P. & Mona J.E. Danner, *Offense Seriousness Scaling: An Alternative to Scenario Methods*, 9 J. QUANTITATIVE CRIMINOLOGY 309 (1993).

MacCormick, Neil & David Garland, *Sovereign States and Vengeful Victims: The Problem of the Right to Punish*, in FUNDAMENTALS OF SENTENCING THEORY 11 (Andrew Ashworth & Martin Wasik eds., 1998).

Maharaj, Davan, *People's Court for Genocide: Eight Years After the Rwandan Slaughter, the Overwhelmed Justice System Turns to Villagers, Including Survivors, to Pass Judgment*, L.A. TIMES, May 29, 2002, at A1.

MALETZKY, BARRY M. WITH KEVIN B. MCGOVERN, TREATING THE SEXUAL OFFENDER (1991).

MANN, KENNETH, DEFENDING WHITE-COLLAR CRIME: A PORTRAIT OF ATTORNEYS AT WORK (1985).

Marcus, Gail Sussman, *"Due Execution of the Generall Rules of Righteousnesse": Criminal Procedure in New Haven Town and Colony, 1638–1658*, in SAINTS & REVOLUTIONARIES: ESSAYS ON EARLY AMERICAN HISTORY 130 (David H. Hall et al. eds. 1984).

Margolick, David, *Law Professor to Administer Courts in State*, N.Y. TIMES, Feb. 1, 1985, at B2.

Marion, Samara, *Justice by Geography? A Study of San Diego County's Three Strikes Sentencing Practices from July-December 1996*, 11 STAN. L. & POL'Y REV. 29 (1999).

Markel, Dan, *Wrong Turns on the Road to Alternative Sanctions: Reflections on the Future of Shaming Punishments and Restorative Justice*, 85 TEX. L. REV. 1385 (2007).

———, *Against Mercy*, 88 MINN. L. REV. 1421 (2004).

———, *Are Shaming Punishments Beautifully Retributive? Retributivism and the Implications for the Alternative Sanctions Debate*, 54 VAND. L. REV. 2157 (2001).

Marks, Alexandra, *For Prisoners, It's a Nearly No-Parole World*, CHRISTIAN SCI. MONITOR, July 10, 2001, at 1.

Marshall, Joshua Micah, *Death in Venice*, NEW REPUBLIC, July 31, 2000, at 12.

Marshall, W.L., *Treatment Effects on Denial and Minimization in Incarcerated Sex Offenders*, 32 BEHAV. RES. & THERAPY 559 (1994).

Martin, John P., *Barber Told To Repay $57,000*, STAR-LEDGER (Newark, N.J.), Oct. 23, 2003, at 13.

Martinson, Robert, *What Works? Questions and Answers About Prison Reform*, 35 PUB. INTEREST 22 (1974).

Massaro, Toni M., *Shame, Culture, and American Criminal Law*, 89 MICH. L. REV. 1880 (1991).

———, *Empathy, Legal Storytelling, and the Rule of Law: New Words, Old Wounds?*, 87 MICH. L. REV. 2099 (1989).

Mattick, Hans W., *Parolees in the Army during World War II*, 24 FED. PROBATION 49 (1960).

MATTINSON, JOANNA & CATRIONA MIRRLEES-BLACK, HOME OFFICE, RESEARCH STUDY NO. 200, ATTITUDES TO CRIME AND CRIMINAL JUSTICE: FINDINGS FROM THE 1998 BRITISH CRIME SURVEY (2000), *available at* http://www.homeoffice.gov. uk/rds/pdfs/hors200.pdf.

May, Bruce E., *The Character Component of Occupational Licensing Laws: A Continuing Barrier to the Ex-Felon's Employment Opportunities*, 71 N.D. L. REV. 187 (1995).

Mazzone, Jason, *The Waiver Paradox*, 97 NW. U. L. REV. 801 (2003).

McConville, Michael & Chester L. Mirsky, *Criminal Defense of the Poor in New York City*, 15 N.Y.U. REV. L. & SOC. CHANGE 581 (1986–87).

———, *The Rise of Guilty Pleas: New York, 1800–1865*, 22 J.L. & SOC'Y 443 (1995).

MCCOY, CANDACE, POLITICS AND PLEA BARGAINING: VICTIMS' RIGHTS IN CALIFORNIA (1993).

McDonald, William F., *Towards a Bicentennial Revolution in Criminal Justice: The Return of the Victim*, 13 AM. CRIM. L. REV. 649 (1976).

McEwan, Craig A. & Richard J. Maiman, *Mediation in Small Claims Court: Consensual Processes and Outcomes, in* MEDIATION RESEARCH: THE PROCESS AND EFFECTIVENESS OF THIRD-PARTY INTERVENTION 53 (Kenneth Kressel et al. eds., 1989).

MCMANUS, EDGAR J., LAW AND LIBERTY IN EARLY NEW ENGLAND: CRIMINAL JUSTICE AND DUE PROCESS, 1620–92 (1993).

McShane, John V., *The How and Why of Therapeutic Jurisprudence in Criminal Defense Work* (2000) (unpublished paper distributed at the American-Psychology-Law Society Conference, New Orleans, Louisiana Mar. 12, 2000).

MEDIATION RESEARCH: THE PROCESS AND EFFECTIVENESS OF THIRD-PARTY INTERVENTION (Kenneth Kressel et al. eds., 1989).

Meares, Tracey L., *Praying for Community Policing*, 90 CAL. L. REV. 1593 (2002).

Meares, Tracey L. & Dan M. Kahan, *The Wages of Antiquated Procedural Thinking: A Critique of* Chicago v. Morales, 1998 U. CHI. LEGAL F. 197.

MEASE, JAMES, OBSERVATIONS ON THE PENITENTIARY SYSTEM, AND PENAL CODE OF PENNSYLVANIA: WITH SUGGESTIONS FOR THEIR IMPROVEMENT (Philadelphia: Clark & Raser 1828) (reprinting an essay originally published in Philadelphia newspapers in 1820).

Medwed, Daniel S., *The Zeal Deal: Prosecutorial Resistance to Post-Conviction Claims of Innocence*, 84 B.U. L. REV. 125 (2004).

Megan Nicole Kanka Foundation, Mission, http://www.megannicolekankafoundation. org/mission.htm (last visited Aug. 26, 2008).

Meldrum, Andrew, *One Million Rwandans to Face Killing Charges in Village Courts*, THE GUARDIAN (London), Jan. 15, 2005, at 16.

Merola, Mario, *Modern Prosecutorial Techniques*, 16 CRIM. L. BULL. 232 (1980).

Mertz, Elizabeth & Kimberly A. Lonsway, *The Power of Denial: Individual and Cultural Constructions of Child Sexual Abuse*, 92 NW. U. L. REV. 1415 (1998).

Messing, Philip et al., *NYPD Stats Were Captain Cooked*, N.Y. POST, Feb. 7, 2010, at 22.

Miller, Marc L. & Ronald F. Wright, *The Black Box*, 94 IOWA L. REV. 125 (2008).

————, CRIMINAL PROCEDURES: CASES, STATUTES, AND EXECUTIVE MATERIALS (1998).

Miller, William Ian, *Clint Eastwood and Equity: Popular Culture's Theory of Revenge*, in LAW IN THE DOMAINS OF CULTURE 161 (Austin Sarat & Thomas R. Kearns eds., 1998).

Mills, Linda G., *Affective Lawyering: The Emotional Dimensions of the Lawyer-Client Relation*, in PRACTICING THERAPEUTIC JURISPRUDENCE: LAW AS A HELPING PROFESSION 419 (Dennis P. Stolle et al. eds., 2000).

Minn. Dep't of Corr., *Restorative Justice: Victims & Offenders in Communication Experiences*, http://www.doc.state.mn.us/rj/Options.htm (last visited May 5, 2011).

————, RESIDENTIAL PROXIMITY AND SEX OFFENSE RECIDIVISM IN MINNESOTA (Apr. 2007), *available at* http://www.nacdl.org/sl_docs.nsf/issues/SexOffender_ attachments/$FILE/MN_Residence.pdf.

————, LEVEL THREE SEX OFFENDERS RESIDENTIAL PLACEMENT ISSUES, 2003 REPORT TO THE LEGISLATURE (Jan. 2003).

————, *Sex Offender Supervision Training*, in PROBATION OFFICER MANUAL.

MODERN POLICING (Michael Tonry & Norval Morris eds., 1992).

Moley, Raymond, *The Vanishing Jury*, 2 S. CAL. L. REV. 97 (1928).

MOORE, CHRISTOPHER W., THE MEDIATION PROCESS: PRACTICAL STRATEGIES FOR RESOLVING CONFLICT (3d ed. rev. 2003).

Moore, Mark Harrison, *Problem-Solving and Community Policing*, in MODERN POLICING 99 (Michael Tonry & Norval Morris eds., 1992).

MOORE, MICHAEL, PLACING BLAME: A GENERAL THEORY OF THE CRIMINAL LAW (1998).

Moore, Robert A. & Thomas C. Murphy, *Denial of Alcoholism as an Obstacle to Recovery*, 22 Q. J. STUD. ON ALCOHOL 597 (1961).

Morin, Monte, *Fund Raiser Receives Maximum Penalty: 8 Years, Plus Restitution*, L.A. TIMES, July 25, 2002, at B5.

Morris, Herbert, *Sex, Shame, and Assorted Other Topics*, 22 QUINNIPIAC L. REV. 123 (2003).

————, *Persons and Punishment*, 52 MONIST 475 (1968).

MORRIS, NORVAL, THE FUTURE OF IMPRISONMENT (1974).

Moses, Marilyn C. & Cindy J. Smith, *Factories Behind Fences: Do Prison "Real Work" Programs Work?*, NAT'L INST. JUST. J., June 2007, at 32.

MOSKOS, CHARLES C. & JOHN SIBLEY BUTLER, ALL THAT WE CAN BE: BLACK LEADERSHIP AND RACIAL INTEGRATION THE ARMY WAY (1997).

Mosteller, Robert P., Essay, *Victims' Rights and the United States Constitution: An Effort to Recast the Battle in Criminal Litigation*, 85 GEO. L.J. 1691 (1997).

MULTICULTURAL JURISPRUDENCE: COMPARATIVE PERSPECTIVES ON THE CULTURAL DEFENSE (Marie-Claire Foblets & Alison Dundes Renteln eds., 2009).

Murder Victims' Families for Reconciliation, Not in Our Name: Murder Victims' Families Speak Out Against the Death Penalty (4th ed. 2003), *available at* http://www.mvfr.org/PDF/NIONbook.pdf.

Murphy, Jeffrie G., *Repentance, Punishment, and Mercy, in* Repentance: A Comparative Perspective 143 (Amitai Etzioni & David E. Carney eds., 1997).

Murphy, Jeffrie G. & Jean Hampton, Forgiveness and Mercy (1988).

Murrin, John M., *Magistrates, Sinners, and a Precarious Liberty: Trial by Jury in Seventeenth-Century New England, in* Saints & Revolutionaries: Essays on Early American History (David H. Hall et al. eds., 1984).

Myers, Laura B., *Bringing the Offender to Heel: Views of the Criminal Courts, in* Americans View Crime and Justice: A National Public Opinion Survey 46 (Timothy J. Flanagan & Dennis R. Longmire eds., 1996).

Nadler, Janice, *Flouting the Law*, 83 Tex. L. Rev. 1399 (2005).

Nagel, Ilene H. & Stephen J. Schulhofer, *A Tale of Three Cities: An Empirical Study of Charging and Bargaining Practices Under the Federal Sentencing Guidelines*, 66 S. Cal. L. Rev. 501 (1992).

Natapoff, Alexandra, *Speechless: The Silencing of Criminal Defendants*, 80 N.Y.U. L. Rev. 1449 (2005).

Nat'l Ctr. for State Cts., How the Public Views the State Courts: A 1999 National Survey (1999).

Nat'l Center on Addiction and Substance Abuse, Behind Bars: Substance Abuse and America's Prison Population (1998).

Nat'l Inst. of Corr., U.S. Dep't of Justice, A Practitioner's Guide to Treating the Incarcerated Male Sex Offender (1988).

Nat'l Serv. of Gacaca Jurisdictions, *Sentences Applicable in the GACACA Courts*, http://www.inkiko-gacaca.gov.rw/En/EnSentence.htm (last visited May 5, 2011).

Nat'l Victims Ctr., Statutory and Constitutional Protection of Victims' Rights: Implementation and Impact on Crime Victims (1996).

Nelson, William E., Americanization of the Common Law: The Impact of Legal Change on Massachusetts Society, 1760–1830 (1975).

———, *Emerging Notions of Modern Criminal Law in the Revolutionary Era: An Historical Perspective*, 42 N.Y.U. L. Rev. 450 (1967).

Netzig, Lutz & Thomas Trenczek, *Restorative Justice as Participation: Theory, Law, Experience and Research, in* Restorative Justice: International Perspectives 241 (Burt Galaway & Joe Hudson eds., 1996).

New Jersey Black and Latino Caucus, *A Report on Discriminatory Practices within the New Jersey State Police*, 26 Seton Hall Legis. J. 273 (2002).

New York Criminal Justice Agency, Inc., CJA Annual Report 2008.

Newman, Donald J., Conviction: The Determination of Guilt or Innocence Without Trial (Frank J. Remington ed., 1966).

Nolan, James L., Jr., *Redefining Criminal Courts: Problem-Solving and the Meaning of Justice*, 40 Am. Crim. L. Rev. 1541 (2003).

———, *Separated by an Uncommon Law: Drug Courts in Great Britain and America, in* Drug Courts in Theory and Practice 89 (James L. Nolan, Jr. ed., 2002).

———, Reinventing Justice: The American Drug Court Movement (2001).

Nozick, Robert, Philosophical Explanations (1981).

Nussbaum, Martha C., Hiding from Humanity: Disgust, Shame, and the Law (2004).

———, *Emotion in the Language of Judging*, 70 St. John's L. Rev. 23 (1996).

O'Connell, Jamie, *Gambling with the Psyche: Does Prosecuting Human Rights Violators Console Their Victims?*, 46 HARV. INT'L L.J. 295 (2005).

O'Donohue, William & Elizabeth Letourneau, *A Brief Group Treatment for the Modification of Denial in Child Sexual Abusers: Outcome and Follow-Up*, 17 CHILD ABUSE & NEGLECT 299 (1993).

O'Hara, Erin Ann & Douglas Yarn, *On Apology and Consilience*, 77 WASH. L. REV. 1121 (2002).

O'Hear, Michael M., *Plea Bargaining and Procedural Justice*, 42 GA. L. REV. 407 (2008).

———, *Is Restorative Justice Compatible with Uniformity?*, 89 MARQ. L. REV. 305 (2005).

———, *Remorse, Cooperation, and "Acceptance of Responsibility": The Structure, Implementation, and Reform of Section 3E1.1 of the Federal Sentencing Guidelines*, 91 NW. U. L. REV. 1507 (1997).

O'Sullivan, Julie R., *In Defense of the U.S. Sentencing Guidelines' Modified Real-Offense System*, 91 NW. U. L. REV. 1342 (1997).

Office of Justice Programs, Bureau of Justice Statistics, *Reentry Trends in the U.S.: Releases From State Prison*, http://bjs.ojp.usdoj.gov/content/reentry/releases.cfm (last visited Nov. 30, 2011).

OFFUTT, WILLIAM M., JR., OF "GOOD LAWS" AND "GOOD MEN": LAW AND SOCIETY IN THE DELAWARE VALLEY, 1680–1710 (1995).

Olson, Susan M. & Albert W. Dzur, *Reconstructing Professional Roles in Restorative Justice Programs*, 2003 UTAH L. REV. 57.

Orenstein, Aviva, *Apology Excepted: Incorporating a Feminist Analysis into Evidence Policy Where You Would Least Expect It*, 28 SW. U. L. REV. 221 (1999).

OXFORD ENGLISH DICTIONARY (2d ed. 1989).

THE OXFORD HANDBOOK OF CRIMINOLOGY (Mike Maguire et al. eds., 4th ed. 2007).

PACKER, HERBERT L., THE LIMITS OF THE CRIMINAL SANCTION (1968).

Padfield, Stefan J., Comment, *Self-Incrimination and Acceptance of Responsibility in Prison Sex Offender Treatment Programs*, 49 U. KAN. L. REV. 487 (2001).

Paduano, Anthony & Clive A. Stafford Smith, *Deathly Errors: Juror Misperceptions Concerning Parole in the Imposition of the Death Penalty*, 18 COLUM. HUM. RTS. L. REV. 211 (1987).

Parascandola, Rocco, *Brooklyn's 81st Precinct Probed by NYPD for Fudging Stats; Felonies Allegedly Marked as Misdemeanors*, N.Y. DAILY NEWS, Feb. 2, 2010, at 8.

PARRILLO, NICHOLAS, AGAINST THE PROFIT MOTIVE: THE TRANSFORMATION OF AMERICAN GOVERNMENT, 1780–1840 (forthcoming Yale Univ. Press; partial manuscript on file with the author).

THE PASSIONS OF LAW (Susan A. Bandes ed., 1999).

Pavlick, Donna L., *Apology and Mediation: The Horse and Carriage of the Twenty-First Century*, 18 OHIO ST. J. ON DISP. RESOL. 829 (2003).

Perry, Steven W., *Prosecutors in State Courts, 2005*, BUREAU JUST. STATS. BULL., July 2006.

XI PERSPECTIVES IN AMERICAN HISTORY (Donald Fleming ed. 1978).

PETERSIK, THOMAS W. ET AL., NAT'L CORRECTIONAL INDUS. ASS'N, IDENTIFYING BENEFICIARIES OF PIE INMATE INCOMES: WHO BENEFITS FROM WAGE EARNINGS OF INMATES WORKING IN THE PRISON INDUSTRY ENHANCEMENT (PIE) PROGRAM? (2003), *available at* www.nationalcia.org/wp-content/uploads/2008/09/researchfullrpt1.pdf.

Petersilia, Joan, *Parole and Prisoner Reentry in the United States*, 26 CRIME & JUST. 479 (1999).

Petrila, John, *Paternalism and the Unrealized Promise of Essays in Therapeutic Jurisprudence, in* LAW IN A THERAPEUTIC KEY: DEVELOPMENTS IN THERAPEUTIC JURISPRUDENCE 685 (David B. Wexler & Bruce J. Winick eds., 1996).

Petrucci, Carrie J., *Apology in the Criminal Justice Setting: Evidence for Including Apology as an Additional Component in the Legal System*, 20 BEHAV. SCI. & L. 337 (2002).

Pettigrew, Thomas F. & Linda R. Tropp, *A Meta-Analytic Test of Intergroup Contact Theory*, 90 J. PERSONALITY & SOC. PSYCHOL. 751 (2006).

Pillsbury, Samuel H., *Emotional Justice: Moralizing the Passions of Criminal Punishment*, 74 CORNELL L. REV. 655 (1989).

1 POLLOCK, FREDERICK & FREDERIC WILLIAM MAITLAND, THE HISTORY OF ENGLISH LAW BEFORE THE TIME OF EDWARD I (2d ed. 1959).

Pollock, Nathan L. & Judith M. Hashmall, *The Excuses of Child Molesters*, 9 BEHAV. SCI. & L. 53 (1991).

Posner, Richard A., *The Problematics of Moral and Legal Theory*, 111 HARV. L. REV. 1637 (1998).

———, *Conceptions of Legal "Theory": A Response to Ronald Dworkin*, 29 ARIZ. ST. L.J. 377 (1997).

———, *An Economic Theory of the Criminal Law*, 85 COLUM. L. REV. 1193 (1985).

Poulson, Barton, *A Third Voice: A Review of Empirical Research on the Psychological Outcomes of Restorative Justice*, 2003 UTAH L. REV. 167.

PRACTICING THERAPEUTIC JURISPRUDENCE: LAW AS A HELPING PROFESSION (Dennis P. Stolle et al. eds., 2000).

Telephone Interview with the Hon. Robert W. Pratt, U.S. Dist. Judge, S.D. Iowa (July 15, 2005).

PREJEAN, HELEN, DEAD MAN WALKING (1993).

PRENDERGAST, WILLIAM E., TREATING SEX OFFENDERS IN CORRECTIONAL INSTITUTIONS AND OUTPATIENT CLINICS: A GUIDE TO CLINICAL PRACTICE (1991).

PRESIDENT'S TASK FORCE ON VICTIMS OF CRIME, FINAL REPORT (1982).

PRISON LABOR: SALVATION OR SLAVERY? INTERNATIONAL PERSPECTIVES (Dirk van Zyl Smit & Frieder Dünkel eds., 1999).

Prison Fellowship, *What Is Prison Fellowship?*, http://www.prisonfellowship.org/why-pf (last visited June 10, 2011).

Probation Officers Advisory Group, *Probation Officers' Advisory Group Survey*, 8 FED. SENT'G REP. 305 (1996).

Public Agenda Foundation, Survey of 28 Questions on Crime and Justice (Feb. 10, 2002), POLLING THE NATIONS, http://poll.orspub.com/search.php?action=new search&mode=poll&sort=field%3Atopic%2Ca&pollid=PAF02102002 (last visited Oct. 9, 2011).

PUBLIC ATTITUDES TO SENTENCING: SURVEYS FROM FIVE COUNTRIES (Nigel Walker & Mike Hough eds., 1988).

PUNISHMENT: *A PHILOSOPHY & PUBLIC AFFAIRS* READER (A. John Simmons et al. eds., 1995).

Questor, Aline O. & Curtis L. Gilroy, *Women and Minorities in America's Volunteer Army*, 20 CONTEMP. ECON. POL'Y 111 (2002).

Rachlinski, Jeffrey J. et al., *Does Unconscious Racial Bias Affect Trial Judges?*, 84 NOTRE DAME L. REV. 1195 (2009).

RAND, MICHAEL R., U.S. DEP'T OF JUSTICE, NCJ 227777, CRIMINAL VICTIMIZATION 2008 (2009).

RANKIN, HUGH F., CRIMINAL TRIAL PROCEEDINGS IN THE GENERAL COURT OF COLONIAL VIRGINIA (1965).

RAWLS, JOHN, POLITICAL LIBERALISM (1996).

Rehm, Peter H. & Denise R. Beatty, *Legal Consequences of Apologizing*, 1996 J. DISP. RESOL. 115.

REIMERS, TODD, SENATE RESEARCH CTR., PAROLE: THEN AND NOW (1999).

REINHARD, CHRISTOPHER, PARDON STATISTICS FROM OTHER STATES, OLR RESEARCH REPORT No. 2005-R-0065 (Jan. 14, 2005), *available at* http://www.cga. ct.gov/2005/rpt/2005-R-0065.htm.

Reitz, Kevin R., *Sentencing Facts: Travesties of Real-Offense Sentencing*, 45 STAN. L. REV. 523 (1993).

RENTELN, ALISON DUNDES, THE CULTURAL DEFENSE (2004).

REPENTANCE: A COMPARATIVE PERSPECTIVE (Amitai Etzioni & David E. Carney eds., 1997).

RESTORATIVE JUSTICE AND CIVIL SOCIETY (Heather Strang & John Braithwaite eds., 2001).

RESTORATIVE JUSTICE AND CRIMINAL JUSTICE: COMPETING OR RECONCILABLE PARADIGMS? (Andrew von Hirsch et al. eds., 2003).

RESTORATIVE JUSTICE: INTERNATIONAL PERSPECTIVES (Burt Galaway & Joe Hudson eds., 1996).

RESTORATIVE JUSTICE: PHILOSOPHY TO PRACTICE (Heather Strang & John Braithwaite eds., 2000).

RETRIBUTIVISM AND ITS CRITICS (Wesley Cragg ed., 1992).

Rice, James D., *The Criminal Trial Before and After the Lawyers: Authority, Law, and Culture in Maryland Jury Trials, 1681–1837*, 40 AM. J. LEGAL HIST. 455 (1996).

Rich, Robert F. & Robert J. Sampson, *Public Perceptions of Criminal Justice Policy: Does Victimization Make a Difference?*, 5 VIOLENCE & VICTIMS 109 (1990).

Richman, Daniel, *Federal Sentencing in 2007: The Supreme Court Holds—The Center Doesn't*, 117 YALE L.J. 1374 (2008).

Robbennolt, Jennifer K. et al., *Symbolism and Incommensurability in Civil Sanctioning: Decision Makers as Goal Managers*, 68 BROOK. L. REV. 1121 (2003).

Roberts, Julian V., *Victim Impact Statements and the Sentencing Process: Recent Developments and Research Findings*, 47 CRIM. L.Q. 365 (2003).

———, *Public Opinion, Criminal Record, and the Sentencing Process*, 39 AM. BEHAV. SCIENTIST 488 (1996).

Roberts, Julian V. & Loretta J. Stalans, *Crime, Criminal Justice, and Public Opinion, in* THE HANDBOOK OF CRIME & PUNISHMENT 31 (Michael Tonry ed., 1998).

———, PUBLIC OPINION, CRIME, AND CRIMINAL JUSTICE (1997).

ROBERTS, JULIAN V. ET AL., PENAL POPULISM AND PUBLIC OPINION: LESSONS FROM FIVE COUNTRIES (2003).

Robinson, Paul H., *Competing Conceptions of Modern Desert: Vengeful, Deontological, and Empirical*, 67 CAMBRIDGE L.J. 145 (2008).

———, *The Virtues of Restorative Processes, the Vices of "Restorative Justice,"* 2003 UTAH L. REV. 375.

———, *Should the Victims' Rights Movement Have Influence over Criminal Law Formulation and Adjudication?*, 33 MCGEORGE L. REV. 749 (2002).

———, *Some Doubts about Argument by Hypothetical*, 88 CAL. L. REV. 813 (2000).

Robinson, Paul H. & Josh Bowers, *Perceptions of Injustice: The Shared Aims and Occasional Conflicts of Legitimacy and Moral Credibility*, http://lsr.nellco.org/upenn_wps/365 (Apr. 22, 2011) (last visited June 24, 2011).

Robinson, Paul H. & John M. Darley, *Does the Criminal Law Deter? A Behavioural Science Investigation*, 24 OXFORD J. LEGAL STUD. 173 (2004).

————, *The Role of Deterrence in the Formulation of Criminal Law Rules: At Its Worst When Doing Its Best*, 91 Geo. L.J. 949 (2003).

————, *The Utility of Desert*, 91 Nw. U. L. Rev. 453 (1997).

————, Justice, Liability, and Blame: Community Views and the Criminal Law (1995).

Robinson, Paul H. & Robert Kurzban, *Concordance and Conflict in Intuitions of Justice*, 91 Minn. L. Rev. 1829 (2007).

Robinson, Paul H. et al., *The Disutility of Injustice*, 85 NYU L. Rev. 1940 (2010).

Robinson, Paul H. et al., *Extralegal Punishment Factors: A Study of Forgiveness, Hardship, Good-Deeds, Apology, Remorse, and Other Such Discretionary Factors in Assessing Criminal Punishment* 65 Vand. L. Rev. (forthcoming 2012).

Roeber, A.G., *Authority, Law, and Custom: The Rituals of Court Day in Tidewater Virginia, 1720 to 1750*, 37 Wm. & Mary Q. (3d Ser.) 29 (1980).

Romer, Daniel et al., *Television News and the Cultivation of Fear of Crime*, 53 J. Comm. 88 (2003).

Ronner, Amy D., *Dostoyevsky and the Therapeutic Jurisprudence Confession*, 40 J. Marshall L. Rev. 41 (2006).

Ronner, Amy D. & Bruce J. Winick, *The Antitherapeutic Per Curiam Affirmance, in* Judging in a Therapeutic Key: Therapeutic Jurisprudence and the Courts 316 (Bruce J. Winick & David B. Wexler eds., 2003).

Rosenthal, Douglas E., Lawyer and Client: Who's in Charge (1974)

Rossi, Peter H. & Richard A. Berk, Just Punishments: Federal Guidelines and Public Views Compared (1997).

————, U.S. Sentencing Comm'n, A National Sample Survey: Public Opinion on Sentencing Federal Crimes (1995).

Rothman, David J., The Discovery of the Asylum: Social Order and Disorder in the New Republic (Aldine de Gruyter rev. ed. 2002).

Rothwax, Harold J., Guilty: The Collapse of Criminal Justice (1996).

Rush, Benjamin, An Enquiry into the Effects of Public Punishments upon Criminals and upon Society (Philadelphia 1787).

Sabol, William J. et al., U.S. Dep't of Justice, NCJ 228417, Prisoners in 2008 (2009).

Saints & Revolutionaries: Essays on Early American History (David H. Hall et al. eds. 1984).

Salter, Anna C., Treating Child Sex Offenders and Victims: A Practical Guide (1988).

Sampson, Robert J. et al., *Does Marriage Reduce Crime? A Counterfactual Approach to Within-Individual Causal Effects*, 44 Criminology 465 (2006).

Samuel, William & Elizabeth Moulds, *The Effect of Crime Severity on Perceptions of Fair Punishment: A California Case Study*, 77 J. Crim. L. & Criminology 931 (1986).

Scanlon, Kathleen M., Mediator's Deskbook (1999).

Scheff, Thomas J., *Working with Shame and Anger in Community Conferencing, in* Judging in a Therapeutic Key: Therapeutic Jurisprudence and the Courts 231 (Bruce J. Winick & David B. Wexler eds., 2003).

Schma, William, *Judging for the New Millennium*, Ct. Rev., Spring 2000, at 4.

Schragger, Richard C., *The Limits of Localism*, 100 Mich. L. Rev. 371 (2001).

Schulhofer, Stephen J., *The Trouble with Trials; the Trouble with Us*, 105 Yale L.J. 825 (1995) (book review).

————, *Plea Bargaining as Disaster*, 101 Yale L.J. 1979 (1992).

————, *Criminal Justice Discretion as a Regulatory System*, 17 J. LEGAL STUD. 43 (1988).

SCHWARTZ, BARRY, THE BATTLE FOR HUMAN NATURE: SCIENCE, MORALITY AND MODERN LIFE (1987).

Scully, Diana & Joseph Marolla, *Convicted Rapists' Vocabulary of Motives: Excuses and Justifications*, 31 SOC. PROBS. 530 (1984).

SEBBA, LESLIE, THIRD PARTIES: VICTIMS AND THE CRIMINAL JUSTICE SYSTEM (1996).

Seidman, David & Michael Couzens, *Getting the Crime Rate Down: Political Pressure and Crime Reporting*, 8 LAW & SOC'Y REV. 457 (1974).

SELLIN, THORSTEN & MARVIN E. WOLFGANG, THE MEASUREMENT OF DELINQUENCY (1964).

SEMMES, RAPHAEL, CRIME AND PUNISHMENT IN EARLY MARYLAND (1938).

SENTENCING AND SANCTIONS IN WESTERN COUNTRIES (Michael Tonry & Richard S. Frase eds., 2001).

2 THE SEXUAL ABUSE OF CHILDREN: CLINICAL ISSUES (William O'Donohue & James H. Geer eds., 1992).

Shane, Scott & Neil A. Lewis, *Bush Commutes Libby Sentence, Saying 30 Months "Is Excessive,"* N.Y. TIMES, July 3, 2007, at A1.

Shapland, Joanna, *Victims and the Criminal Justice System, in* FROM CRIME POLICY TO VICTIM POLICY: REORIENTING THE JUSTICE SYSTEM 210 (Ezzat A. Fattah ed., 1986).

Sharpe, J.A., *"Last Dying Speeches": Religion, Ideology and Public Execution in Seventeenth-Century England*, 107 PAST & PRESENT 144 (1985).

Sherman, Lawrence W., *Trust and Confidence in Criminal Justice*, 248 NAT'L INST. JUST. J. 22 (2002).

Sherman, Lawrence W. & Richard A. Berk, *The Minneapolis Domestic Violence Experiment*, POLICE FOUND. REP., Apr. 1984, at 1–2, *available at* http://www.policefoundation. org/pdf/minneapolisdve.pdf.

Shipley, Curtis J., Note, *The* Alford *Plea: A Necessary but Unpredictable Tool for the Criminal Defendant*, 72 IOWA L. REV. 1063 (1987).

Shuman, Daniel W. & Jean A. Hamilton, *Jury Service—It May Change Your Mind: Perceptions of Fairness of Jurors and Nonjurors*, 46 SMU L. REV. 449 (1992).

Shuman, Daniel W., *The Role of Apology in Tort Law*, 83 JUDICATURE 180 (2000).

Siegel, Reva B., *"The Rule of Love": Wife Beating as Prerogative and Privacy*, 105 YALE L.J. 2117 (1996).

Silver, Marjorie A., *Love, Hate, and Other Emotional Interference in the Lawyer/Client Relationship, in* PRACTICING THERAPEUTIC JURISPRUDENCE: LAW AS A HELPING PROFESSION 357 (Dennis P. Stolle et al. eds., 2000).

SIMON, JONATHAN, GOVERNING THROUGH CRIME: HOW THE WAR ON CRIME TRANS-FORMED AMERICAN DEMOCRACY AND CREATED A CULTURE OF FEAR (2007).

SIMON, WILLIAM H., THE PRACTICE OF JUSTICE: A THEORY OF LAWYERS' ETHICS (1998).

Skeel, David A., Jr., *Shaming in Corporate Law*, 149 U. PA. L. REV. 1811 (2001).

Sklansky, David A., *Cocaine, Race, and Equal Protection*, 47 STAN. L. REV. 1283 (1995).

————, *Police and Democracy*, 103 MICH. L. REV. 1699 (2005).

SKOLNICK, JEROME H. & JAMES J. FYFE, ABOVE THE LAW: POLICE AND THE EXCESSIVE USE OF FORCE (1993).

SKOTNICKI, ANDREW, RELIGION AND THE DEVELOPMENT OF THE AMERICAN PENAL SYSTEM (2000).

Slobogin, Christopher, *An End to Insanity: Recasting the Role of Mental Disability in Criminal Cases*, 86 VA. L. REV. 1199 (2000).

————, *Therapeutic Jurisprudence: Five Dilemmas to Ponder*, 1 PSYCHOL. PUB. POL'Y & L. 193 (1995).

Smith, Abbe, *The Difference in Criminal Defense and the Difference It Makes*, 11 WASH. U. J.L. & POL'Y 83 (2003).

————, *Can You Be a Good Person and a Good Prosecutor?*, 14 GEO. J. LEGAL ETHICS 355 (2001).

SMITH, ADAM, THE THEORY OF MORAL SENTIMENTS (Dublin: J. Beatty & C. Jackson, 6th ed. 1777).

SMITH, BARBARA E. ET AL., AM. BAR ASS'N, THE PROBATION RESPONSE TO CHILD SEXUAL ABUSE OFFENDERS: HOW IS IT WORKING? (1990).

SOLOMON, AMY ET AL., URBAN INSTITUTE, FROM PRISON TO WORK: THE EMPLOYMENT DIMENSIONS OF PRISONER REENTRY (2004).

Solomon, Robert C., *Justice v. Vengeance: On Law and the Satisfaction of Emotion, in* THE PASSIONS OF LAW (Susan A. Bandes ed., 1999).

SOLZHENITSYN, ALEXANDER, ONE DAY IN THE LIFE OF IVAN DENISOVICH (Ralph Parker trans., 2008).

THE SPANGENBERG GROUP, RATES OF COMPENSATION PAID TO COURT-APPOINTED COUNSEL IN NON-CAPITAL FELONY CASES AT TRIAL: A STATE BY STATE OVERVIEW (June 2007).

Special Issue on Plea Bargaining, 13 LAW & SOC'Y REV. 185 (1979).

Stalans, Loretta J., *Measuring Attitudes to Sentencing, in* CHANGING ATTITUDES TO PUNISHMENT: PUBLIC OPINION, CRIME AND JUSTICE 15 (Julian V. Roberts & Mike Hough eds., 2002).

Stalans, Loretta J. & Shari Seidman Diamond, *Formation and Change in Lay Evaluations of Criminal Sentencing: Misperception and Discontent*, 14 LAW & HUM. BEHAV. 199 (1990).

STATE BAR OF TEX. LEGAL SERVS. TO THE POOR IN CRIMINAL MATTERS COMM., PROSECUTOR SURVEY RESULTS, THE STATUS OF INDIGENT CRIMINAL DEFENSE IN TEXAS (n. d.) (unpublished manuscript, on file with the author).

State Board Tells of Parole System, N.Y. TIMES, June 12, 1926, at 7.

STATE COURTS: A BLUEPRINT FOR THE FUTURE (Theodore J. Fetter ed., 1978).

Steen, Sara, *West Coast Drug Courts: Getting Offenders Morally Involved in the Criminal Justice Process, in* DRUG COURTS IN THEORY AND PRACTICE 51 (James L. Nolan, Jr. ed., 2002).

STEINBERG, ALLEN, THE TRANSFORMATION OF CRIMINAL JUSTICE: PHILADELPHIA, 1800–80 (1989).

2 STEPHEN, JAMES FITZJAMES, A HISTORY OF THE CRIMINAL LAW OF ENGLAND (1996) (London: MacMillan & Co. 1883).

Stiller, Daniel W., *Guideline Sentencing: Deepening the Distrust Between Federal Defendant and Federal Defender*, 11 FED. SENT'G REP. 304 (1999).

STITH, KATE & JOSÉ A. CABRANES, FEAR OF JUDGING: SENTENCING GUIDELINES IN THE FEDERAL COURTS (1998).

Stockwell, Jamie, *Defense, Prosecution Play to New "CSI" Savvy: Juries Expecting TV-Style Forensics*, WASH. POST, May 22, 2005, at A1.

Strahilevitz, Lior Jacob, *"How's My Driving?" for Everyone (and Everything?)*, 81 N.Y.U. L. REV. 1699 (2006).

Strang, Heather, *The Crime Victim Movement as a Force in Civil Society, in* RESTORATIVE JUSTICE IN CIVIL SOCIETY 69 (Heather Strang & John Braithwaite eds., 2001).

Strang, Heather & Lawrence W. Sherman, *Repairing the Harm: Victims and Restorative Justice*, 2003 UTAH L. REV. 15.

STUNTZ, WILLIAM J., THE COLLAPSE OF AMERICAN CRIMINAL JUSTICE (2011).

———, *Unequal Justice*, 121 HARV. L. REV. 1969 (2008).

———, *The Political Constitution of Criminal Justice*, 119 HARV. L. REV. 780 (2006).

———, *Plea Bargaining and Criminal Law's Disappearing Shadow*, 117 HARV. L. REV. 2548 (2004).

———, *The Pathological Politics of Criminal Law*, 100 MICH. L. REV. 505 (2001).

———, *Self-Defeating Crimes*, 86 VA. L. REV. 1871 (2000).

———, *The Uneasy Relationship Between Criminal Procedure and Criminal Justice*, 107 YALE L.J. 1 (1997).

Suellentrop, Chris, *The Right Has a Jailhouse Conversion: How Conservatives Came to Embrace Prison Reform*, N.Y. TIMES, Dec. 24, 2006, § E (Magazine), at 46.

Sundby, Scott E., *The Capital Jury and Absolution: The Intersection of Trial Strategy, Remorse, and the Death Penalty*, 83 CORNELL L. REV. 1557 (1998).

Sunstein, Cass R., *Moral Heuristics*, 28 BEHAV. & BRAIN SCI. 531 (2005).

———, *On the Psychology of Punishment*, 11 S. CT. ECON. REV. 171 (2004).

———, *Deliberative Trouble? Why Groups Go to Extremes*, 110 YALE L.J. 1071 (2000).

Sunstein, Cass R. et al., *Do People Want Optimal Deterrence?*, 29 J. LEGAL STUD. 237 (2000).

Symposium, *Juvenile Justice: Reform After One-Hundred Years*, 37 AM. CRIM. L. REV. 1409 (2000).

Taft, Lee, *Apology Subverted: The Commodification of Apology*, 109 YALE L.J. 1135 (2000).

Tanick, Marshall H. & Teresa J. Ayling, *Alternative Dispute Resolution by Apology: Settlement by Saying "I'm Sorry,"* HENNEPIN LAW., July-Aug. 1996, at 22.

TAVUCHIS, NICHOLAS, MEA CULPA: A SOCIOLOGY OF APOLOGY AND RECONCILIATION (1991).

Telephone Interview with Bruce Kittle, member of the board of directors of the Victim-Offender Mediation Ass'n and chaplain, Iowa Dep't of Corr. Servs. (Feb. 27, 2004).

Terry, Don, *Carjacking: New Name for Old Crime*, N.Y. TIMES, Dec. 9, 1992, at A18.

Tewksbury, Richard & Jon Marc Taylor, *The Consequences of Eliminating Pell Grant Eligibility for Students in Post-Secondary Correctional Education Programs*, 60 FED. PROBATION 60 (1994).

Thacher, David, *The Rise of Criminal Background Screening in Rental Housing*, 33 LAW & SOC. INQUIRY 5 (2008).

Thaxton, Rodney, *Professionalism and Life in the Trenches: The Case of the Public Defender*, 8 ST. THOMAS L. REV. 185 (1995).

THERAPEUTIC JURISPRUDENCE: THE LAW AS A THERAPEUTIC AGENT (David B. Wexler ed., 1990).

A 30-Second Ad on Crime, N.Y. TIMES, Nov. 3, 1988, at B20.

Thomas, Andrew P., *The CSI Effect on Jurors and Judgments*, 115 YALE L.J. POCKET PART 70 (2006), *available at* http://www.thepocketpart.org/2006/02/thomas.html.

Thomas, Evan, *America's Crusade: What Is Behind the Latest War on Drugs*, TIME, Sept. 15, 1986, at 60 (cover story).

THOMPSON, ANTHONY C., RELEASING PRISONERS, REDEEMING COMMUNITIES: REENTRY, RACE, AND POLITICS (2008).

Three Get Youth Detention in Rape of Retarded Teen, CHI. TRIB., Apr. 24, 1993, § 1, at 10.

TOBOLOWSKY, PEGGY M., CRIME VICTIM RIGHTS AND REMEDIES (2001).

Tonry, Michael, *Determinants of Penal Policies, in* CRIME, PUNISHMENT, AND POLITICS IN COMPARATIVE PERSPECTIVE 1(Michael Tonry ed., 2007).

————, *Punishment Policies and Patterns in Western Countries, in* SENTENCING AND SANCTIONS IN WESTERN COUNTRIES 3 (Michael Tonry & Richard S. Frase eds., 2001).

————, *Rethinking Unthinkable Punishment Policies in America*, 46 UCLA L. REV. 1751 (1998).

TRAVIS, JEREMY ET AL., FROM PRISON TO HOME: THE DIMENSIONS AND CONSEQUENCES OF PRISONER REENTRY (2001).

————, URBAN INST. JUSTICE POL'Y CTR., FAMILIES LEFT BEHIND: THE HIDDEN COSTS OF INCARCERATION AND REENTRY (2005).

TRUSTI, BRITTANI & MICHAEL EISENBERG, CRIM. JUST. POL'Y COUNCIL, INITIAL PROCESS AND OUTCOME EVALUATION OF THE INNERCHANGE FREEDOM INITIATIVE: THE FAITH-BASED PRISON PROGRAM IN TDCJ (Feb. 2003).

1 TRUTH AND RECONCILIATION COMM'N, TRUTH AND RECONCILIATION COMMISSION OF SOUTH AFRICA REPORT (1998).

————, *Amnesty Hearings and Decisions: Summary of Amnesty Decisions, 1.11.2000*, www.doj.gov.za/trc/amntrans/index.htm (last visited May 5, 2011).

Turner, Jenia Iontcheva, *Judicial Participation in Plea Negotiations: A Comparative View*, 54 AM. J. COMP. L. 199 (2006).

THE 2002 CORRECTIONS YEARBOOK: ADULT CORRECTIONS (Camille Graham Camp ed., 2003).

Tyler, Tom R., *Viewing CSI and the Threshold of Guilt: Managing Truth and Justice in Reality and Fiction*, 115 YALE L.J. 1050 (2006). ————, *The Psychological Consequences of Judicial Procedures: Implications for Civil Commitment Hearings, in* LAW IN A THERAPEUTIC KEY: DEVELOPMENTS IN THERAPEUTIC JURISPRUDENCE 3 (David B. Wexler & Bruce J. Winick eds., 1996).

————, WHY PEOPLE OBEY THE LAW (1990).

————, *What Is Procedural Justice?: Criteria Used by Citizens to Assess the Fairness of Legal Procedures*, 22 LAW & SOC'Y REV. 103 (1988).

Tyler, Tom R. & Robert J. Boeckmann, *Three Strikes and You Are Out, but Why? The Psychology of Public Support for Punishing Rule Breakers*, 31 LAW & SOC'Y REV. 237 (1997).

TYLER, TOM R. & YUEN J. HUO, TRUST IN THE LAW: ENCOURAGING PUBLIC COOPERATION WITH THE POLICE AND COURTS (2002).

Tyler, Tom R. et al., *Influence of Voice on Satisfaction with Leaders: Exploring the Meaning of Process Control*, 48 J. PERSONALITY & SOC. PSYCHOL. 72 (1985).

U.S. COMM'N ON CIVIL RIGHTS, UNDER THE RULE OF THUMB: BATTERED WOMEN AND THE ADMINISTRATION OF JUSTICE (1982).

U.S. GOV'T ACCOUNTABILITY OFFICE, GAO-09-54, CRIME VICTIMS' RIGHTS ACT: INCREASING AWARENESS, MODIFYING THE COMPLAINT PROCESS, AND ENHANCING COMPLIANCE MONITORING WILL IMPROVE IMPLEMENTATION OF THE ACT (2008).

U.S. SENT'G COMM'N, MANDATORY MINIMUM PENALTIES IN THE FEDERAL CRIMINAL JUSTICE SYSTEM (1991).

U.S. SENT'G GUIDELINES MANUAL (2010).

Ulmer, Jeffery T., *The Localized Uses of Federal Sentencing Guidelines in Four U.S. District Courts: Evidence of Processual Order*, 28 SYMBOLIC INTERACTION 255 (2005).

Ulrich, John F., A Case Study Comparison of Brief Group Treatment and Brief Individual Treatment in the Modification of Denial Among Child Sexual Abusers (May 1996) (unpublished Ph.D. dissertation, Andrews University School of Education) (on file with the James White Library, Andrews University).

UMBREIT, MARK S., THE HANDBOOK OF VICTIM-OFFENDER MEDIATION: AN ESSENTIAL GUIDE TO PRACTICE AND RESEARCH (2001).

UMBREIT, MARK S. ET AL., VICTIM MEETS OFFENDER: THE IMPACT OF RESTORATIVE JUSTICE AND MEDIATION (1994).

Vander Pol, Brian L., Note, *Relevance and Reconciliation: A Proposal Regarding the Admissibility of Mercy Opinions in Capital Sentencing*, 88 IOWA L. REV. 707 (2003).

2 VELIMIROVIĆ, NIKOLAI, THE PROLOGUE FROM OCHRID (Mother Maria trans., 1985).

VOGEL, MARY E., COERCION TO COMPROMISE: PLEA BARGAINING, THE COURTS AND THE MAKING OF POLITICAL AUTHORITY (2007).

———, *The Social Origins of Plea Bargaining: Conflict and the Law in the Process of State Formation, 1830–1860*, 33 LAW & SOC'Y REV. 161 (1999).

VON HIRSCH, ANDREW, CENSURE AND SANCTIONS (1993).

———, PAST OR FUTURE CRIMES: DESERVEDNESS AND DANGEROUSNESS IN THE SENTENCING OF CRIMINALS (1985).

———, DOING JUSTICE: THE CHOICE OF PUNISHMENTS (1976).

Vora, Jay A. & Erika Vora, *The Effectiveness of South Africa's Truth and Reconciliation Commission: Perceptions of Xhosa, Afrikaner, and English South Africans*, 34 J. BLACK STUD. 301 (2004).

Vorenberg, James, *Decent Restraint of Prosecutorial Power*, 94 HARV. L. REV. 1521 (1981).

Wagatsuma, Hiroshi & Arthur Rosett, *The Implications of Apology: Law and Culture in Japan and the United States*, 20 LAW & SOC'Y REV. 461 (1986).

Wakefield, Hollida & Ralph Underwager, *Assessing Violent Recidivism in Sexual Offenders*, 10 ISSUES IN CHILD ABUSE ACCUSATIONS 92 (1998).

Walburn, Steven E., *Should the Military Adopt an* Aford[sic]-*Type Guilty Plea?*, 44 A.F. L. REV. 119 (1998).

WALKER, LENORE E., THE BATTERED WOMAN SYNDROME (3d ed. 2009).

———, THE BATTERED WOMAN (1979).

WALKER, SAMUEL, POPULAR JUSTICE: A HISTORY OF AMERICAN CRIMINAL JUSTICE (2d ed. 1998).

WALSH, JENNIFER E., THREE STRIKES LAWS (2007).

Washburn, Kevin K., *Restoring the Grand Jury*, 76 FORDHAM L. REV. 2333 (2008).

Weigend, Thomas, *Problems of Victim/Witness Assistance Programs*, 8 VICTIMOLOGY: INT'L J. 91 (1983).

Weinstein, Jack B., *A Trial Judge's Reflections on Departures from the Federal Sentencing Guidelines*, 15 FED. SENT'G REP. 6 (1992).

———, Comment, *A Trial Judge's Second Impression of the Federal Sentencing Guidelines*, 66 S. CAL. L. REV. 357 (1992).

Welling, Sarah N., *Victim Participation in Plea Bargains*, 65 WASH. U. L.Q. 301 (1987).

WEMMERS, JO-ANNE M., VICTIMS IN THE CRIMINAL JUSTICE SYSTEM (1996).

Wexler, David B., *The TJ Criminal Lawyer: Therapeutic Jurisprudence and Criminal Law Practice*, in THE AFFECTIVE ASSISTANCE OF COUNSEL: PRACTICING LAW AS A HEALING PROFESSION 367 (Marjorie A. Silver ed., 2007).

———, *Some Reflections on Therapeutic Jurisprudence and the Practice of Criminal Law*, 38 CRIM. L. BULL. 205 (2002).

WHEELER, STANTON ET AL., SITTING IN JUDGMENT: THE SENTENCING OF WHITE-COLLAR CRIMINALS (1988).

Whiteley, Diane, *The Victim and the Justification of Punishment*, CRIM. JUST. ETHICS, Summer/Fall 1998, at 42.

WHITMAN, JAMES Q., HARSH JUSTICE: CRIMINAL PUNISHMENT AND THE WIDENING DIVIDE BETWEEN AMERICA AND EUROPE (2003).

————, *What Is Wrong with Inflicting Shame Sanctions?*, 107 YALE L.J. 1055 (1998).

Wiebe, Richard P., *The Mental Health Implications of Crime Victims' Rights, in* LAW IN
   A THERAPEUTIC KEY: DEVELOPMENTS IN THERAPEUTIC JURISPRUDENCE 231
   (David B. Wexler & Bruce J. Winick eds., 1996).

2 WIGMORE, JOHN HENRY, A TREATISE ON THE SYSTEM OF EVIDENCE IN TRIALS AT
   COMMON LAW (1904).

Wilczak, Ginger L. & Carol A. Markstrom, *The Effects of Parent Education on Parental
   Locus of Control and Satisfaction of Incarcerated Fathers*, 43 INT'L J. OFFENDER
   THERAPY & COMP. CRIMINOLOGY 90 (2006).

Wilgoren, Jodi, *Citing Issue of Fairness, Governor Clears Out Death Row in Illinois*, N.Y.
   TIMES, Jan. 12, 2003, § 1, at 1.

WILSON, JAMES Q. & RICHARD J. HERRNSTEIN, CRIME AND HUMAN NATURE: THE
   DEFINITIVE STUDY OF THE CAUSES OF CRIME (1985).

WINES, E.C. & THEODORE W. DWIGHT, REPORT ON THE PRISONS AND REFORMATORIES
   OF THE UNITED STATES AND CANADA, MADE TO THE LEGISLATURE OF NEW
   YORK, JANUARY, 1867 (1867).

Winick, Bruce J., *Therapeutic Jurisprudence and Problem-Solving Courts*, 30 FORDHAM
   URB. L.J. 1055 (2003).

————, *Redefining the Role of the Criminal Defense Lawyer at Plea Bargaining and
   Sentencing: A Therapeutic Jurisprudence/Preventive Law Model, in* PRACTICING
   THERAPEUTIC JURISPRUDENCE: LAW AS A HELPING PROFESSION 245 (Dennis P.
   Stolle et al. eds., 2000).

————, *Therapeutic Jurisprudence and the Role of Counsel in Litigation, in* PRACTICING
   THERAPEUTIC JURISPRUDENCE: LAW AS A HELPING PROFESSION 309 (Dennis P.
   Stolle et al. eds., 2000).

————, *Redefining the Role of the Criminal Defense Lawyer at Plea Bargaining and
   Sentencing: A Therapeutic Jurisprudence/Preventive Law Model*, 5 PSYCHOL. PUB.
   POL'Y & L. 1034 (1999).

————, *The Jurisprudence of Therapeutic Jurisprudence, in* LAW IN A THERAPEUTIC KEY:
   DEVELOPMENTS IN THERAPEUTIC JURISPRUDENCE 645 (David B. Wexler & Bruce
   J. Winick eds., 1996).

Winick, Bruce J. & David B. Wexler, *Drug Treatment Court: Therapeutic Jurisprudence
   Applied*, 18 TOURO L. REV. 479 (2002).

Winn, Mack E., *The Strategic and Systematic Management of Denial in Cognitive/
   Behavioral Treatment of Sexual Offenders*, 8 SEXUAL ABUSE: J. RES. & TREATMENT
   25 (1996).

Witte, Ann Dryden, *Estimating the Economic Model of Crime with Individual Data*, 94 Q.J.
   ECON. 57 (1980).

Wolf, Elaine M., *Systemic Constraints on the Implementation of a Northeast Drug Court, in*
   DRUG COURTS IN THEORY AND PRACTICE 27 (James L. Nolan, Jr. ed., 2002).

WOLFE, ALAN, ONE NATION, AFTER ALL (1998).

Worth, ROBERT, *A Model Prison*, ATLANTIC MONTHLY, Nov. 1995, at 38.

Wright, Ronald F., *How Prosecutor Elections Fail Us*, 6 OHIO ST. J. CRIM. L. 581 (2009).

Wright, Ronald & Marc Miller, *Honesty and Opacity in Charge Bargains*, 55 STAN. L. REV.
   1409 (2003).

————, *The Screening/Bargaining Tradeoff*, 55 STAN. L. REV. 29 (2002).

Wright, Ronald F. & Rodney L. Engen, *Charge Movement and Theories of Prosecutors*, 91
   MARQ. L. REV. 9 (2007).

Yung, Corey Rayburn, *The Emerging Criminal War on Sex Offenders*, 45 Harv. C.R.-C.L. L. Rev. 435 (2010).

Zamble, Edward & Kerry Lee Kalm, *General and Specific Measures of Public Attitudes Toward Sentencing*, 23 Canadian J. Behav. Sci. 327 (1990).

Zehr, Howard, Book Review, 43 Brit. J. Criminology 653 (2003) (reviewing The Spiritual Roots of Restorative Justice (Michael L. Hadley ed., 2001)).

Zimring, Franklin E., The Contradictions of American Capital Punishment (2003).

———, *Tough Crime Laws Are False Promises*, 7 Fed. Sent'g Rep. 61 (1994).

INDEX

adolescence *See* youth

Alameda County, California, plea bargains in, 19, 178*n*62

Alcoholics Anonymous, 66, 79, 102, 203*n*16

Alford, Henry, 61

Amar, Akhil, 114

Appleman, Laura, 148

Arendt, Hannah, 214*n*46

Arnold, Thurman, xv, xv*n*1

Auburn prison, New York, 20, 178*n*68

Bandes, Susan, 94, 123

Banner, Stuart, 23

Barkow, Rachel, 24, 116

Beccaria, Cesare, xxx, 14, 89, 218*n*13

benefit of clergy, 7–8

Bentham, Jeremy, 14, 49, 89

Bias, Len, 36

Bierschbach, Richard, 148

Bill of Rights, 13, 114

Blackstone, William, 7

Blumberg, Abraham, 54

Bowers, Josh, 63, 148

Braithwaite, John, xxiv, 94–95, 97, 99, 125, 141

Braman, Donald, 11, 135

Brockway, Zebulon, 21

bureaucratic pressure to maximize efficiency, 115–17

California

pardons in, 24

plea bargaining in, 20, 45, 46–47, 47, 192*n*39

Proposition 8 (Victims' Bill of Rights), 93

public knowledge regarding sentencing, 37

three-strikes laws, 46–47, 93, 192*nn*38–39

capital punishment *See* death penalty

Cherry Hill prison, Pennsylvania, 20

Chesterton, G.K., 39

Christie, Nils, 86

Churchill, Winston, 141

Civilian Conservation Corps, 139

civil mediation *See* mediation

class *See* race, sex, and social class

clemency

in colonial America, 26

decline in, 24, 116

Enlightenment reformers and, 14, 23

remorse and, 9

restorative justice and, 161–62

sentence softening, 8

victim input regarding, 78

colonial American criminal justice

clemency in, 26

colonists' homogeneity, 2, 168*nn*3–4

death penalty in, 3, 6–9, 169*n*6, 172*n*21

differences across and within colonies, 2, 169*n*2

drunkenness in, 2, 10, 169*n*6

judges in, 5–6

lay justice, xix, 3–6, 13, 70, 170*nn*10–11, 171*nn*15–18, 174*n*40

mercy, 6–9, 172*n*26

pardons in, 8–9

punishment in, xix, 6, 9–13

recidivism in, 12, 174*n*38

small-town morality, 2–3

women in, 8, 12, 174*nn*37, 40

youth in, 8

277

Printed in the USA/Agawam, MA
April 9, 2013

574267.032